TELLING C000005374

Kim Philby *by Edward Harrison*
'A welcome debunking of the Kim Philby Myth' – *Literary Review*

Parnell *by Robert Kee*
'An imaginative and pertinent study' – *Literary Review*

Marie Stopes and Germaine Greer *by Christina Hardyment*
'A sensitive as well as clever comparative study' – *Spectator*

Peter Fleming *by Duff Hart-Davis*
'Fleming's description of an allegorical monument in Rio de Janeiro
is worth the price of this anthology by itself – *Literary Review*

Bruce Chatwin *by Redmond O'Hanlon*
'[A] vivid and funny memoir' – *Financial Times*

Bram Fischer *by Martin Meredith*
'[An] astonishing depiction' – *New Statesman*

Alec Douglas-Home *by D.R. Thorpe*
'Intelligent, balanced and elegantly written' – *Daily Telegraph*

Herbert Gladstone *by John Grigg*
'John Grigg's exemplary study of Herbert Gladstone is . . .
thoughtful and persuasive' – *Daily Telegraph*

Basil Liddell Hart *by Alex Danchev*
'Witty and inventive . . . vigorously distinctive prose' – *The Times*

Axel von dem Bussche *by Alistair Horne*
'A moving memoir' – *Independent*

Margaret Thatcher *by John Campbell*
'Enormously enjoyable' – *Daily Telegraph*

Adam Mickiewicz *by Norman Davies*
'[A] learned portrait' – *Spectator*

W.B. Yeats *by Roy Foster*
'Foster's sketch is especially subtle' – *Financial Times*

Carole Lombard *by Alan Davidson*
'A joyous elegy' – *New Statesman*

Clement Greenberg *by Tim Hilton*
'Hilton writes a very personal and very moving memoir of
Clement Greenberg, the American art critic. It is the more moving
because it is unvarnished' – *Spectator*

Davy, Faraday and Turner *by James Hamilton*
'Clear and enjoyable' – *Literary Review*

Charles Babbage *by Anthony Hyman*
'Hyman expertly establishes Babbage as a figure of major
importance' – *Financial Times*

Richard Cobb *by David Gilmour*
'Gilmour's rich, round, funny appreciation brings this unique and
very loveable man to life' – *Financial Times*

Isaiah Berlin *by Michael Ignatieff*
'A touching éloge' – *Independent*

Alistair Horne is the acclaimed author of history books such as
The Price of Glory, *A Savage War of Peace*, *Small Earthquake in
Chile* and *How Far From Austerlitz?*: *Napoleon*, *1805–1815*, as well
as the authorized two-volume biography of Harold Macmillan. He is
currently writing a history of Paris for Macmillan. The contributors
have all held the Alistair Horne Fellowship at St Anthony's, Oxford.

TELLING LIVES

From W.B. Yeats to Bruce Chatwin

Edited by Alistair Horne

PAPERMAC

First published 2000 by Macmillan

This edition published 2001 by Papermac
an imprint of Macmillan Publishers Ltd
25 Eccleston Place, London SW1W 9NF
Basingstoke and Oxford
Associated companies throughout the world
www.macmillan.com

ISBN 0 333 76552 4

A CIP catalogue record for this book is available from
the British Library.

Typeset by SetSystems Ltd, Saffron Walden, Essex
Printed and bound in Great Britain by
Mackays of Chatham plc, Chatham, Kent

To the Wardens and Fellows

of St Antony's College, Oxford

– past, present, and future

Contents

Contents

Permissions Acknowledgements

The authors and publishers wish to thank the following who have kindly given permission for the use of copyright materials:

Extract from *Marriage in Our Times* by Marie Stopes, copyright The Galton Institute, London.

Extracts from the essay 'Politics' by Jamie Mackie and Andrew MacIntyre in *Indonesia's New Order: The Dynamics of Socio-Economic Transformation* edited by Hall Hill (Sydney, Allen & Unwin, 1994), pp. 1–53.

Extracts from 'To Ireland in the Coming Times', 'A Coat', 'Easter 1916', 'Long-legged Fly' and 'The Circus Animals' Disertion' by W.B. Yeats reproduced by permission of A.P. Watt Ltd on behalf of Michael B. Yeats.

Letter by Lord Dunglass to Mrs Walter Elliot from the Baroness Elliot of Harwood papers.

Extract from *Screwball: The Life of Carole Lombard* by Larry Swindell (New York, William Morrow, 1975) reproduced by kind permission of HarperCollins.

Every effort has been made to trace all copyright holders but if any has been inadvertently overlooked, the author and publishers will be pleased to make the necessary arrangement at the first opportunity.

List of Illustrations

Section One

Kim Philby (*John Philby/Camera Press*)

Charles Stewart Parnell (*Hulton Getty*)

Marie Stopes (*Tom Blau/Camera Press*)

Germaine Greer (*Jerry Bauer*)

Peter Fleming

Richard Burton (*Mary Evans Picture Library*)

Henry Morton Stanley (*Mary Evans Picture Library*)

Fridtjof Nansen (*Hulton Getty*)

Bruce Chatwin (*From* Sittings by Snowden, *Weidenfeld & Nicholson/Camera Press*)

Bram Fischer (*Mayibuye Centre Photo Library, University of the Western Cape*)

Suharto of Indonesia (*Erma/Camera Press*)

Winston Churchill (*Hulton Getty*)

Alec Douglas-Home (*Hulton Getty*)

Herbert Gladstone (*National Portrait Gallery, London*)

Basil Liddell Hart (*Hulton Getty*)

Wully Robertson (*Hulton Getty*)

Section Two

Benito Mussolini (*Hulton Getty*)

Axel von dem Bussche

Axel von dem Bussche

Margaret Thatcher (*Hulton Getty*)

Foreword

Raymond Carr

Sometime in the late 1940s I met Alistair Horne, a Cambridge man, watching a rugby match in Oxford. To this unlikely encounter – neither Alistair nor I had watched a rugby match before and were never to do so again – a future historian might trace the origin of the Alistair Horne Fellowship. In March 1969 I received, out of the blue, a letter from Alistair. He was by then a much respected military historian. As an admirer of Clausewitz he saw a military history as more than a bare description of the movements of armies on the field of battle. It must embrace the social, human and political backcloth of the powers engaged in open conflict. It was this vision that secured him a wide public and the royalties that came with successful authorship.

Research, he knew from his own experience, is an expensive business. Its costs might deter a young and able historian from embarking on a book. Alistair was turning over in his mind some way in which he might help a promising historian to meet the costs of his research when research grants were not as easily attainable as they were later to become, especially for a writer who held no academic post. He had consulted John Bayley, a friend and colleague of mine when I was a Fellow of New College, as to how he might achieve his aims. John had suggested that he talk over his plans with me as Warden of St Antony's.

On the afternoon of a dull March day Alistair arrived in my office at St Antony's. A conventional literary prize would not achieve his aims since the reward would only be given *after* a book had been published. My old friend, the late Michael Astor, had set up a foundation to provide a young writer, who had not produced a book but who might be encouraged to write one given the help of a modest grant, financial aid. I was a member of Michael's foundation. It was a model at the back of my mind in my discussions with Alistair. I suggested that, instead of setting up an independent foundation, the award should be attached in some way to St Antony's.

The form of this attachment was the establishment of the Alistair Horne Research Fellowship at St Antony's, formally set up in September 1969 with the College matching Alistair's gift of £10,000. It was 'specifically designed to support a candidate whilst writing a serious work on modern history for young, unestablished writers, who rarely recoup their expenses from publishers' royalties and can expect no government support or backing'. The Fellow would be selected by the governing body of St Antony's advised by a committee consisting of Mr Horne and two representatives of the College and their choice was to be by no means limited to the academic world. It was this flexibility that was the glory of the Horne Fellowship as it had been of Michael Astor's foundation.

From the outset, though primarily intended for the struggling young, there was no age limit. With the passage of time and the increased possibility of research grants, established writers came as Horne Fellows when they were engaged on writing a book. They enriched the social and intellectual life of the College. The diversity of contributions to learning in the form of books by both the young Fellows and their elders is truly astonishing. They range from the politics of the Italian Army to John Ruskin, from the history of deer stalking to the history of the Salzburg Festival, from Kosovo to Gustave Courbet and the Revolution of 1848, from Dumas on food to the Polish–Soviet War of 1919. The seed planted in 1969 has borne a rich and varied fruit of twenty-five books in thirty years. The Horne Fellowship has been an unparalleled success. Those who have benefited from it have contributed the essays in this book.

Introduction

Alistair Horne

Thirty odd years ago I had a stroke of rare good fortune as an author. With the help of my publishers, here (still Macmillan and the publishers of this present volume) and abroad, I actually made some money, on a trilogy of books on Franco-German history. At the same time, being then much involved in authors' rights – such as the struggle for Public Lending Right (PLR) – I was appalled by the realization of how difficult – and costly – it was for young authors to get a footing on the first rung of the ladder. One newspaper article analysing the profit and loss account of a first-time novelist particularly shocked me: for a year's work of 2,000 hours he had earned £200, at 10p an hour – whereas his putative loss of a year's salary had amounted to £2,950: i.e. a net loss of £2,750.

It was much worse for us non-fiction writers, burdened with the extra costs of research. Even in the 60s, research (including travel) for our kind of books could be prohibitively expensive – I was then having to pay my research assistant the princely wage of 50p an hour! It had taken me three books before I published one (*The Price of Glory; Verdun 1916**) that could have begun to offer anything like a living wage – and that was, in a modest way, a best-seller.

How, then, could a young, unknown historian or biographer even *begin*? What talents might be lost for ever because of a simple lack of opportunity – or else drained off abroad, a common phenomenon in the 60s? What I felt was needed was a kind of kick-starter to help provide a worthwhile author with either the time, or

---

* Still in print after over three and a half decades.

the cash (in fact, they amount to roughly the same thing) in which to write a specific book.

I hunted around for the best part of a year, testing the water, plaguing friends, colleagues and publishers for advice and help, and looking for a vessel to contain my idea – and which I might be able to fund from my own earnings. I must have made myself a perfect pest; those initial letters and responses fill half a box file. But I was seriously serious; I find copies of letters declaring how I was 'planning to give up writing for the foreseeable future . . . instead I hope to devote what energy I have got left to promoting a literary fund . . .' (In fact, as it turned out, Macmillan did persuade me to go on to clock up another dozen books.) Reading through the responses now, thirty years later, I hear voices from a distant past – sadly many dead – none of them reproachful, most of them encouraging and helpful. Generally they thought the idea had merits; but how and where to put it into effect? I approached the Arts Council, UNESCO, my old college at Cambridge, Jesus, and the Society of Authors. Alas, none of them could quite come up with what I wanted. The Society of Authors, an admirable but underfunded institution, came closest,* and we were on the verge of negotiating a trust deed . . .

Then, early in 1969, there came a response to one of my letters from John Bayley, Wharton Professor of English Literature at St Catherine's, Oxford – and husband of the late Iris Murdoch. I already owed John a considerable debt of gratitude; six years previously, as a judge of the prestigious Hawthornden Prize (though unbeknown to me) he had proposed *The Price of Glory*, and it had won the prize for 1963, the first work of non-fiction to do so. Since then we had become friends – though I was often disconcerted on the telephone, taking Iris's deep, rather masculine voice to be John's, and his gentle falsetto to be the great, and, to me, rather daunting novelist. After putting forward several names in his letter, he came up with 'a bigger gun, Raymond Carr, former colleague of mine, now Warden of St Antony's College . . .' (Only recently founded, though soon to become Oxford's most prestigious postgraduate

---

* In fact, one of its officers, Victor Bonham-Carter, was to become an early recipient of the Fellowship as well as the most senior, with his official history of the Society; his contribution to this book in on p.183.

college, St Antony's, it transpired, held particular affection for John, one of its first Fellows, in that it had been the launching pad from which he had conducted his dedicated suit of Iris.)* Warden Carr, he continued: 'is almost too enthusiastic . . . but I think you would like him and I think he would throw himself into the idea. He knows everyone . . .'

John Bayley proved to be right, on every score. I had known Raymond, tangentially, when he had been a somewhat reprobate don tutoring various friends of mine in history, and well nicknamed 'the Soul of All Fellows'. He had only taken over, from Bill Deakin, as Warden of St Antony's the year before, but already was leaving his stamp on it.

Raymond was one of the last of the true Oxford eccentrics, and his rich brand of eccentricity greatly appealed to me. One of the world's leading Spanish historians, he somehow managed to combine imposing erudition with living it up wildly; fox-hunting with playing the clarinet, trumpet, and tenor-sax. (He once admitted that, 'Had I been a better trumpeter, I would never have become a don!') For many years the Carr house in Charlbury Road, where the long-suffering Sara hospitably entertained generations of students, sported a couple of concrete blocks supporting the sofa – relic of some past bacchanalia. Students, who thrived under his tuition, would recall addressing a rather green-hued face resting on the floor at a tutorial – Raymond believing that hangovers could best be cured with the feet raised higher than the brain. Not infrequently he would return to Oxford at the beginning of term with his arm in a sling, having fallen off his horse hunting on Exmoor. While Warden of an Oxford college, he had absolutely no inhibitions about working as a barman in Stockholm, when funds ran low.

But beneath the surface of Raymond lay great wisdom, humanity – and flair. He did not always convey the appearance of a kindly man, but generosity came bubbling out from his rather unusual philosophy as a reviewer: never take on a book if you're going to slam it, he would proclaim. 'Think of the poor sod who wrote it, all that bloody effort.' The results were, usually, positive critiques of great insight. He was also, in his own inimitable way, no mean

---

* See his deeply moving account, *Iris – a Memoir of Iris Murdoch* (Duckworth, 1998).

administrator. Though always pushed for funds, under him St Antony's prospered exceedingly.

We had our first meeting, I find recorded, at 3 p.m., on Tuesday, 11 March 1969. Raymond instantly took up my idea. He refined it and modified it, and made it work. Most significantly, he railroaded his Governing Body into allocating a matching sum from the College, thereby doubling the modest commitment I was able to make, topped up from time to time with various prize monies that fell to me.

For me at least, it was a marriage made in heaven; over the best part of the next two decades, I don't think we ever had a disagreement (except perhaps when he once lectured me on the immorality of divorce).

In those early days, we also managed to lure three publishers (one of them Macmillan) into backing financially our first years. This was an invaluable pump-primer for which we remained long beholden; thereby the publishers gained prior knowledge of projects on offer – publishing several books from both the accepted and rejected candidates, which might not otherwise have seen the light of day. The Fellowship, as a result, was able to offer initially between £1,200–£2,000 per annum. It was a shoestring – barely ever enough to be able to compete with average university stipends – and, although risen over the years to £6,000–£8,000, it still is.

The Fellowship was to be awarded, as a rule, for one author per year, though, if funds permitted (perpetually a big if) an extension was possible – as was the simultaneous award of more than one Fellowship. Limited as the financial inducement might be, the biggest attraction, however, was to prove the associated attachment to the unique and marvellously eclectic body of St Antony's. Entirely postgraduate, and 50 per cent foreign from every country in the world, then and now St Antony's offered a uniquely stimulating environment. When asked to describe St Antony's in a sentence, I grew accustomed to trotting out, glibly but with all sincerity, that it was 'what the United Nations ought to be, but isn't!' I vividly recall one of my first exchanges, in Hall; it was the day Nasser died, and an Israeli lent across me to offer his condolence to an Egyptian (who was, as I recall, an expert on Brazilian economics). With parallel courtesy, the Egyptian thanked him – but remarked that he'd always loathed his late President! That always seemed to me to epitomize the spirit, the warm friendliness and open-mindedness that characterizes the College. At some time or other, almost every Fellow was to comment on the intangible benefits to them of 'cross-pollination' with other members of the College working on a vast panorama of totally diverse subjects.

When the Fellowship was launched in the Michaelmas term of 1969, reactions both from the Press and the world of letters were hearteningly encouraging. Michael Howard, subsequently Regius Professor of Modern History at Oxford, rarely given to fulsome praise, welcomed it as 'a stroke of genius', and said that 'generations will be in your debt' – a most flattering prediction.

For those crucial kick-off years, 1969–70, our first selections proved about as good as they possibly could be. Tim Clark came from Essex University as a young history of art lecturer; for a modest pittance of £500 he produced not one but two excellent books: *The Absolute Bourgeois; Artists and Politics in France: 1848–1851* and *Image of the People: Gustave Courbet and the 1848 Revolution* (both from Thames and Hudson). Both were provocatively left-of-centre in the political approach; this seemed not altogether inappropriate, as St Antony's, with its strong Centre for Russian and Soviet Studies, was under regular attack from Moscow as 'that well-known nest of right-wing spies'! Unintentionally, the balance was somewhat redressed by our next Fellow, Norman Davies, whose *White Eagle, Red Star: The Polish-Soviet War, 1919–20* had little of comfort to say about aggressive Soviet foreign policy in the Leninist era. Our third Fellow, John Whittam, produced *The Politics of the Italian Army, 1861–1918*, another excellent contribution to European history.

All three followed up with most distinguished academic and writing careers. Norman Davies, perhaps particularly, proved a success story of which the Fellowship could – justly – feel most proud. When he came to us, aged twenty-nine, he was very much down on his fortunes; one of his referees was unsupportive, but a rave testimony from that great maverick historian, A.J.P. Taylor, swung us: 'It is rare to be able to commend a book without reserve,' he wrote in the introduction to *White Eagle*, 'I do so now ... a permanent contribution to historical knowledge and international understanding.'

On the back of *White Eagle* Norman was awarded a lectureship at the School of Slavonic and East European Studies (SSEES) of London University.

Graciously he wrote me at the time: 'without the boost to my reputation which the Fellowship has obviously given, I would probably be on the dole.'

From then on Norman Davies never looked back; establishing himself, with his definitive *God's Playground*, as a leading world-authority on Polish history, and then – in 1997 – producing his record best-selling blockbuster of 1,300 pages, unambiguously entitled *Europe – A History*. This was to set a record for sales of a 1,300-page, seriously academic work, gaining the rare accolade of a *Times* leader that singled out a new book for special praise. *The Isles* ditto!

Apart from the perennial problem of finance, each academic year we faced the concern of whether we were reaching the candidates we wanted, and – more important – those who really needed us; whether we were getting the word around. Occasionally we advertised, but by and large the best applicants came to us by word of mouth. As John Bayley had intimated, Raymond really *did* know everyone – from the great and the good to down-and-out students with a touch of unsung genius. Over its first eighteen years while he was Warden, the Fellowship owed everything to him. Inevitably applicants brought in their share of the way-out, and sometimes verging on the eccentric. There was one, for instance, who took even Raymond aback at interview; when in answer to the conventional question 'Do you intend to spend time in the College?', his reply was: 'As a matter of fact, Warden, I was going to ask you about that; you see I live on a barge, and it's leaking – so I wondered if you'd mind my putting it up on blocks in the quad?'

He got the Fellowship; the College did not get the barge.

Another applicant was a historian with the reputation for showing a disturbingly friendly bias towards Adolf Hitler. Nevertheless he had an interesting project. We, the appointing triumvirate (then Raymond, Theodore Zeldin – who later became immeasurably successful in his own right as a historian of modern France – and myself), decided to take advice telephonically. The high-pitched, donnish voice of the Greatest Living Expert on Hitler rang out across the room: 'I strongly recommend him – provided you don't mind having the College bugged!'

We turned the applicant down – not out of apprehension for college privacy, but on the grounds that he was already too successful and affluent.

We had applicants ranging in age from their twenties to their seventies; apart from the manifest needs we were trying to address, there were refugees from matrimony, or those trying to break an alcohol problem. One Fellow, Robert Kee, took twenty years to complete his biography of Parnell – but finally presented us with a winner in the shape of *The Laurel and the Ivy* (1993). He was kind enough to write that only the Fellowship had kept his project going.

There were disappointments, and sadnesses. Charles Brooks, our first American, was an enormously talented man working on a topic close to my heart, 'The French Film in the 1930s'. Charles more than sang for his supper by his superb presentations of old movies to the College, but had to give up because academe could not compete with the enticements of a legal profession in Washington DC. We lost other valuable candidates through the brain-drain, stolen away by American colleges that could offer more.

Sadder still was the premature death of Steve Gallup (also American), but who did complete his excellent *History of the Salzburg Festival*; and of my old friend from Germany, Axel von Bussche, who found it altogether too painful to write his eagerly awaited autobiography.

Over the passage of thirty years I was fortunate to get to know all the Fellows; many became good friends, and from all of them I benefited a lot from their work and knowledge, learning about areas that ranged far beyond my own horizon. Perhaps I was occasionally able to help them. Correspondence with them, or about the Fellowship, came to fill some four to five tightly packed filing boxes; but I look back on it all as almost the most rewarding enterprise of my life. Not least was the incidental privilege, hugely appreciated, of being elected an Hon. Fellow of St Antony's, with all the *richesses* it had to offer and which were enjoyed by the Fellows.

The Fellowship – and its benefactor – have survived three wardens, as well as gaining the kind benevolence and friendship of the founding Warden of St Antony's, Bill (Sir William) Deakin, distinguished academic and brave wartime soldier. When Raymond finally retired after eighteen years in the saddle (literally, as well as figuratively), I was fearful lest his successor, whoever that would be, might possibly think this modest fellowship not worth the candle. Flatteringly, but rashly, some friends in the College even put me up as a candidate for the succession; though not eager for the responsibility, or feeling in any way qualified for it, I let my name go forward – mainly out of affection for the institution to which I had become so greatly attached. My wife threatened divorce in the event of my being elected (though, as we were not yet married at the time, I had to point out that it would have had to be post-active!); but happily – and wisely – the College made the ideal selection of Ralf Dahrendorf. With a genetic sense of order, Ralf could hardly have been more different in style to Raymond; yet I came enormously to enjoy his dry, Teutonic sense of humour and greatly to respect his mind and his integrity. His talented wife Ellen, a Russian expert in her own right, became a huge asset in the College, and much loved.

My fears for the Fellowship immediately proved groundless. To deal with, Ralf was ever courtesy itself, he had many inventive ideas, and could not have been more supportive of the Fellowship. It was as pleasurable to work with him as with Raymond, and during his ten years as Warden we appointed as many excellent Fellows. Sadly Oxford got him down – as it often does men of larger than average stature, these days: the demands of fund-raising, the petty bickering and backstabbing of the dons (notably outside the College) proved too much for an intellect of such broad vision – not for the first or last time. He retired prematurely to devote himself to other work in London, and the Lords.

Once again I had worries about the succession and the Fellow-ship; once again I was proved wrong. Marrack ('Mig') Goulding equally was a very different personality. With no claims to be an academic, he was trained as a diplomat, then becoming for many years Assistant Secretary General of the UN. 'Peacemonger' he modestly described himself, but he had a refreshingly direct, no-nonsense approach not always to be found in *la carrière*; it was also reputed that, curiously, he actually enjoyed fund-raising. He brought a breeze of informality into the College. We hit it off at once – and certainly as far as the Fellowship was concerned, with him, Tim

Garton-Ash and Michael Aris* on the selection committee, the omens look as cheerful as they can be.

So what have we achieved in thirty years? Fellows – from America, France, Germany, and Ireland as well as Britain – have published twenty-five highly prestigious books, with more under way. At least one has created his own, new, professional chair at Oxford; and by my reckoning we can now count some seven professors, and eight doctorates. It would be impertinent to suggest that any came as a direct consequence of the Fellowship; but at least some of the past Fellows reckon the kudos attached might have helped in some small way.

Back in 1969, one of our original publisher supporters, the late John Pollock of British Printing Corporation, ventured – perhaps partly in jest – 'One will hear "But of course, he was a Horne Fellow . . ."!' It may be unbecomingly boastful to say this, but I like to think that, after thirty good years, this wishful prognosis may have received some vindication.

The Fellowship continues to suffer the intolerable pains of under-funding. Sometimes we can't afford the stars we would like; and it would be a marvellous dream to be able to appoint more than one a year. But, speaking personally, I hope the Fellowship will continue for many a year yet, and certainly long after I have left the scene.

Whatever the future, the genesis of this book – proposed by my daughter Camilla – was to recognize the superb achievements of its Fellows over the past thirty years.

Looking at the backlist of books published, I was somewhat surprised to discover that there were actually more biographies than pure histories; but, after all, what is history but a patchwork quilt of biography, and the dividing line often a smudgy one?

So we decided to invite each surviving Fellow to submit a 5,000-word essay on any *biographical* topic of his or her choice. That would seem more easily focussed, and more manageable, than one on more diffuse historical subjects. As to a general binding theme, there was none – except for the nexus of the Fellowship and the common bond of St Antony's.

* Tragically, Michael – husband of the heroic Burmese Nobel Prizewinner, Aung San Suu Kyi – died in 1999 before this book was completed.

To my delight, and surprise, twenty-five out of a possible total of thirty all accepted – in itself the most rewarding compliment, and testimony, to the Fellowship. All are published here. As will be seen, the range is marvellously eclectic, which seems eminently suited to the spirit of both the Fellowship and St Antony's. Publication date was deferred to tie in with St Antony's own fiftieth anniversary in millennium year.

*

We start with an unquestioned villain – Kim Philby – and end with two (sadly deceased) heroes of the late twentieth-century Oxford scene – Richard Cobb and Isaiah Berlin. As mentioned earlier, until the Berlin Wall came down in 1989, whenever St Antony's was mentioned in the Soviet Press it would regularly be identified as a 'nest of right-wing spies'. Tourist buses travelling down the Woodstock Road would even be heard pointing out 'On your left, the "Spy College".' How many 'spies' St Antony's actually nurtured, educated or produced, I have no means of knowing. Yet now it seems to be a badge to be worn with honour. In 1999, shocking revelations came to light of the truly staggering extent of KGB activities in Britain during the Cold War. Quite coincidentally, the College held a major conference (in September of that year) to assess the work of intelligence services during the Cold War, and their future. In an extremely open atmosphere, delegates attended from all the major powers – including ex-directors of the CIA and former KGB generals. Out of the two sets of events one fact emerged with great clarity: that St Antony's should have been made such a target of this kind of intelligence-war 'disinformation' must now surely be seen to the College's credit, rather than the reverse. Clearly there was something about the College that made it, in KGB eyes, an enemy that needed to be destroyed. The whole value of Britain's MI5 and MI6 since 1945 may now be due for a sweeping reassessment; consequently it seems timely that this collection of essays should open with a fresh look at perhaps the wickedest and most damaging of all the KGB 'Cambridge Five' spies.

Some of the subjects chosen were close to my heart. Peter Fleming, explorer and literary adventurer extraordinaire, was a hero of my youth; Basil Liddell Hart, the 'Seer of Medmenham' – though I didn't always agree with him – exerted a considerable influence on me, and was enormously supportive while I was writing my early books. According to Alex Danchev, he sold one million copies of *The Real War* – the largest ever for a history to date. But I mostly remember him as a role model, for his extraordinary accessibility to young writers like myself, and the boundless trouble he would take to answer tedious queries.

And since this book had its roots deeply in Oxford, it seems right and proper that its last two essays should be about two legendary figures of their era, Richard Cobb and Isaiah Berlin – like Raymond Carr, both true eccentrics in their fashion. Richard Cobb first came into my life in the late 70s, after the publication of my book on the Algerian War, *A Savage War of Peace*. There followed a copious correspondence, all on small cards, sometimes as many as twenty or thirty to an envelope. I hugely admired his writing on France, and we became friends. Almost the last time I saw him was when he brought his successor as Professor of Modern History, Norman Stone, to lunch at Turville. Between them, they emptied the cellar. I only wish I had seen more of him (preferably not at home!), and known him better – as David Gilmour in his generous tribute to his old tutor makes so very comprehensible.

Michael Ignatieff's grandfather, I learn from his family memoir, *The Russian Album*, was the Tsar's last Minister of Education before the Revolution of 1917. Therefore, as a second-generation émigré himself, he was abundantly well-equipped to explain what the 'need for belonging' meant for someone like Isaiah Berlin. An Honorary Fellow of St Antony's, Isaiah was truly a Don for All Seasons; he could, and would, talk at any level whatsoever and make his interlocutor feel prized beyond belief. At a first meeting, my wife expressed alarm at finding herself seated next to such an august academician at a St Antony's dinner. I reassured her, 'Don't worry, he'll take charge!' Looking up from my end of the table, I was relieved to see them in lively conversation with each other. When afterwards I asked what they'd talked about so busily, and what Isaiah's opening gambit had been, she said, 'As we sat down, he said, "Tell me, my dear, did you have many lovers when you were young?"' – then proceeded to talk about his own, *in extenso*. When I once asked how he and his biographer were getting on, he replied – with alarming hubris: 'Poor boy, the only rule I've imposed is that it should not be published in my lifetime – just what Harold Macmillan imposed on you – but, you see, I intend to live for ever.'

Of course, sadly, he didn't – though there were times when it seemed almost as if he were immortal. Only the details of Isaiah's painful last days make unhappy reading in what Ignatieff has written about 'Berlin in Autumn'.

*

Finally, it gives me greatest pleasure to express my most profound gratitude to St Antony's College, Oxford, and wardens past and present for the support and enthusiasm which has made the Alistair Horne Fellowship succeed so well to this day – and for notably enriching the life of its benefactor. As any don knows, Governing Bodies of Oxford colleges, working in mysterious and not always wonderful ways, are not naturally the most moveable objects; but to St Antony's I owe a perpetual debt of gratitude for their support, friendliness – and vision. Particularly, we all owe a debt to Raymond Carr for the imagination that enabled it to take off at all, back in 1969.

I am also much beholden to Dr Eugene Rogan of St Antony's Middle East Centre for preparing the groundwork for this book; to Macmillan, one of our original team of backers, and my own publisher for the past forty years, who have been superbly responsive in their enthusiasm for it – and, specifically there, to Ian Chapman, Tim Farmiloe, Becky Lindsay and Tanya Stobbs – who have borne the brunt of the editorial work with flair and energy.

Edward Harrison

KIM PHILBY: THE END OF A MYTH

During the quarter-century after his defection in 1963 the Soviet spy
Kim Philby became a mythical figure. It was claimed he played his
double role without a slip and that he was destined to become Chief
of the British Secret Service. He was styled 'the spy who betrayed a
generation' and 'the most remarkable spy in the history of espionage'.[1] But was Philby's career as a spy as successful as these terms
suggest? Was he even the most effective of the Cambridge spies, the
group of Cambridge graduates, who, like Philby, dedicated their
lives to the secret service of communism? Although Philby's
employer, the Secret Intelligence Service, (SIS), has not yet released
its records, some of Philby's colleagues in SIS have written about his
work for British Intelligence. Furthermore, selected KGB records
concerning Philby have been made available recently and Soviet
officers who knew Philby have published memoirs. This new Russian
material contains elements of disinformation, but overall it is a
valuable addition to the discourse on Philby. The complete picture
of Philby's career may never be known; but we can now come closer
to the truth than before.[2]

Harold Adrian Russell ('Kim') Philby was born at Ambala in
the Punjab on 1 January 1912. His father, St. John Philby, was
an official in the Indian Civil Service. Philby senior later became an
enthusiast for the Arab cause and converted to Islam. The first Prime
Minister of Israel, David Ben Gurion, thought St. John 'not a nice
man. The father became a Moslem, so why should not the son
become a communist?' Philby decided to work for communism
during his last week as a student at Cambridge. Following the
disintegration of the Labour Party, the British Left seemed no match
for the challenges posed by depression at home, or the alarming

menace of fascism on the Continent. Instead Philby turned to international communism. The most important influence on Philby at Cambridge was Maurice Dobb, a young Marxist don. When Philby left Cambridge in the summer of 1933, Dobb gave him an introduction to a communist group in Paris, which in turn passed him on to a secret communist organization in Vienna, for whom Philby worked as a courier. The daughter of the couple he stayed with in Vienna, Lizy Friedmann, was already working as a communist agent. When in February 1934 Lizy became wanted by the police, Philby married her to give her the protection of a British passport and also out of affection, though the marriage was not to last. In spring 1934 the Philbys travelled to Britain, where Kim sought to join the Foreign Office. To support his application he needed two references from figures more senior than Dobb. When he approached two other Cambridge dons, they consulted one another and he was told that 'his sense of political injustice might well unfit him for administrative work'.[3]

Thwarted in his attempt to start a conventional career, Philby was talent-spotted for Soviet Intelligence by Edith Tudor Hart, like her friend Lizy Philby a Viennese communist who had married an English husband to escape prosecution for her illegal party activities. Tudor Hart recommended Philby for secret service to Arnold Deutsch, yet another conspirator from the Austrian underground who was working for Soviet Intelligence in Britain. Deutsch met Philby in Regent's Park in June 1934 and Philby agreed to penetrate bourgeois institutions and supply information. By early 1935 Alexander Orlov, the head of the underground Soviet Intelligence apparatus in Britain, had earmarked Philby to penetrate SIS, also known as MI6, the British government organization responsible for collecting secret intelligence on foreign territory. Although the KGB had set Philby an important task, his disparaging code-name 'Soehnchen' (little son – a reference to the domineering St. John) suggests he was regarded with a touch of disdain.[4]

To provide cover for his espionage Philby took up journalism. In autumn 1935 he started to edit the magazine of the Anglo-German Fellowship, an organization that sought to promote good relations between Britain and Germany. The Nazi propaganda ministry provided funds for Philby's magazine, so from late 1935 Philby visited Berlin frequently and held meetings with Nazi officials.[5] But in autumn 1936 the Nazis stopped the subsidy to his magazine, and Philby was out of work. Soviet Intelligence now decided to send him to Spain under cover as a journalist to gather information on General Franco's rebellion against the Soviet-backed Spanish Republic. Thanks to his early articles on the Spanish Civil War, and firm support from his father, in May 1937 *The Times* made Philby its special correspondent with Franco. Philby also reported to the Soviets on Franco's war effort. It was a bitter assignment. During 1938 and 1939 Philby had to witness victory after victory for Franco until in July 1939 he was able to return to London.[6]

During the years leading up to the Second World War Philby was overshadowed in importance as a Soviet agent by the second spy Soviet Intelligence recruited at Cambridge, Donald Maclean. Philby had placed Maclean top of a list of Cambridge communist contacts he compiled for the KGB. In August 1934 Maclean told Philby he was willing to carry out special work for communism. In autumn the following year he began his open career in the Foreign Office. The Office had no security procedure as its secrets were protected by the personal honour of the gentlemen to whom they were entrusted. In January 1936 Maclean handed his first bundle of documents to Deutsch. The flow of material continued after Maclean's transfer to the Paris Embassy in September 1938. Maclean's material was remarkable both for its quality and quantity. Between January 1936 and his departure from France in June 1940 Maclean stole for photocopying about 13,500 pages of documents.[7]

Maclean's work as a Soviet agent clearly vindicated Philby's decision to give him pride of place in his list of suitable communist contacts for Soviet Intelligence. Philby placed Guy Burgess, the third Cambridge spy to be recruited, bottom of the list. After Maclean told Burgess he was working secretly for communism, Deutsch felt he had to recruit Burgess to shut him up. Though Deutsch ran Burgess as an individual agent, Burgess regarded intelligence as a social activity carried on together with his friends and insisted on maintaining the links with the others.[8]

At the beginning of 1937 Burgess introduced Deutsch to Anthony Blunt, who was the fourth of the Cambridge spies to be recruited. Blunt was an art historian and Fellow of Trinity College,

Cambridge. Blunt and Burgess worked together as talent spotters for the Soviets. Their most useful find was the Trinity undergraduate John Cairncross, who joined the Foreign Office in autumn 1936 and was recruited by the KGB in spring 1937. Cairncross asked other officials out to lunch and recorded their conversations in detail for Soviet Intelligence.[9] Whereas Cairncross was a notorious bore, Burgess had the charm to make friends with anyone. After he became a producer for the BBC in October 1936 Burgess befriended men with intelligence links, one of whom helped Burgess to get a job in Section D of SIS, which was responsible for planning sabotage and subversion. In June 1940 Philby was also recommended for work in Section D by one of its women officers working under journalistic cover, and Burgess took the opportunity to support his friend's recruitment. In summer 1940 Section D was taken away from SIS to form part of the new Special Operations Executive (SOE). Gladwyn Jebb, SOE's Chief Executive Officer, sacked Burgess as he considered him 'quite exceptionally dissolute and indiscreet'. But Philby successfully made the transition and so kept a foothold in the intelligence world. His job was to train agents in subversive propaganda, which he discussed with SOE's driving force, Colin Gubbins.[10]

In September 1941 Tommy Harris, a friend of Philby and Burgess who headed the Iberian section of the British Security Service (MI5), suggested that Philby's knowledge of Spain would be useful in strengthening Section V of SIS, which dealt with counter-espionage. Philby was vouched for by Colonel Valentine Vivian, Deputy Chief of the SIS with special responsibilities for counter-espionage. Vivian had known Philby's father in India, so he invited father and son to lunch. When Kim went out to wash his hands, Vivian quizzed his father about him. 'He was a bit of a communist at Cambridge, wasn't he?' Vivian enquired. Naturally anxious to get his son a better job, St. John replied, 'That was all schoolboy nonsense. He's a reformed character now.' Vivian summed up Philby's recruitment: 'I was asked about him, and I said I knew his people.' Vivian endorsed Philby even though he was aware of his youthful interest in communism. Furthermore, Vivian overlooked Kim's work for the Anglo-German Fellowship and his father's role in the anti-Semitic and pro-German British People's Party. In 1940 Philby senior had been arrested in India while en route for the United

States. He was returned to Britain and detained by the Home Office for fear he would spread anti-war propaganda in America. Within less than a year after his release he was recommending his son for the Secret Service. The strange feature of Kim's successful return to SIS from SOE was not so much that his communism was condoned, but that his own and still more his father's pro-German record went unnoticed.[11]

Thanks to Vivian, Philby began work in autumn 1941 as head of the Iberian subsection of Section V of SIS. Within three years he had risen to become a head of section. Why was he able to make such a rapid career? There were three main reasons for this. First, this was a boom period for counter-intelligence due to the successful exploitation by SIS and MI5 of broken German Secret Service (*Abwehr*) codes, and consequently it was a golden opportunity for a competent officer to make a good impression. Second, some of the other SIS personnel were of disappointing ability. The senior staff failed to check up on Philby, and the juniors were mostly unable to compete with him. Vivian's recruitment of Philby was a disastrous attempt to improve the intellectual calibre of the service. Vivian himself was scarcely fitted for his role as senior counter-espionage officer in SIS. Lord Dacre, who worked in SIS during the war, described him as 'a Uriah Heep of a man, soapy, feeble and treacherous'. While Vivian was very weak, his principal rival within SIS, Colonel Claude Dansey, was very difficult. The former SIS officer Nicholas Elliott characterized Dansey as 'a snobbish, arrogant, incompetent shit'. Dansey was a champion of traditional espionage and particularly resented officers like Philby employed in counter-intelligence.[12]

In a smug passage of his published memoirs, *My Silent War*, Philby boasts of his cleverness in getting on the right side of Dansey. And indeed the third part of the explanation for Philby's rise is to be found in his bureaucratic skills. During his time in Section V Philby laid the foundations for his career in SIS by his tact, industry and his willingness to co-operate with other parts of British Intelligence. Whereas SIS was responsible for counter-espionage on foreign territory, its sister organization, MI5, was responsible for counter-espionage on British territory. The two organizations also had different priorities. Charles Stuart, who served in the Radio Security Section (RSS) of SIS during the war wrote:

MI5 was a security organization concerned with catching spies and with locking them up. For this purpose it needed information for action. MI6 was an intelligence-collecting organization concerned with recruiting agents and extracting information from them. Above all, it was determined to guard its sources in order to preserve them for further use.

For wartime recruits such as Philby, 'the immediate needs of the war came first. This tended to place them, whatever their department, on MI5's side of the fence favouring "free trade" in information and accepting the risks of action upon it.' In contrast, Felix Cowgill, the head of Section V, was a protectionist and sought to keep the flow of information to MI5 to a minimum.[13]

From autumn 1941 onwards the Iberian subsection of Section V working under Philby made a solid contribution to the intelligence war. It had a considerable volume of intelligence at its disposal, both from intercepted *Abwehr* signals and from agents run by Section V's stations in Madrid, Lisbon and Tangier. The intelligence flowing through Philby's subsection allowed the Ministry of Economic Warfare, for example, to pre-empt a German bid to purchase wolfram or tungsten ore at the end of 1941. Steel is alloyed with tungsten to harden it and facilitate the protection or piercing of armour. Hitler's Germany was short of tungsten and thus intelligence about Nazi attempts to buy wolfram was at a premium. Furthermore, a German project to use infra-red light to monitor British shipping passing through the Straits of Gibraltar at night was the subject of a formal protest following preparatory work by Philby's team, though the protest had at best only mixed success. Philby also played a part in bringing the double agent Garbo to England. Garbo became a key figure in the Allied deception covering the Normandy invasion. One of Philby's colleagues later recalled: 'The success of our department was largely due to Philby. He was very thorough and he himself worked harder than anyone.'[14]

Despite his free-trading inclinations, Philby occasionally blocked the circulation of intelligence in the interests of the Soviet Union. In particular Philby was determined to stifle any material that might prompt the British Government to take interest in the military opposition to Hitler, which if successful could have resulted in a strong post-war Germany firmly allied to the West. At the end of

1942 the RSS produced a report that showed the growing rivalry between the Nazi Party and the German Army and pointed to its wider political significance. The paper was passed to Philby for approval. Stuart later recalled that, 'Philby was not interested in the evidence but only in its suppression.' Similarly, early in July 1944 the SIS station in Lisbon learned from Otto John, who belonged to the German Resistance, of the pending attempt on Hitler's life. Stuart wrote that, 'John's report was . . . of interest . . . and import-ance. But Philby . . . dismissed it as unreliable.'[15]

Philby worked hard for British Intelligence. He worked even harder for the KGB, sending copies of nearly a thousand documents between 1941 and 1945. The quality of Philby's material varied greatly. Much of the material he sent on SIS personalities was extremely banal, though spiced with the vicious and superficial little personal appraisals that later characterized *My Silent War*, e.g. 'Stewart Menzies is a weak CSS [Chief of Secret Service] who is irascible rather than strong', or on David Boyle, who was respon-sible for handling Triple X material, the intelligence extracted from diplomatic bags: 'Boyle is an exceptionally nasty person . . . In peacetime, he was CSS's stockbroker, so he has a considerable pull in the office.' Of much higher quality was Philby's analysis of SIS's structure, and he also provided valuable single items of intelligence. But his material served to poison Anglo-Soviet relations. In particu-lar he fuelled the groundless Soviet fears concerning Rudolf Hess, reporting on 18 May 1941: 'Hess may possibly become the focal point of intrigues and compromise peace conclusions and . . . he will be useful to the peace party in England and to Hitler.' Philby's malign speculations compounded the foolish policy of silence over Hess developed by the Foreign Office, so that Stalin remained suspicious that Britain might use Hess to reach a deal with Hitler. Philby made matters worse by the spin he put on the Canaris affair. Philby learned from intercepted *Abwehr* traffic that its chief, Admiral Canaris, was due to visit Spain. Philby proposed that SOE should assassinate Canaris. His plan was approved by Cowgill but rejected by Menzies, no doubt concerned about the potential impact on Anglo-Spanish relations, and unenthusiastic about the prospect of Nazi retaliation: it seems dog seldom eats dog in that world. Philby reported to the KGB that it was possible that SIS and *Abwehr* were in collusion.[16]

The material Philby provided to the Soviets during the war years was not as significant as that sent by Blunt and Cairncross, both of whom provided intelligence on German military operations. Philby and the others fondly imagined that their prodigious labours were appreciated in Moscow. In reality the KGB was unable to read all the material they supplied. Yuri Modin, who worked from December 1943 as an English translator in the KGB's Lubyanka HQ in Moscow, aka the Centre, recalls that a steady flow of intelligence arrived from Britain:

> Seven individuals who worked day and night at the Lubyanka would dip more or less at random into the pile, translate what they could of it, and file the rest away 'to be read later'. This was a euphemism for forgetting about a good proportion of the information gathered by our agents in England . . . their telegrams and reports had barely a fifty per cent chance of being read.

The sheer volume of the Five's material convinced a group within Moscow Centre that the Cambridge spies were double agents really working for the British. The leading advocate of this conspiracy theory was Elena Modrzhinskaya, whose job was to analyse and distribute agent information. Modrzhinskaya argued that Philby's intelligence was disinformation. It served Britain's interests and did not help with the KGB's main concern, namely catching British agents spying against the USSR. Soviet Intelligence refused to believe Britain did not have any agents in Russia and concluded Philby must be withholding names in the interests of his real masters.[17]

In Stalin's Russia paranoia was praised as vigilance and could be sure of a favourable reception. In October 1943 Moscow Centre wrote to the KGB London residency stating that it had decided that Philby, Burgess, Blunt and Cairncross were British agents who had been planted into the KGB network. In contrast, Maclean might just be the innocent dupe of British Intelligence. Although the four were regarded as double agents, the Centre nevertheless wished contact to be maintained with them because of the value of their material on the Germans. Meanwhile the KGB sought to check the authenticity of the Cambridge spies' information by matching it with material obtained through independent sources. This check suggested that Philby and the others were bona fide. For example,

Philby provided the SIS file on 'Co-operation between the British and Soviet Intelligence Services' and this tallied completely with a copy obtained independently. Furthermore, Pavel Fitin, the Centre's Chief of Intelligence, pointed out in his final report on the inquiry that Philby had passed on many files, 'the contents of which rules out any premeditation on the part of the Intelligence Service to pass them over to us through Philby'. Fitin concluded that the work of the Cambridge group was authentic and thus in August 1944 they returned to favour.[18]

Happily unaware of the profound misgivings he had aroused in Moscow, Philby passed to his Soviet control a written report on SIS plans to set up a new section specializing on international communism. The KGB told Philby to try to become head of the new section. Cowgill, his main rival for the post, had made himself unpopular through withholding counter-intelligence from other departments. In contrast, Philby had been winning friends through handing it out. In a post that required particularly close co-operation with MI5, he was the obvious choice. Towards the end of 1944 Philby was indeed appointed, and with Vivian's help pushed through a plan for his new section, which included a large number of overseas stations run by officers under diplomatic cover responsible to Philby. The KGB had previously suspected him because he could not provide the names of any agents working against the Soviet Union. Once he was head of Section IX Philby made up for this with a vengeance. After the Soviet Union replaced Germany as the main SIS target, Philby betrayed many agents recruited for work against communism. Britain's targets included the former Baltic States of Lithuania, Latvia and Estonia seized by Russia in 1940 and now being reoccupied by the Red Army. In 1944 Philby set up the anti-Bolshevik Bloc of Nations (ABN) as a front organization to co-ordinate the recruitment of Baltic spy networks previously controlled by the Nazis. The anti-communism of former Nazi agents seemed guaranteed. Many ex-Nazis including war criminals were smuggled out of Eastern Europe, provided with funds and new identities, and sent back home to work for Britain. They then recruited further agents, ostensibly for Britain, but their main effect was to identify dissidents for the KGB. On their eventual exposure the spyrings could be tainted with the charge of Nazi associations.[19]

Just as Philby's career in both British and Soviet Intelligence was taking off, it was nearly ended by a defection. In August 1945 a KGB operative named Konstantin Volkov who was working under consular cover in Istanbul called at the British Consulate and offered to defect. He claimed that during the war there had been two Soviet agents in the Foreign Office and seven in British Intelligence, one of whom headed a section of British counter-espionage. Volkov was about to expose the Cambridge spies. When his offer reached Menzies, the Chief of the Secret Service, he called in Philby, his anti-Soviet expert, to discuss the matter. The obvious course for the British to take was to spirit Volkov out of Istanbul. Philby was placed in charge of the operation but managed to warn the KGB, who snatched Volkov. Philby was rattled by his close escape and wrote an ill-judged report on the affair for SIS that called Volkov a traitor, an odd way for an SIS officer to describe a Soviet defector. Philby also tried too hard to discredit Volkov's intelligence. In 1945 his prestige in SIS was so high that his bizarre attitude to Volkov was overlooked. But when Philby later fell under suspicion it would bolster the case against him.[20]

Philby's destruction of Volkov made it possible for the Cambridge Five to continue their espionage for almost six more years, and this long period of remission produced an enormous dividend of intelligence for the KGB. After the war John Cairncross returned to the Treasury. By 1948 Cairncross was supplying intelligence on the financing of the British Army, the Royal Navy and the RAF. Modin claims that by autumn 1948 Cairncross was in a position to tell the KGB everything about Nato.[21] Burgess was also becoming highly productive. He had joined the news department of the Foreign Office in 1944 and on 31 December 1946 he was confirmed as private secretary to Hector McNeil, Minister of State at the Foreign Office in the Labour Government. McNeil was lazy and got Burgess to read through his letters and documents instead of doing it himself. Amongst other things, Burgess was able to provide the KGB with correspondence between Britain and its allies concerning the international conferences of the post-war period.[22]

In contrast, Philby's value to the Soviets was somewhat diminished in 1947 by a posting to Istanbul where he headed the SIS station. Philby could have avoided or at least postponed such a move away from headquarters, but he probably wanted to get out of the kitchen for a while, and the money was better overseas. By the time he arrived in Istanbul Philby had been working for the Russians for thirteen years and the strain was taking its toll. On one occasion Philby was invited to lunch at a colleague's house. He drank most of a bottle of gin, washing this down with several glasses of red and white wines. After a trip to the bathroom he returned licking his lips. He had been drinking eau de cologne.[23]

Under the strain of his double life Philby was lurching downhill. He did not seem to perform as well in the field as at headquarters. SIS tasked Philby with recruiting agents to gather intelligence in the southern regions of Russia from the Ukraine to the Caucasus. Philby sought out natives of these regions who still had relatives there and suggested they return on behalf of British Intelligence. Philby passed details of his recruits and their date and place of arrival to the KGB, condemning to death or imprisonment those he had personally persuaded to work for Britain. However, he did not drink from remorse over his dead agents, but rather from anxiety for his own skin should he be caught.[24]

Philby's deterioration did not prevent a final prestigious appointment. In 1949 he was posted to Washington as SIS liaison officer with the FBI and CIA. It seemed that Philby was being groomed for the top job. By 1950 Menzies and his deputy, Major-General John Sinclair, had worked out a preferred sequence for the future chiefs of SIS. Menzies would be followed in turn by two armed service officers already working in SIS, first Sinclair himself and then Air Commodore Jack Easton. Next, Philby would succeed. To prepare him for his future role Philby was to be brought back from Washington and appointed Assistant Chief of the Secret Service, fourth in the SIS hierarchy. Such a senior appointment needed the approval of the Permanent Under-Secretary at the Foreign Office, Sir William Strang. Strang asked Patrick Reilly, Assistant Under-Secretary responsible for Foreign Office relations with SIS, to make a recommendation. In summer 1950 Philby visited London and was seen by Reilly. Philby showed signs of heavy drinking and made a bad impression on Reilly, who told Menzies and Sinclair there was something wrong with Philby and also reported in the same vein to Strang. So although SIS saw Philby as its eventual head, the Foreign Office did not agree to this plan, and vetoed his appointment as Assistant Chief. Philby would never have become Chief of the Secret Service. Had Reilly decided in favour of Philby in 1950, he would have been brought home from Washington permanently and might have avoided later exposure. For if treason prospers none dare call it treason.[25]

Philby had arrived in Washington soon after Maclean had finished a tour of service there. Maclean's work at the British Embassy had won golden opinions from both his British and Russian masters. His willingness to take on wearing extra jobs impressed his British colleagues. The KGB appreciated the intelligence he provided on America's nuclear weapons. Maclean also provided copies of correspondence between the British and American Governments. In the summer of 1947 he denounced the Marshall Plan to the Soviets, claiming that its goal was to achieve American economic domination of Europe. Before passing this material on to Stalin, Deputy Foreign Minister Andrei Vyshinsky sought to check the credibility of the Cambridge spies. He was concerned the group might have been compromised by Alexander Orlov, who had escaped to America in 1938. Vyshinsky asked Pavel Sudoplatov of the KGB whether Philby, Maclean and Burgess might be engaged in a double game. Soviet doubts about their English spies had resurfaced, though in this case Sudoplatov was able to reassure Vyshinsky. But although they had survived further scepticism in Moscow, the Cambridge agents were now working on borrowed time. In 1945 an item of Maclean's diplomatic material had been put into code carelessly by a Soviet cipher clerk, who included a serial number from Maclean's copy allocated to the British Embassy in Washington. Western security decoded the message and realized that the Soviets had an agent delivering secret documents from the British Embassy in Washington. But the Embassy had hundreds of personnel and at first it was assumed that only a cleaner or some similar person would spy for the Russians.[26]

In his new post liaising with American Intelligence Philby was ideally placed to inform the KGB of the progress of the hunt for the embassy spy. According to Harry Rositzke, a former operative in the US Central Intelligence Agency (CIA), Philby had frequent contact with senior CIA officers, including the Director. Philby played a central role in various covert operations which the SIS and the CIA mounted jointly in the late 1940s and early 1950s to undermine the Soviet Bloc. The most disastrous of these was intended to split Albania from the communist sphere. The operation was run by an SIS-CIA committee in Washington with Philby as joint commander. Until 1952 agents were sent in groups to Albania. Most were caught and killed. According to Modin, Philby provided the KGB with precise details of the first three incursions. In each case the information was passed on to the Albanians who were able to ambush the agents as they arrived. Even without Philby's treachery, the Albanian operation was misconceived and suffered from poor security. The landings continued to be intercepted after Philby had been recalled to London and was no longer in a position to betray them. Philby also sat in on several Anglo-American meetings that co-ordinated the dropping of British and US agent teams into the Baltic States and the Ukraine. But one should be wary of using Philby as the sole explanation for the disasters that befell Anglo-American spy networks in Eastern Europe. As with Albania, so too elsewhere, betrayals took place for which Philby could scarcely have been responsible.[27]

While Philby damaged American interests behind a facade of charm, Burgess was unable to conceal his visceral hatred of the United States. He had been transferred to the Washington Embassy in the summer of 1950. There was scarcely any posting for which he was less suited. To compound the disaster, Philby invited Burgess to stay with him. This was a serious error on Philby's part. It was unwise for two agents to associate together so openly. But where Burgess was concerned, Philby's characteristic shrewdness ceased to apply. Having dumped Burgess onto the Washington Embassy, the Foreign Office now pondered what to do with Maclean, who had been sent home from a senior posting in Cairo after becoming a violent drunk. He was treated by a psychiatrist and then appointed head of the American department of the Foreign Office. It was the height of the Korean War, and Maclean was ideally placed to supply intelligence on Anglo-American discussions about Korea. In December 1950 Prime Minister Attlee went to Washington to urge America not to use nuclear weapons in Korea. Maclean provided Soviet Intelligence with Attlee's briefings for this visit and the details of the discussions. The papers found in Maclean's files after his flight included a copy of Attlee's report to the Cabinet on his visit. Maclean's material was of such value that despite the progress of the inquiry into the embassy spy, Moscow Centre ordered that, 'Maclean must be kept in place for as long as possible.'[28]

However, by early 1951 the suspects had been reduced to three, including Maclean. Philby and Burgess now decided that he had to be warned. Burgess was being sent home by the Ambassador anyway for collecting multiple speeding tickets. So he could pass a warning. Before he left Washington Philby made Burgess swear to stay in London himself, pointing out that if he left for Russia with Maclean, MI5's logical next step would be to arrest Philby. Burgess promised not to defect himself. On arriving in England, Burgess alerted the KGB through Anthony Blunt. Moscow Centre now quickly agreed to Maclean's defection. When Maclean said that he was not strong enough to go through with it by himself, the Centre radioed: 'Burgess will leave with Maclean, but only as his travelling companion', implying he could return to England. Once the two spies reached Prague there was no turning back for Burgess. His flight ended Cairncross's employment as a British official because some of his material for the KGB was found in Burgess's flat.[29]

Philby's career was also finished. The Centre seems to have overlooked the impact of Burgess's flight on Philby's position, or perhaps lingering suspicion of Philby made them indifferent. The CIA Director demanded his immediate recall to England. On his return Philby was gently questioned by Dick White of MI5 who reported to Menzies that he was suspect. Menzies was not convinced but bowed to pressure from the CIA and MI5. Philby was asked to resign from SIS and given a golden handshake. London was trying to be fair to him, but in Moscow his treatment was seen as strangely indulgent, and awoke once again the old suspicions. Otto John, Head of the Federal Internal Security Office in West Germany from 1950, later claimed that he was kidnapped in 1954 so the KGB could check whether Philby was reliable. The KGB wanted to compare John's account of his dealings with the British during the war against Philby's version of the same events. John wrote: 'This is the only explanation I can give for the fact that my interrogations [in the USSR] concentrated upon my connections with the British secret service and upon potential promises by the British government in the event of a successful coup d'état against Hitler.'[30]

Although Philby had resisted throughout repeated questioning, rumours circulated in London that he was the mysterious 'Third Man' who had warned Burgess and Maclean. In October 1955 the matter was brought to a head when a parliamentary question identified Philby. In the absence of conclusive evidence the Foreign Secretary Harold Macmillan exonerated him and SIS friends helped him to find a job as a journalist in Beirut. Only in 1962 did conclusive evidence against Philby emerge. A pre-war friend of Philby's named Flora Solomon, angered by some anti-Israel articles he had written, revealed that he had tried to recruit her as a communist agent.[31]

In January 1963 Nicholas Elliott, one of Philby's old friends in SIS, was sent out to confront him in Beirut. Elliott told Philby that SIS now had irrefutable proof that he was a Soviet agent and produced Solomon's testimony. Elliott offered Philby immunity from prosecution in return for a full confession. Philby pretended to accept the offer and Elliott transferred the case to the SIS station chief in Beirut. While SIS in London were still drawing up the list of questions for him, Philby contacted the KGB who told him to board the Soviet cargo ship *Dolmatova*, lying in the port of Beirut. On 27 January Philby arrived in Moscow.[32]

Philby's reception in Moscow was not what he expected. He was not made an officer in the KGB, but remained an ordinary agent. There was a strong element of careerism in Philby. In the foreword to *My Silent War*, he commented on his recruitment by the Soviets that, 'One does not look twice at an offer of enrolment in an elite force.' But the 'elite force' looked askance at Philby time and time again. It did not give him an influential post in Moscow Centre, but put him out to pasture to write his memoirs.[33]

These were published as *My Silent War* in 1968. After the KGB had approved a synopsis, first Modin and then another KGB officer closely controlled Philby's progress with the content of his memoirs. Philby had two principal goals, to praise the KGB and to denigrate Western Intelligence. His eulogy of the KGB verged at times on the ridiculous, and served not least as a crude ploy to incite others to treachery. Philby lied about his status in the KGB and gave a highly selective account of his work for it. While his writing about Western Intelligence unfairly maligned many of the personalities involved, his account of the institutions and operations of British Intelligence in the struggle against the German Secret Service is largely borne out by the official history of British Counter-Intelligence.[34]

Once they had exploited his memoirs for a propaganda triumph, the KGB had no further practical use for Philby. Indeed it was felt he might be a double agent sent to penetrate the KGB. So his telephone was tapped, his flat was bugged, his mail was opened and a check was kept on his visitors. Philby was only rehabilitated after Yuri Andropov, the head of the KGB, decided that defectors to the Soviet Union had a further propaganda use. They were to be given an enviable existence that would be publicized to attract further defectors. Oleg Kalugin was told to improve the lot of foreign defectors in Moscow, in particular Kim Philby. Not only were unhappy defectors bad publicity for the KGB, there was also the danger of a propaganda disaster if they were lured home. Philby told the East German spy-master Markus Wolf that SIS had approached him several times in Moscow with offers for him to return to England. But Philby was in no state for such an exploit. When Kalugin visited Philby in early 1972 he found a 'wreck of a man reeking of vodka'. His 'bent figure caromed off the walls as he walked'. Aided by Philby's Russian wife Rufina, Kalugin gradually sobered him up and gave him renewed purpose by consulting him on KGB foreign operations. Philby also invited to tea KGB officers bound for England or the dominions and briefed them on English customs. Furthermore, he took part in KGB 'active measures' by faking documents for distribution abroad that suggested the US had aggressive military plans. Philby's propaganda career continued even after his death on 11 May 1988. His Soviet obituary proclaimed once more the lie that he had been working for peace.[35]

Philby's later exploits for the KGB scarcely bore comparison with his earlier work. Although Maclean provided intelligence of greater value, much of his espionage was only made possible by Philby's destruction of Volkov in 1945. Philby's treachery demoralized some colleagues in SIS, undermined its reputation, and weakened for a time the Anglo-American Intelligence relationship. Philby provided the KGB with a wealth of material on British and American Intelligence and later served as a formidable propaganda tool. Nevertheless, as Patrick Seale wrote, 'both man and career have been greatly inflated'. The Foreign Office rejected the plan for him to become Chief of the British Secret Service, and he was never fully trusted by the KGB. Although Philby sacrificed wives, friends, agents and his country to the Soviet cause, even such a bounty of treachery failed to convince the KGB that he was really on their side.[36]

The evidence from Russia undermines the Philby myth because

it shows that Philby's pompous self-estimation was by no means shared by his Soviet masters, and that Philby was miserable in Moscow. Kalugin observed that, 'There was, after all, something ineffably sad about Philby, something in his expression, in his bearing, that told you this was a man carrying a heavy burden.' Kalugin also brings out Philby's essential callousness: 'Philby knew that his spying . . . had doomed many men and it didn't seem to haunt him.' But if Philby was indifferent to the human misery he had caused, why was he so troubled at the end of his life? Partly, of course, it was the unhappiness of an exile, heightened in Philby's case by a particular – and under the circumstances highly ironical – fondness for the English way of life. This affection was made bitter by the certain knowledge that he could never again experience English customs at first hand. But, more significantly, Philby was saddened by the failure of his own career. If he had not been misled by a criminally foolish don at Cambridge, he might have ended his days not in Moscow exile as simple 'Agent Tom' but at home in England as a former senior official, or even head, of the British Secret Service.[37]

* * *

NOTES

1. Harry Rositzke, *The KGB: The Eyes of Russia* (London, 1982), p. 119; Hugh Trevor-Roper, *The Philby Affair* (London, 1968), p. 41; Bruce Page, David Leitch and Phillip Knightley, *Philby: The Spy Who Betrayed a Generation* (Harmondsworth, 1969); Phillip Knightley, *Philby: KGB Masterspy* (London, 1989), p. 1.

2. I am greately indebted to Lord Dacre of Glanton, the late Sir Patrick Reilly, Dr Richard J. Aldrich, the late Mr Robert Cecil and the late Mr Nicholas Elliott for their generous help. Responsibility for the selection and interpretation of evidence is exclusively my own. For a thoughtful analysis of the new KGB sources, cf. Sheila Kerr, 'KGB Sources on the Cambridge Network of Soviet Agents: True or False?', *Intelligence and National Security*, vol. 11, no. 3 (July 1996), pp. 561–85.

3. P(ublic) R(ecord) O(ffice) FO 953/2165, Sir M. Crosthwaite Beirut to Foreign Office, 1 March 1963; Malcolm Muggeridge, *Chronicles of Wasted Time* vol. 2: *The Infernal Grove* (London 1973), p. 125; Oleg Kalugin, *Spymaster: My 32 Years in Intelligence and Espionage Against the West* (London, 1995), p. 133. Kalugin's memoirs contain inaccuracies such as the implied date of

publication of Philby's memoirs and Kalugin's assertion that Philby never visited East Germany: cf. Markus Wolf, *Memoirs of a Spymaster* (London, 1998), pp. 92–3; Knightley, *Philby: KGB Masterspy*, p. 45.

4. John Costello and Oleg Tsarev, *Deadly Illusions* (London, 1993), pp. 136–7 and 151. I follow the practice of Oleg Gordievsky and Christopher Andrew in using the term KGB to denote Soviet State Security throughout this piece, cf. idem, *KGB: The Inside Story of its Foreign Operations from Lenin to Gorbachev* (London, 1990), p. xii.

5. Costello and Tsarev, *Deadly Illusions*, pp. 160–1; Muggeridge, *The Infernal Grove*, p. 126; Nigel West, *MI5: British Security Service Operations 1909–1945* (London, 1981), p. 91.

6. Costello and Tsarev, *Deadly Illusions*, pp. 163–6.

7. Ibid., pp. 201–3 and 219. For the controversy over Maclean's recruitment see Kerr, 'KGB Sources', p. 575.

8. Costello and Tsarev, *Deadly Illusions*, p. 213.

9. Ibid., p. 214; Andrew and Gordievsky, *KGB: The Inside Story*, p. 174.

10. Genrikh Borovik, *The Philby Files: The Secret Life of the Master Spy – KGB Archives Revealed* (London, 1994), pp. 162–3. *The Memoirs of Lord Gladwyn* (London, 1972), p. 101; PRO HS 6/855 Ministry of Economic Warfare (Hugh Gaitskell) to R.A. Leeper, XO/157/4, 27 May 1941; Imperial War Museum, Gubbins' diary, entries for 27 July and 1 September 1941.

11. Desmond Bristow with Bill Bristow, *A Game of Moles: The Deceptions of an MI6 Officer* (London, 1993), p. 273; Patrick Seale and Maureen McConville, *Philby: The Long Road to Moscow* (London, 1973), p. 135; Richard Griffiths, *Patriotism Perverted: Captain Ramsay, the Right Club and British Anti-Semitism 1939–40* (London, 1998), pp. 55 and 139; Noel Annan, *Our Age: The Generation That Made Post-War Britain* (London, 1991), p. 315; A.W. Brian Simpson, *In The Highest Degree Odious: Detention without Trial in Wartime Britain* (Oxford, 1992), p. 216.

12. Christopher Andrew, *Secret Service: The Making of the British Intelligence Community* (London, 1985), p. 461; Letter of Mr Nicholas Elliott to E.D.R. Harrison, 23 December 1992; Lord Dacre to E.D.R. Harrison, 18 September 1995; Page, Leitch and Knightley, *Philby*, p. 124. For an assessment of SIS in the Second World War, see E.D.R. Harrison, 'More Thoughts on Kim Philby's *My Silent War*', *Intelligence and National Security*, vol. 10, no. 3 (July 1995), pp. 514–25.

13. Kim Philby, *My Silent War* (London, 1968), pp. 60–5; Charles Stuart, 'The Philby Phenomenon', *Spectator*, 26 April 1968.

14. Bristow, *A Game of Moles*, pp. 27–30, 264 and 274; F.H. Hinsley and C.A.G. Simkins, *British Intelligence in the Second World War*, vol. 4, *Security and Counter-Intelligence* (London, 1990), pp. 160–2.

15. Stuart, 'The Philby Phenomenon'.

16. Nigel West and Oleg Tsarev, *The Crown Jewels: The British Secrets at the Heart of the KGB Archives* (London, 1998). See Appendix II, 'The Philby Reports', pp. 295–345; Borovik, *The Philby Files*, p. 185; Yuri Modin with

Jean-Charles Deniau and Aguieszka Ziarek, *My Five Cambridge Friends* (London, 1994), pp. 62–3; private information; Andrew and Gordievsky, *KGB: The Inside Story*, p. 241. For the British reaction to Hess cf. E.D.R. Harrison, ' "... *wir wurden schon viel zu oft hereingelegt*". *Mai 1941: Rudolf Hess in englischer Sicht*' in Kurt Paetzold and Manfred Weissbecker, *Rudolf Hess: Der Mann an Hitlers Seite* (Leipzig, 1999) pp. 368–92.

17. Borovik, *The Philby Files*, pp. 212–13; Modin, *My Five Cambridge Friends*, p. 39; For Modin's tendency to puff the Cambridge spies, cf. Kerr, 'KGB Sources', p. 569.

18. Borovik, *The Philby Files*, pp. 213 and 216–18; West and Tsarev, *The Crown Jewels*, pp. 166–7.

19. Borovik, *The Philby Files*, pp. 231–3; Modin, *My Five Cambridge Friends*, pp. 46 and 126–7; Robert Cecil, 'The Cambridge Comintern' in C. Andrew and D. Dilks (eds.), *The Missing Dimension: Governments and Intelligence Communities in the Twentieth Century* (London, 1984), p. 180; N. Docherty (Producer), 'Philby and the Nazis', *This Week* (BBC Television, 1988).

20. Modin, *My Five Cambridge Friends*, p. 124; Andrew and Gordievsky, *KGB: The Inside Story*, pp. 305–7.

21. Modin, *My Five Cambridge Friends*, pp. 146–50 and 167–8.

22. PRO CSC 11/38 report on service, 3 September 1947; Modin, *My Five Cambridge Friends*, pp. 150–8.

23. Private information; Seale and McConville, *Philby: The Long Road to Moscow*, p. 186.

24. Modin, *My Five Cambridge Friends*, p. 159.

25. Knightley; *Philby: KGB Masterspy*, p. 150; Trevor-Roper, *The Philby Affair*, pp. 41–3; Sir Patrick Reilly to E.D.R. Harrison, 18 March and 15 April 1993, 19 June 1999.

26. Modin, *My Five Cambridge Friends*, p. 119; Pavel Sudoplatov and Anatoli Sudoplatov, *The Memoirs of an Unwanted Witness – A Soviet Spymaster* (London, 1995), p. 231.

27. Rositzke, *The KGB*, pp. 119 and 124; Knightley, *Philby: KGB Masterspy*, p. 157; Modin, *My Five Cambridge Friends*, p. 186; Tom Bower, *The Red Web: MI6 and the KGB Master Coup* (London, 1989), p. 120; Anthony Cavendish, *Inside Intelligence* (London, 1990), p. 59.

28. Modin, *My Five Cambridge Friends*, pp. 183 and 196; Cecil, 'The Cambridge Comintern', p. 192.

29. Modin, *My Five Cambridge Friends*, pp. 199–203.

30. Ibid., pp. 216–17; Page, Leitch and Knightley, *Philby*, p. 277; Tom Bower, *The Perfect English Spy: Sir Dick White and the Secret War 1935–90* (London, 1995), pp. 121–8 and 134; Otto John, *Twice Through the Lines* (London, 1972), p. 314.

31. Modin, *My Five Cambridge Friends*, pp. 232–4; Peter Wright with Paul Greengrass, *Spycatcher: The Candid Autobiography of a Senior Intelligence Officer* (New York, 1987), p. 164.

32. Modin, *My Five Cambridge Friends*, p. 257; Andrew and Gordievsky, *KGB: The Inside Story*, p. 361; Bower, *The Perfect English Spy*, pp. 291–302.

33. Andrew and Gordievsky, *KGB: The Inside Story*, p. xxii; Philby, *My Silent War*, p. xix.

34. Modin, *My Five Cambridge Friends*, pp. 258–9; Hinsley and Simkins, *Security and Counter-Intelligence*; for a more detailed analysis of *My Silent War*, cf. E.D.R. Harrison, 'Some Reflections on Kim Philby's *My Silent War* as a Historical Source' in Richard J. Aldrich and Michael F. Hopkins (eds.), *Intelligence, Defence and Diplomacy: British Policy in the Post-War World* (London, 1994), pp. 205–25.

35. Kalugin, *Spymaster*, pp. 132–3 and 137; Wolf, *Memoirs of a Spymaster*, p. 93; Knightley, *Philby: KGB Masterspy*, p. 260.

36. Cavendish, *Inside Intelligence*, p. viii; Bristow, *A Game of Moles*, p. 252; Patrick Seale, 'The shy Philby I knew', *Observer*, 15 May 1988.

37. Kalugin, *Spymaster*, pp. 143–6.

Robert Kee

PARNELL AND THE
GOOD FRIDAY AGREEMENT

HIS PLACE IN IRISH NATIONALISM

*What do you think Parnell would have said about the Good Friday
Agreement and where we are with it now?*

The question, posed just before the critical summer of 1999,
came out of the genial hubbub of a drinks party. As with almost
any question about Northern Ireland today, the only possible
immediate reply was a considered pause. This disguises wrestling
with the problem inherent in any discussion which has Irish nationalism at its heart, of how far back to go. The only feasible line
perhaps a throw-away in the same vein: 'It depends on whether he
had yet met Katie O'Shea.'

Playing games with history is not a serious academic exercise,
though both Churchill on the Battle of Gettysburg and Robert
Harris on the end of the Second World War had some serious fun
with it. The fantasy of getting Parnell to look at the Good Friday
Agreement dissolves rather too quickly. Somebody had to win or
draw at Gettysburg; somebody had to win the Second World War.
But there can be small reality in the thought of Parnell looking at
the Good Friday Agreement and saying anything – not so much
because of the time-distance, which is part of the game, but because
he would have been largely nonplussed, if also delighted, by what
he found, and he was not the sort of man to admit to being nonplussed by anything.

However, it could be rewarding to try to share with him some
of the thoughts and memories that might pass through his head as

he briefly brings himself up to date and strives to come to terms
with his nonplussment.

What, for a start, is this 'Ulster' that is not Ulster? It is only
two-thirds of it. It is an Ulster deprived of the very three counties
(Cavan, Monaghan and Donegal) that helped give him a majority of
Ulster MPs before the 1886 Home Rule Bill. And this diminution of
nationalism in Ulster is the result of a temporary concession made
by a nationalist leader (Redmond) who had been one of his most
ardent admirers! Redmond's hope, it seems, had been to make it
easier eventually to get an All-Ireland Home Rule Bill through both
Houses of Parliament and onto the Statute Book. But an All-Ireland
Home Rule Bill did get through both Houses of Parliament and
onto the Statute Book, in 1914, and was never implemented! No
wonder the Fenians – militarily nil in his day, though very useful at
times in other ways – had at last, some eighty years ago, been able
to take to arms effectively. There is no doubt that he would strongly
have applauded that.

At intervals throughout his life he had made clear, both privately
and at times publicly, that his ultimate hope for Ireland was for
sovereign independence. 'An Englishman of the strongest type
moulded for an Irish purpose' was how a nationalist stalwart of the
day had seen him on first meeting, though he left out perhaps the
most important part, which was that he was also half American. In
1879 in Co. Cavan in Ulster (yes, Ulster) a great crowd had cheered
him to the echo when he had told them there were no constitutional
lengths to which Ireland should not be prepared to go, and that
when they had their country to themselves their children would
thank them 'as the people of America thanked those noble men like
George Washington and others who in 1775 secured the independence of America'. At Waterford in 1880 he had made his point
even more clearly. Stressing that, 'our present path is within the
Constitution' and that he would stick with that 'as long as it suits
us', he suggested that should there ever be a chance of going to war
for what they wanted 'with prospect of success', any true Irishman
would consider it his 'highest duty' to give his life for his country.

It is true that at the time of the first Home Rule Bill he expressed
his 'belief' that the limited Home Rule it conferred would prove 'a
final settlement'. There were to be those then, and indeed for the
rest of his life, who inferred that his preparedness for compromise

owed much to his consuming passion for the 'darling wife' – as he even then liked to think of her – living at Eltham in Kent. But politically his all-important consideration had been to reassure wavering Liberals in Gladstone's party that Home Rule did not break the link with Britain; and anyway 'belief', by definition, inevitably covers a certain future inexactness. Looking today at the developments since his own time he could reasonably enough claim that the 'settlement' he had been prepared to accept would finally have provided, to coin a phrase, 'the freedom to win freedom'.

So bravo, he would undoubtedly have said, for the bold Fenian men – those of 1919–21 anyway who had been right to fight and who had won the freedom for an 'Irish Free State' to win freedom. Now for fifty years there has been an Irish democratic sovereign state, the Republic of Ireland, more flourishing today than ever before. It embodies the greater part of the population of the country and, more important, marks the culmination of more than seven hundred years' struggle to give lasting political coherence to Irish national identity.

I am not sure he would have summed it up in quite such historical abstraction as this. There were mixed views among his contemporaries about how much Irish history he actually knew, but he had a sound feel for its emotional resonance, the one constant factor in an Irish 'nationalism' that over those seven hundred years had otherwise seldom maintained a consistent external character for long.

But to return to the last fifty years and further thoughts which perhaps in more senses than one, we can share with him.

That it should have proved impossible during these fifty years to adjust what to him had been the relatively subsidiary problem of the six counties of Ulster might seem in retrospect extraordinary. After all, the British Government in its statutory recognition of the Republic of Ireland had raised no constitutional objection in principle to the whole island eventually uniting as one state. And the Irish Government had long formally accepted the British Government's only proviso, namely that before final unity can come about, a democratic majority in the six counties must first agree to it. The important thing now for him would be that the goal for which he entered politics at a time when the goal seemed virtually unobtainable, namely to make Ireland 'a Nation once again', has been achieved. Only a relatively small proportion of its territory is still to come. Political engineering of the sort in which he had specialized all his political life should, he might have thought, been able to complete the job in a great deal less than fifty years.

The Good Friday Agreement is the most recent precarious attempt to make progress on the matter and by far the most ambitious. It marks a positive acknowledgement of the northern minority's Irish national aspirations: it involves among other changes a North–South Council, which can concern itself with such common matters as health, education, social security and environmental development. But why so long in getting even here? And why, with sound electoral majorities in both parts of Ireland endorsing the Agreement, such difficulty from the start in carrying it into effect? Someone coming to look at all this out of the blue would need more information about what on earth has been going on these past fifty years.

The trouble, as he might see it, has come from a group of self-styled 'republicans' based mainly in the false Ulster, trying to solve the problem by Fenian violence in opposition not only to the British Government but to that of the Republic of Ireland too. How could they possibly have thought they could win this way with the Republic of Ireland itself and the vast majority of Irishmen all over Ireland against them? For thirty years they have enacted a travesty of a noble past, and got nowhere in the process except to graves.

Well, yes, it can be said reasonably that this Agreement itself is an achievement of their long and bloody campaign. When they announced their ceasefire, unsuccessful in their chief aim as they had been for so many years, they were also, as they had been for so many years, undefeated on the ground. This Good Friday design, which they have thereby 'won', has indeed a much more national character than anything the Unionists were ever prepared to support in the past. A majority of them (even if a slim majority) are now prepared to support it, whereas in the past a very large majority of Unionists were unable to support a similar idea when it came, strangely, from Sunningdale in Surrey. The present Agreement undoubtedly brings the prospect of a united Ireland nearer. So why have the 'republican' hard men seemed so reluctant to accept it in full as an achievement, reserving the right even to take arms against it should they decide to do so?

In this respect further questions might pass through our Parnell's head. How far, for instance, has the motivation of these northern 'republicans' been pathological, that is to say, a holier-than-thou ideological self-indulgence for a Holy Grail Irish Republic, the search for which could continue for ever? How many of them really thought all these years that their campaign of violence actually had a chance of bringing the 'six counties' into the Republic of Ireland? Some clearly have seen reason and moved into the Agreement's political process. But how could others still think they might one day succeed?

The answer may lie in the basis for another question. How was it that the British Government, apart from being unable to deal with the political problem all these years, was also unable to deal with, or at least confidently contain, the physical problem of the violence? How, with the Regular Army, the police and a highly sophisticated intelligence service at their disposal, and the moral and intelligence support of the Republic of Ireland behind them, were they unable positively to defeat the hard men on the ground, or even stop them practising their own version of justice in people's homes and on the streets?

The answer to that bewildering question will be, if only as a footnote, in future history books. But what of our Parnell's comments: his emphasis on the Republic of Ireland as the most significant feature since his own time and his assessment that the problem of the 'six counties' need not have been the problem in the last fifty years that it turned out to be? Could not he himself possibly bear some responsibility for what has for so long gone so wrong?

That he would have applauded enthusiastically the existence today of a sovereign Republic of Ireland is in character and logical. Its achievement owes as much to him as it does to those who, in practical terms, helped bring it about, though few of those who most dogmatically proclaim themselves Republicans would be interested in recognizing this.

The first principle of his attitude to British Government had always been 'They will do what we can make them do.' On one level, certainly, it could be said that all he had succeeded in making them do was to take the idea of Home Rule for All-Ireland seriously enough to introduce a bill for it in the House of Commons in 1886. This failed; he died in 1891. As part of his political legacy a new

Home Rule Bill did pass the Commons in 1893 only to be thrown
out by the House of Lords. There it remained on the floor for the
better part of twenty years. This is not, in the minds of some
contemporary Republicans, a notably significant achievement.

Yet the reality of his achievement behind these events is of great
historical importance. It was instrumental in laying the foundations
of modern Irish nationalism, and is linked for good or ill to the
reality of everything that has happened in Ireland since, including
the Good Friday Agreement.

The clichéd 'post-colonial' definition of Irish nationalism
obscures the many different realities from which over the centuries
Irish nationalism in a modern form finally emerged. The 'colonists',
first invited over by native Irish to help them in wars against other
native Irish, were themselves mainly to become Irish by identity,
and subsequent generations of 'colonists' continued to do so. After
the Reformation they became, in general, one or the other of two
separate Irish identities, Protestant or Catholic. In the seventeenth
century the Catholic majority identity fought for English Stuart
kings, opposed in one phase by Cromwellian soldiers who themselves sometimes settled down in Ireland to engender Catholic Irish
families. In the eighteenth century it was those of the minority
Protestant identity who as Irishmen called themselves 'Patriots' and
won a theoretical parliamentary independence from Westminster
under the Crown. Parnell's great-grandfather figured prominently in
that Parliament. Broadly speaking, over the centuries the story was
one of different Irish interests, sometimes in relationships of complexity with each other, seeking coherence by identifying themselves
with the nuclear shape of an Irish nation whose ancient roots were
in a nebulous past.

'Nationalism', etymologically a mid-nineteenth-century term,
first appears in an embryonic modern spirit in Ireland at the end of
the eighteenth century under the modernizing influence of the French
Revolution and its Republic. A short-lasting theoretical alliance of
the late 1790s between Catholics and mainly Presbyterian Protestants, each with their own interests disguised under the wish-
fulfilment term 'United Irishmen', failed dismally and bloodily to
live up to its name. But it managed to place on the historical shelf,
as a sort of icon of what Irish nationalism ought to be, and for some
actually was, a bust of the idealist republican Wolfe Tone, who had

been one of the United Irishmen's only begetters. On the shelf that bust rested for a long time while people periodically admired it without taking too much notice of it. Reality took other shapes.

The Act of Union of 1801 that followed the rebellion of 1798 set up a new dimension within which to ponder the nature of Irish 'national' identity. The Protestants, who had been Irish 'Patriots' in the previous century, were now amalgamated with their fellow Protestants across the water as citizens of a united kingdom. This union now also embraced all Irish Catholics whose chief concern was to be emancipated from grievances previously afflicting them under an Irish Parliament, such as their powerlessness to elect Catholics to represent them and the obligation to pay tithes to an established church that was not theirs.

A Catholic lawyer from Co. Kerry, Daniel O'Connell, by being overwhelmingly re-elected to Westminster after being barred the first time from taking his seat, succeeded in winning Catholic Emancipation in 1829, thus acquiring the popular name of 'Liberator'; he had at least liberated the majority of the people of Ireland from the feeling that they were of secondary importance in their own country. He next gave what had been primarily a social political movement a distinct national spin by campaigning for a repeal of the Union and the establishment of an Irish parliament in Dublin.

This time, of course, the parliament would have a mainly Catholic Irish identity, although with ultimate loyalty, like the former Protestant Irish Parliament, to a British monarch. O'Connell regularly ended his vast Repeal meetings of the 1840s – at which it was said, in the days before microphones, that his voice could be heard 'a mile off, as if it were coming through honey' – with three cheers for Queen Victoria.

However, a group of impatient young supporters of his, mainly Protestants, were already taking the national spin on the Repeal movement into regions of their own. Under the group name 'Young Ireland' they enthusiastically studied, on the shelf, the bust of Wolfe Tone with his ideal of uniting Protestants, Catholics and Dissenters in an independent country in the common name of Irishmen.

The devastation of the Great Famine swept away not only a quarter of the Irish population but with it Repeal and all immediate issues on the political scene other than how to cope with the disaster, recover from it, and look to any sort of coherent future. In a last desperate effort to assert some sort of continuing Irish political presence, Young Ireland took Wolfe Tone down from the shelf for revolutionary inspiration, and did indeed make an unsupported gesture of rebellion, but were almost immediately swept away to exile in Australia or the United States, taking with them, to the latter, Tone's bust to do duty, principally from there, in the future.

In the aftermath of the Famine, nationalism in Ireland drifted publicly into a doldrums for many years, leaving only a non-political consciousness of individual Irish identity rock-like in place. Neither in the House of Commons nor in Ireland as a whole was there much evidence of national feeling as a dynamic political force, though a small secret Irish Republican Brotherhood founded largely on Young Ireland's principles dates from this time. More relevant to the reality of things seemed the attitude of the Catholic Church, whose leaders felt understandable reservations about nationalism's potential competition with the Church's own higher claims for moral authority.

It was not until eighteen years after the end of the Repeal movement, that a so-called National League appeared, to work again for a separate Irish parliament in Dublin. The most interesting thing about this was not that it soon folded into the background, as it did, but what it stood for: 'the recovery of our national cause of 1782', which was the date of the Protestant 'Patriot' Parliament's technical gain of independence from Westminster. Unresolved, as if it did not need to be resolved at all, lay the question of how realistic it was to think that the now predominantly Catholicized political scene could be effectively invested with the appeal of eighteenth-century Protestant patriotism. This was one further instance of an imprecision of focus in the Nation which, as the popular song had it, Ireland would once again, one day, be.

Marginally more relevant to a possible contemporary national mood was the event that next relegated such Protestant-conditioned nostalgia to the historical background where it belonged. This was the Fenian Rising of 1867, co-ordinated up to a point by exiles in the United States and the recently formed Irish Republican Brotherhood in Ireland.

The venture was a military anti-climax with few casualties on either side; it signally failed to rouse the countryside. But it was dramatic enough to add to the accumulation of legendary attempts at political definition of Irish national identity.

What in fact was now to determine Ireland's new political future was not a political event but an economic one: an agricultural crisis of menacing dimension eventually projecting Ireland into a political phase from which the troubles of the twentieth century would proceed. It established Parnell himself as a figure of national and historical stature.

He had shown little response to the Fenian Rising other than anger when his American mother's house in Dublin was rigorously searched by police because a letter from her about a medical prescription had been found on a local chemist they were arresting as a Fenian. But in the early 1870s he had decided to enter politics as an appropriate profession for a gentleman landowner with some 5,000 acres in Co. Wicklow and an inclination, inherited both from his American family background and his Protestant 'Patriot Parliament' family background, to view public events with a detached but interested eye. Another gentlemanly organization to campaign again for a Dublin parliament had just come into being, with a quarter of its first members from the Protestant nationalist tradition but in general of wider-based character and outlook. Developing into the Home Rule League it put up its own candidates for the Westminster Parliament and succeeded in nominally re-organizing Ireland's non-Unionist representation there as nationalist rather than liberal. To this new party, committed sometimes rather lethargically to Home Rule, Parnell naturally gravitated. From the start he set his own unlethargic personal stamp on the direction in which he would like it to go.

When he first stood, unsuccessfully, for the Party in Dublin he immediately made clear that at heart he saw Ireland as a separate country. What they were seeing in Home Rule, he told the electors, was only what every other country had: the power to make its own laws. And he reminded them that it was the immense number of Irish who had left Ireland for America who had made that country what it was; as soon as they got Home Rule they would produce 'similar results and similar prosperity here'.

Finally elected in 1875, he at once injected into the Party at Westminster, which had amiably settled down to a flaccid and often apologetic representation of Ireland, a quite new style of independent attack. He backed up his often resented parliamentary offensive with a vigorous counterpart campaign under his leadership in Ireland itself. There he made strategic use of former and still sometimes undercover Fenians who were now ready to accept, for the foreseeable future, the futility of planning another rising with even less chance of success than in 1867, and were eager to agitate for the national cause in whatever form it presented itself.

The form in which it presented itself at the end of the 1870s was the dramatic one of the agricultural crisis. The down to earth everyday interests of that greater part of the Irish population, who were dependent one way or another on tenant farming, were the central feature of Irish daily life. But these were now being severely threatened by the combination of the turn-down in agricultural prices with a three-year succession of poor harvests. The ghost of the Famine of thirty years before, bringing with it the memory of so many personal ghosts and awakening long-slumbering resentment at the apparent inadequacy or even lack of will of the State to do more for the people, began to stalk the fields and villages of Ireland. The familiar everyday issues of fair rent, security of tenure, freedom from eviction, the right to sell a right to the holding, together with the major objective of state-subsidized mortgages for tenants to purchase their holdings for themselves – all these things suddenly took on a new urgency, becoming for a time new matters of life and death. And it was this most emotional Irish cause of all – the Irishman's right to a fair living off the land for himself and his family in his own country – that Parnell now took up and brilliantly intertwined with the political cause of Home Rule and some form of eventual 'independence' for Ireland.

'I believe the land of a country ought to be owned by the people of the country,' he told a crowd at Limerick in 1879 to loud cheers and cries of 'Parnell for ever', going on with a fine example of the linguistic sleight of hand by which he equated the twin causes of Land and Nation:

> Then we will have the farmers of this country occupying the position they ought to hold. We will have them independent in feeling self-reliant and national. We will have an Irish nation which will be able to hold its own against the nations of the world . . . a country which will be able to speak with the enemy at the gate.

He was at times happy to take both issues to extremes. He spoke publicly in September 1880 of the landlord class (the crowds knew of course that he was one himself but a good one and as such could be trusted to know what they were really like): 'the landlord class who do not work, who live upon the stolen fruits of your labour and can be got rid of by organization and determined action . . .' And he went on to talk of 'publicly sowing the seeds of, and the principles of, republicanism, which alone can raise an enslaved people'.

A foreign journalist asked him if he was really quite sure he had not got the balance of the two separate issues in his political campaign the wrong way round. Might it not have been better to put Home Rule first and then, when he had won that, approach the complex land question, which he would then be in a stronger position to resolve? No, replied Parnell, the land question was about the Irish people's daily bread and therefore easier for them to understand, it found its way to their hearts and therefore when linked with Home Rule it brought their hearts with enthusiasm into that movement.

One of his most active Fenian-type supporters put it nobly: 'Irish nationality is the soul of this movement. It inspires the men who are engaged in it in the same way as the soul inspires the body.' Parnell himself put it the other way round. He saw material interests as inspiring the tenant farmer towards the nationalism that was, for the time being, Home Rule.

The progressive land laws, which he succeeded in engineering from the British Government in the course of the 1880s, paved the way for an eventual transformation of the tenant farmer's daily way of life. Fair rent and security of tenure as a legal right, and an extension of state-subsidized mortgages to help the tenant farmer purchase his holding for himself now became part of the present as well as the future. His popular rhetoric constantly linked the land to the nationalist aspiration for Home Rule. The double significance of the word 'land' was invaluable. Railing against 'landlordism' in Cork in 1880 he even turned the word 'land' to historical advantage, proclaiming: 'The people of Ireland are today engaged in a great struggle for the land of this country, which was wrested from them seven centuries ago by force of arms . . .' Determined to take the power of governing Ireland out of the hands of the English

Parliament and into the hands of his own people, they could only secure these ends, he said, 'by making the land of Ireland as free as it was when the waters of the flood left it'.

To have successfully fastened the historically restless soul of Irish national identity at last to a feasible political cause was Parnell's incomparable achievement in terms of modern Irish nationalism. The fact that his political objective of winning a Home Rule Parliament for All-Ireland from Britain was itself never achieved is irrelevant to consideration of his success. It was the firm attachment of the majority of the Irish people to that cause that had been the achievement. When the British Government, having put Home Rule onto the Statute Book, finally reneged at the end of a world war in which many tens of thousands of nationalist Irishmen had fought with it for 'the rights of small nations', it was entirely in the logic of Parnell's fundamental thought that the majority of the Irish people should, however reluctantly, support violence to secure the freedom to win freedom. No Irish national figure could be more appropriately summoned from the blue to comment on the Good Friday Agreement.

But at the same time he shares with others a certain lack of realism about the North usefully reflected in our imaginary game by his assumption that he himself would long ago have been able to engineer a conclusion of which the Good Friday Agreement is only a forerunner.

From Wolfe Tone onwards all modern Irish nationalists, confronted by the problem of north-east Ulster, tended to recognize it as a problem that would somehow go away or solve itself once the rest of the nationalist formula was completed. O'Connell, of course, was interested in collecting party funds from the Catholic areas of Ulster but was described as passing through the rest 'like a thief in the night', and in Belfast like 'a man afraid of his own shadow'. None of this discouraged his Young Ireland supporters who certainly took the north-east problem seriously by writing songs like 'Orange and Green Will Carry the Day' as if that would make it come true. They also invented, or borrowed in spirit from the new Second Republic in France, an appropriate tricolour (green, white and orange), which eventually did have a great success but not in that part of Ulster. Parnell himself made a more realistic impact at times, urging that the tenant farmers in both parts of Ireland should come together to protect each other and 'join hand in hand with us from Cork to Belfast to obtain for the people of Ireland their own land'. But of course, with the idea of 'partition' not yet serious current political thinking, none of them had to think in terms of 'Northern Ireland', only of the whole of Ulster in which Parnell himself was actually capable of winning a parliamentary majority.

We now have the problem much as it was left to us by a British Government eighty years ago. The Good Friday Agreement is not only all we have to help solve it, but the most feasible plan we have had in all those eighty years. It is only a pity we are not able to have at least some of Parnell's political engineering skills to help us see it through.

Christina Hardyment

MARIE STOPES AND GERMAINE GREER

ENDURING PASSION AND THE STUMP CROSS CRONE

How did the personal lives of Marie Stopes and Germaine Greer affect their writing? And was the black pessimism of the second sexual prophet of our age caused by the manic optimism of the first?

If your love life is good, declared forty-eight-year-old Marie Stopes in 1928, you can differ from your partner in almost every way imaginable. Conversely, though you may be compatible in every other way, if sex is unsatisfactory, happiness will be hard to come by and divorce unsurprising. Few people realize that the woman whose name became synonymous with birth control was also the person who set the agenda for today's high expectations of sustained sexual activity in marriage. She even coined a new term for the new age of which she was the self-appointed high priestess: 'erogamy', by which she meant erotic love in marriage. In adopting it, she added, with what some might feel is unresolved ambivalence, we can 'leave the ugly, slimy-sounding word "sexual" to those who still roll in the filth and who delight in the unclean echoes of the centuries'.

When Marie Stopes died in 1958, Germaine Greer was a nineteen-year-old student at Melbourne University, delighting in all things sexual and in using far stronger words as poisoned darts in her flamboyant invasion of the man's world of the 1950s. Two decades after Stopes was tossing condoms into student audiences during her hugely popular lectures, Greer was jangling bracelets made from used diaphragm springs and was already set in the rutting that would make her in her turn a sexual high priestess. Nervous men lined the walls of the Oxford Union like hypnotized rabbits while she held forth on how sexually unattractive she found the English; she reportedly paid no attention to a request from one William J. Clinton to 'give a Southern boy a chance'.

The similarities between the two women, both intellectually brilliant, socially flamboyant and bubbling with sexual energy, are startling. Both chose to write their first major book about the female orgasm. Both followed up with books about contraception, the menopause and lifelong relationships between men and women. Most striking of all, perhaps, is the way both assumed that their own lives could provide patterns for those of women in general. 'She used her own life as the raw material to wreak changes in social attitudes, often with startling courage and with equally startling indifference to other people's feelings' is a sentence that could well have appeared in Christine Wallace's recent biography of Greer, *Untamed Shrew* (1997). In fact it comes from June Rose's 1992 *Marie Stopes and the Sexual Revolution*.

But the differences between them were profound. To the end of her days, Stopes sang the joys of 'enduring passion' between the sexes. In her seventies, she was still skinny-dipping off Portland Bill with a handsome toyboy. Greer announced in her early fifties that sex had lost its attraction. She has deliberately vamped up a new role as 'a batty old hag', celebrating the joys of good food, friendship, animals and gardening, and writing men off as mad, bad and dangerous to know.

*

Before I delved into her extraordinary career, I imagined Marie Stopes as a motherly pragmatist. Contraception has connotations of carefulness and forethought – family planning indeed. While writing a history of childcare theories, I had read her two babycare manuals, and recalled her elaborating on the importance of natural food, fresh air and exercise, and instructing mothers to have no truck with what she called the 'aberrant mind of Freud'. Hardly a new woman.

But when I turned to *Married Love*, her best-selling and most famous book, I soon realized that it was far from being the practical guide to contraception that I had assumed. Only two or three pages refer to the subject, and then only in the vaguest of terms. As its original title *They Twain* suggests, *Married Love* was in fact an astonishingly explicit, if rosily romantic, vindication of the sexual rights of women. Dedicated to 'young husbands and all those who are betrothed', it described in detail how to give their loved ones the greatest possible erotic satisfaction.

Its style is a startling combination of the passionate and the practical. Here, for example, is how Stopes introduced the concept, hitherto unheard-of in 'nice girls', of female desire: 'Welling up in her are the wonderful tides, scented and enriched by the myriad experiences of the human race from its ancient days of leisure and flower-wreathed love-making, urging her to transports and to self-expression, were the man but ready to take the first step in the initiative or to recognise and welcome it in her.' Detailed descriptions of successful foreplay techniques followed.

Stopes tried (unsuccessfully) to pre-empt accusations of obscenity by claiming that her Exocet missile into the bedrooms of the nation was merely the fruit of her own 'scientific investigations', undertaken when (she claimed) she realized, three years after her wedding, that her own marriage had never been fully consummated. Although she read widely on the subject of 'sexual congress', ranging from Havelock Ellis to the *Kama Sutra*, objectivity was never the hallmark of her research. She described reading Ellis's *Studies in the Psychology of Sex* as 'like breathing a bag of soot: it made me feel choked and dirty for months' (1939). Nor was Freud any better. 'Don't please think about your subconscious mind,' she wrote to one sexually anxious correspondent. 'All the filthiness of this psychoanalysis does unspeakable harm.'

The publication of *Married Love* was financed by Humphrey Roe, a wealthy supporter of feminist ideals in general and birth control in particular whom Stopes would soon marry. The book first appeared in 1918, just eight months before the end of war. It was perfect timing. Women had become used to working; those over thirty had just been awarded the vote. The time was ripe for a new frankness between the sexes, though it still needed to be frankness shrouded in euphemism.

The book was a runaway best-seller. Within ten years it had been reprinted eighteen times and translated into twelve languages, including Afrikaans, Arabic and Hindi. In 1935 it was placed sixteenth on a list of the most important books of the last fifty years

– higher, and undoubtedly more read, than Einstein's *Relativity*, Hitler's *Mein Kampf* and Freud's *Interpretation of Dreams*. Thousands of those who bought it wrote Stopes letters registering both their gratitude and their need for much more information, especially on birth control. It was this response that made her realize how essential contraception was to sexual ecstasy.

Wise Parenthood, a guide to contraceptive practice, followed swiftly. Its opening line declares that, 'A family of healthy and happy children should be the joy of every pair of married lovers.' Note the last two words. Stopes believed that passion between twin souls, true hearts, soulmates, need never end if you got the technique right. Many of her readers found otherwise. 'After the poetry of your book what has actually happened?' wrote a Newark vicar. 'We go to rest, my wife always lies with her back towards me, I make a "tender advance" and suggest that she turn round so that we may chat and cuddle – the end of the poetry is "I do not like your breath in my face!!!!"'

Stopes took note. In later marital manuals she made the point that people's sex drive was as likely to be as variable as their appetite for food. Some couples made love only once in two years, some seven times a day. She added provocatively that the chance of finding a sexually compatible mate was considerably slimmer than finding someone who shared your taste in food. She estimated in *Enduring Passion* that 30 per cent of men wanted more sexual action than their partner. But, she added with considerable originality, 30 per cent of women also felt themselves inadequately served. Only 15–20 per cent of couples were well matched erogamously. Around 20–25 per cent did without sex altogether.

The trouble with guesstimates like these is that most people like to think of themselves as on the passionate rather than the puddingy end of the erotic scale. The long-term effect of *Married Love* was undoubtedly to put more emphasis on the importance of enduring sexual satisfaction in marriage, and to legitimate the idea of ending a marriage because of sexual incompatibility.

Stopes herself was evidently among the 30 per cent of unsatisfied Messalinas. A long train of adoring, soon-to-be-deflated men accompanied her whirlwind progress through life. The odd percipient drone escaped. 'She is more in love with Love than with me,' said a young zoologist, Charlie Hewitt. 'I can see that to her man is only the personification of her great ideal love – that I cannot be.'

Intensely feminine in her frills and furbelows and proud of her 'buoyantly physical nature', Stopes relished her struggle against a highly disapproving establishment. In 1920 she sent her own privately printed *New Gospel* to each of the 267 bishops attending the Lambeth Conference of Bishops. 'Paul spoke to Christ nineteen hundred years ago. God spoke to me today,' it began. His message through His new medium, imparted as she was sitting under a yew tree, was very different from Paul's killjoy 'marry lest ye burn' stuff. The gospel according to Stopes was that 'no act of union fulfils the Law of God unless the two not only pulse together to the highest climax but also remain thereafter in a long brooding embrace without severance from each other'.

The bishops doggedly stuck to St Paul; the Catholic Church was predictably even more outraged. Undaunted, Stopes continued a high-profile media guerrilla war to promote birth control. Her unorthodox methods of furthering the cause included passing round Dutch caps at dinner parties and creeping into Westminster Cathedral with a Press Association photographer in tow to chain her critical pamphlet *Roman Catholic Methods of Birth Control* to the altar rail.

*

Fifty-three years after *Married Love* was first published, another outrageous woman's name was on everyone's lips and another seminal twentieth-century sexual classic was the most discussed book of the day. Sales of *The Female Eunuch* began slowly in 1970, but by the end of 1971 the striking latex torso of the paperback edition seemed to be on every station bookstall in the country. The book's purpose was to call for sexual liberation by delivering a coruscating attack on the way in which women held themselves in thrall to what they thought men wanted. Its author, a thirty-one-year-old Australian, was every bit as outrageously outspoken and passionately body-conscious as her predecessor in what one might call the Virtual Chair of Radiant Womanhood – and just as bonny a fighter.

Where did Germaine Greer come from intellectually? Born in 1939, she escaped as soon as she could from her family home in Melbourne, and went to Sydney University to write an MA on Lord Byron and enjoy a wild life with the free-living, free-loving counter-culture group known as Push. In 1964 she went to the Leavisite Cambridge Faculty of English to do a PhD on Love and Marriage in Shakespeare. From the point of view of myself and my cocoa-sipping friends in Newnham, she and Clive James between them *were* the swinging 60s. She pranced around the stage of the Footlights dressed only in a Union Jack, she became co-editor of the pornographic magazine *Suck*; she boasted not just of jettisoning her bra but of wearing no panties. Six years later, as a lecturer at Warwick University, she produced *The Female Eunuch*, a book as remarkable for its range of literary, philosophical and political reference as for its sexual politics. Within two years her name was synonymous with Women's Liberation.

Since then, Greer has confounded her supporters and delighted her critics by repeatedly reneging on the cause she once epitomized. Having roused women to live a man's life in *The Female Eunuch*, reinforcing her message with erudition and style in the dreadful warnings of *The Obstacle Race* (1981), the story of Mozart's lost sister and other female geniuses domesticated into extinction, she went sour, disagreeing with everybody. In *Sex and Destiny* (1984), she remapped Western womanhood and modern contraception methods as a disaster area and glorified Third-World-style extended families. In *Daddy, We Hardly Knew You* (1990) she explored her thwarted desire for her father's approval and inability to get on with her mother in painfully personal terms.

In *The Change* (1991) she announced that sex was overrated, and claimed that she got more joy in the tiny compass of seeing a chrysalis transformed into a butterfly than she ever had in bed with a man. In *Slipshod Sibyls* (1995) she dismissed all women poets before 1800 as second-rate. Now sixty, she has just published *The Whole Woman* (1999), a pessimistic diatribe constructed from media horror stories that bears as much resemblance to the average family's experience as Hieronymus Bosch's vision of Hell. Its bent is profoundly reactionary. The *Sunday Telegraph* headlined its appraisal of it as 'The Female Enoch'.

But was Greer ever a genuine revolutionary? 'I am a woman of the 50s, I wait to be asked,' she said in an interview in *You* magazine in 1989. Yes, 1989. 'I have an unusual amount of emotional insecurity . . . There have been complaints that I very seldom make advances, even in a relationship. Men have to court me and make the running. I have never rung a man up in my life. I realise how absurd that is.'

Marie Stopes, on the other hand, was quick to take the initiative and constantly insisted that the men in her life danced to her tune. She even offered to write a letter for her proposed second husband Humphrey Roe, breaking off his earlier engagement to another girl. In her fifties, deprived of sexual fulfilment by Roe's latter-day impotence, she dictated an agreement for him to sign, which condoned the lovers she intended to enjoy from then on.

It has to be said that Stopes did not publicize details such as these in the way that Germaine has done. But both might fairly be described as obsessed with sexuality, very definitely men's women. Both expressed their admiration of splendid male physiques and were often derogatory about other women. Both dressed with dashing eccentricity. Both women remained remarkably attractive as they grew older, and succeeded in maintaining lifelong friendships with some of their former lovers.

But there is a highly significant difference between them. Greer, rarely without an obscenity on her lips, talks of sex with a disgust worthy of Mrs Grundy. Stopes's writing, radiantly euphemistic, holds it transcendentally joyful. Greer is a Snow Queen, her vision forever marred by some internal splinter of glass that makes the world seem implacably hostile. Stopes is Cinderella's fairy godmother, egging Western girlhood on to trust themselves to the rapturous embrace of their Prince Charmings.

Was this contrast an effect of childhood experience? Both Marie and Germaine were oldest daughters. Both were deeply involved with their fathers and virtually at war with their mothers. Through childhood, each operated in a troika situation, an unholy competitive trinity of father, daughter and mother. Not that they were only children. Marie had one younger sister who was, perhaps tactically, a chronic invalid. Germaine had two much younger siblings, a sister and a brother, whom her parents found it easier to get along with. Stopes won her battle for paternal attention, if there can be winners in such a game, hence her unshakeable confidence in the ideal mate. Judging by what she says in *Daddy*, Greer seems to think she lost hers. Hence, perhaps, her deep-rooted distrust of such a notion.

Both daughters felt their mothers to be as dominant as the mythic witch Baba-Yaga. Marie's mother, Charlotte Carmichael, born in 1841, had to earn her own living as a governess after the death of her father when she was thirteen. Undaunted and self-directed, she was the first woman in Scotland to get the certificates of education to MA standard. Her intellectual interests ranged from Shakespeare to experimental physics – she met Henry Stopes at a meeting of the British Association for the Advancement of Science in 1876. She was then thirty-five, a fundamentalist Protestant of ancient Scottish lineage. He was twenty-four, thoughtful, intense, and hiding his youth behind a luxuriant beard and moustache. A Quaker from a wealthy brewing family, he was a keen amateur archaeologist and palaeontologist. Maybe their shared disapproval of the potentially atheistic implications of Darwin's theories brought them together, maybe Henry's money spelt security for the fatherless Charlotte.

They married three years later, and Marie was conceived early on the six-month honeymoon they spent exploring archaeological sites in Italy, Egypt and Palestine. Cracks in the marriage were already apparent by the time they returned to England. Charlotte disliked the incessant domestic interruptions to her studies. 'I can't read, let alone write books,' she complained. Although a second daughter appeared in 1884, when she was forty-three, sexual relations between the couple had evidently by then become rare. 'Dearest,' ran a pleading letter from Henry in 1886, when Charlotte was away on a seaside holiday with the little girls, 'will you not put from you the teachings of your splendid brain and look only into the depths of your heart and see if you can but find there the love that every woman should hold for the father of her babies? . . . We would put from us the seven blank years that ended and commence the truer honeymoon.'

How aware of all this was their daughter Marie? Browsing through *Marriage in Our Times*, a potboiler she wrote fifty years later in 1935, I found this passage: 'I remember my father saying that his father used to say that the marriage bed should be seven feet square!' She then recalls the wonderful atmosphere of her parents' four-poster when she was tiny. It was succeeded by a brass bedstead from Maples. Or were there two? Was there some connected train of thought that led to the next passage:

Though of course the twin bedstead was used long before I came
into the world, its recent widespread invasion of the home is one
of the features of marriage to-day. The twin bedstead, each bed
narrow, each bed covered with sheets and blankets of 'single bed
size', is one of the enemies of true marriage. It gives a false pretence
of nearness in union which is a travesty. Its narrowness creates
cold draughts at a time when warm comfort and space is vital. It
secures the ever-present sense of intrusion when real solitude is
desired. It enforces continual proximity and deadens feelings,
without that intimate and close contact which rests, soothes and
invigorates. Marriage to-day would do well to go back to the
Victorian era and throne itself in a marriage bed, large and square
and comfortable, attended by a single bed either in the same room
or in a near-by dressing room for one or other of the partners
when either desires solitude. The Victorian double bed from which
there was no retreat created problems people thought to solve by
the twin bedstead, but in turn the twin bedstead creates graver
problems which often go unrecognised.

As Marie grew older, she rather than her mother became Henry's
closest confidante. He was intensely proud of her, frequently taking
her on the fossil-hunting expeditions that sowed the roots of her
first career in palaeobotany.

How well did our other heroine's parents get on? In 1935 Reg
Greer was thirty, an established and successful seller of newspaper
advertising space in Melbourne, Australia. He dressed with style,
hinted mysteriously at a gentlemanly English ancestry, and spoke as
if he'd been to a public school. One day he wandered out into the
street at lunchtime and saw eighteen-year-old Peggy Lafrank, a
milliner, with a gaggle of girl friends. His sophistication swept Peggy
off her feet; she also enjoyed his evident admiration of her use of
lipstick and her sassy frocks. She had abandoned her Catholic
convent scholarship to try her luck in the fashion business when her
mother separated from her over-possessive Italian husband. Peggy
was pretty enough to be featured in at least one magazine advertisement (*Table Talk*, 1936): the odds are that Reg got the job for her.
He certainly impressed Mrs Lafrank with his good manners and
'avuncular' care for all her children. He also had such a good job
that he was a fine catch for Peggy. He took instruction in Catholi-
cism and married her in 1937.

Two years later, on 29 January 1939, Germaine was born. Three years later again, Reg went to war along with thousands of other more or less willing Commonwealth volunteers. He was old enough at thirty-seven not to have been sent overseas but he elected to go ('Did he run away from a difficult marriage and a trying three-year-old?' asks Germaine with wistful anguish in *Daddy, We Hardly Knew You*). He found his way to what should have been a cushy bum-shiner job in ciphers. But months spent 80 feet underground in GHQ Malta shattered his nerves and sent him to the military hospital at Deovlali (from which the slang 'doolally' comes). He was discharged as suffering from anxiety syndrome. Germaine remembers going to the station with her mother in 1944, both dolled up to the nines, to meet him. Neither of them recognized the toothless wreck they found there.

But the marriage survived. Two years later Germaine's sister was born and then her brother. They all lived together until Germaine flounced off to Melbourne University at the age of seventeen, but she seems to have felt herself to be an ugly duckling. Telling shards of her experience of early childhood are on offer in *Daddy*: a mother primarily concerned with perfecting her suntan and curling her hair, and who didn't hesitate to discipline Germaine physically; a father who found it increasingly difficult to cope with his restless, brilliant, demanding daughter and seemed in constant retreat to his cronies. Was Germaine's young mother in much the same sexually neglected boat as Marie's father? For whose benefit were the perfect suntan, the meticulous make-up and hairdos? Germaine drops dark hints at GI dancing partners while her father was away in the war, and found the sight of her mother pencilling her eyebrows and painting her greasy red lips in a pouting bow 'obscene'. 'Why couldn't I have a mother who was motherly instead of a frustrated pin-up?' she once complained. Lipstick remains one of her bêtes noirs.

When she was older and stronger she came to blows with her 'mad dog' of a mother in the kitchen while her father shut himself away next door muttering, 'It takes two to make a quarrel.' Was she avenging her bruised childhood self or unconsciously defending her father's lost honour? Did twin beds arrive from the Melbourne branch of Maples? History does not relate what measures Harry Stopes and Peggy Greer took to satisfy what seem likely to have been buoyant sexual temperaments, but it is tempting to ask how deeply their parents' perceived behaviour affected Marie and Germaine, both of whom became flamboyant sexual spokeswomen for their generations.

It is easier to idealize a father if he doesn't hang about too long. Marie Stopes's adored father became seriously ill while she was doing her finals at University College, London. She was given her (excellent) results early so that he could know them; he died a week after seeing them. She spent as little time as possible at home with her mother and sister after this, and went to Munich to study. There she began to realize how much she had been deprived of a sense of the importance of femininity by her mother. She learned to dress more dashingly, adopting furs and short skirts. 'There is hardly anything in the world so gloriously beautiful as a woman's body,' runs a passage she wrote in an unpublished autobiographical novel. 'And while I am one, and a young one, I think it would be wickedness not to enjoy the loveliness of it.'

She went to the theatre to watch Isadora Duncan wowing spellbound Munich audiences. When she went home, she wrapped herself in flimsy voiles and imitated Isadora's highly erotic dancing. But at this time she went no further. Most of her relationships were with older men, professors to whom she could relate in a filial way. She was, she wrote of herself later, 'a child in a woman's body'. But her father's early death had allowed her to write her own script. She could abandon his strait-laced family code and enjoy her intense physicality without losing the evergreen memory of his admiration.

At the same sort of age, Germaine's relationship with her father was very different. He was all too real: adored but in her eyes infuriatingly unresponsive. In a violent reaction, she decided not to act as the sort of woman he would have admired but as a female version of the brilliant, aggressively masculine man she thought he ought to be. It was all too evident on the rare times they met that he simply did not know what to make of her; was in fact intensely nervous of her. When he died in 1983, she was chilled that he had chosen not to mention her in his will. It was to cope with her sense of being rejected by him that, attracted by the romantic hints of noble ancestry he used to throw out, she decided to dig into the past to find early family faces to whom she could perhaps relate better. It was a disillusioning experience. It emerged that Reg was in fact the illegitimate son of a housemaid seduced by a local businessman.

His real name was not even Greer, but Greeney. *Daddy* is full of intense longing for kinship, but Greer does not seem to perceive its implications: perhaps only her looks are her father's; her energy and moral dynamism, her inclination towards Mediterranean-style extended families must all come from her much despised mother's healthily mongrel ancestry: part Italian, part Irish and part Danish.

*

So much for the genesis of our heroines' obsessions. How did they learn to universalize them so tellingly? Both women were ambitious, outstandingly intelligent and intensely moral girls. Religion had a high profile in their upbringings: regular attendance at Presbyterian and Quaker services for Marie; a convent education from the age of four for Germaine. Although both disengaged themselves from conventional religious observances rapidly, each retained a habit of morality coupled with a deep sense of mission. Marie's mother, a committed early feminist, sent her to North London Collegiate, the most forward-looking girls' school in the country. Marie outdid her mother's scholastic achievement by becoming the first woman to read science at University College, taking her honours degree – with distinction – in only two years instead of three.

Germaine has put on record how much she enjoyed her long convent education, dismissing the family home as a cultural desert. Her maternal grandmother was the person who first took her to the Art Gallery in Victoria; perhaps she also introduced her to the public library in the same building, the 'Valhalla' to which Germaine made repeated pilgrimages in her youth. 'More of my waking life has been spent in libraries than anywhere else,' she tells us in *Daddy* in a rare moment of serenity. 'Libraries are reservoirs of strength, grace and wit, reminders of order, calm, continuity, lakes of mental energy, neither warm nor cold, light nor dark. The pleasure they give is steady, unorgiastic, reliable, deep and long-lasting.'

By the age of twelve she had begun to formulate an ambition to go to university and be an intellectual. The nuns had given her a social conscience. They also spotted the potential of her singing voice, and introduced her to music, a lasting love. What the convent did not prepare her for was the unromantically sudden approach of Melbourne boys to dating. 'I waited a year for romance, then gave up, as I realised I was considered a tease' was the way she explained her first sexual experiences to an interviewer from *Today* in 1989. She became more laddish than the lads, suffered for it, swallowed hard and continued to try to outdo them at their own game. Talking later of the wild years that followed in Sydney, she acknowledged the role played by her own instincts as well as that of the prevailing climate of permissiveness.

> Those were the rules that governed the lives of many who are now seen as the apostles of permissiveness. Utter honesty, no jealousy or possessiveness, no sexual game playing, no bra, no cosmetic aids, no bullshit. Yet anyone who paid any attention to me when I was two years old would have seen it coming. The nuns used to say, You'll be a great saint or a great sinner. I chose sin because it seemed more straightforward. And if God doesn't like it, he can lump it.

Once they were sexually active, contraception became a key issue in the lives of both women. In this context, it is Stopes who was both more radical and more rational. *Wise Parenthood* (1918) was a useful guide to what limited contraceptive techniques were then available. It was also far from reliable. In her own book on the subject, Greer ridicules Marie Stopes for getting caps muddled with diaphragms. (She was right about Stopes's blunders. A 1920s playground skipping rhyme ran

> Jeannie Jeannie, full of hopes
> Read a book by Marie Stopes
> But to judge from her condition
> She must have read the wrong edition.)

But *Sex and Destiny* was a very different kind of book from either *Wise Parenthood*, or Stopes's follow-up history *Contraception: Its Theory, History and Practice* (1923). Its condemnation of sexploitation reflected Greer's realization of the damage her gynaecological history had dealt her chance of having the child that she had jauntily announced she was ready to create at the age of thirty-seven. A panoramic sweep across the history and anthropology of contraception, it concludes that chemical and mechanical means of contraception are mixed blessings if not unmitigated evils. She also idealized Third World extended families in terms reminiscent of Margaret Mead's thoroughly misleading *Coming of Age in Samoa*, and argued that the idea of population explosion was a fantasy and that Western contraceptive methods were unnecessary. She actually ended up recommending several of the same methods for achieving sexual satisfaction short of full intercourse as Stopes. Liberated women's jaws dropped in horror at such retrograde ideas. But arguably, there is a sense of the wheel turning full circle, of Stopes's erotically ambitious social experiment having been tried and found wanting by a stern, though no longer young, Antipodean judge. The book may also owe something to Greer's Catholic upbringing.

In mid-life, both women pursued successful academic careers in subjects quite separate from the field for which they became most famous. Stopes was a palaeobotanist with a special interest in the nature of coal who had lectureships set up for her in what was then a little-explored field. Greer's field is English literature; she has held academic posts at Tulsa, Oklahoma and at Newnham College, Cambridge. Stopes wrote to the papers frequently on all sorts of matters. She asked Lloyd George if she could lead an armed force against the striking miners. She also wrote second-rate novels and very derivative poetry. Greer's pungent tirades on every issue imaginable are sought-after media properties. Both took to celebrity status like ducks to water. Stopes suggested to Kipling that 'If' should be rewritten to deal with women and invited Thomas Hardy to her Portland Bill lighthouse holiday home. Greer's presence guarantees the success of literary parties.

Maritally, both had low boredom thresholds, though Stopes's marriage to the always adoring and extremely long-suffering Humphrey Roe lasted in name until his death, aged seventy, in 1949. Despite the early memories of that cosy four-poster (and perhaps her own place in it), she insisted on separate bedrooms for husbands and lovers alike. Greer too has said that she prefers to sleep on her own. She has had one very short marriage, and numerous proudly flaunted affairs.

Both women proclaimed the joys of maternity but found them hard to experience personally, although that did not stop them expressing very definite ideas on the upbringing of children to both their friends and the world at large. Greer has put on record her profound regret at not having a child of her own. But she has some seventeen godchildren and numerous cats. These favoured pets, together with her books, her love of and talent for teaching, her personal connections with many Third World women and children, and a succession of human and animal waifs and strays who come and go at her well-tended small-holding near Saffron Walden, all testify to her abundant maternal instinct.

Stopes had one son when she was forty-four, and named him after her father. She fostered a series of boys in a search for a companion for this second adored Harry; all were ruthlessly disciplined, found wanting and returned. But when he grew up, Harry proved to be one of the few men his mother could not dominate. She was so unpleasant about his chosen wife that after marriage Harry removed himself from her orbit almost completely, and she left him only her *Oxford English Dictionary* in her will.

The age of fifty found our heroines marching to very different drums. Stopes's *Enduring Passion* was for mature lovers. It was frank-spoken on impotence among older, professional men. She was also one of the first people to identify the possibility of a 'male menopause' in her 1936 book *The Change of Life in Men and Women*. (H.G. Wells hotly denied the notion in a letter to her: 'It's a great and selling idea ... But I don't find much in the book ... I am 70 ... I have never been able to detect any lunar periodicity in my life although I kept a very careful private diary.') For herself, Stopes declared that she was still 'psychologically twenty-six'. In Greer's own book on the menopause, *The Change*, written when she was fifty-two, she resigns herself (and as usual all other women) to celibacy with considerable wit and serenity. She also offers the compensation of a likeable quality called Post Menopausal Zest.

What of their final legacies? Although the Marie Stopes Clinics are at the forefront of family planning work in the Third World, Stopes herself can be seen in the long-term as no more than a courageously prominent surfer on the wave of an unstoppable movement. To some extent her jealous insistence that she and only she should control the organization of family-planning clinics actually delayed their development. Moreover, for her, contraception was merely the means to a much more important end. The greatest tribute to her impassioned advocacy of sex for sex's sake came in 1958, two months before her death, when the Lambeth Conference she addressed so fruitlessly in 1920 changed its tune. It not only acknowledged the need for birth control but declared that, 'The procreation of children is not the sole purpose of Christian marriage;

implicit within the bond of husband and wife is the relationship of love with its sacramental expression in physical union.' Since then a sea change in marital expectations has taken place. It is a sobering thought that, forty years on, the failure of more than one marriage in three may reflect both the accuracy of her guesstimate percentages of sexual compatibility in marriage and the extent to which many of us mistakenly adopted her demanding New Gospel of erogamy. Many of us didn't. Authoritative British and American sex surveys in the 1990s have revealed that the majority of us rest content with a distinctly low-key love life.

Germaine Greer took a distinctly maverick line when she in turn surfed the crest of the wave of the 1960s Women's Liberation movement. Many of the more serious-minded feminists condemned *The Female Eunuch* as (literally) sleeping with the enemy. But millions of women now in their fifties still give that shocking but unforgettable book the credit for shaking them out of a rut.

It is impossible as yet to define the legacy for which Greer will be most famed – she's surprised us before and no doubt will again. She is certainly growing old gracefully. She could yet single-handedly revive the tradition of respect for the sagacity of wise old women; from all accounts she could also write a better book about home-making than Constance Spry or Martha Stewart. As to her past, it is now more often pointed to as a warning than as an inspiration. Despite the current vogue for a superficial laddishness, her maverick exploration of the frontiers of sexuality discouraged more women than it converted, not least because, by her own admission, it has proved a far from fruitful experiment. The latest Hollywood hero-ines once again extol the value of virginity, of 'saving yourself' for Mr Right.

But arguably the life Greer lived as a young woman was also a brave and a necessary experiment; its outcome proof positive of the hollowness of Marie Stopes's promise of never-ending ecstasy. Women today are the wiser for both women's high-profile experi-ments. More independent, more tolerant, and better friends with each other, they enjoy far more stimulating and balanced relation-ships with men both in the workplace and the bedroom than they have in any previous century. Between the Scylla of Stopes on the one hand and the Charybdis of Greer, they are slowly but surely constructing a middle way.

Duff Hart-Davis

PETER FLEMING

When Peter Fleming died suddenly in August 1971 at the age of sixty-four, his renown as a writer had been almost totally eclipsed by that of his younger brother Ian, whose character James Bond had taken the world by storm. Yet in the 1930s, before Ian even thought of becoming an author, Peter established a reputation as one of the most original and amusing young English travel writers of the day – less scholarly than Robert Byron, less astringent than Evelyn Waugh, but arguably wittier than either.

His fame derived largely from two books, *Brazilian Adventure*, published in 1933, when he was twenty-six, and *News from Tartary*, which came out in 1937. Both immediate best-sellers, they raced through numerous hardback editions and have remained in print ever since. By the time the Second World War broke out, Peter's huge literary success, and his marriage to the up-and-coming actress Celia Johnson, had made him a glamorous national figure.

Some idea of his early ebullience can be gained from his description of a public monument in Rio de Janeiro:

> Victory has got a half-Nelson on Liberty from behind. Liberty is giving away about half a ton, and also carrying weight in the shape of a dying President and a brace of cherubs. (One of the cherubs is doing a cartwheel on the dying President's head, while the other, scarcely less considerate, attempts to pull his trousers off.) Meanwhile an unclothed male figure, probably symbolical, unquestionably winged, and carrying in one hand a model railway, is in the very act of delivering a running kick at the two struggling ladies, from whose drapery on the other side an eagle is escaping, apparently unnoticed . . .

Nothing in his family background suggested that he would be so gifted with the pen. His grandfather Robert Fleming, son of an impoverished Scottish farmer, left school in Dundee at the age of fourteen to start work as an accountant; but such was his financial acumen that he moved to London, founded the merchant bank that still bears his name, made a fortune in the City, sent his sons to Eton, bought a 2,000-acre estate and, like the Macmillans, established his family as a pillar of Edwardian society.

His elder son Valentine – Peter's father – became a close friend of F.E. Smith and Winston Churchill. After reading law at Oxford, he began his career by going to work in the bank, amply cushioned by a gift of £250,000 from his father on his twenty-first birthday. He tackled everything he did with immense energy, both physical and mental, and was greatly liked, most of all by the officers and men of his yeomanry regiment, the Oxfordshire Hussars.

For Val, a man of essentially conservative outlook, it was a bold step to marry a girl as flamboyant as Evelyn Ste Croix Rose, whose character embodied many contradictions. She came from a respectable family, but her brothers were known, with good reason, as 'the Wild Roses', and she herself was wilfully eccentric. As if not satisfied with her arresting looks – a long face, high cheekbones and large, dark eyes – Eve deliberately attracted attention by wearing outrageous clothes and striking histrionic attitudes. Sometimes shrewd, often silly, by turns selfish and generous, always snobbish, she looked like an exotic, hothouse bloom, yet was practical and good with her hands: an efficient carpenter, she also played the violin.

Wasting no time, she bore Val four sons, of whom Peter was the first, born on 31 May 1907. Three years later Val was elected Member of Parliament for Henley-on-Thames, and the surroundings in which his boys grew up were as solid and comfortable as could be: a large house full of servants in London, another at Ipsden, where the Oxfordshire Chilterns roll down to the plain, and, just up the hill, their grandparents' Nettlebed estate.

For all these material comforts, Peter's early life was blighted by a persistent gastric ailment, which meant that he spent long days in darkened rooms – a misfortune that seems to have had three long-term effects. First, it curtailed his growth, leaving him much smaller than Ian; second, it reinforced his deep natural shyness; and third, it made him all the more determined – when he eventually recovered – to excel in the family's tradition of taking violent exercise.

Before that, however, his world was abruptly darkened by the death of his father, killed fighting in France on 20 May 1917. In an unfinished fragment of autobiography, written towards the end of his own life, Peter recalled 'the terrible sounds of grief' that broke out in the hall of their London home when the fatal telegram brought the news, and how, not yet ten years old, he lay in bed 'engulfed in misery, out of my depth among grown-up emotion'.

Urged by well-meaning adults to take his father's place, he showed a precocious sense of responsibility. Yet behind his facade of seriousness and reserve there lurked an irrepressible propensity for cracking jokes, which had already begun to show itself at Durnford, his preparatory school in Dorset, and later flowered at Eton, where he enjoyed brilliant intellectual success.

Winner of prizes for French and Spanish, he became Captain of the Oppidans – in effect, head of the school, apart from the seventy Collegers, or scholars – and won a scholarship to Christ Church, Oxford. He also edited the *Chronicle*, in which there appeared many characteristic flashes. One leading article, entitled *Fons et Origo*, purported to describe the departure of an expedition to discover the source of the Jordan – the stream that runs past Eton:

> They carried with them a portable canoe, very rightly described as collapsible, and a cast-iron stove, whimsically called by its maker 'The Inferno'. Each individual carried provisions to last him forty-eight hours if he ate without stopping. Each in addition was equipped with one mapping pen, one umbrella, one instrument for removing tadpoles from the hosiery, one list of printed instructions for taking the bull by the horns, one Red Cross outfit in case he did, and one pneumatic compass.

This nonsense proved curiously prophetic. Many of the farcical elements with which Peter saddled the Jordan explorers were reproduced in uncomfortably accurate detail when he went to Brazil.

He grew up to be 5′ 9″ tall, dark-haired, and strikingly handsome. Unlike Ian, who was twice *Victor Ludorum* in the Eton athletics championships, he lacked the physical co-ordination to shine at games, but more than made up for it by intellectual achievement. At Christ Church he continued his meteoric progress, winning many friends, acting in the Oxford University Dramatic Society (his biggest role was Iago in *Othello*), and gaining a First in English.

At university, as at school, he spoke in a slow drawl, cultivating an air of insouciance and urbanity that remained his hallmark for life: it was a quintessentially Etonian trait that, no matter whether you succeeded or failed, you must never appear to be trying. In this, Peter excelled; but few of his contemporaries realized that, just as his taciturnity and apparent nonchalance were a cover for intense shyness, so his constant frivolity was a device for avoiding any display of emotion.

Another Oxford innovation was that of smoking a pipe – a habit to which he became addicted for life. He came down from university on the crest of a wave – but now he had to earn a living. He had no idea what he wanted to do, and was dismayed by his mother's determination that he should go into the family bank. The idea appalled him; yet he was unable to resist it, and in September 1929 he was despatched to New York, to learn about railway finance. No matter that Wall Street collapsed a few days after his arrival: the Great Depression was as nothing compared with his own. 'This is the most God-awful existence,' he wrote to my father, Rupert, his closest friend, in the middle of December:

> My aversion to Business and all that it stands for grows almost hourly, and I know beyond any shadow of doubt that I shall never be any good at it or happy doing it ... The buildings in the financial district are of a truly immense height: it is wonderful to stand among them and to reflect that they are packed from top to bottom with hundreds and thousands of Crashing Bores. Not only that, but if one of these Bores decides to commit suicide by jumping out of the window (which they quite often do), it is almost morally certain that, on reaching the ground, he will injure or destroy two or three creatures as crass and beef-witted as himself.

Soon he wrote home to say that he was quitting. His family did not conceal their disappointment, but he avoided them for the time being by spending Christmas quail-shooting in Alabama and making a quick visit to Guatemala. Back in London, he flirted with various temporary jobs before joining the *Spectator* as columnist and reviewer, later becoming literary editor. He used to say that the editor, Wilson Harris, carried his articles about as gingerly as if they had been sackfuls of ferrets, and he was nearly fired after writing:

> It is the proud boast of the editorial staff that no two issues of the *Spectator* have ever been proved identical. Sometimes it is the phraseology that is different, sometimes the order or titles of the articles are changed. If the same thing is said, it is said in a different way. If the same words are used, they are used of something else. That has always been the tradition. If not variety, then at least divergence. *Semper idem, sed numquam verbatim.*

Peter enjoyed the *Spectator*, but what he really wanted was to travel in far places – and somehow, in the summer of 1931, he obtained four months' leave to attend an international conference in China. The proceedings of the meeting meant little to him, but the journey was everything: his first visit to Moscow, his first trip on the Trans-Siberian Railway, his first glimpse of Shanghai and Peking. He returned elated, fascinated by China, and determined to range yet farther afield.

His chance came in the spring of 1932, when he answered an advertisement in *The Times* for 'two more guns' to join an 'exploring and sporting expedition' to Brazil. Its aim was to ascertain the fate of Colonel P.H. Fawcett, who had disappeared in the interior searching for a lost city seven years earlier. Peter sensed from the start that the enterprise was amateurish, but he scented fun and adventure, and signed on, also recruiting Roger Pettiward, a tall, red-headed artist whom he had known slightly at Eton. In a flurry of last-minute activity he arranged to act as an unpaid special correspondent to *The Times*, and signed a contract for a book with Jonathan Cape.

The expedition turned out even more farcical than Peter had feared, thanks largely to the futility of its local organizer. The party sailed to Rio de Janeiro and proceeded northwards overland to Leopoldina, on the fringes of the Mato Grosso, where they embarked on capacious, clinker-built vessels called *bataloas* and set off on a three-week journey down the River Araguaia, camping at night on sandbanks in mid-stream. The farther they went, the more infuriated Peter grew with their leader – 'bland, irrelevant and enigmatic' – and when it became clear that he had no intention of carrying out any serious search for Fawcett, the expedition split in

two, amid fierce recriminations. While the leader went on to wait at
a rendezvous down river, Peter and Roger set out on their own with
Indian guides, boating, wading and walking in the opposite direction, up the Tapirapé river, towards the area in which Fawcett had
last been reported.

It was a brave attempt. The heat was overpowering, the insects
voracious, the temper of the natives uncertain. Finding no trace of
their quarry, the rebels were eventually forced to turn back – and
there ensued a tremendous race between them and the rump of the
expedition, down a thousand miles of the Araguaia to Belém on
the Atlantic coast. The expedition as a whole ended in total failure,
yet for Peter himself it had been a kind of triumph. 'FIERCE FUN,'
he cabled Rupert. 'ABOUNDING HEALTH STARK MELODRAMA.' He
had come through a ferocious physical ordeal unscathed and got a
wonderful story.

Back in London, he discharged his commitment to *The Times*
with two rather dull articles; but he was saving his fire for his book
– and when *Brazilian Adventure* came out in August 1933, it burst
on the public like a rocket, racing through eight impressions in the
remainder of that year, four in the next and three in 1935.

In those days travel writers tended to take themselves rather
seriously. Peter did exactly the opposite, indulging in relentless self-
mockery and sending up the whole ridiculous enterprise. Heavy-
weight reviewers such as James Agate, J. B. Priestley and Harold
Nicolson found the book immensely refreshing and praised it in
extravagant terms.

Not giving a damn about his sudden fame, Peter wanted only to
travel to exciting places and write about them. In the summer of
1933 he persuaded *The Times* to send him to China, where the
political situation was unstable, with a Japanese army of occupation
holding Manchuria, and the communists, under their youthful leader
Mao Tse-tung, entrenched in 'Red Areas' in the south. So he set off
on his second grand tour of the Far East, where he managed to
interview the Chinese nationalist leader Chiang Kai-shek and join a
Japanese column on a hunt for bandits, before returning via Japan
and America. The journey yielded a second best-seller, *One's
Company*, which, without being quite as outlandish as *Brazilian
Adventure*, consolidated the young author's reputation.

In the summer of 1934 he again obtained from *The Times* a

commission to rove in the Far East as the newspaper's special correspondent, and he set off in August with only the vaguest of plans. In his mind, however, he carried a definite ambition. Anything he managed to achieve in China would be no more than a prelude to the main undertaking – a marathon overland trek from Peking to India. Although in despatches to Geoffrey Dawson, his editor, he played down the difficulties involved, they were in fact formidable. The only feasible route lay through the province of Sinkiang, or Chinese Turkestan, which had been closed to foreigners by a series of civil wars. As Peter himself wrote, 'Sinkiang, if you substitute political for physical difficulties, shared with the peak of Everest the blue riband of inaccessibility.'

As usual before departure for distant destinations, he was in emotional turmoil. For more than two years he had been in love with Celia Johnson, the young actress who was establishing her reputation on the West End stage. He was deeply attached to her, addressing her as 'Numble' and referring to her among friends as 'the Crackwit'. To her he opened himself up emotionally as to no one else. Yet still he was driven by wanderlust. Twice already he had abandoned her for long periods – four months in Brazil, six months in China. Now once more he left her for an indefinite period. Celia was desperately in love with him, and painfully upset by his departure, but blanketed to some extent by the fact that *The Wind and the Rain*, the comedy in which she had a leading role, was a runaway hit, and had been playing for nearly a year.

After a wild shooting expedition in the Caucasus Peter went on via Samarkand and Tashkent to Novosibirsk and Vladivostok, then once more roamed about China. In Harbin he ran across Ella Maillart (always known as 'Kini'), a Swiss woman of thirty-one who had skied, played hockey and sailed for her country, and had already proved herself an intrepid traveller. Peter, meeting her briefly in a nightclub in London the year before, had said in an offhand way, 'See you in China.' Now he found that she, too, was secretly hoping to walk to India, and after some preliminary wandering about together, they set out as a pair on their tremendous trek.

For seven months and 3,500 miles, most of which they covered on foot or on horseback, they lived cheek by jowl. Did they become lovers? It seems unlikely, because Kini (who never married) made no secret of her lesbian leanings, and Peter reported to Rupert, 'As far as the Affections go, she will never mean more to me than a yak.' The point was that throughout a severe and protracted physical ordeal they remained on reasonably good terms.

Peter was tormented by the fact that, although he had told Celia more or less what he was attempting, he had concealed from her the existence of his companion. 'I am already the colour and consistency of a Gladstone Bag, though probably pucer,' he wrote in one of the few letters he was able to send her; and although he declared himself 'extremely attached', he never came clean about his fellow traveller.

Kini was tall, slender, and described by Peter as 'slightly wolf-like in appearance'. Though tough and resourceful, she was also romantic, and her approach to travel was quite different from his. Whereas he, once launched, wanted only to make the fastest possible progress towards home, she would have liked to wander for ever and divert towards the skyline whenever distant mountains drew her.

By a combination of luck, cunning and sheer endurance, this improbable pair wound their way past bureaucrats, between civil wars, through deserts both burning and freezing, until eventually they reached the first outpost of civilization, the British Consulate at Kashgar. Then, after a refreshing break, they took the high passes of the Pamirs in their stride and came down through Baltit and Nagar and Gilgit to their final goal, Srinagar, in the Vale of Kashmir. In Delhi Peter caught the Imperial Airways flight for London, which took three days. From Alexandria he cabled Rupert: 'DEBAG SWISS CAT IF CELIA'S COMING CROYDON': that is, if Celia was coming to meet him at the airport, Rupert was to tell her about Kini.

Details of their reunion are no longer clear; but Peter's initial release of information was evidently not as full as it might have been. He went straight to Scotland, to shoot grouse, and at first Celia was shocked and confused. 'I got very depressed last night on account of Ella who's a new one on me,' she wrote. 'She's not the Swiss, is she?' Peter told her not to worry, assuring her, 'She never poached at all.' Soon they were firmly back together, making arrangements for a clandestine wedding, and never formally announcing their engagement – an unusual omission in those days. Secrecy was needed partly to outwit Peter's mother, Eve, who he knew would cause trouble, and partly to escape the attention of the

Press. On 2 December, after 900 performances, Celia withdrew from the cast of *The Wind and the Rain*, and the couple were married in the Old Church, Chelsea, a week later.

The book that Peter's long walk inspired, *News from Tartary*, was by far his best. Harold Nicolson described it in the *Daily Telegraph* as 'an amazing narrative achievement', and said that, as a travel writer, the author was now 'in a capacity apart'. The novelist Eric Linklater thought he had brought off 'a grand and miraculous journey'. (Kini's own book about the trip, *Oases Interdites*, was so different that it might have described an entirely separate venture.)

The romance of distant travel blended intoxicatingly with that of the theatre, and Peter's third consecutive best-seller, combined with Celia's success in a new production of *Pride and Prejudice*, made the young Flemings one of the best-known couples in the country. In London Peter returned to *The Times* as leader-writer and special correspondent. Yet he managed to keep travelling, taking Celia with him – first on a three-month tour of European capitals, then on a much more arduous journey through the Far East. Fortunately for him Japan had declared all-out war on China, and this provided him with an ideal excuse for yet another of his roving commissions. Celia delighted him by the fortitude she displayed during their trek through Burma. When he courted danger by visiting the war front, she stayed with friends, and between despatches to *The Times* he fired off the odd salvo at Rupert: 'Last night we went to a Chinese dinner at six and a French dinner at nine, and I can feel the sharks' fins navigating unhappily in the Burgundy.'

Back home in the autumn of 1938, he found his world considerably changed. His grandfather had died five years earlier, and now his grandmother expired intestate, so that none of the family money came to him or his brothers; but his uncle Philip, with characteristic generosity, decided to give him the entire Nettlebed estate, so that he suddenly found himself in possession of 2,000 acres of rolling beechwoods and farmland in the Chiltern Hills above Henley-on-Thames, to say nothing of fifty-odd cottages.

This magnificent and unexpected inheritance, coupled with the fact that Celia was pregnant, finally persuaded him to suppress his nomadic tendencies. Perhaps the growing threat of war with

Germany was another factor that made him feel he should take root in England.

The land at Nettlebed was beautiful, but Joyce Grove, the principal dwelling, on the edge of the village, was a monster, and Peter decided to build a new house in the middle of the estate, at the head of a gently-sloping vista framed by woods. As architect he chose Paul Phipps, father of the actress Joyce Grenfell; and if the red-brick building that emerged lacked character, it did provide a solid home for the rest of Peter's life. He called the house Merrimoles, after an old wooden barn which already bore that curious name.

On 3 January 1939 Celia gave birth to a son, Nicholas, soon known as Nichol. Peter was delighted – but the year brought little else to please him. International tension ruled out long-distance travel, and he could not think of a subject for another book. It was therefore something of a relief to him when war at last broke out.

Fiercely patriotic, and spurred on by loyalty to the memory of his father, he was determined to do his best for England, and if possible to fight in the front line. But his age (thirty-two) and his intellect frustrated this ambition: although he rejoined the Grenadier Guards, with whom he had already served as a territorial, he was drafted into intelligence work.

When, in March 1940, he fell ill, he was outraged to find that his ailment was German measles. His reaction was characteristic: he rattled out a short, satirical novel called *The Flying Visit*, in which Hitler makes a reconnaissance flight over England, has his aircraft sabotaged, parachutes down and lands on the Chilterns, where nobody will take him seriously. If the story was slight, it took an original line in that it ridiculed the Führer at a time when many English people were deeply scared of him; and also, in an extraordinary way, it pre-figured the flight to England of Hitler's deputy, Rudolf Hess, which took place a year later.

After dangerous escapades in Norway and Greece, Peter went out on a top-secret assignment to organize strategic deception under General Sir Archibald Wavell, Allied Commander-in-Chief in South-East Asia. He and Wavell got on extremely well. Both taciturn by nature, they positively enjoyed the long silences that punctuated their conversations. More important, each respected the other's abilities, and Wavell gave Peter every support in creating phantom armies with which to bamboozle their principal enemy, the Japanese.

So too did Wavell's successor, Lord Mountbatten. Peter finished the war as a lieutenant-colonel in command of D Division – a grandiose title for his relatively small deception unit, which was based in Delhi. Again and again he had courted danger by going off on semi-official or unofficial forays, but he never quite managed to involve himself in the thick of the fighting, as he would have liked.

He returned to Nettlebed in the autumn of 1945. Throughout the war Merrimoles had acted as an ideal base not only for Celia and Nichol, but also for the widow and four children of Peter's youngest brother Michael, who had died of wounds in 1940. Now Nichol was joined by Kate, born in 1946, and Lucy, in 1947. Celia, meanwhile, made her name immortal with her performance opposite Trevor Howard in Noël Coward's film *Brief Encounter*.

Friends were surprised that Peter did not continue in intelligence work or take a senior editorial post at *The Times*. What they failed to realize was that he loathed the idea of an office job, lacked all conventional ambition, and wanted two things only: to manage his estate and continue writing.

In both aims he was no more than moderately successful. Untrained in agriculture or forestry, he came to the land as an amateur, and never acquired the knowledge (or the capital) to make the estate really productive. Because he was cack-handed – lethal to machinery – he rarely worked on the farms or in the woods, and shyness made him a poor man-manager. New plantations, put in to replace trees compulsorily felled during the war, ran riot for lack of maintenance, turning into impenetrable jungles – and this in turn ruined the shooting, his main passion during the winter. And yet, even if the estate never made money, he did realize his declared ambition of creating 'a non-artificial, unsubsidized example of what we would all like England to be'. Under his benevolent regime everyone on the property became devoted to 'the Colonel'.

His writing was similarly inconsequential. At *The Times* he began turning out fourth leaders – the light-hearted pieces that then followed heavier editorials – and for the *Spectator* he started a weekly column signed 'Strix' (Latin for 'screech owl'), which became a fixture for many years. Yet these essays, though urbane and amusing, were essentially frivolous: Peter longed to produce another worthwhile book, but could not find a subject that suited him. After months of struggle with a novel, he decided it was no good, and gave it up. When Eric Linklater suggested he should write a book about the heroic spirit, he scribbled lugubriously in his diary, 'I wish I could write a book about mustard and cress.'

In 1949 he did complete a rather feeble thriller about a Soviet attempt to undermine the British character, which came out in 1950 entitled *The Sixth Column*, but it was not until 1954, seventeen years after the publication of *News from Tartary*, that he hit on a really solid project. It was Celia's brother John Johnson, a literary agent, who suggested that he should write an account of Hitler's plans to invade England in the summer of 1940; the idea was excellent, and *Invasion 1940* won immediate acclaim, reviving Peter's reputation and launching him on a new career as a military historian. His next subject, the Boxer rebellion of 1900, was more abstruse, but suited him just as well, and *The Siege at Peking*, published in 1959, again drew wide praise. In 1961 he brought out *Bayonets to Lhasa*, about the Younghusband expedition to Tibet, and followed that two years later with *The Fate of Admiral Kolchak*, the White Russian commander who declared allegiance to Great Britain after the Bolshevik Revolution.

All four historical studies benefited from the fact that the author himself knew those parts of the world in which they were set. It was as great a deprivation to posterity as it was to himself that interminable bureaucratic obstruction prevented him from writing what would surely have been his masterpiece in this *genre* – the official history of strategic deception in the Second World War: a fascinating subject of which, once again, he had first-hand knowledge.

While Peter was establishing himself as an historian, Ian had at last, aged forty-three, set out on his own literary road. His first thriller, *Casino Royale*, caused no great stir when it came out in 1953, but by the early 1960s James Bond had become an international phenomenon. Peter, far from being jealous, was thrilled by his brother's success.

In his fifties Peter lived more and more for shooting. In midsummer he would begin counting the days to the start of the grouse season, and early in August he would drive north, to reach Black Mount, the huge family estate in Argyll, by the 12th. Then, all through the winter, he would shoot pheasants, often by invitation on other estates, but mostly at home, where he would tramp through

outlying coverts, usually accompanied only by his much-loved but
atrociously wild Labradors.

This regular exercise kept him fit. Contemporaries regarded him
as indestructible, and it was true that he never seemed to be ill. Yet
with hindsight it appears that he may have had intimations of an
early death: why else should he have written elaborate instructions
for his own funeral when he was little more than sixty?

The one fate he dreaded was that of becoming decrepit in old
age. The sight of his uncle Phil confined to what he called 'a Bath
chair' depressed him deeply. 'Anything but that,' he told a friend.

His wish was granted. On 18 August 1971, at the start of
another season, he went out with a family party at Black Mount,
shot two grouse, right and left, sent his dog to retrieve the birds,
and fell dead in the heather from a sudden heart attack.

Emotion ran high at Nettlebed, especially when it was discovered that he had left behind a short poem, with a request that it
should be engraved on his tombstone:

> He travelled widely in far places;
> Wrote, and was widely read.
> Soldiered, saw some of danger's faces,
> Came home to Nettlebed.
>
> The Squire lies here, his journeys ended –
> Dust and a name on a stone –
> Content, amid the lands he tended,
> To keep this rendezvous alone.

So ended a life of high promise, high adventure, high achievement, and towards the end, some disappointment. What was it that
died after *News from Tartary*? The trouble, perhaps, was that the
ebullience of youth faded until it was no longer strong enough to
overcome Peter's fundamental aversion from allowing his emotions
to show, in print as much as in life. Whatever the reason, countless
friends and admirers mourned the fact that he never regained the
impetus that had taken him to such heights before the war.

Frank McLynn

GREAT VICTORIANS:
BURTON AND STANLEY COMPARED

Of the five great Victorian explorers of Africa, John Hanning Speke and Sir Samuel Baker leave me cold. The animal-slaughtering Speke and the Negrophobic Baker had great geographical achievements to their credit, but neither seems to me interesting as human being or psychological study. David Livingstone is another matter, but the issue of religion makes him problematical as an object of study. For me the two most fascinating African explorers are the Welshman Sir Henry Morton Stanley and the Anglo-Irishman Sir Richard Francis Burton.

A story is told of Orson Welles coming to lecture at a small Midwestern town in the depths of winter. At the local PTA hall he found barely a dozen souls huddling to meet him. He addressed them thus: 'In my life I have been actor, impresario, film director, theatre producer, radio writer, federal administrator, author, goodwill ambassador, illusionist and prestidigitator. Isn't it surprising that there are so many of me and so few of you?' With even greater justice could Burton make such a claim. Soldier, consul, explorer and traveller, linguist and translator, poet and scholar, anthropologist, ethnologist, archaeologist, occultist, swordsman and war correspondent, these roles merely exhaust the categories where he was recognized as a master of authority; they say nothing about his myriad other enthusiasms and interests.

If Burton was Renaissance Man, or an awesome mixture of Matthew Arnold's Scholar-Gypsy, Balzac's Vantrin and the Three Musketeers, Stanley was more of a modern specialist. As a pure technician in the art of African exploration, he had no rivals. There was no one, not Baker, not Speke, not even his mentor Livingstone, to touch him. If you wanted to achieve the seemingly impossible in Africa, you sent for Stanley. This was why he was courted by General Gordon, by Leopold of the Belgians, by Cecil Rhodes and a host of other British capitalists with economic interests in Africa.

I propose here to look at the salient interactions between these two great contemporaries and to establish the significance of their connection for the solution of that great Victorian mystery, the source of the Nile; then to examine their views on Africa. But first a word about the personalities, their differences and similarities. They were men of very different background and origin. Stanley was brought up in poverty and illegitimacy in a Welsh workhouse and clawed his way to the top via journalism: before his scoop of the century in 'finding' Livingstone in 1871 he had notable success as a war correspondent in Abyssinia, Spain and the American West. Burton, of mixed Irish, Scots and French blood, was born into upper middle-class comfort with certain expectations, which were later disappointed. Their differential relationship with money was significant: Stanley squirrelled away all his earnings, kept a careful note of every penny he ever spent, and ended his life a very rich man from the sale of his books. *In Darkest Africa*, his account of the Emin expedition, sold an incredible 250,000 copies in the days before paperbacks. Burton, deprived of his greater expectations by his mother's partiality for a ne'er-do-well half-brother, nonetheless inherited £16,000 in 1859, which he proceeded to run through in an orgy of drunken gambling in the USA in 1860. He was permanently short of money thereafter and had Harold Skimpole's attitude to creditors. He scarcely improved the shining hour by marrying a spendthrift wife, and was not finally free of financial worries until his translation of the *Arabian Nights* in 1885 netted him £12,000.

Burton was contemptuous of all religion – he shared the view, common to Feuerbach, Marx and Freud, that religion was the fantasy of Man afflicted by the realization of his own inadequacy, and its function was to allay fears and enhance hopes. Nevertheless Burton was always prepared to put in a spot of special pleading for his beloved Islam – more to tweak the noses of 'followers of the Nazarene' (as he called Christians) than out of theological conviction. Stanley, on the other hand, retained the narrow Calvinism of his youth, though his Christianity was of the Old Testament kind, based on the smiting Yahweh, rather than Jesus and the law of love. Interestingly, though, both men were at one in having the utmost contempt for missionaries in Africa. Largely, too, they moved in different circles and had different friends – insofar as Stanley can ever be said to have had friends in the true sense. Prickly, hypersensitive and aloof, he regarded himself as a 'perfect Ishmael' with every man's hand turned against him. Burton, on the other hand, was sociable and gregarious and his spectrum of friends embraced the poet Swinburne, Bram Stoker of *Dracula* fame, the African explorer Verney Lovett Cameron and a host of Arabic scholars like Edward Palmer, Charles Tyrrwhit-Drake and John Payne. In many ways the one repelled the people the other attracted. Livingstone loved Stanley but hated Burton for his attitude to missionaries and his complaisant, Wildean attitude to slavery (Stanley had kept his own feelings on the subject hidden from Livingstone). Verney Cameron disliked Stanley but worshipped Burton. The secretary of the Royal Geographical Society, Clements Markham, revered Burton and hated Stanley. And so on.

But these differences were perhaps less significant than the similarities between the two men. Even at a physical level both men made a striking impression. At 5'5" Stanley was at an obvious disadvantage with Burton who was 5'11" and looked taller because of his powerful frame. Frank Harris, who knew both men well, fastened on their different height as the key to their differential reception in English society. Burton was received cordially in the best society 'while little Stanley was greeted with derision'. But the barrel-chested Stanley with his cold, ruthless eyes, 'like chips of ice' and in later life his Stanlinesque physiognomy, impressed all who met him as a man not to tangle with. In fact there is a lot of evidence that Stanley's fanatical driving power was over-compensation for his small stature and that his size had a lot to do with his autocratic personality. This is of course a commonplace of Adlerian psychology. It is well known that Napoleon, Stalin, Hitler, Mussolini, Franco and other famous autocrats also suffered from and compensated for their physical smallness. Burton, on the other hand, with his sallow, oriental complexion, black eyes, pendulous Chinaman moustache and hideous disfiguring scar across the cheek – the result of a wound from a lance at Berbera – looked in his good moods like a truculent Mandarin and in his bad ones like the Prince of Darkness.

To an amazing extent the two men shared the same values, ideology, prejudices and predilections. Their common dislikes embraced Gladstone, whom both at different times ventured to contradict flat – the unpardonable sin with the 'Grand Old Man' – and Lord Salisbury. In 1890 Stanley engaged in a vociferous public slanging match with Salisbury, accusing him of weakness in refusing to annex Uganda. Burton, as a consular official, was not able to pull Salisbury's beard so effectively, but 'got across' him by treating him with the same familiarity Salisbury meted out to him. Closeted with Burton for a discussion on Egypt, Salisbury addressed the Consul as 'Burton'. Burton replied in the same vein with 'Salisbury'. Disconcerted by such 'impertinence', Salisbury reverted to formality, but Burton played the joke out and continued to use the appellation 'Salisbury' throughout the interview. Both Burton and Stanley fell foul of the notorious Laurence Oliphant, both were taken up by the Africanist Winwood Reade, both were courted by Gordon for service in the Sudan and both evinced jealousy and contempt towards him.

This convergence persisted into more serious areas. Both men were ambivalent towards women and exhibited marked homosexual tendencies. Burton, whose closest family tie in childhood was with his brother Edward, spent his life in a quest for surrogate brothers. These included Walter Scott, John Steinhauseser, Speke, Tyrrwhitt-Drake, Cameron and other less well-known junior comrades, all of whom, uncannily, died young. Stanley likewise had a string of young male companions: Lewis Noe, Frank Pocock, Edward King, Mounteney-Jephson, to say nothing of his servants Selim and Kalulu. Both Stanley and Burton were men of the Right, and in political terms 'reactionary' would not be too strong an epithet to describe them. Both, independently, made the same analysis of socialism as being a hankering for the division of labour in primitive societies, but their detestation of egalitarianism did not rest there. Both despised the Irish and were fervid opponents of Home Rule. Both, too, were wholehearted imperialists before this dispensation became a universal fashion in England, though they concurred in believing that the Empire needed to be governed by true professionals (i.e. men like Burton and Stanley). Both were servants of hard taskmasters. Stanley played Hercules to Leopold's Eurystheus, while Burton spent thirty years trying to be the Foreign Office's sorcerer's apprentice.

Other interesting psychological similarities include a common propensity to be 'economical with the truth'. We should perhaps make a careful distinction here. Burton's tall stories arose largely out of boredom with the Gradgrindery of facts, a love of paradox and the desire to *épater le bourgeois*. Stanley's mendacity had a deeper basis in the pathological and seemed to arise from a desire to deny aspects of reality (such as his parentage and background) that he found inconvenient or unpalatable. If we posit that Burton's white lies were contrary to the truth, while Speke's claim to have taught Burton everything he knew about exploration was a blatant contradiction of it, in Stanley's case we have to reach out to a further category – what we might call the negation of the negation – where lies become self-deception.

Those who see merit in Jung's views on synchronicity will also find interesting the number of occasions when the two men were in each other's tracks. I omit the case of East Africa and Lake Tanganyika, when Stanley was self-confessedly following Burton's footsteps. But the unconscious overlap in other areas is fascinating. In 1867 in the American West, Stanley covered much of the ground trodden by Burton seven years earlier. In 1874 he was on the Gold Coast, covering the Ashanti War, and this was the domain of Burton's West African consulate from 1861 to 1864. In 1870 Stanley toured the battlegrounds of the Crimea where Burton had spent an unhappy period as a soldier in 1855. In the same year Stanley made an extensive tour of the Holy Land, as did Burton the year after. In 1869, unknown to each other, they witnessed the inauguration of the Suez Canal. Both men were war correspondents: Stanley as a professional in West Africa, Spain (twice) and Abyssinia; Burton as an amateur in South America.

Their experience with violence is paradoxical. Burton, the professional soldier, by singular ill-luck failed to see front-line service either in India in the 1840s – a decade of wars, with the Afghan and two Sikh campaigns – or in the Crimea. He was exploring Africa when the Indian Mutiny broke out. His one and only experience of combat was at Berbera in 1855 when his camp was ambushed by Somalis and he received a lance thrust through his cheek. Yet Burton thirsted for action and was a martial arts expert. One of the greatest

swordsmen in Europe, he was also a trained boxer and a master of
self-defence with Indian clubs. Yet it fell to Stanley to be the veteran
of half a hundred battles. He fought at Shiloh on the Confederate
side in 1862, was in the thick of action using a rifle in Ashanti,
Ethiopia and Spain, and later battled with the tribes of Africa
continually (if not continuously) from 1874 to 1899, including
thirty-two engagements during the descent of the Congo alone
(1877). However, it is interesting that both Stanley and Burton, like
Livingstone, despised big-game hunting as an activity for the feeble-
minded. The great explorers divide sharply on this issue. Samuel
Baker and Speke in the nineteenth century, and Wilfred Thesiger in
our own, were fanatical hunters of big game. What inference or
moral we can draw from this I leave to the reader to decide.

Having sketched in something of the private worlds of my heroes
and their overlap, I must now address the question of the importance
of their interconnectedness for the world of geographical discovery
in the nineteenth century. What Livingstone positively was for
Stanley, Speke was negatively for Burton. Where Livingstone was
the source of light for the thirty-year-old Welshman at Ujiji in 1871,
Speke was, so to speak, the angel of death for Burton's career as
an African explorer. Speke and Burton travelled together on the
expedition of 1857–9 to discover Lake Tanganyika. Speke then
sped back to London to garner the laurels. The RGS president Sir
Robert Murchison, who detested Burton, raised the funds to send
Speke back to Africa to make good his claim that Lake Victoria
(which Speke had discovered on a side trip in 1858) was the source
of the Nile. So, while the true pioneer of European exploration in
East Africa departed on a dissolute nine months' sick leave in the
USA, Speke returned to Africa, explored the western reaches of
Lake Victoria, and visited the three great African kingdoms: King
Rumanika's Karagwe, Mutesa's Buganda and Kamrasi's Bunyoro.
Concluding that Ripon Falls at the head of the lake was the source
of the Nile, Speke followed the river north to the Sudan and Egypt.

Speke now claimed to have conclusive proof that Lake Victoria
was the source of the Nile. He was right: it was. But Burton clung
to his belief that the ultimate feeder for the Nile was Lake Tanganyika. In this he had the support of Livingstone, who claimed that
the River Lualaba he had discovered west of the lake was the Nile's
ultimate source. Speke's discoveries seemed to have destroyed the

Livingstone/Burton thesis, but the two were far from downcast. They took comfort from Kamrasi of Bunyoro's story that there was yet another lake, to the north-west of Victoria, out of which flowed northward a mighty river. Burton hypothesized that this lake, *Lutu Nziga* (later named Lake Albert), connected with the river system of Lake Tanganyika to the south. When Burton returned to England on leave from West Africa in the autumn of 1864, intellectual battle was joined in earnest. For the first time all three notable explorers of Africa, Livingstone, Burton and Speke, were in England at the same time. Supported by Consul Petherick, the theoretical geographer A.G. Findlay and, most importantly, by Livingstone himself, Burton's case that Lake Tanganyika was the ultimate feeder of the Nile made more and more converts as 1864 progressed. Burton's thesis was in two parts: a negative argument showing why Speke's theory could not be correct; and his own detailed explication of the Nile foundations.

Burton's critique of Speke's methodology had a powerful ad hoc force. He began by pointing out that Speke, at an altitude of 250 feet above Lake Victoria, could see for no more than 20 miles, yet claimed the breadth of the Nyasa was 80–100 miles. On his second journey he simply took it for granted that he was marching round the western perimeter of the lake, yet made no attempt to verify the hypothesis. At Rumanika's Speke evinced singular laziness, never once visiting the lake. He followed the shore of his 'vast lake' for just 50 miles, yet was adamant that the stretch of water was one vast lake, and not two or more, as Burton claimed. Most carelessly of all, after sighting Ripon Falls, Speke simply assumed that its waters descended into the Nile. He followed the river north just 50 miles to Kamrasi's capital. When he regained the banks of the Nile from Bunyoro, he had missed nearly 90 miles of its course. After tracing its course for another 50 miles, he again left it to strike across the country. After a detour of 150 miles, he came on a river that he described as 'like a fine highland stream' and which he simply assumed to be the one that began at Ripon Falls.

The crux of Burton's positive argument was that nobody had followed up his own work on Lake Tanganyika and tested *his* hypothesis. This was, in essence, that Lake Tanganyika was the western source of a lake he called *Baharingo*, allegedly the eastern source of the Nile. It was an essential part of this argument that the

River Rusizi flowed out of Tanganyika; according to Burton it did, to Lake Albert, west of Bunyoro. Lake Tanganyika was thus a feeder of the Nile; Burton asserted that it could not be the source, as no lake could be the origin of a river. The eastern source of the Nile, Lake Baharingo, he hypothesized, received its water from the fabled 'Mountains of the Moon'. Speke's Lake Victoria – incidentally two lakes, not one, claimed Burton – was thus irrelevant to the entire question of the Nile.

Speke's tragic death by shooting on the very day he was due to debate the source of the Nile at the British Association meeting in Bath closed the argument for a while. Livingstone set out on his final expedition to chart the Lualaba and prove his theory that this river ('Livingstone's river') was the true source of the Nile. The story of the failure of his expedition, his destitution and desperation at Ujiji on the shores of Lake Tanganyika, and the famous expedition under Stanley financed by Gordon Bennett of the *New York Herald*, which brought new supplies and the wherewithal for a fresh start, is too well-known to need rehearsal here. It lives in most memories through the immortal (and later much-regretted) 'Dr Livingstone, I presume.' Part of the reason for the notorious animus of the RGS towards Stanley in 1872 (until it finally repented and gave him the Gold Medal) was that Bennett's expedition scooped one of its own, being laboriously prepared under the aegis of a lacklustre quartet; Henn, Dawson and Livingstone's son Oswell. The command of this relief expedition had been offered to Burton, but he had turned it down contemptuously. Privately he gave as his reasons the fact that East Africa was now old hat and it was 'rather *infra dig* to look for a missionary' (clearly revenge on Livingstone for the doctor's low opinion). Publicly, Burton made his contempt even more patent. At a fund-raising dinner for the Livingstone Relief Expedition, the Prince of Wales offered to subscribe a large sum if Burton would accept leadership. 'I'll save Your Royal Highness the trouble,' Burton replied, in his best 'bored aristocrat' drawl.

But Stanley's mission to find Livingstone did sound an early warning that Burton's theory on the source of the Nile was untenable. He and Livingstone explored the Rusizi river at the northern end of Lake Tanganyika and discovered that it flowed *into* the lake, not out, as Burton's theory required.

The month Burton spent in London before his departure for his consulate in Trieste in 1872 was notable for the acquaintance he struck up with H.M. Stanley, the new lion of the hour following his dramatic 'finding' of Livingstone. Stanley had been involved in a furious altercation with the RGS, whose committee first doubted his claim to have met Livingstone, then, when unimpeachable evidence was produced, began to snipe and cavil at his latitudinal observations and calculations. In an increasingly desperate and reprehensible attempt to discredit Stanley, the RGS turned to its other old enemy, Burton, in hope that he might find Stanley guilty of charlatanry. The council members were buoyed up in their hopes by Burton's low opinion of Stanley. In *Two Trips to Gorilla Land* Burton sneered at Stanley 'the discoverer of Livingstone', and contrasted his exploits with the 'admirable work' of the 'gallant Lieutenant Cameron'. Even more mocking was this estimate of Stanley's immortal four words to Livingstone, as published in Clements Markham's *Ocean Highways*:

> Had the travellers fallen upon one another's bosoms and embraced, they would have acted like Arabs from the days of Esau and Jacob until AD 1873. But walking deliberately up to each other, taking off hats and addressing a few ceremonious words, so far from impressing Arabs with a sense of dignity would only draw forth such comment (to put it in a complimentary form) as 'Wallah, what sort of meeting is this? Verily they are wonderful things, those Franks.'

The two greatest living African explorers (for Livingstone by now was at the threshold of death) came face to face on 21 September 1872. Much to their surprise, the two men rather took to each other. Burton told his RGS contacts that Stanley was the stuff of which the true African explorer was made and that it was idle to disparage his achievements. Stanley recorded similarly favourable impressions in his journal. 'He [Burton] appears to be a hardy man – with a bronzed complexion, of medium height and powerful figure. His face struck me for its keen, audacious look. He spoke well and avoided jarring on my nerves. If he was not so wicked – I have a strong feeling that I should like him.'

About a week later Stanley and Burton met again at a dinner given by Clements Markham (who hated Stanley and adored Burton), at which Verney Cameron was also present. Stanley noticed

Markham's peculiar habit of measuring the extent of his regard for
his guests by the variety of handshake. Thus Stanley got one finger
of Markham's right hand to shake, Cameron as a naval officer got
two, while Burton as an old friend received the entire hand. Stanley
soon spotted that Burton took a perverse pleasure in presenting
himself to the public in as unflattering a light as possible: 'It has
been Burton's humour to feed the malice of the world with libels on
himself.' But even so there was ambivalence about Burton's attitude.
He wished to be thought hard and wicked and was pleased that
society was shocked by his defiance of its values. At the same time
he was secretly annoyed that society took him so readily at his
word. But morality apart, Stanley was bowled over by the intellectual range and grasp of his fellow explorer: 'He is brilliant in
conversation – and upon any subject not connected with himself, his
tastes and prejudices, he exhibits sound judgement and penetration.
I am sorry that he is so misguided – for his talents deserve a wider
recognition than he is likely to obtain.'

The two men maintained a wary, respectful relationship over
the years. Burton grudgingly acknowledged the greatness of Stanley's achievement during the trans-Africa charting of the Congo in
1874–7. Stanley undoubtedly thought of Burton as one of the few
great men he had met. When Burton mocked him in *Two Trips to
Gorilla Land*, Stanley very neatly turned his flank by attributing bad
faith to his tormentor.

> The interior [of Africa] everyone hopes to retain as a preserve for
> his own exclusive benefit and I am not sure but many travellers in
> Africa have been magnifying the dangers of African travel in order
> to deter others from penetrating the continent. There are many
> passages in Captain Richard F. Burton's *Gorilla Lands* which
> create these suspicions and Joseph Thomson, if the newspapers
> report his speeches correctly, appears inclined to follow the same
> course.

Later Laurence Oliphant, who met Stanley in Paris in 1872,
tried to purge his guilt for his role in the Speke-Burton estrangement
by turning on Stanley and claiming that in his writings, particularly
Through the Dark Continent, Stanley had depreciated the role of
Speke and Burton. In his journal Stanley dealt with the charge
judiciously:

Burton perhaps has suffered from the greater honour paid to Speke's memory by me – but I have always had sufficient reasons for paying my little tribute to Burton also – as a writer, an accurate observer, ethnologist etc. The hardest thing I have said of Burton that I remember just now is that as a travelling litterateur he had no superior but that his judgement of men, white or black, was not to be trusted, because his prejudice so often misled him.

Stanley's great 1874–7 trans-Africa epic finally drove the nail into Burton's coffin on the Nile question. For some time Burton hoped against hope that his ideas would still prevail. When he heard that the Italian Romaldo Gessi was circumnavigating Lake Albert – which Samuel Baker had explored but perfunctorily – he kept his fingers crossed. *Quien sabe?* he wrote cryptically to a confidante. But when Stanley emerged at the Atlantic in August 1877 after his 999-day epic, Burton realized the game was up. Stanley had circumnavigated both Lakes Tanganyika and Victoria and then followed Livingstone's Lualaba on to the Congo, proving conclusively that neither that river nor the Tanganyika were Nile feeders. Magnanimously Burton saluted Stanley's great achievement, but the heartache of discovering that Speke had been right after all was too much. Only in 1881, in a footnote to his translation of Camoëns's *Lusiads*, did he concede that his erstwhile companion and tormentor really had taken the palm in 1863. 'I am compelled formally to abandon a favourite theory,' he wrote, 'that the Tanganyika drained to the Nile basin via the Lutu-Nzige . . . there is a time to leave the Dark Continent and that this is when the *idée fixe* begins to develop itself. "Madness comes from Africa." '

It was 1888 before their paths crossed significantly again. By this time Stanley was in the thick of the Emin Pasha expedition, while Burton was an invalid, enjoying a sinecure as British Consul in Trieste. While Burton was on home leave that year, the newspapers wanted to know his opinion on the likely fate of Stanley, who had not been heard of for more than a year. The common opinion was that he was dead. But Burton knew his man better than that. He predicted, accurately, that Stanley would soon be heard of again, and that he was bound to come through successfully. When Stanley returned to England in triumph in February 1890, Burton paid his fellow explorer magnanimous tribute. 'I should have wished at this and every other opportunity to express my hearty admiration of all that Stanley has dared and done. He is to me, and always will be, the Prince of African travellers.'

A last meeting between the two men in Switzerland in August 1890, a month before Burton's death, put the seal on their friendship. At Maloja, on another sick leave, the Burtons ran into Stanley, who was staying at the same hotel. Stanley, currently in the full flush of his Emin expedition triumph (critical backlash on this dubious affair had not yet developed), had just married the thirty-nine-year-old Dorothy Tennant, and was on honeymoon. Curiously, he was accompanied by his young male friend A.J. Mounteney-Jephson, his principal lieutenant on the Emin expedition. No greater concentration of Victorian eccentrics can be imagined than the quartet composed of the Stanleys and Burtons. Stanley in his own way was just as much a psychological oddity as Burton. His wife had slept with her mother in the maternal bedroom all her adult life and kept a diary in which she communed with her long-dead father.

Burton and Stanley had met just twice before, once at Clements Markham's in 1872, and again at a public dinner in 1886. They had never had the opportunity before for a heart-to-heart chat, and made full use of the serendipity presented in Maloja. By a final twist of synchronicity, both came close to physical disaster in Switzerland on this very holiday. After the Burtons departed, Stanley broke his leg in a freak accident. When Burton was driving a landau in Davos, one of the two horses broke loose and careered over a precipice. If it had taken its comrade and carriage with it, Burton would certainly have perished.

Stanley and Burton thoroughly enjoyed their sustained conversations after dinner. The two wives and Grenfell Baker and Mounteney-Jephson rubbed along pleasantly. Lady Bancroft took a photo of the entire group, complete with Stanley's African servant Sali. Mrs Stanley amused the company by folding a piece of paper and then asking Burton for his autograph. Sir Richard supplied a sample of his tiny hand, in English and Arabic. Mrs Stanley then turned over the back of the paper to reveal the words, 'I promise to put aside all my other literature, and as soon as I return to Trieste, to write my own autobiography.' All the others signed as witnesses and on her return to Trieste Isabel had the paper framed.

Stanley and Jephson both gave detailed impressions of Burton at this time. 'Sir Richard is certainly a wonderful man and his talk

most interesting but he seems to be awfully bitter and cynical,'
Jephson told Stanley's patron, the Scottish magnate Sir William
Mackinnon. Stanley's assessment complements and amplifies this.

> Had a visit from Sir Richard F. Burton, one of the discoverers of
> Lake Tanganyika. He seems much broken in health. Lady Burton
> who copies Mary, Queen of Scots in her dress was with him. In
> the evening, we met again. I proposed he should write his remin-
> iscences. He said he could not do so because he would have to
> write to so many people. 'Be charitable to them, and write only of
> their best qualities,' I said. 'I don't give a fig for charity; if I write
> at all, I must write truthfully, all I know,' he replied. He is now
> writing a book called 'Anthropology of Men and Women', a title,
> he said that does not describe its contents, but will suffice to induce
> me to read it. What a grand man! One of the great ones of England
> he might have been, if he had not been cursed with cynicism. I
> have no idea to what his Anthropology refers, but I would lay
> great odds that it is only another means of relieving himself of a
> surcharge of spleen against the section of humanity who have
> excited his envy, dislike or scorn. If he had a broader mind he
> would curb these tendencies, and thus allow me to see more clearly
> his grander qualities.

The final point of comparison must hinge on judgements of our
duo as men of Africa. A *general* comparison between the achievements of Stanley and Burton is not really feasible. Stanley was far
the greatest European explorer of Africa, made seven separate forays
into the Dark Continent, including four major expeditions, occupying thirteen years in total at the prime of his life. He was the first
man to circumnavigate both Lakes Tanganyika and Victoria, the
first to chart the Congo and the first to cross Africa in both
directions. His journeys straddled the continent, from Ethiopia to
the Cape and from Zanzibar to Ghana. Burton's record scarcely
measures up to this: a total of four and a half years restricted to
Somaliland, modern Tanzania and the Bights of Benin and Biafra.
But Burton made contributions to exploration and scholarship in
other areas than Africa: in India, Arabia and South America most
notably. In addition he had Promethean talents far in excess of
those possessed by Stanley. Master of twenty-five languages (forty if
we include dialects), poet, anthropologist and scholar, Burton certainly approached the status connoted by that much-misused word

'genius'. His tragedy was that of the creative artist *manqué*; he was unable to find a single focus for his Protean abilities, so that he was at the deepest level immobilized by his contradictory impulses. 'An orchestra without a conductor' is how Alan Moorehead neatly puts it. Stanley by contrast was one of the century's great achievers – surely no one else rose so high from such humble beginnings – but his ruthlessness and ambition never carried him beyond talent to the penumbra of genius occupied by Burton.

If we are to compare like with like, our most fruitful source is the two men's differential perception of Africa. Here we can put the matter in a nutshell. Stanley loved Africa and Africans and hated the continent's Arab slavers. Burton despised the Dark Continent and hated blacks, while revering the Arabs and claiming that the 'horrors' of the slave trade were largely liberal cant and humbug. It is interesting that the continent largely repaid the compliments. There are copious records of the impact of Stanley, Livingstone, Speke and Baker in tribal oral tradition, but none of Burton, almost certainly because, living like an Arab, he was mistaken for one.

Why did Burton so despise the black man?

The difference between Burton as student of primitive society and racial theorist was as wide and profound as that between the dispassionate scholar and the saloon-bar 'barrack-room lawyer'. To put it another way, in Burton the Victorian confusion between race and culture is raised virtually to the power of infinity. Burton distrusted and (except for Islam) despised all organized religions, yet was capable of getting inside the idiom of any religious system he cared to study. He defended the idea of forced labour on theoretical grounds as a means of ending poverty, but denounced the slave trade, which he had seen at first hand. Even there his attitude was ambivalent, for though he felt qualified to talk of the evils of slavery, he did not feel that missionaries, and their armchair supporters at Exeter Hall, possessed the necessary expertise to be able to pronounce on the matter.

So it was that one of the most brilliant students of Africa despised and hated the African, and pitched into the black man with a virulence that would not have disgraced a Gobineau or a Houston Chamberlain. East Africa had left Burton with a marked distaste for 'the Hamitic race'. He was contemptuous of their religion of fetishism, their inability to think of morality except in terms of material possessions – which led them to kill slaves on the death of a king – their inability to imagine the idea of the immortality of the soul, and their general thralldom of demonology and witchcraft. But in East Africa Burton merely despised and derided the black man for his ignorance and idleness; full-blooded hatred had not yet made its mark.

When Burton reached West Africa, he found it even more uncongenial than the Lake Regions had been. Burton often claimed in defence of his Negrophobia that the cruelties he had witnessed in Dahomey had been enough to turn the brain of any normal man.

> The modern Dahomans . . . are a mongrel breed, and a bad. They are Cretan liars, cretins at learning, cowardly and therefore cruel and bloodthirsty; gamblers and consequently cheaters; brutal, noisy, unvenerative, and disobedient . . . a 'flatulent, self-conceited herd of barbarians' who endeavour to humiliate all those with whom they deal; in fact a slave race-vermin with a soul apiece. *Furca, furax, infama, iners furiosa ruina* describes the race.

The notion of a man driven mad by Africa's 'heart of darkness' like Conrad's Kurtz, is plausible enough in the case of a sensitive soul, but it hardly squares with Burton's other self-image, assiduously promoted to Monkton Milnes, Swinburne and Fred Hankey, of the 'wickedest man alive'. Burton boasted to Milnes that Dahomey was disappointing because there was no lake of gore; but the merest trickle of blood, according to another version of himself by himself, was enough to launch him into undying hatred of the black man.

Chronology is also against Burton, for his 'defence' implies that it was only his witnessing of the atrocities in Dahomey that tipped him over the edge. But his vicious outpourings of racial bile occurred, arguably, as a result of the long voyage along the West Africa coast to Fernando PO in August–September 1861. What seems to have thrown Burton seriously off balance was the sight of black men aping their white 'betters' and aspiring to the same sort of lifestyle. Burton could tolerate in his derisory way the 'noble savage' of East Africa. But the be-suited and top-hatted black lawyers of Sierra Leone elicited feelings of anger and rage. He was not the only African explorer to feel this way. Joseph Thomson, who idolized the East Africa Masai as the noblest of noble savages, felt that the West Africa 'nigger' was unbearably 'uppity'. One look at the black population of Sierra Leone produced a virtually identical reaction in Burton. Beginning with their 'personal deformity accompanied by conceit', Burton pitched into every single aspect of these 'arrogant' blacks: their physical appearance, brains, morals, in fact everything. 'The white man's position is rendered far more precarious on the coast than it might be, if the black man were always kept in his proper place.' As for the moral influence of gentleness on the benighted Africa savage, Burton quoted approvingly the words of his friend MacGregor Laird that moral influence in West Africa meant a 68-pounder worked by British seaman.

Burton's hatred of the black man was composed of three main overt elements. Blacks, he contended, were moral and mental imbeciles, but even worse were the missionaries and 'negrophils' who aided and abetted them in their vain quest to escape the biological imperatives of nature. Burton accepted uncritically the dominant racial theories of his time.

> I hold as a tenet of faith the doctrine of great ethnic centres, and their comparative gradation. I believe the European to be the brains, the Asiatic the heart, the American and African the arms and the Australians the feet of the man-figure ... [the black] is prognathous and dolicho-cephalic with retreating forehead, more scalp than face; calfless, cucumber-skinned, lark-heeled with large broad feet; his smell is rank, his hair crisp and curly.

Burton regarded the Sierra Leone black intellectual's refusal to admit his own biological inferiority as in itself evidence of his mental crassness, 'as if there could be brotherhood between crown and clown'. Burton's oeuvre is studded with references to the unregenerate stupidity and mental incorrigibility of the 'moronic' black man: 'study or indeed any tension of the mind, seems to make these weak-brained races semi-idiotic'; after all is not the white man universally portrayed in African legend as a god? On one notable occasion Burton brings down two of his unfavourite birds with one stone. 'To the question, *"Quid muliere levius?"* the scandalous Latin writer suggests *"Nihil"*, for which I would suggest *"Niger"*.'

Even worse than the African's stupidity, for Burton, was his crazed, insensate cruelty. 'They were the slaves of impulse infantile passion and instinct, wilful, lazy, improvident, selfish, irreverent, impatient and without conscience; retaliation and vengeance . . . are their greatest agents of moral control.' Only the sentimentalist could take seriously the idea of the 'noble savage', slaves were just as brutal and cruel as their masters. In West Africa Burton witnessed the loathsome spectacle of unfaithful wives being floated down the Bonny river to the sea bound to bamboo sticks and mats, to be eaten piecemeal by sharks; the same fate was meted out to the slaves of a great man when he died. This drew from Burton an agonized cry of hatred for the black races.

> There is apparently in this people a physical delight in cruelty to beast as well as to man. The sight of suffering seems to bring them an enjoyment without which the world is tame; probably the wholesale murderers and torturers of history, from Phalaris and Nero downwards, took an animal and sensual pleasure – all passions are sisters – in the look of blood and in the inspection of mortal agonies. I can see no other explanation of the phenomena which meet my eye in Africa. In almost all the towns in the Oil Rivers, you see dead or dying animals fastened in some agonising position.

People often asked Burton why the criminals and sacrificial victims of Africa made no attempt to escape the horrible fate that awaited them. He attributed their apathy to the capricious uncertainty of their fate – itself a form of refined cruelty – which meant that the end of the line for the poor unfortunate under sentence could either be death or a royal pardon.

But at least the New Testament precept 'Father, forgive them for they know not what they do' could be urged in defence of the benighted savages. What conceivable defence could be mounted for the missionaries, *bien-pensant* liberals and assorted 'do-gooders' in England, who singularly mixed cant with ignorance in their support of the black man? Burton considered that the anti-slavery humanitarians were riddled with cant and hypocrisy. They talked of the 'sin and crime' of slavery, but overlooked the many areas where traditional Christianity was ambivalent on slavery, notably the New Testament occasion when the centurion's slave is converted into a 'servant' to appease the conscience of the 'unco' guid' (in flat and absurd defiance of the fact that the Greek word used, *doulos*, is always a slave). They ignored the poor and needy in the slums of England who were in many cases worse off than the slaves. They failed to condemn economic imperialism, such as British action in the Opium Wars, which made the indigenous population much more enslaved than anything devised by the Arab traders in Africa. And, most tellingly of all, the British did not return to their native habitat the slaves recovered from slaving vessels by the Royal Navy; instead they shipped them off to the West Indies. Besides, the naval interception of slave-ships immediately placed at risk the ostensible objects of the mission: the slaves themselves. 'The buccaneers quite as humane made their useless prisoners walk the plank. The slave-ships, when chased and hard-driven, simply tossed the poor devil niggers overboard; the latter must often have died, damning the tender mercies of the philanthropy which had doomed them to untimely deaths instead of a comfortable middle passage from Blackland to Whiteland.'

In any case, the spurious humanitarians of Exeter Hall and the missionary societies knew nothing of slavery as it actually obtained on the ground in Africa. Throughout the East the slave's condition was superior to that of the poor free man, 'a fact which I would impress upon the several Anti-slavery Societies, honest men whose zeal mostly exceeds their knowledge and whose energy their discretion'. This was saying nothing of the sleight of hand involved in overlooking the more serious 'slavery' of the tens of thousands of poor white women in London who were in thrall to the lusts of rich males of the elite. The African reality was very different from that imagined by the emancipators. 'Justice requires the confession that the horrors of slave-driving rarely meet the eye in Africa . . . the fat lazy slave is often seen stretched at ease in the shade whilst the master toils in the sun and wind . . . the porter belonging to none but himself is left without hesitation to starve upon the roadside.'

Burton categorically denied that the abolition of the slave trade and of slavery itself would benefit the African. He thought that 'free emigration' schemes were a snare and a delusion, and argued for a form of export of surplus labour similar to the slave trade, in particular a primary-producing colony in the Cameroons, consisting of 45,000 former slaves. He also detested the only available contemporary alternative model, the colony of free blacks at Sierra Leone. He hated seeing Africans in European dress, was outraged to find them holding down posts in local government and the judiciary, and was stupefied to find white men condemned by all-black juries.

Sierra Leone to Burton was a modern Sodom and Gomorrah. Its men were thieves, gamblers, drunkards and rogues, and its women harlots. Miscegenation produced half-castes, mulattos, quadroons and octoroons, each racial thinning producing degeneracy. Things could only improve, he argued, when there was complete apartheid between black and white, with separate courts and separate institutions of all kinds.

Most detested of all species of 'improvers' for Burton were the missionaries. They encouraged miscegenation, mindless manumission without thought of consequences, and fomented the absurd fantasy of the intrinsic equality of blacks and whites. He poked fun at the missionaries' ignorance of native languages, their prudish insistence on clothing the naked aboriginals, their destruction of indigenous polygamy, their attempt to frighten the tribesmen with fire-and-brimstone tales of the punishments of Hell – or with actual corporal punishment, in the case of the Jesuits, if the mind control did not work.

Burton considered that the only way for the black man in Africa was through emigration or the embrace of Islam. It was an item of faith for him that any black who had achieved anything in history, like Toussaint L'Ouverture and the other black emperors in Haiti, must have had Semitic blood, like the Hausa. Since 'improvement' via Islam was the sole realistic way forward for the African, it particularly infuriated Burton that the missionaries directed so many of their broadsides about 'diabolic heresies' at Islam. He noted ironically that missionaries always had a good word for the religions that were no threat to them, like Buddhism, Hinduism and Confucianism, but never one for the faith of Mohammed. 'Dr Livingstone, for one instance of many, evidently preferred the Fetishist, whom he could convert, to the Unitarian Faithful whom he could not.' But after all, Livingstone's position was merely the obverse of Burton's, who could see nothing good on the African continent except Moslems and who went out of his way to contrast devotees of Islam favourably, even in physical appearance, to the native inhabitants.

Moreover Burton felt that Islam did more good in Africa than the Europeans. The latter deceived themselves that Africans respected their religion and culture; they did not – they respected only their guns and superior technology – and in all other respects hankered after the culture of the Arabs. By and large, Africans generally respected Arabs, even when they feared and envied them. The slave trade, anathema in Western eyes, was merely an extension of the domestic slavery sanctioned by tribal custom. Islam by contrast was attractive to the African since, unlike Christianity, it was untouched by racial bias and accepted the African perception of the role of women. Islam and African tribalism were at one in accepting a plurality of wives and a general chattel status for females. The Muslim religion itself required no more than the mouthing of a few rote-learned words. Best of all, Islam put prestigious firearms in the converts' hands, and the Muslim Paradise, with its four luscious virgins assigned to each member of the faithful, was infinitely more appealing than the anaemic and ethereal Christian Heaven.

Besides, on any analysis the Arabs did more for the African than the European interlopers like Leopold of the Belgians. The Arabs taught the more advanced tribes administration. With scribes working in Arabic, they were able to offer enlightened local rulers the elements of a modern bureaucracy. They spread Swahili as a common language through East and Central Africa. They were responsible for a revolution in African diet, having introduced mango, orange and avocado trees, beans, onions, garlic and tomatoes to the continent. Indeed some British colonial administrators later regretted that the Arabs had not established an empire over the entire area, thus providing the incoming European overlords with a sophisticated native class with which to collaborate. In the light of his attitudes, which endorsed these pro-Arab sentiments, it is a great historical irony that Burton did not meet Tippu Tip, the greatest Arab slaver of Central Africa c.1860–90 and a key figure in the conflict of Arab against European in the Dark Continent. Although Tippu helped Livingstone, Verney Cameron and, most notably, Stanley in 1876–7, he was suspicious of white men and resented their attitude of 'effortless superiority'. He ended by detesting Stanley in particular, as an ingrate and manipulator. But the Burton view of Islam and slavery was the precise one Tippu advanced in his debates with European visitors in the 1880s, notably the Belgians Vangele and Becker. Tippu spoke with contempt of the great zeal Europeans had to abolish overnight everything it had taken the Arabs and Africans centuries to build up. He challenged the Europeans to explain to him the difference between African slavery and

Russian serfdom. In his view, his own slaves had a better deal than the proletariat of Europe's cities. At least, slaves as they were, they had full bellies, while the European employee, if he was lucky enough to find employment and be tied to a master, had the 'freedom' to languish from lack of proper payment and the 'privilege' of watching his children die of starvation. Tippu made the further point that Christian arguments about the dignity of freedom were so much humbug in a continent where a slave could be happy while the 'free' tribesman was at the behest of some murderous chieftain. There was far less racial prejudice between Arab and black than between the white man and the black; he himself would not treat a black slave the way he had seen Stanley treating his own whites. You Christians believe in the morality of work, he taunted, yet the black man left to himself is lazy and prefers to steal his bread rather than earn it. How then did Christians square 'freedom' with the morality of work? His final point was that European aspirations for the eventual independence of Africa were, if not false and hypocritical, a recipe for disaster: 'Independence for the African is nothing else but licence, theft, brigandage, debauchery, madness and misery. Just see what will happen in the future.'

How different was the attitude of Stanley. It was not just Livingstone's influence that made him loathe the Arab slavers. They became direct trading and political rivals in the Upper Congo in the early 1880s. Stanley was bitterly frustrated that he did not have the military resources to force a decisive confrontation with them. In fact Leopold's Congo was not strong enough to deal decisively with the heirs of Tippu Tip until 1893. In addition, Stanley had a very high opinion of the African's capabilities and talents. During his five years building the Congo Free States (1879–84) he often contrasted the superior intelligence of his African aides with the white flotsam and jetsam of Europe that was sent out to him. Few things irritated Stanley more than references to 'niggers' or suggestions that the African was a benighted savage, incapable of normal human emotions. He described blacks as capable of great love and affection, with a full sense of gratitude and other noble traits. He found them in general clever, honest, industrious, docile, enterprising, brave and moral, 'in short, equal to any other race or colour on the face of the globe'. As he wrote in his journal in October 1883, commenting on the Bangala chieftain's love for the grandson whom

Stanley was holding to ransom: 'I have seen hundreds of instances which absolutely contradict that absurd statement of the Portuguese Monteiro that the African knows neither affection nor gratitude. Monteiro, I know, has been endorsed by Captain R.F. Burton – but Burton would endorse anything that was uncomplimentary to the African. I know not which to wonder at most – the impudence of Monteiro or the credulity of his stupid readers.'

It has to be remembered, too, that Burton-like views were entertained by many of Stanley's white collaborators and contemporaries on the Congo: the missionary Bentley described the Bolobo as innately cruel, drunk and immoral, while Liebrechts considered that the intelligence of the African was used mainly for evil purposes.

But Stanley was not just impressed by the innate goodness of the black man; this could after all be subsumed in paternalism with the added rider 'until corrupted, just like children'. He declared himself fully convinced of the African's intellectual equality with the white man. Among the Irebu in June 1883 he listened to a brilliant piece of narration from an African storyteller. 'The story as a story was capitally narrated; as a comedy it was surprisingly well done and proved that in this faraway part of Africa there must have been many a Shakespeare and Milton, who have mutely and ingloriously died unwept, unhonoured and unsung by the ignorant civilised world.' And as for ability in business:

> In the management of a bargain I should back the Congolese native against Jew or Christian, Parsee or Banyan, in all the round world. Unthinking men may perhaps say cleverness at barter and shrewdness in trade, consort not with their unsophisticated condition and degraded customs. Unsophisticated is the very last term I should ever apply to an African child or man in connection with the knowledge of how to trade . . . I have seen a child of eight do more tricks of trade in an hour than the cleverest European trader on the Congo could do in a month.

Stanley was a Victorian paternalist only in that he was convinced of the superiority of European *culture*.

The more one examines the African record of the two men, the more the Ossa of irony piles on the Pelion of paradox. Stanley's mastery of Swahili on his fourth expedition was not as great as Burton's on his first, yet he made far more real contact with the peoples he encountered. On the other hand, Burton's anthropological understanding of the tribes he met was more profound; he had a remarkable talent for getting inside the idiom of alien culture, his 'green fingers' in this respect partly deriving from his fidelity to the old adage *cherchez la femme*. In other words, Burton understood the importance of sex and realized that a principal key to any society, possibly *the* key, is how it treats women. The sexually repressed Stanley, who as a shrewd journalist anyway believed in giving the repressed Victorian public what it wanted to hear, always shied away from these fundamentals. For Burton an African tribe had an intrinsic intellectual interest as a thing in itself. For Stanley the tribe was of importance only insofar as it would help or hinder his own expeditions. Yet another paradox arises from the use of violence. We might have expected Burton, who deplored the demise of *'that good old remedy, the sword'* and who hated Africans, to have spread blood and thunder through the continent. Yet as a friend said in a panegyric: 'No tales of blood disfigure the narratives of his explorations: on his death-bed he could have recalled . . . no lives of poor Africans or Asiatics taken away by his orders, no villages in any part of the world plundered.' The implicit reference to Stanley was obvious, for Stanley was notorious for his hard-line methods and disposition to use force. The casualty rates on Stanley's expeditions were always enormous because of his hard-driving methods. Neither wild animals nor hostile tribes nor the ravages of smallpox, malaria, typhus, yellow fever or bilharzia could constrain him or persuade him to slacken his blistering pace. In 1871 he covered the distance to Tabora three times as fast as Burton in 1858. But in addition Stanley dealt out death to all who opposed him. In a single day in 1875, with the use of explosive bullets, he killed fifty Bumbireh tribesmen and wounded hundreds of others. It was this exploit that led the Socialist writer H.M. Hyndman to make his abortive attempt at a vote of censure on Stanley in the RGS in 1878.

The prickly Stanley would have been affronted at any attempt to compare his record in Africa with Burton's. But Burton, the lover of paradox, would surely have relished the difficulty one was in drawing up a judicious balance sheet. The apposite text, I think, is the one Burton used in his poem 'The Kasidah' to mock the pretensions of rival theologies:

All faith is false; all faith is true; Faith is the shattered mirror
    strown
In myriad bits; while each believes his little bit the whole
    to own
'You are all right, you are all wrong' we hear the careless
    Soofi say
For each believes his glimmering lamp to be the glimmering
    light of day.

Roland Huntford

NANSEN

Hamlet is one of the great literary mirrors of the human condition, Don Quixote another. It was, however, with Goethe's Faust that Fridtjof Nansen, the Norwegian polar explorer, chose to identify. Faust, in Nansen's own words, 'never reached a place where he wanted to "remain". I cannot even glimpse anywhere worth the attempt.' That echoed the words of Goethe in which Faust makes his compact with the Devil. As this is usually understood, Faust would be granted what he wished in return for giving up his soul after a term of years. In Goethe's portrayal, it was *at some time that depended on himself*. As long as Faust was dissatisfied, he was safe, but:

> If to the fleeting hour I say
> 'Remain, so fair thou art, remain!'
> Then bind me with fetters on that day,
> For I will gladly perish then.
> Let the death-bell start to toll.

In this version, Faust is not buying a favour. He is making a challenge. He is daring Mephistopheles to satisfy him. Goethe's tortured hero is in the image of modern man. Sometimes Nansen almost gave the impression of acting out the play.

He was born on 10 October 1861 in Christiania, as Oslo was then called. Although a small, little-known country on the edge of Europe, Norway in the nineteenth century was no backwater. Once a Danish possession, she had been transferred by the Napoleonic Wars into an unwilling union with Sweden, and the power of nationalism was at work.

One consequence was intellectual ferment and a latter-day

renaissance. Norway produced a burst of talent out of all proportion to its population – at around 1.7 million, no more than that of contemporary Paris. Take, for example, Nils Henrik Abel, a founder of modern mathematics. Then there was Henrik Ibsen, the prophet of modern drama, and Edvard Grieg, an exponent of nationalism in music. There were others, like Edvard Munch, a pioneer of the neurotic in art. Among these, Nansen takes his place as the father of modern polar exploration, but also something more.

At school, Nansen was a conspicuous all-rounder, but sport was the object of his zeal. When the time came to choose a career, he decided on zoology. By his own account, he made his choice because he thought that it would guarantee him an open-air life. His father, Baldur Nansen, a Christiania lawyer, was simply relieved that he had found a direction. Baldur had come to expect great things of him, to the point of considering him a genius. This was rather hard on Baldur's other child, Nansen's younger brother Alexander, diligently following his father into law. It was also hard on Nansen. To add to his burden, their mother had died when he was sixteen, never having shown maternal love.

In 1882, after a year at the University of Christiania – then the only one in Norway – Nansen moved to Bergen, on the west coast of Norway, as curator at the museum. Amongst its other functions, the museum dealt with marine biology. It was an age when formal qualifications were still not required for research. Nansen found himself specializing in the central nervous system of lower marine creatures.

One consequence of Darwin's theory of the origin of Man, was that a simpler organism was a model of himself. Studying primitive nervous systems, therefore, would reveal the workings of the human brain; ultimately perhaps the secret of thought itself. It was while embarking on this work that Nansen was introduced to Goethe's *Faust*. 'The questing human spirit,' Nansen wrote to his father in the first flush of enthusiasm, 'sometimes dares to penetrate where its power ends, like ... Faust, who entered into an alliance with the Devil, and that is the spirit that has emerged nowadays more powerfully than ever.'

That was well said. It was in that decade, of the 1880s, that the seeds of the modern world were being sown. In Germany, for example, Heinrich Hertz was producing the first radio waves.

Nansen found himself embroiled in the question of how nerves communicated with each other, which was just as far-reaching.

The reigning view was that nerves were fused together in a continuous network. Nansen's research quickly gave him leave to doubt. His difficulty was how to stain his specimens so that their detail was revealed in the microscope. The best available method for nerve cells was the so-called '*reazione nera*' of Camillo Golgi, a celebrated Italian anatomist at the University of Pavia. Early in 1886 Nansen visited Golgi's laboratory to learn the method properly. He then worked for a few months at an international research station in Naples to perfect its application to marine creatures.

Thus fortified, Nansen went back to Bergen. What he now saw in the microscope persuaded him that the nerves were independent units, connecting with each other by touching. This was an historic breakthrough, subsequently confirmed, and laid the foundation of modern neurology. It came to be known as the neuron theory, from a Greek word meaning 'sinew'. Consisting of the cell body and its fibre-like outgrowths, the neuron is the building block of the nervous system.

As is often the case, Nansen was not alone. Two Swiss scientists, August Forel, a psychiatrist, and an embryologist, Wilhelm His, were independently coming to similar conclusions. These three, from different points of view, had launched the first onslaught on the orthodox network theory. Their work appeared in print within a few months of each other during 1886 and 1887. They thus became co-founders of the modern view of the nervous system, although by a quirk of publication, Nansen secured technical priority. He also gave the first correct explanation of the reflex arc, the mechanism by which sensory impulses are transformed into physical actions.

To profit academically by his work, Nansen also wrote it up as a doctoral thesis. Reluctantly, because of the originality of his ideas, the University in Christiania granted him his degree at the end of April 1888. A few days later he sailed off to attempt the first crossing of Greenland from coast to coast.

On the face of it, this seemed grotesquely improbable. In the spring of 1882, however, the University in Christiania had sent Nansen in a sealer to the Arctic to collect zoological specimens. Along the way, he sighted one of the last unexplored parts of the

coast of east Greenland. By his own account that stimulated an
ambition to make the crossing of Greenland. It had fought all the
while with his desire to solve the mysteries of the central nervous
system, recalling Faust's wail that 'two souls, alas, live within my
breast!'

By now, the Polar Regions were the last great blank spaces, and
the crossing of Greenland was one of the last of the great geographical goals. It meant traversing a high-lying ice cap, covering most of
the country, the interior of which was virtually unknown. Nansen
proposed using skis.

Although ancient and widespread in Siberia and Scandinavia,
skiing in its modern form is a Norwegian invention. Nansen
belonged to the generation that gave it its final shape. He was both
a leading competition skier – in Nordic and alpine disciplines – and
a pioneer of mountain skiing. Except for some tentative trials,
however, skis had not so far been used in polar exploration.

Besides skiing, Nansen was making other innovations. He developed a new kind of sledge, based on a traditional form with broad,
ski-like runners, also an insulated cooker to save fuel. Hitherto, all
attempts to cross Greenland had started from the west coast, which
was inhabited, while the east coast, except for a few Eskimos'
settlements, was not. Nansen proposed doing it the other way about,
scorning received wisdom by deliberately cutting off his lines of
retreat so that the instinct of self-preservation would drive him on.
This original approach was roundly condemned. The State rejected
Nansen's application for a grant, but private enterprise came to the
rescue. A Danish coffee wholesaler called Augustin Gamél paid for
the expedition.

With five companions, Nansen was landed on the pack ice off
the east coast of Greenland on 17 July by a Norwegian sealer
appropriately called *Jason*. After various setbacks, they reached
land. On 15 August, at a place called Umivik, they started the climb
up to the ice cap. On 24 September, they reached the other side.
The crossing had taken forty-one days.

Caught for the winter in Greenland, they stayed at the Danish
settlement of Godthaab. In the spring of 1889, Nansen returned to
civilization and international fame. His was the first attainment of a
great geographical goal since Stanley had settled the sources of the
Congo and the Nile in the previous decade.

More to the point, compared with the horrors of previous Arctic expeditions, Nansen's tale was one of insulting ease. His book about the expedition – published in English as *The First Crossing of Greenland* – was hugely popular. Its main lesson was that through the use of skis he had revolutionized Arctic travel and demythologized the polar environment. The book also made skiing known abroad, and launched it as a universal sport.

Nansen once whimsically dismissed his expedition as a much-needed holiday from research. In reality, he had deserted neurology for good. As he himself put it, once he established the principle, 'the charm had vanished'. His pioneering of the neuron theory was submerged; chiefly by leaving the field, so that others appropriated the honour, and he never received the credit that was his due.

In any case, after the first crossing into Greenland, it was the turn of the poles of the earth. Nansen wanted to be the first man at both, starting with the North. Once more, he overturned accepted ideas. Hitherto, explorers had fought the powers of nature; Nansen decided to work with them.

In 1884 he had learned of relics in the pack ice that suggested a current flowing from Siberia to Greenland. Most of the Arctic was still unknown, and this was as good a postulate as any. He would use the putative current to take him to his goal. He proposed to freeze a ship into the Arctic pack ice and let her be carried by drift.

Again Nansen found himself at odds with received wisdom. After crossing Greenland, however, he was a Norwegian national hero, so the State largely financed his new expedition, whatever the experts said. The danger, inherent in his plan, and with ample precedent, was that his ship would be crushed. To avoid this, he had one built to his own innovative design. Like all craft intended for the ice, she was made of wood, flexible and strong. She was, however, distinguished by being small and broad on the beam, with round, smooth bilges, sides flaring outwards all the way to the deck, and a rounded stern, so that she looked like an eggshell cut in half. Thus the ice could get no purchase, so that she would rise when squeezed, instead of being gripped, and thus avoid being crushed. Nansen called her *Fram* – 'Forwards'. On 20 July 1893 she left the coast of Norway. At the end of September, off the New Siberian Islands, she was frozen in.

Nansen's predicted current, or at least surface drift, did in fact appear, but not on the desired course. It was going to miss the Pole. Nansen decided to try to reach it over the ice, and then make for land.

This was uncharacteristically reckless. Nansen had abandoned his principle of not defying the power of nature. He had, however, not foreseen the effect of isolation. Today, with our instant communication, and the view from space, it is impossible to conceive of what that meant. The first men on the moon, in constant touch with Earth, were less alone than Nansen and his twelve companions on *Fram*.

Without radio, cut off from the world, Nansen was in the grip of violent conflicts of emotion. For all his philosophizing, he found that he could not passively wait while natural forces did their work. He needed action at almost any price. Also, he was missing his wife. In 1889 he had married Eva Sars, a concert singer. She played up to his Faust fixation by performing, with eerie undertones, musical settings of passages from Goethe's work. Nansen wanted to go home, and the quickest way seemed via the North Pole. On 14 March 1895, with one companion, Hjalmar Johansen, he left *Fram*, and headed over the frozen sea.

They were forced to turn after three weeks, still well short of the Pole. Eventually, after a journey of 700 miles over the pack ice, they reached the little-known Franz Josef Land archipelago. They were caught for the winter on one of the islands there, in a primitive stone hut. They survived. The following summer, elsewhere in the archipelago, they met Frederick Jackson, an English explorer, in whose expedition ship they returned to civilization.

On 13 August 1896 Nansen and Johansen landed on the Arctic coast of Norway. They were like men returning from the dead. In a sense all their efforts had been in vain. *Fram* arrived barely a week afterwards, unscathed, her design vindicated, having drifted not far short of Nansen's own record. Nonetheless his arrival was one of the sensations of the age. His failure to reach the Pole did not count. He had reached a latitude of 86° 14′, breaking the previous record for the farthest north by 170 miles. It was the biggest single advance for nearly 400 years. His journey had the quality of epic, and his meeting with Jackson was reminiscent of Stanley's with Livingstone. His book about the expedition, published in English as *Farthest North*, became an instant best-seller.

All this was separately impressive. Nansen had the power of transmuting it into something greater. His personality was overwhelming, to which his appearance conformed. Tall, big-boned, blond, handsome in a Nordic way, blue eyes fiercely aglint, he looked like a triumphant Viking chieftain. Eminently photogenic, as the half-tone system of reproducing photographs was becoming universal, he was a favourite of journalists, and a creation of the popular Press. He became one of the most famous of living men. He was a hero of his times.

Behind the image, Nansen's achievements were real enough. He was the first of the pole-seekers to bring everyone back alive. With only twelve companions on *Fram*, he had discredited the use of large, cumbersome expeditions in favour of a small cohesive party.

Technically, Nansen had revolutionized polar travel yet again. On the crossing of Greenland, he had been forced to man-haul his sledges, but on this occasion he had used dogs. Other explorers had done so before; Nansen made the momentous discovery that the speed of a dog team pulling a loaded sledge matched that of a Nordic skier at his natural pace. This made the skier the natural polar traveller, which had not hitherto been obvious. It secured Scandinavian domination in high latitudes, and opened the race for the Poles; Nansen had launched modern polar exploration.

The fate of the precursor is hard. Nansen's primacy lasted five years. In September 1900 his record for the farthest north was broken by the Duke of the Abruzzi, a scion of the Italian ruling house of Savoy. Nansen entered in his diary a paraphrase of Faust's despairing words: 'Cursed be that within our dreams, / Which cheats with thought of lasting fame!'

To Nansen, the North Pole was now just one more discarded ambition. On *Fram*, before his polar dash, he had shown that the Arctic was not a shallow sea, but a deep oceanic basin, yet again overturning accepted ideas. This turned him to oceanography, and one more field in which he became a pioneer. Eventually he was made a professor ad hominem in the subject at the University in Christiania.

Meanwhile the Norwegian drive to independence was approaching its culmination. Other motives aside, Nansen had conceived his expeditions as patriotic enterprises, and exploited them to promote the Norwegian cause abroad. There, too, he was a pioneer; in this

case, the use of non-political activities for political ends. When the
time came, he had a political role as well.

Although Norway was a junior partner in the Union with
Sweden, she had a national Parliament and Government with greater
autonomy than the states of the European Union today. On 7 June
1905 independence was declared by a parliamentary coup. Nansen
was used to give it legitimacy abroad. This began during the prelude,
when he was sent on a private mission to England, then still one of
the Powers, to prepare the ground.

Nansen was the one Norwegian of international stature, and
about him there still hung the aura of his polar exploits. Since the
Fram expedition, he had been treated in England almost as a home-
grown national hero – partly because he spoke English fluently and
was obviously an Anglophile. Still the darling of the Press, he
brought off one propaganda coup after the other, proving himself a
master of the nascent craft of public relations. In addition, he had
an entrée to the ruling circles everywhere. He played a vital role
both in the negotiations with the Swedes to dissolve the Union and
in the king making that went hand in hand with independence. It
was largely Nansen who persuaded the Danish Prince Carl to replace
the Swedish house of Bernadotte and ascend the Norwegian throne
as King Haakon VII – a hark back to a glorious medieval past when
Norway had last been a sovereign kingdom.

Nansen was sent to London in 1906 as the first Ambassador
of an independent Norway. From one point of view, he was an
ambivalent figure. The separation of Sweden and Norway had
occurred without a drop of blood being spilt, but it was an ominous
example of nationalistic unrest from Ireland to the Carpathians.
On the other hand, by sheer force of character, Nansen achieved
what he had been sent to do. This was the signature by the Great
Powers of a treaty guaranteeing Norwegian territorial integrity.
That accomplished, Nansen lost interest in diplomacy. In 1908 he
resigned his post, and returned to his forbidding home by the fjord
in Christiania.

While Nansen was in London, his wife Eva died, leaving him
with five children to bring up. He had a heavy conscience, having
conducted at least one extra-marital affair that deeply wounded
Eva. Nansen now retired into semi-private life, and concentrated on
oceanography. In a small digression, he wrote a monumental work

on early northern exploration, published in English as *In Northern Mists* – still required reading in the field. He did many of the illustrations, possessing artistic talent amongst his other gifts. He was an accomplished author, overcoming even the barriers of translation.

Although retired from exploration, Nansen continued hankering for the South Pole. That delusion was shattered when, in December 1911, Roald Amundsen, Nansen's compatriot, forestalled him, as he forestalled the English contender, Captain Scott. At best, Nansen had always regarded Amundsen with the conflicting emotions of mentor and rival. Amundsen had borrowed his old ship, *Fram*, at first intending to go north, and then secretly turning south when, in 1909, the American R.E. Peary claimed to have reached the North Pole. It was in the aftermath of the affair that Nansen recorded in his diary the dismal echo of Faust that he 'never reached a place where he wanted to "remain" '.

The outbreak of war in 1914 left Norway neutral, but Nansen believed that this did not of itself guarantee security, and had been agitating for a strong defence. This was the opposite of government policy and public opinion so, contemptuous of his fellow country-men, mistrusted by politicians, he was condemned to inaction. In 1916 he was privately approached as a mediator by the representa-tive in Norway of a German military faction that wanted to make peace with England, but his overtures were rejected by the Foreign Office. All this was unknown to the Norwegian authorities who, the following year, grudgingly called Nansen out of retirement for a diplomatic mission to Washington. Again, he was the only Nor-wegian with the necessary stature. His brief – successfully accom-plished – was to negotiate an agreement to import American food through the naval blockade after America's recent entry into the war on the Allied side.

The mission to Washington had rekindled Nansen's taste for action. Meanwhile he had been undergoing a kind of conversion. All along he had been a consistent realist, but now he had developed alarmingly idealistic tendencies. He began to see himself as the conscience of the world. This was out of character. An apostle of Darwin, Nansen had once written that, 'Nature has only given the strong the right to live.' He was untouched by suffering in the mass. To his shame, the horrors of the war left him unmoved. He tried to overcome it, but his expression of concern came not from the heart, only from the head. Nansen had become a humanitarian. This word of dubious origin all too often hides the contradiction of an outer show of charity and an inner harshness.

On his return to Norway from Washington in 1918, Nansen found a use for his new-found humanitarianism in the founding of the League of Nations. This was one of the American war aims. A League of Nations Union was formed internationally to advance the cause, and Nansen became chairman of the Norwegian branch. In that capacity, after the German defeat, with unclear aims, he headed for the Peace Conference in Paris.

He travelled via London, where he visited Kathleen Scott, the widow of Captain Scott, the ill-fated Antarctic explorer. They had first met nine years earlier in Norway, when Kathleen was accompanying her husband on a visit to prepare for his attempt on the South Pole. That included consulting Nansen, then still the polar oracle. In Berlin, Nansen later had a brief affair with Kathleen, ironically while Scott was away in the Antarctic, discovering that he had been beaten by Amundsen. 'I feel like a Faust, who has got a draught of the fountain of life,' Nansen wrote afterwards to her.

But for Kathleen, Nansen would have simply joined the hangers-on at the Peace Conference. She knew Colonel Edward House, President Woodrow Wilson's aide in the American delegation, and gave Nansen a letter of introduction. He presented it on arrival in Paris.

The conference was ostensibly about making peace with Germany, but the real concern was Russia, the sinister absentee, after the Bolshevik Revolution and Lenin's assumption of power in 1917. The West wanted to stop Lenin, but was uncertain how to do so. Herbert Hoover, the head of the American Relief Administration (ARA), had a plan. Instead of military force, he proposed using food as a weapon. Thus originated one of the great political devices of the century.

Russia was then in the grip of civil war and incipient starvation. Hoover's idea was to offer food, in return for an armistice, and the end of attempts to export communist revolution. Because Lenin's regime and America were enemies, Hoover needed a front man. Nansen, bearing Kathleen's letter, arrived as if on cue. He was exactly what was needed. He belonged to a neutral country, he had presence, and his humanitarian credentials were in order. He was also guileless to a fault. He signed the documents that Hoover drafted, but did not understand that he was being used as a pawn. Lenin understood it all too well. He rejected the overture, privately jeering at Nansen as a 'sixteen-year-old schoolgirl'.

Nansen returned to Norway, now seriously beginning to see himself as a saviour of suffering mankind. He did not have long to wait for another mission to materialize. In April 1920 he was asked by the now operative League of Nations to head their repatriation of Russian prisoners of war and those of the former Central Powers.

This was a shady operation. The work properly belonged to the International Committee of the Red Cross in Geneva. It had been appropriated by the League to give itself a title to existence. The man behind this coup was Philip Noel-Baker (later Lord Noel-Baker), a future English Labour MP, and a well-known pacifist. Having fleetingly met Nansen at the Peace Conference in Paris, Noel-Baker, too, was overwhelmed by his personality and saw how it might be turned to his advantage. He now visited Nansen at home in Christiania to persuade him to accept the invitation.

Like Nansen, Noel-Baker had developed a taste for good works, while concealing a morose streak of harshness. In Nansen's case, it was his family who suffered. Where Noel-Baker was concerned, it was his wife Irene who paid the price. Noel-Baker saw in the newly-found League a stepping stone in his career. Unfortunately he lacked presence and trustworthiness. Nansen possessed both. They thus complemented each other. Noel-Baker offered Nansen a mission and a new lease of life. In return, Noel-Baker had found someone through whom he could attain his own ends. This was the compact they tacitly entered into. Noel-Baker was playing a very credible Mephistopheles to Nansen's Faust. Nansen accepted the invitation of the League, and was duly appointed High Commissioner for the Repatriation of POW's.

As it turned out, the Red Cross actually did the work, but the League, as planned, appropriated most of the prestige. To their eternal credit, the Red Cross never publicly complained. Nansen himself was really a figurehead, brought out when required to cajole money and assistance from men in power, and exercise his old talent for opening doors.

For their part, the Soviet authorities became the next to see

in Nansen a means to their own ends. They regarded the League of
Nations as a capitalist conspiracy, which they refused to recognize.
Hungry for international respectability, however, they were prepared to deal with Nansen as an individual. On a visit to Moscow
to smooth out difficulties, he was received by the Kremlin, whose
masters were distinctly co-operative. By 1922 the prisoners of war
had been repatriated, some 430,000 of them. Meanwhile another
mission had come Nansen's way.

In July 1921 he received a telegram from Moscow begging with
curious arrogance for help to relieve a famine. The signatory was
the Russian author, Maxim Gorky, but the formula was Lenin's.
Hating the peasants as bastions of capitalism, Lenin had been trying
to starve them into submission. Instead, he had caused a crop failure
in the Volga region which, coming on top of industrial collapse and
a mutiny at Kronstadt (the second of its kind, the better-known first
Kronstadt mutiny was a prelude to the Bolshevik Revolution) near
St Petersburg, shook his regime to the core. This was what had
driven him to make his appeal. He had opened the first charity
chantage of the century. He had invented the exploitation of disaster
as moral blackmail of the West.

Yet again through the agency of Noel-Baker, Nansen found
himself with a role in all this. He was appointed head of Russian
famine relief by a private conference of charitable organizations in
Geneva. He was anticipated by Herbert Hoover, who saw that the
moment for the food weapon had arrived, and no longer needed a
front man.

Hoover, sensing the weakness behind Lenin's bombast, quickly
negotiated an agreement. His objectives were to secure the release
of American hostages in Russia, to mop up an American glut of
grain, and to force the Kremlin to hand over gold reserves abroad
so as to deplete Soviet resources for foreign propaganda. He succeeded in all three and, in return, through the ARA, effectively fed
the starving.

This demonstration of efficiency by a capitalist ogre in the
person of Hoover was not at all to Lenin's liking, so he proceeded
to use Nansen as a counterweight. The Soviet authorities quickly
signed another aid agreement with Nansen, as the representative of
the Geneva conference. The ARA operation in Russia was independent, down to their own soup kitchens in the field. Nansen's

Kim Philby (1912–88)

Charles Stewart Parnell (1846–91)

Marie Stopes (1880–1958)

Germaine Greer (1939–)

Peter Fleming (1907–71)

Henry Morton Stanley (1841–1904)

Richard Burton (1821–90)

Fridtjof Nansen (1861–1930)

Bruce Chatwin (1940–89)

Bram Fischer (1908–75)

Suharto of Indonesia (1921–)

Right:
Winston Churchill (1874–1965)

Below:
Alec Douglas-Home (1903–95)

Below right:
Herbert Gladstone (1854–1930)

Basil Liddell Hart (1895–1970)

Wully Robertson (1860–1933)

organization was considerably less efficient, and under the thumb of the Kremlin. At the height of the famine in 1922, the ARA was feeding 8.5 million people against the bare 400,000 by all the charities under Nansen's aegis combined. Soviet propaganda, however, disparaged Hoover and built Nansen up as the saviour of the starving Russians.

Nansen seemed to believe it himself. With his political naivety, he allowed himself to be used by the Soviets and their sympathizers as a cover to exploit the famine for their own purposes, notably to break a trade embargo. Lenin had the last laugh. Western charity, and Nansen in particular, had saved him when, in his own words, he was 'barely hanging on'.

Like many charitable workers, Nansen tried to prolong the emergency upon which the justification for his work depended. He had, however, become suspect in the West as a Soviet tool. His organization was dissolved in September 1922, after little more than a year. Before then, however, yet another mission appeared.

In August 1921 the League of Nations appointed Nansen their High Commissioner for Russian Refugees. Once again, Nansen could thank the scheming of that obsessive manipulator, Philip Noel-Baker. About 1 million Russians, having fled the Bolshevik regime, were exiles in Europe. Lenin deprived them of their nationality and, at the stroke of a pen, turned them into a stateless horde. Nansen was appointed to give them international protection. From the start, he was lukewarm. Starving Tolstoyan peasants made more attractive objects of self-indulgent pity.

His new post began in the familiar way. Once more, he happily allowed himself to be used as a front man. Edouard Frick, a Swiss among his entourage, grasped that the refugee question was a legal one. He invented a document to be issued by the country of residence as a certificate of identity and travel without conferring nationality. With or without permission, he called it a 'Nansen passport', and the name stuck. Thus under Nansen's aegis – halfheartedly perhaps – the position of the refugee was first regularized. The principles still hold.

At one point, to general suspicion, Nansen filled four concurrent roles: leader of famine relief, leader of POW repatriation, protector of Russian refugees, besides being Norwegian delegate to the League. As the first two faded, he began to concentrate on the third.

In that capacity, he invented the media-conscious international civil servant, which turned into one of the figures of the century.

At a certain point, Nansen's brief was extended from Russian refugees to those of any origin, and he became simply High Commissioner for Refugees, the first of his kind. His most spectacular service was in the aftermath of the Greek defeat in the war against Turkey of 1919–22. Turkey was to be purged of non-Muslims. In the wake of the defeated Greek Army, a million Greek fugitives poured into Greece from Asia Minor. To deal with this influx, Nansen was called in – Noel-Baker ever at his side. By now the two were inextricable and, in the true Faustian manner, it was difficult to say who was using whom.

Now there was in Greece a Muslim minority of about 400,000. Nansen proposed their reciprocal expulsion to Turkey. 'To unmix the populations of the Near East,' as he put it, 'will . . . secure the pacification of the Near East.' With his capacity for holding contradictory opinions, Nansen had shown that he could after all still jettison fruitless ideals when circumstances required. Greek and Turk did not get on, so it was pointless forcing them to live together.

The idea was not as radical as it may seem. In the Balkans, as a solution to political problems, exchanges of population had already been invoked and regulated by treaty. Nansen's proposal differed only in scale. He put it late in 1922 to the Conference of Lausanne, which was making peace between Greece and Turkey. It was accepted with tacit relief. The compulsory exchange of minorities was enshrined in a treaty, and an international loan raised to enforce it as humanely as possible. A festering minority problem had been exorcized.

The outcome aside, the process itself was of great historic interest. Nansen had set a precedent. This was the first occasion on which national governments had used an international civil servant to take the odium of uncomfortable decisions and legitimize their actions. Partly in recognition of his work for the exchange of minorities, Nansen received the Nobel Peace Prize for 1922.

Thereafter, Nansen reverted to his ideals, and became one of the familiar, well-meaning figures during the 20s in the precincts of the League of Nations in Geneva. He pursued various quixotic crusades. One was a plan to repatriate Russian refugees for their country's good; another, to found a national home for Armenians on Soviet territory – in which Nansen's assistant was the subsequent Norwegian Nazi collaborator, Vidkun Quisling. Both schemes derived from Nansen's belief in the goodwill of Stalin, now beginning his reign of terror in Russia, and both predictably failed.

For all that he had done, Nansen was never satisfied. In between his international activities, he was still pursuing his scientific interests. He was an early adherent of the effect of the sun on climate change. He combined his humanitarianism with an interest in eugenics. 'We are threatened with the survival of the unfittest,' he wrote. In another contradiction, while considered a Soviet dupe abroad, at home he was involved in efforts to stop the advance of communism.

Nansen's private life was anything but happy. His children were miserable at home. He remarried in 1919, disastrously as it turned out. He was forever seeking solace – platonically no doubt – in the company of other women. He died in 1930, of heart disease. The year before, he had visited America, and was interviewed by a woman journalist who imagined that he was in love with her. She recorded that he spoke to her of Faust. She seemed surprised. She need not have been. Nansen had spent most of his life in the shadow of Goethe's creation.

Redmond O'Hanlon

BRUCE CHATWIN: CONGO JOURNEY

Redmond O'Hanlon, now firmly established as an intrepid explorer, and one of today's most entertaining travel writers, is as difficult to locate as Colonel Fawcett or Dr Livingstone. When finally tracked down to the Outer Hebrides, he said he was under just too much pressure to produce something new in the time available, but he could offer us, gratis, his epitaph to his friend and fellow traveller Bruce Chatwin, which originally appeared in Congo Journey *(Viking, 1996), pp. 340–4. Anyway, he said, it was one of his best bits of writing. It is.*

*   *   *

O'Hanlon is lying sleepless in the Congo, devoured by insects and bed bugs and maggots, wondering whether they can – knowing their habits, and those of the Congolese – possibly infect him with AIDS . . .

*

. . . So I lay on the planks and tried to think of something peaceful; of the little bedroom in the vicarage of childhood; of the blackbird that used to perch each summer evening on the roof of the bicycle shed below my window and sing me to sleep; of the woodpigeons in the conker tree; but it didn't work. Nothing held for long enough; my brain was too disturbed to be directed in its dreams; my imagination obstinately filled with thoughts of Bruce Chatwin, the only person I knew who had died of AIDS.

'Redders!' would come a familiar voice down the phone far too early in the morning. 'Not even Bunin' (for example) 'was interesting yesterday. I can't stand it a moment longer. I'm sick of writing. I'm

tired! Tired! Tired!' (said with enough energy to crack your ear-
drum). 'And when a man is sick of writing he must walk.' (Oh
God.) 'I'm coming to get you.' (Panic.) 'What are you doing?'

'I'm in bed.'

'Up you get! Two glasses of green tea. See you in half an
hour.'

I would begin wondering who or what Bunin was: with Bruce
you could never be sure. The new Stravinsky from Albania? The
nickname of the last slave in Central Mali? A lighthouse-keeper
from Patagonia? Scroll 238B from a cave in the Negev? Or just the
émigré King of Tomsk who'd dropped in for tea? Still vaguely
wondering, I lurched out of the house.

A white 2CV puttered into the drive. There was a sailboard
strapped to the roof. Chatwin got out, his wife Elizabeth's two dogs
wagging about his feet.

'Come on! It's almost dawn! I'm taking these brutes to a hill
farm in Wales. We'll look at the tree of life on the south door of St
Mary and St David at Kilpeck; we'll deliver the dogs; we'll call in
on my old friend Lady Betjeman; and then I'll walk you over the
Black Hill.'

'So what's the sailboard for?' I said, suspicious.

'Oh, that. That's my new hobby. You bring your car and make
your own way back tonight and I'll go sailing in the Bristol Channel
in the morning.'

And you'll probably be in Dublin for supper, I thought.

Beneath the first ridge of the Black Mountains we parked by a
track and got out our boots: mine, black wellingtons; his, a pair of
such fine leather that Hermés would have done a swap. I put on my
bergen (with nothing in it but a loaf of bread and two bottles of
wine) and he put on his small haversack of dark maroon calfskin
(with nothing in it but a Montblanc pen, a black, oilcloth-bound,
vrai moleskin notebook, a copy of Aylmer Maude's translation of
War and Peace, Strindberg's *By the Open Sea* and the most elegant
pair of binoculars that I had ever seen).

'Werner Herzog gave them to me,' said Bruce, his eyes blue and
bright and eager. 'He wants to film *The Viceroy of Ouidah*. And
Jean-Louis Barrault had this pack designed just for me. But you
could get some decent boots, Redders. The Canadian Moccasin
Company. Just say you're a friend of mine.'

He took off up the hill with a strong, loping stride, through the heather and the whinberries, a real nomad's stride. In a few minutes I fell behind, trying not to pant like an engine shed.

'The twins I wrote about lived there,' he said, turning without slackening his pace and pointing to a long slate-roofed farmhouse set back from the road in the diminishing valley below us.

'And . . . that's . . . where!!!' His words whipped past me, split up and were lost to sense in the wind. The speed of ascent was effort enough, replying to the wild and ceaseless monologue an impossibility – which was just as well, because it was far too late in our friendship to admit that, much as I admired *In Patagonia*, what with one siesta and another I had just not quite read *On the Black Hill*.

'There's a hippy camp down there,' he called, nodding north-west at the clouds pulling their dark fringe of falling rain towards us. He shouted with laughter. 'All the locals are terrified of them. They think they'll be strangled in their beds! When I was staying with the King of Afghanistan he had an old English colonel about the court. "Your Royal Highness," said the colonel, "you must let me remove all the hips from your country. You must let me put all the hips in trucks and take them to the border."'

Down on the Llanthony road, we walked through the hail, and Bruce talked about a female albatross that had wandered northwards to the wrong hemisphere and built a nest in Shetland, waiting for the mate that never came, and about the train he caught from King's Cross on his way to see her – and how the only other passenger in his sleeper compartment was a Tierra del Fuegian ('on his way to the North Sea oil-rigs – they're the only men who can throw a boat's painter through a ring on a buoy') whose settlement Bruce had visited on the journey that became *In Patagonia*.

He talked about his love for the herdspeople of the Sudan; about smuggling Roman coins out of Turkey; about the design of a prehistoric wheel that linked the Irish to an ethnic subgroup in the Caucasus (I think); and about his real dream – the Russian novel he would write one day.

There was the noise of an engine shaking itself to bits, three violent backfires, and a rust-holed van lurched up the road towards us. I jumped onto the bank at the base of the hedge; but Bruce, engrossed, was still walking in the road. Surprisingly slowly, it seemed, the van nudged the Jean-Louis Barrault haversack. Equally slowly, Bruce, still talking ('Just tell the story straight as Tolstoy. No tricks!'), turned a full somersault in the air. 'No tricks!' he said as he windmilled into the ditch.

'You stupid bastards!' he shouted, getting to his feet. 'That was unnecessary.'

A young boy, his hair in a ponytail, jumped down from the cab. 'Sorry, squire,' he said. 'I'm sorry. Honest. What more can I say? It's like this – my wheels hasn't got no brakes.'

'I say,' said Bruce. 'How exciting. Can we have a lift!'

*

Just back from months in the jungle between the Orinoco and the Amazon, I thought I'd celebrate with warm scallops in a London restaurant and got a six-month dose of hepatitis A. Half asleep, eyes shut in the isolation wing of the Churchill Hospital in Oxford, I heard a familiar voice.

'Shush,' it said. 'Don't tell anyone. I'm not here.'

I opened one eye. So it was true. Hepatitis A induced delirium. You saw visions on it.

'Shush, I'm in France. Bill Buford's after me. I'm meant to be writing a piece for *Granta*. But with you here too I might just as well phone Reuters and be done with it.

'I've brought you some liver pills. They're from Elizabeth's guru in India. I'm having Aboriginal warts removed from my face. I'm in the room next door. Look – I'll do the same for you if you die first. Will you be my literary executor?'

'I'll do anything you say. I want to go to sleep.'

'You know – there's something else I want you to know. When I first came in here they told me I was mortally ill. They said I had a fungus of the bone marrow which I must have picked up in a cave in China. It's exclusive! It's so rare that I'm only the tenth recorded case in the medical literature! And they also let me know why I got it, Redders – I got it because I have AIDS. They told me I had six months or a year to live. So I thought, right, Bruce is a dog's name and I'm not going to stand for this. I can't get on with my big nomad book as it is – I can't see how I can pull material out of my notebooks and onto the page; and I'm not going to waste away and go feeble in the head and defecate all over the place.

'So I went to Geneva – there's a place in the Alps that haunts me, a ravishing cliff near Jungfrau – and I wanted to jump off it. Or, failing that, I thought I'd go to Niger and simply take off my clothes, put on my loincloth, walk out into the desert and let the sun bleach me away.

'But the bone marrow got me first. I fainted on the pavement; someone took me to hospital in a taxi; and Elizabeth came and rescued me and brought me back here. I was so weak I couldn't whisper. I came in on a Friday and they thought I'd be dead by Monday. Then Juel-Jensen put me on his anti-fungal drip and Elizabeth nursed me night and day and I pulled through: I owe it all to them.

'I've almost finished my big book – there's a terrible old character with a twisted gut called Hanlon – and now I have a whole novel growing in the notebooks, too. I can see almost all of it. It's set in Prague and I shall call it *Utz* – *Utz*! Anyway, one day you must tell people, Redders, but not now. It's a fable. It's all there, ready-made. And the moral is simple; never kill yourself. Not under any circumstances. Not even when you're told you have AIDS.'

*

I last saw Bruce in Elizabeth's light-filled house, which looks south down an Oxfordshire valley; he was in his second bedroom, books on the counterpane, the manuscript of a young novelist he had befriended and encouraged stacked in a box by the bed, cassettes of young musicians he had supported piled on the bedside table, his newly-bought Russian icons on the walls.

Though he was very weak and so thin you could see the white bones in his arms, his telephone was still plugged into its socket. He was making and receiving calls, talking to his friends all over the world.

'Just for now, Redders, I can't hold a pen. It would be ridiculous to start yet, and I hate dictation. But the moment I'm better I'll begin that Russian novel. It's going to work. I can see almost all of it. No tricks!'

His grin gave out in a burst of coughing. As I left, the sun bright on the walls, I took his hands in both of mine. A thought struck him, and he gave a snort of laughter.

'Redders! Your hands – they're so soft I don't believe you ever go anywhere. You just lie in bed and make it up.'

They were his last words to me. And quite right too, I thought. I must read Bunin. And get a sailboard.

But it won't be the same.

Martin Meredith

BRAM FISCHER

In June 1995, a year after South Africa held its first democratic elections, Nelson Mandela delivered a memorial lecture in Johannesburg to pay tribute to a white colleague who had died in relative obscurity twenty years before, while serving a sentence of life imprisonment. Few people knew of the real role that Bram Fischer had played in the struggle against apartheid, but Mandela was one of them.

Bram Fischer was a distinguished lawyer credited with saving Mandela and other conspirators from the death penalty demanded by state prosecutors in 1964 for their part in launching armed rebellion against the South African Government. He was also a dedicated revolutionary who led a secret double life, managing to serve simultaneously as chairman of the Johannesburg Bar Council and chairman of the underground Communist Party, which had helped organize the rebellion.

What was even more remarkable about all this was that Bram Fischer came from one of the most prominent Afrikaner families in South Africa, a Free State aristocrat immensely proud of his Afrikaner heritage. His grandfather had been a prime minister, his father a judge-president.

As Mandela noted in his memorial lecture, if Fischer had decided to follow the path of Afrikaner nationalism, like most of his community, he could himself have become prime minister or chief justice. But he had taken a different course, the most difficult any person could choose to follow. He had challenged his own people.

'I fought only against injustice, not against my own people,' said Mandela. 'Bram showed a level of courage and sacrifice that was in a class by itself.'

*

In his youth, growing up in Bloemfontein in the bitter aftermath of the Anglo-Boer War, Bram had been as fervent an Afrikaner nationalist as others of his generation. He learned of how British troops, marching into Bloemfontein in March 1900, had proclaimed the Orange Free State as a British colony, renaming it the Orange River Colony, and commandeered his grandfather's imposing double-storey mansion in the centre of town and the family farm a few miles to the north. According to the family's English governess, British soldiers occupying the townhouse ripped up editions of Dickens to use as material for pillows.

On a barren stretch of veldt outside Bloemfontein, the British authorities built what they termed a 'concentration camp' where hundreds of local Boer women and children were dumped in tents without any shade. By the end of the war, some 26,000 Boers had died from disease and malnutrition in British concentration camps in South Africa, most of them children under the age of sixteen.

Bram's grandfather, Abraham Fischer, a prominent figure in the Orange Free State Government, had done his utmost to prevent war, endeavouring to mediate between an all-powerful British Government intent on seizing control of the goldfields in the neighbouring Transvaal Republic and the obdurate Transvaal leader, Paul Kruger, who was determined to fight for its independence. But after all attempts at mediation had failed, he had voted, along with his colleagues in the Free State Volksraad, to stand together with the Transvaal and defy the might of the British Army, even though the risks of defeat were high.

When the British decided, only four years after their devastating war of conquest, to hold elections in the Orange River Colony and to allow it to become a self-governing territory, Abraham Fischer was chosen as Prime Minister. His principal task was to overcome the hardships and fierce emotions resulting from the war whilst accommodating the realities of British hegemony.

It was in these turbulent times that Bram was born in Bloemfontein in 1908, the eldest son of Percy and Ella Fischer. Despite his grandfather's efforts, fear and resentment of British domination ran deep. Many Afrikaners never accepted the idea of being part of the British Empire and mourned the loss of their own republics. Everywhere they were reminded of the presence of British authority. 'God Save the King' became the official anthem; the national flag was the British Red Ensign, with the Union Coat of Arms in a lower corner.

When Britain went to war with Germany in 1914 and enlisted South Africa's support, many Afrikaners were outraged that South Africa should be drawn into the conflict on Britain's side. A group of old Boer War generals thought the time was ripe for rebellion and issued a call to arms.

Once again, the fortunes of the Fischer family were blighted by war. Rumours were rife that the Afrikaner rebels were acting in league with Germany. Afrikaner politicians opposed to the war were accused of being 'German agents'. As rebel forces gained control of great swathes of the Free State and the western Transvaal, a mood of jingoism swept through many South African towns, fanned by extremist groups like the British Citizens Movement. Shops and businesses with German names became the target for attack.

At the age of six, sitting on his father's shoulders, Bram Fischer watched as mobs in Bloemfontein set fire to business premises with German names including those of his mother's family, the Fichardts.

Both his parents were resolutely sympathetic to the rebels. Percy Fischer helped organize an ambulance unit and worked tirelessly in the courts defending rebels whom the Government brought to trial while Ella joined a group of prison visitors taking rebel prisoners food and flowers, sometimes allowing Bram to accompany her.

Bram retained vivid memories of those visits to prison. One of his most treasured possessions was a wood carving of a chameleon with moving parts made especially for him by the *kommandant* of the Kroonstad commando while awaiting trial.

In a conciliatory gesture, the Government decided to deal leniently with the rebels. Most were given no more than fines. General de Wet, the Free State rebel leader, was sentenced to six years' imprisonment but served only two. Years later, Bram was to use the example of leniency shown to General de Wet in arguing for a prison sentence for Mandela's involvement in rebellion rather than the death penalty.

Percy Fischer's actions in defending the rebels, however, cost him dearly. Clients shunned him, and attorneys declined to send him briefs. So difficult did his circumstances become that he was obliged to rent out his townhouse and move his growing family –

four children and a pregnant wife – to a small shack on a farm outside Bloemfontein. To make ends meet, Ella was reduced to selling flowers at Bloemfontein station. Only when the animosities of the 1914 rebellion had abated did Percy Fischer manage to re-establish his law practice and his place among the Bloemfontein elite.

At school and at university, Bram excelled as scholar and as sportsman. He seemed on the brink of a brilliant career, a favoured son of Afrikanerdom, well-connected and widely admired both for his many talents and for his modest, unassuming nature. Many looked on him as a potential future prime minister.

Yet an episode had occurred that suggested that Bram was straying from the conventions of the time. In 1927 he was invited to join the Bloemfontein branch of the Joint Council of Europeans and Africans, a national organization intended to provide a forum where whites and blacks, mainly teachers and clergymen, could meet to discuss African conditions.

At his first meeting, when he was introduced to leading members of the African community, Bram felt a sudden revulsion at having to shake their hands. He was never to forget the enormous effort of will it took.

That night he spent hours trying to account for his reaction. During his childhood on the farm outside Bloemfontein, he had spent countless days in the company of two African youths of his own age, roaming about, hunting, modelling clay oxen, playing and swimming together, and not once during those years could he remember that 'the colour of our skins affected our fun or our quarrels or our close friendship in any way'.

Then, when his family had moved back to town, he had drifted into the habit common to most white South Africans of regarding whites as masters and Africans simply as servants. Now he seemed unable to take the hand of a black man in friendship. 'What became abundantly clear was that it was I and not the black man who had changed,' he recalled. 'I had developed an antagonism for which I could find no rational basis whatsoever.'

Later that year, Bram became involved in adult education courses for Africans in Waaihoek 'location' in Bloemfontein, where he taught reading and writing in a dilapidated building with winter winds blowing dust through the makeshift classroom. And there he began to realize that real friendship could extend across the colour bar.

A spell at Oxford University as a Rhodes scholar and journeys he made to Germany and the Soviet Union during the early 1930s opened him to new influences. Observing the rise of Nazism in Germany and the threat it posed to the Jewish community, he began to question the theories of race superiority commonly held by white South Africans and developed a profound antipathy to nationalism. 'I believe firmly that the world's one hope of salvation lies in the suppression of . . . nationalism,' he wrote to his father in 1933, 'and if a person takes that point of view, it's difficult to generate much enthusiasm for the birth of exactly that spirit in our country.' What was needed instead was to become internationalist in outlook, and strive for the actual scientific organization of the whole world.

Back in South Africa, Bram established a reputation as a formidable corporate lawyer, sought after by South Africa's giant mining corporations. He moved with ease in the highest political and social circles. But simultaneously he developed radical leanings and, disillusioned with the efforts of white liberals, was drawn increasingly towards the Communist Party, the only political organization in South Africa not to practise some form of colour bar.

What attracted him were both the humanitarian ideals that underpinned the communist faith and its Marxist creed. He came to regard Marxism as a science, providing not only an explanation for the world's conflicts but a solution. Communism for him became a cause, one from which he was never to waver; and with it went an unswerving loyalty to its originator, the Soviet Union.

His wife, Molly Krige, a close relative of the Smuts family, with a similar aristocratic background, shared his ideals, and the bonds they forged in marriage were to become the foundation of a remarkable partnership in politics. Both threw themselves tirelessly into supporting the struggle for African rights.

Bram's influence on the younger generation of African nationalists like Nelson Mandela was profound. At a time when Afrikaners were coming to be regarded by Africans as the enemy, Bram's friendship gave Mandela a wider understanding of Afrikanerdom that he was never to forget and helped persuade him to abandon the Africanist camp, which wanted the black population to develop their own political organizations separate from other racial groups.

'Bram's commitment to the struggle helped to change many of us in the African National Congress from being Africanists to believers in non-racial democracy,' said Mandela.

As the menace of apartheid gathered momentum in the post-war era, the Fischer household in Beaumont Street in Orchards in the wealthy northern suburbs of Johannesburg became an oasis for friends and acquaintances of all races determined to keep alive the idea of a multiracial world. The Fischers were renowned for their hospitality, welcoming visitors at all hours. Beaumont Street was a regular venue for jumble sales, fund-raising events and children's parties. On the veranda, political discussion went on for hour after hour. On summer weekends, friends flocked to the swimming pool. After one particularly hot weekend, Molly described in a letter to Bram's parents how the swimming pool resembled the beach at Muizenberg, a popular resort near Cape Town. 'It's all very interesting,' she said, 'but sometimes I long for a rainy Sunday.'

To all comers, Bram was invariably warm and approachable, always willing to help with other people's problems. Despite his strong political views, he never attempted to impose his ideas on others, or even to proselytize. 'He never tried to throw his weight about, to try to recruit somebody to his point of view,' said Mandela. 'I can hardly recall an occasion when I had a conversation about ideology with him.' Even in his dealings with the police, Bram remained polite and dignified, however fraught the circumstances.

Yet beneath this calm, unassuming exterior lay an iron resolve. Bram was a true believer in communism and the Soviet Union and held fast to his faith with religious zeal. Nothing deflected him from it, neither doubts nor uncertainties. Whatever twists and turns were required to follow the Soviet line, Bram made them unhesitatingly.

When the Communist Party was banned in 1950, he was one of a select group of activists who re-established it underground. He became adept at the business of clandestine meetings, secret communications and hidden transactions. He was also increasingly involved as a defence lawyer for anti-government dissidents, taking part in both the Defiance Campaign trials and the marathon Treason Trials of the 1950s, which the Government instigated hoping to decapitate the nationalist movement.

In court, his manner was self-effacing, hesitant, almost apologetic, but his research and preparation were invariably meticulous and he pursued his arguments with implacable determination. 'His skills as a lawyer were phenomenal,' recalled Nelson Mandela, who spent months watching him at work. 'He was quietly efficient, humble, not given to any form of confrontation. When others would be aggressive, he would be highly diplomatic and I appreciated that very much.'

Bram's quiet demeanour, his courteous, soft-spoken nature, gave little clue as to the complex life he was leading. During the state of emergency in 1960, when thousands of government opponents were detained without trial, Molly Fischer was imprisoned, leaving Bram on his own to care for his three children, one of whom, his son Paul, suffered from permanent poor health and was sometimes close to death. His work in the courts meanwhile included the defence of Mandela and others in the Treason Trial. He was also constantly preoccupied with helping the wives and families of detainees. Added to all that was his activity in the communist underground, providing a crucial link between members of a secret committee who had evaded arrest and the outside world, avoiding police surveillance all the while.

In the wake of the state of emergency, after the African National Congress had been banned, Bram became a reluctant convert to the idea of armed struggle. He had doubts as to whether an underground movement could mount a campaign of violence as well as survive the repression that would inevitably follow, but eventually agreed with revolutionary enthusiasts in the Communist Party that they should set up an armed force consisting of small squads of saboteurs as a prelude to engaging in guerrilla warfare. He became a regular participant at meetings at the secret headquarters the Communist Party established at a Rivonia farmstead on the outskirts of Johannesburg. The same headquarters were used by Mandela when launching sabotage operations in 1961.

Ostensibly, Bram remained a pillar of respectability. In 1961 he was elected chairman of the Bar Council. His talents as a lawyer capable of mastering the most abstruse legal and financial cases were still sought by large corporations. In secret, he was the head of a revolutionary communist movement and a leading conspirator in a plot to launch armed rebellion against the Government.

No one outside a small group of Rivonia conspirators knew of Bram's real role in the underground. His political sympathies were evident but not his involvement in clandestine activity. When the Rivonia conspirators were arrested in 1963, lawyers acting on their behalf asked Bram to lead the defence team, unaware of the acute dilemma he faced. For he knew that evidence obtained by the police at Rivonia was likely to implicate him; his handwriting was on several documents seized there. What was even more hazardous was that he would be called upon to question state witnesses in court who could betray him at any moment. Only reluctantly did Bram eventually agree to lead the defence team. When the conspirators first heard that he would act on their behalf, one of them remarked: 'He deserves the Victoria Cross.'

Bram's defence of the Rivonia conspirators, including Mandela, was widely credited with saving their lives. What was at issue was not the question of their involvement in armed struggle, for Mandela freely admitted to it. It was whether they would receive the death penalty demanded by the Government. Mandela himself fully expected a death sentence. He prepared a statement for the court defiantly proclaiming his willingness to die for the cause of democracy. Bram, fearing that Mandela's statement would tip the judge's decision against him, pleaded with him to modify it, but to no avail. 'I felt we were likely to hang no matter what we said, so we might as well say what we truly believed,' said Mandela. 'Bram begged me not to read the final paragraph, but I was adamant.'

The life sentence that Mandela was subsequently given by the judge, an Afrikaner, was due primarily to Bram's skilful handling of the case and to his ability, as an Afrikaner, to influence the judge's outlook by arguing that Mandela's act of rebellion was no worse than that of Afrikaner rebel leaders who had taken up arms against the Government in 1914 and been given lenient prison sentences by the courts. The outcome of the trial was to have the most profound consequences for South Africa.

Even when the Rivonia trial was under way, Bram continued his underground activities. He played a leading role in trying to reconstruct a new military high command to replace the Rivonia men. He even managed to pass on to underground activists copies of maps and sabotage targets captured by police at Rivonia, which had been handed to him by the prosecution in the normal course of court proceedings.

But a few days after the trial ended, Bram was struck by

personal tragedy. Driving by car from Johannesburg to the Cape for a holiday, he swerved to avoid a motorcyclist. His car left the road and plunged into a waterhole some 30 feet deep. Bram managed to escape, but Molly was pinned in the back and drowned. The loss of his beloved companion for thirty years was a devastating blow.

His political world was also on the verge of disintegration. Unknown to him, the senior ranks of the Communist Party had been penetrated by a police agent, providing the security police with enough information to wipe out its entire structure. What evidence they lacked was subsequently obtained from a senior figure in the Communist Party, Piet Beyleveld, a fellow Afrikaner whom Bram had recruited in the 1950s, who agreed to testify against his former colleagues, including Bram, in exchange for his own freedom.

In September 1964, Bram was arrested and charged with membership of the illegal Communist Party. Until the last minute he was convinced that Beyleveld would never testify against him. 'For years, Piet and I were comrades,' he told a friend. 'I do not believe that when he comes to court, when he looks me in the eyes, he will be able to give evidence against us.' But Beyleveld came to court, he stood in the witness box and he evaded Bram's gaze.

Despite the charges, Bram was given permission to fly to London to argue an international patents case before the Privy Council, which his client subsequently won. In London, friends tried to persuade him to remain there. But Bram believed not only that it would be dishonourable to jump bail but that his place was in South Africa. He returned to face trial.

But then in January 1965, in a last act of defiance against the apartheid state, he decided to go underground. He explained his reasons in a letter to the court:

> What is needed is for white South Africans to shake themselves out of their complacency ... Unless this whole intolerable system is changed radically and rapidly, disaster must follow ... To try to avoid this becomes a supreme duty, particularly for an Afrikaner, because it is largely representatives of my fellow Afrikaners who have been responsible for the worst of these discriminatory laws ... If by my fight I can encourage even some people to think about, to understand and to abandon the policies they now so blindly follow, I shall not regret any punishment I may incur.

To help him with a disguise, Bram enlisted the support of a German-born theatre designer, Raymond Schoop, who, as a youth growing up in Hamburg in an anti-Nazi family during the war, had acquired an acute understanding of what was required to survive underground.

Schoop insisted that Bram needed to develop not just changes to his physical appearance but a distinctive new identity. The key to survival, he believed, was not for Bram to fade as inconspicuously as possible into the background, but for him to emerge as a new person, with a different profession, a different family background, different habits, tastes and mannerisms. Schoop bought an entirely new wardrobe, choosing colours and styles that Bram never usually wore. The plan was for Bram to become a professional photographer, carrying camera bags over his shoulder that would make him easily recognizable.

Bram was taken to a cottage on a remote farm west of Pretoria to work on his new identity. He was immediately put on a spare diet. His portly frame began to shrink. The thick grey hair on his head was shaved back to give him a receding hairline and what was left was dyed an auburn colour. He grew a goatee beard, which made him look like Lenin, and took to smoking a pipe, which altered the quality of his voice. His familiar black-rimmed spectacles were replaced with light-rimmed ones. He spent hours practising a different style of walking, changing the rolling gait he had habitually used since a rugby injury at Oxford to shorter, quicker steps, by walking on his heels.

For week after week, Bram rehearsed his new identity, living a hermit-like existence in his sparsely-furnished cottage before returning to Johannesburg. The name he chose for himself was an English one, Douglas Black.

His disguise proved highly effective. While the security police continued to scour the country for him month after month, Bram moved about unrecognized. He tested the disguise to the limit time and again. On one occasion, he returned to his old chambers and took the lift standing close to lawyers whom he knew well. On another occasion, he stepped into a lift with a close woman friend at the building where she worked; all that she noticed at the time was 'a funny little man' who made some remark about the weather. A security policeman who knew him well walked past him in a

Johannesburg street showing no sign of recognition. A doctor who examined Bram for high blood pressure gave no hint he suspected anything amiss.

Yet the loneliness of his underground existence constantly preyed upon him. His original plan had been to cut himself off from his previous milieu in Johannesburg. But he was unaccustomed to a solitary life and soon sought the company of close friends and family members, ignoring the risks they faced. He made little headway in establishing a new network of activists, as he had planned to do, and fell prone to bouts of depression. A particular blow came in November 1965 when the Bar Council decided to strike his name from the roll of advocates.

Eight days later, the security police arrested one of his closest colleagues. For seventy hours she held out, interrogated without stop in a small airless room by a relay of security policemen who threatened reprisals against her two children and warned her she would end up in a mental asylum. Though Bram knew of her arrest, he made no determined effort to get away. Shortly before his capture, he spent part of the afternoon gardening and passing the time of day with a neighbour.

At his trial in 1966, the charges against him were similar to those faced by Nelson Mandela and other Rivonia conspirators. In addition to being a member of the outlawed Communist Party, Bram was accused of sabotage and conspiring to cause 'a violent revolution' in South Africa.

With his three children listening ardently in the courtroom, Bram stood in the dock to give his testament as an Afrikaner revolutionary, explaining, in much the same way that Nelson Mandela had done during the Rivonia trial, the reasons behind his defiance of the apartheid state.

He spoke of his fears about civil war and of his deep apprehension about the future of his own Afrikaner people; for it was Afrikaners, he said, who were blamed for all the evils and humiliations of apartheid.

> All this bodes ill for the future. It has bred a deep-rooted hatred for Afrikaners, for our language, our political and racial outlook amongst all non-whites ... It is rapidly destroying amongst non-whites all belief in future cooperation with Afrikaners.

To remove this barrier will demand all the wisdom, leadership and influence of those Congress leaders now sentenced and imprisoned for their political beliefs. It demands also that Afrikaners themselves should protest openly and clearly against discrimination.

To ensure that at least one Afrikaner made this protest actively, he had undertaken the task himself.

It was to keep faith with all those dispossessed by apartheid that I broke my undertaking to the court, separated myself from my family, pretended I was someone else, and accepted the life of a fugitive. I owed it to the political prisoners, to the banished, to the silenced and those under house arrest, not to remain a spectator, but to act. I knew what they expected of me and I did it. I felt responsible, not to those who are indifferent to the sufferings of others, but to those who are concerned.

At the end of his four-hour speech, Bram declared:

If one day it may help to establish a bridge across which white leaders and the real leaders of the non-whites can meet to settle the destinies of all of us by negotiation and not by force of arms, I shall be able to bear with fortitude any sentence which this court may impose upon me.

On 9 May 1966, at the age of fifty-eight, Bram was sentenced to life imprisonment.

In Pretoria prison, where white political prisoners were held, he was subjected to harsh and vindictive treatment. For the first few months, he was kept in isolation. His Afrikaner guards regarded him as a traitor and persecuted him at every opportunity, giving him clothes that were far too large, making him clean toilets on his knees, shouting obscenities, inflicting punishment for the slightest infringement of regulations. Bram remained courteous and polite, but he was slowly ground down. By the time he was allowed to join other political prisoners he had become old and haggard.

For the rest of his prison life, he suffered from official vindictiveness. When his son Paul died in 1971, losing his struggle against cystic fibrosis, Bram was not allowed to attend the funeral. When he fell ill with cancer, the prison authorities only belatedly allowed him proper treatment. Even when he was clearly dying, the

Government ignored all appeals for his release. The Minister of Justice told Parliament he still represented a security risk.

Only for the last few weeks of his life was he allowed into the care of his brother in Bloemfontein, although he was still classified as a prisoner and his brother's home was declared a prison, subject to prison regulations.

Soon after his sixty-fifth birthday, he lapsed into unconsciousness and died two weeks later, on 8 May 1975. Even then, the prison authorities were not finished with him and insisted that after cremation his ashes be returned to their department.

At a simple ceremony in Bloemfontein, the distinguished lawyer Arthur Chaskalson read out a speech written in London by one of Bram's former prison colleagues Hugh Lewin.

> Do not weep for Bram. He would not have you weep on his behalf. And do not weep for the recent long years in jail. That, especially, he would not like. For though they were long, painful years away from his family and his friends outside, for Bram inside they were not lost years. They meant for Bram, in a very real sense, a rounding and a completion.
>
> However full the man who first went to jail – however distinguished the lawyer, however fine the father, husband, friend, adviser – however full the man before, jail encompassed the fullness and enlarged it.

The Afrikaner writer, André Brink, added his own eulogy. Far from alienating himself from his Afrikaner people, he said, Bram had 'enlarged and deepened' the concept of Afrikanerdom. 'If Afrikanerdom is to survive, it may well be as a result of the broadening and liberating influence of men like Bram Fischer.'

Fischer's true cause, he said, went beyond the confines of a political system. He believed in liberty, justice, compassion, trust, equality of mercy and, above all, human dignity. 'It is my firm belief that in his pursuit of these ideals, history will not only absolve him but vindicate him.'

James Clad

SUHARTO OF INDONESIA

Twenty years ago, in the initial phase of what was, for me at least, a major affair, the Javanese woman I loved told me who had killed her father during a watershed coup attempt years earlier in Indonesia.

On the night of 30 September 1965 she stumbled down from her bedroom in time to see her father, the supreme Indonesian army commander, dragged off by rebel soldiers. Later that evening his kidnappers killed him, and four other generals, thereby starting an epic process of revenge that would bring the then strategic reserve commander, General Suharto, to paramount power in Indonesia for thirty-two long years.

'So who, exactly, plotted the 1965 event?' I asked her, choosing my words and the moment with care.

'Why, what can you mean?' she replied, her marvellous wide eyes bewildered at my failure to grasp even the most elementary fact of Indonesian political life. 'Why, *he* did it; *he*'s the one,' she murmured, pointing her index finger in the general direction of the presidential palace. We were 10 miles away from President Suharto's office, standing together at the monument marking the place – known locally as *lubang buaya* ('crocodile's hole') – where allegedly communist-backed killers eliminated her father and the other generals, then dropped their bodies into the pit. Five statues representing the murdered generals now marked the ground, their stone fingers pointing accusingly at the crocodile hole, the defining place in the mythology of Suharto's long 'New Order' regime, the Ground Zero of Communist Infamy. '*He did it; he's the one,*' she said.

But did Suharto really know and connive in the killings? Did he play the classic double game, giving a wink to the conspirators and then turn on them? How could even the most stupid coup plotter leave Major General Suharto off the pick-up list? Debate has always been intense if hushed about this sensitive question, a debate mostly conducted by American and Australian academics from the safety of their distant universities.

The question of Suharto's culpability arose again when the old man finally left office in May 1998, gently assisted out by a military a generation younger than him, still in awe of the old man. The questions swirled in the higher-toned press, now suddenly free to question the past. Did Suharto work with the CIA to eliminate what was, at the time, the world's third largest communist party? (The answer is probably that, if he did it, he did it on his own.) Did he pretend to help the then president Sukarno eliminate a challenge from the Army, but then opt to follow his own agenda? (The answer is almost certainly that he did.)

Various old spectres from the past emerged to join the debate; old men imprisoned by Suharto's regime for three decades, coming out of jail telling hesitant, age-warped stories. Most pointed to some degree of Suharto's collusion, but nothing seemed definitive. The confusion only grew. Yet the question still seemed central, still important enough to try to expiate from the nation's historical memory.

So much turned on that night in September 1965. So many died during the following year as the Army and its politicized Islamic allies sought out members of PKI (Communist Party of Indonesia) mass organizations. Figures vary widely, but it seems safe to assume that half a million Indonesians, mostly peasants in Java and Bali, died in a holocaust exceeded in South-East Asia only by the deranged policies of the 1975–9 Khmer Rouge regime in Cambodia.

By the decade's close, Suharto's passage and the deep impact on Indonesia of South-East Asia's financial crisis have brought back memories of that earlier transition that brought Suharto to power. The shift in the mid-1960s pulled Indonesia out of founding president Sukarno's wild, charismatic ride down a revolutionary road of hyper-inflation, madcap campaigns to 'Crush Malaysia' and grab Dutch New Guinea, and connivance in PKI campaigns against landlords in Java.

Indonesians remain both fascinated and repelled by the old question of whether and to what extent Suharto was complicit in the events of 1965 – at least those who lived through the army-backed pogroms. In my own view Suharto was as appalled as the rest of his colleagues at the death of their brethren. Yet the question looms large once more, as Indonesia's second major political succession since independence back in 1950 runs into complex challenges – of separatism, religious extremism, and ethnic strife. Suharto's departure followed riots in which 'only' a thousand died, with several thousands more brutalized in organized attacks on the vulnerable, often despised ethnic Chinese population.

Within this complex succession crisis, East Timor's people finally were able to choose independence in a UN referendum, at the end of August 1999. This in turn gave new heart to provinces in various stages of covert or open revolt, all along the eastern, central and western reaches of this 3,000-mile archipelago. Suharto's mercurial successor, Bacharrudin Jusuf Habibie, tried to retain the presidency but failed when, in October 1999, a nearly blind Muslim cleric, Abdurrahman Wahid, won a surprise victory.

For Indonesia and the wider world, the East Timor fiasco revealed, in one specific place, the type of system Suharto crafted for his unitary state. Just as his national structure virtually guaranteed political vacuum upon his unwilling departure, so also did the local systems put in place, in East Timor and other restive provinces, guarantee a chaotic end to Indonesian rule if the Timorese were ever to chose independence. I went to East Timor to observe the 1999 plebiscite and found a UN electoral operation oblivious to these latent dangers of Indonesian rule. The consequences of this ignorance would be terrible, for the UN and for the Timorese.

Indonesian rule in East Timor depended on identifying compliant local Timorese whom the Indonesians would bring to East Java for special training, and then embed in a Timorese locality. There these local lords received a share of the island's coffee business, now controlled by military-backed ethnic Chinese from Jakarta. These local headmen, many of whom dated from the Portuguese era and willingly joined the Indonesian occupation, would lose everything if East Timor ever became independent. A ferocious Indonesian reaction to the plebiscite's 78.6 per cent pro-independence vote was, in this sense, inevitable.

When I drove back along the eastern coastal road to the East Timor capital Dili, several days after the independence vote, paramilitary goons manned successively more menacing roadblocks. They sported automatic weapons they had received from regular military units. Passing through their posts became steadily more difficult.

'*Saya selalu mementingkan kesatuan negara,*' I said with as much conviction as I could muster each time I was forced to stop: 'I always think first of [Indonesia's] national unity.' The militia, most in their late teens, let me pass with wry smiles: most were drunk and, in any event, they had bigger, bloodier business at hand. Naturally – as in other cases where the UN has worked with insufficient armed resolve – other Westerners and I could manage to avoid the gathering mayhem by chartering a plane and flying to Bali. Hundreds of high-school youth working temporarily for the UN were not so fortunate.

As I flew to safety, I wondered how Suharto regarded the debacle, the old man now sitting in an army-protected home in an old Dutch suburb of Jakarta. If the measure of his rule over East Timor was 'strength without flexibility', his erratic successor had inverted the formula – to disastrous effect. Many thousands died in Timor's partition from Indonesia.

In January 1999, Habibie had sought in one bold move to put the East Timorese imbroglio behind him. But his plebiscite offering special autonomy or outright independence infuriated the military. It also presented the pro-independence movement with a grim choice: either force the pace towards an overwhelming pro-independence vote (and suffer terrible but transitory consequences), or let a golden moment slip by, perhaps for ever. They opted for the first alternative. So did the United States, Britain, Australia, and other Western states – all gambling that Indonesia would not risk losing face by allowing tensions to degenerate into a shambles. To put it gently, this proved a bad miscalculation.

Meanwhile, the fiasco in Timor has reinforced a nasty strain of xenophobic nationalism in Indonesia, a country rather open to foreigners and foreign influence. The sight of Australian intervention forces arriving in Dili at the end of September 1999 shocked most Indonesians. Photographs of Australian soldiers standing over militiamen sprawled on the ground fed a growing anti-IMF, anti-Western mood in Indonesia's capital. At the same time, Habibie's campaign for re-election ran into steadily more turbulent opposition.

The new parliament, elected in June 1999 but convening only in October, chose a new man instead. As vice president it chose Megawati Soekarnoputri (former president Sukarno's daughter). In this volatile environment, the East Timor disaster fanned emotion and disarray.

Much of the mess resulted from the tenacity of Suharto's rule. The old master had put in place a system that eliminated rivals of any stature, leaving the political arena populated by pygmies. From Jakarta, the forcibly retired old President could only smile at the extent of the disaster: he had never left any room for another kingpin. Remove him and the structure couldn't stand alone.

> The inner man [Suharto] remains curiously unknown, almost cryptic and elusive, even to his closest associates. He generally presents himself as calm, dignified, restrained, soft-spoken, almost avuncular – the 'Smiling General'. Unlike Sukarno, whose entire life, even down to his love affairs, seemed to be conducted on a public stage, Suharto has remained an intensely private man, devoted to his family and his cattle farm. Indonesians refer to him as *tertutup* (reserved, shut off) – a quality respected by Javanese and utterly unlike the extroverted Sukarno. 'No one knows what that man thinks . . . that is the secret of his power,' commented one senior politician who had watched him closely for years. Only occasionally does Suharto lose his cool, or reveal much of his inner feelings and thinking.

When Australians Jamie Mackie and Andrew MacIntyre wrote these words in 1993, they had the benefit of having various officially sanctioned, sanitized biographies and autobiographies in front of them. Suharto's own *Autobiography* complements two books by O.G. Roeder, *The Smiling General* and *Anak Desa* ('Child of the Village').

Suharto's own book portrays a man who, as the Australian academic Angus McIntyre puts it, is always 'taxing his mind to maintain his composure; by thinking ahead, by trying to anticipate events, he tried to create the inner calm that more predictable parental behaviour than he enjoyed bestows naturally on its beneficiaries.'

Although Suharto's predecessor spoke passionately for an egalitarian Indonesian republic, Sukarno sought to ground his own past in the bloodlines of Java's aristocracy. In the early 1960s, Sukarno told a compliant Western biographer that he was 'the last King of Singaraja' (through his mother) and through his father's family 'the last Sultan of Kediri', both places being past kingdoms in Java – the island on which two-thirds of Indonesia's 210 million people dwell. Sukarno also portrayed his arrival in this world as marked by holy signs and, by his birth at dawn, as accompanied by a sign of future greatness.

By contrast, Suharto has taken pride from his father's lowly status as a village irrigation official. This father left Suharto and his mother two years after his birth; the toddler was also separated from his mother at an early age. Suharto's own story shows an early childhood with little permanence – he lived in the homes of his father's friends.

He resigned from a clerical job in a rural bank after a bicycle accident tore his only *sarong*, the skirt-like lower garment that many Indonesians still wear. The future president then joined the Royal Netherlands Indies Army in 1940, rising to an NCO's position by the time of the Pacific War. In the war for independence against the Dutch that followed the Japanese surrender, his own account cast him as a stout defender of the central Java city of Yogyakarta. (A US defence attaché serving in the early 1960s told me that General Yani, the army chief of staff murdered in 1965, enjoyed the nightlife; Suharto by contrast remained a stay-at-home type. The story fits.)

Suharto's historical moment arrived in the days after five generals died in an attempted coup very probably occurring with Sukarno's tacit go-ahead. Moving with inexorable pace, Suharto marginalized the plotters, mounted a counter coup, and initiated a movement to root out the PKI from the countryside. Army and local Muslim wrath fell with a terrible force in some rural areas, as on Java's south central coast where peasants found PKI promises appealing. Entire villages disappeared in nights of killing.

Suharto's presidential career followed a canny, slow-motion phase. He gradually consolidated his power base although Sukarno remained the nominal head. Finally, in March 1967, the country's supine supreme parliament voted Suharto as the country's Acting President. Soon the word 'acting' slipped from the title as, in tightly stage-managed elections held every five years after 1971, Suharto retained and concentrated his control.

Over the years, Suharto's indulgence for his family members became ever more his central weakness. Indonesia's large resource base and the long boom generated a widespread view that the Suharto family members and their business associates had gained a strategic, even commanding, position in the rapidly growing economy.

Although Indonesia's oil revenues steadily declined as a percentage of overall export earnings during the 1970s, the country's new export manufacturing companies, its unsustainable tropical hardwood exports, and new palm oil and rubber revenues spewed out money. Suharto's family seemed to lose all sense of proportion, inserting itself into major new business ventures. The boom consolidated Indonesia's unhappy reputation as *the* most corrupt country after Nigeria – a sorry distinction.

Apart from the *cukongs* – an Indonesian word used to denote ethnic Chinese business cronies – Suharto bestowed favours on all those able to buttress his regime. He gained greater independence from his earlier army links. Through rapid reassignments he moved senior officers around with such frequency that none could ground himself long enough anywhere to mount a challenge. None cared to try; the Army generally remained in awe of Suharto right up to the end.

Suharto never intended to leave office voluntarily. He designed instead a structure locking anyone with high ambition from play. One by one, old comrades from the era of the independence struggle died or went into retirement. The members of his Cabinet, by the end, resembled – in the aging President's mind – his own children, both in age and stature. Finally, it took a profound economic crisis, and months of mismanaged response to it, to bring him down. The army leaders bringing him the news that he should go promised him, in so many words, that no retribution need ever occur, to him or to his family. The Army has kept that promise.

During his time as President, Suharto grudgingly revealed biographic details of his early life, as when rebutting local press articles claiming an aristocratic lineage. Suharto always preferred the public picture of a plainly born man and a dutiful son. His own *Autobiography*, published by his eldest child Siti Hardijanti Rukmana, reinforced this plain-born bias: 'The young Suharto was not the son of an aristocrat who had been prepared by his parents to become a national leader. He was also not a child whose birth was accompanied by signs of his future greatness. He was merely a village child who was born into the family of a poor peasant.'

Because of Suharto's longevity, attention centred over the years on his 'composure'. People were fascinated by the side of his character that an anthropologist of Java, Clifford Geertz, calls a 'certain flatness of effect' marking the truly refined Javanese character. Over time, Suharto became almost completely his own creation, an amalgam of socially-imposed and self-imposed discipline centred on the 'three don't's': *'aja kagetan, aja gumunan, aja dumeh'* ('don't be startled, don't be overwhelmed, don't feel superior').

Curiously, in this respect only, Suharto calls George Washington to mind, another leader with an eighteenth-century obsession with dignity, 'carriage', decorum and demeanour. This emphasis, in Suharto's mind, supplemented a superior intelligence enabling him to outsmart opponents, whether Dutch colonial troops or the communists. In his own autobiographical account, other Indonesians figure only intermittently, a sideshow to his own achievements. A former prime minister, abruptly removed from an official independence day celebration list, told a Western journalist, 'We don't exist any more to him. He is the only one now.'

The 'abiding impression one is left with', comments McIntyre, 'is just how dimly lit other people are on Suharto's mental screen.' The underlying impression is one of a very calculating individual. Adam Schwarz, author of *A Nation in Waiting*, asked one of Suharto's ministers about the character of his boss. 'I find him kind of scary,' the man replied, 'cold, hard eyes that look right through you.'

When Suharto left office in May 1998, few Indonesians were sorry to see him go. The general mood in the cities was one of elation. Abroad, Western policy makers sighed with relief, satisfied that the 'transition' had not been worse. Paul Wolfowitz, a former US ambassador in Jakarta, reflected in writing on Suharto's unhappy legacy immediately following the President's resignation. Quoting Shakespeare, Wolfowitz likened Suharto's end to the Earl of Cawdor's death in *Macbeth*; 'nothing in his life became him like the leaving it'.

Wolfowitz bemoaned Suharto's unwillingness to leave office before events forced him out. 'If he had left office ten years ago, he would have left as a hero. He would still be admired today – most of all for his undisputed role in transforming Indonesia from a country in economic ruins . . . to a country that is self-sufficient in rice by the 1980s.'

*

Another element in Suharto's life that continues to fascinate his countrymen is his abiding belief in the strain of thinking that Indonesians call *kebatinan* ('inner-ness') – a type of mystical training very much concentrated in central Java, Suharto's home region. Some foreign writers, such as Angus McIntyre, see in this mystical strain yet another component of Suharto's 'emotional autarchy'. To me, it seems to be Suharto's way of connecting with the world, especially his continued use of various *dukun*s, mystical teachers and soothsayers.

From the late 1970s onwards, my professional and even some of my personal life turned on the impact of this durable Javanese ruler. Though vilified now, his imprimatur, more than any other's, still marks the entirety of what nineteenth-century scholars routinely called 'the Malay Archipelago', those islands and peninsulas now comprising contemporary Indonesia, Malaysia, Brunei, and the Philippines.

In idle moments I sometimes compare my personal experience of Suharto and the long-time leader of neighbouring Malaysia, Mahathir bin Mohamed. While the Malaysian leader acquiesced to my prosecution in 1985 under Malaysia's Official Secrets Act – a statute closely modelled on British legislation – Suharto had once walked by my side in a sylvan setting. To be exact, Suharto and I swapped farming stories for fifteen minutes during a Jakarta ceremony marking Indonesia's annual *Hari Tani*, or 'Farmer's Day'.

Wearing an overcoat and gumboots, Suharto spotted me hovering near a small display of New Zealand cattle – a glamorous assignment for the embassy's most recently arrived junior diplomat. He gestured to me to join his inner ring of attendants, asking if I spoke Indonesian. I managed an affirmative answer. 'Good,' said the *Bapak Pembangunan* ('Father of Development') and we set out without another word across a field crowded with farm displays. Scowling security men followed close behind.

I watched him obliquely. He seemed to enjoy the moment, a

chance to show his ordinary roots. As he fingered the fatty tail of a sheep, he suddenly said, 'They tell me that New Zealand has three million people and ninety million sheep.'

'Yes, *Bapak*,' I said, at a loss. Where was this leading?

'Well, in Java, it's the other way around!' He laughed. 'Ninety million people and three million livestock; you are the lucky ones down there!'

In the sway of his good humour and losing my fear at this unexpected proximity to the Boss, I gradually fell into something like a normal conversation with him. He seemed so utterly normal – but no one could ignore the awed silenced crowds as we walked about, the junior diplomat from an insignificant country alongside this mainstay of Asian order. For another few minutes we moved among the people, their smiles masking many thoughts, as smiles often do.

That was it. After that day in 1978 I shook his hand once or twice, part of long dutiful queues at Washington receptions. I once seized a lull in the reception line's forward movement to speak to him. I mentioned meeting him first on Farmer's Day. I repeated the lame comment about human and livestock numbers on Java and in New Zealand. He smiled absent-mindedly; he had obviously forgotten the trivial exchange. This, then, is the sum total of my direct contact with one of Asia's most durable Strong Men; I should quickly add that most who have written about him have had no interaction with him at all. How could I match the man I'd seen in this trivial encounter to the wily leader my Javanese girlfriend described? Anyway, it's quite possible to connive in events that may lead to unplanned, unintended consequences. Is that the truth behind what happened that night, all those years ago, when she was a young girl?

*

Suharto usually receives biographers' attentions as if he stands alone within a mystical Javanese background and inside an opaque Indonesian political culture. But he came to power, and held it for many long years, within a region admiring strong leaders. In Malaysia and Indonesia, Mahathir and Suharto represent an authoritarian style that has a lot of life in it yet, despite claims that Asia is now experiencing a durable democratic enlargement.

Mahathir's career rests on his solid commitment to a sustained, government-funded effort to transform Malays into yet another squad of Asian industrial shock troops. Mahathir admires the East Asian phalanx of industrialized and *industrious* peoples. Yet any thinking visitor to Malaysia rapidly recognizes what he or she can also see in Indonesia – a durable *Ali-baba* connection. (The phrase connotes 'Ali' – the compliant, free-riding Malay – and 'Baba', the quick-witted, opportunistic Chinaman maximizing commercial opportunity in return for the 'native' Ali's protection.) We may expect post-Suharto Indonesia to follow Malaysia's pro-native policies of positive discrimination. This will take the form of creating programmes favouring non-ethnic Chinese.

*

While serving in Malaysia, I met successive Indonesian envoys. They provided the most caustic analysis of (what they dismissed as) Malaysia's supine, take-it-from-the-Arabs approach to Islam. This is a harsh and facile view: they contrasted Malaysia's 'off-the-shelf Islam' (a direct quote from one envoy) with Indonesia's amalgam of Islam and local beliefs, including a large element of mysticism. Suharto falls squarely into this syncretic tradition, now more vulnerable to the remonstrations of formal Muslim piety since his fall from power.

This sharp if rarely discussed divergence within the Malay world really amounts to a type of fraternal squabbling. Both Malaysians and Indonesians speak sentimentally about being *serumpun Melayu*, 'bred from the same Malay seed'. In the post-Suharto period, Indonesians envy Malaysia's successful shift of corporate ownership and broad economic control away from ethnic Chinese and towards the 'natives'.

Indonesia's self-styled 'open economy' expanded 7–9 per cent per annum after the mid-1980s. But the 'market forces' much touted by World Bank economists never came even close to the reality. In some observers' eyes Indonesia had become a giant playing field in which Suharto's family and secondary patronage systems seemed all-powerful.

This was the arena in which Suharto's involuntary succession played itself out in 1997–8. Picture a set of concentric circles. The formal constitutional structure requires any new president to win indirect election from the supreme parliament, a mix of elected MPs and government appointees, including thirty-five members of the armed forces. The voluble Habibie, unexpectedly elevated to supreme office, fought for wider political space. And Habibie's successor, whom Indonesians universally call 'Gus Dur' ('Brother Dur', approximately) has since the end of 1999 crafted an unwieldy government of mutually suspicious factions, including senior Suharto-era military officers. Most are alert to the chase for spoils; the most tempting target is a government holding agency taking possession of hundreds of technically bankrupt or insolvent companies.

Most of Indonesia's 290 pre-Crisis banks had local ethnic Chinese owners. Most asset-stripped their banks as the complex political and debt crises unfolded after August 1997, crises exacerbated by Suharto's health worries, erratic monetary policy, and sense that the regime had entered its final days. The post-Suharto period remains very unsettled, however – at both the national and local levels. Locally, outbreaks of resentment against immigrants from other islands have reinforced demands for local autonomy – especially in regions where natural resources (timber, oil, gas, palm oil, natural rubber, gold, copper, nickel, or hydro-power and aluminium) have been siphoned off by the Jakarta elite. At the national level, politicized Muslims call for a 'People's Economy', a phrase encapsulating plans to emulate Malaysia's state-led positive discrimination programmes toward *bumiputra*s, or 'sons of the soil' and/or 'indigenous people'. The message is clear: persistent dislike of the small (3–4 per cent) but economically powerful ethnic Chinese minority.

A minister of cooperatives in 1999, Adi Sasono spoke in forceful terms about 'breaking [ethnic Chinese] conglomerates' control over trade in cooking oil, rice, and wood'. The business should go, Sasono said (to everyone's disbelief) to thousands of small *pribumi* traders grouped in cooperatives. Sasono said he had frog-marched Chinese owned plantation and lumber companies to grant 20 per cent of their interests to the cooperatives ministry – another source of future political patronage.

A blizzard of corruption accusations has followed Suharto's departure. No charge seems too bizarre, no alleged theft too egregious. The local press said a senior coordinating minister for the economy profited from a forced sale of shares in US mining giant Freeport McMoRan Copper and Gold. True or not? Did men close to former president B.J. Habibie demand commissions equal to 60 per cent of public funds recapitalizing a local bank? Did, as other press accounts alleged, the Habibie family abuse its favoured position in the Suharto era to enrich itself? Did the Central Bank (as the Government admitted at the beginning of 2000) simply 'lose' over $7 billion intended for domestic bank recapitalization? Amid the cynical swirl of accusation and counter-accusation, nothing seems too egregious while much seems all too credible.

*

Many writers see Suharto's life and legacy as a type of gross aberration. But the assessment stands or falls on *scale* and *duration*. The truth is, most Indonesians expect some type of reconstructed patronage structure – only smaller in scale to that entrenched during the Smiling General's three decades in power.

Why should we expect anything else? In a 1939 book describing the pre-Second World War western Pacific, John Gunther called 'the East Indies' (Indonesia) 'the Big Loot of Asia'. The post-Suharto era may yield a modicum of greater restraint based (as in the Philippines after the Marcos dictatorship's collapse in 1986) on an understanding that limited terms of office and a better grip on nepotism may be able to restrain the greed. Perhaps – though this remains unclear – a slightly higher degree of public shame may attend the worst excesses.

Speaking to visitors some months after his fall from power, Suharto said that those abandoning him '*tidak tahu malu*' ('they don't know shame'). But what is sauce for the goose is sauce for the gander; new cycles of loyalty and patronage have begun in Indonesia while, in Malaysia, a difficult transition from Mahathir's two decades as premier dominated political horizons in 2000. An overextended credit system, manipulated by government favouritism, kept government-linked firms from tottering into outright bankruptcy. But Malaysia could take years to reckon the costs of this policy of preferential solvency. Meanwhile, Mahathir's colleagues hold their boss in awe even as, just like Suharto, they also know their long-time leader must eventually go.

*

I met General Yani's daughter again in September 1999, utterly by happenstance. My new wife and I were in central Java, and I learned that Amelia Yani had moved to a nearby village. The three of us

met; together we travelled one morning, at Amelia's invitation, to
Java's wild south shore. Most Javanese believe the turbulent surf
covers the sunken home of Loro Kidul, a princess whose malevol-
ence every sensible fisherman propitiates with daily offerings scattered across the waves.

Time had treated Amelia kindly. Her position as daughter of the
Suharto regime's most venerated hero had enabled her to enjoy a
life without much material anxiety. At an appropriate moment I
asked her again about 1965, and whether she still suspected
Suharto's real role at that time with as much conviction as she had
shown when we first met.

Amelia said that much time had passed. She thought her family
could now live more easily with many things. As a Javanese, she
said, one had to be *rela* ('accepting') and to try to put aside all
strong feelings.

This didn't seem to be the answer I had hoped to hear. I wanted
time to deliver more precision, not less. So I pressed on. Did
comments by some old PKI political prisoners still living, now freed
after Suharto's fall, confirm her former view of Suharto's intention
and whereabouts on that long-ago evening in September 1965? She
was then only a girl of fifteen, coming downstairs when hearing the
commotion in her house, rubbing sleep from her lovely eyes, just in
time to see her father, in the defining moment of her life, taken from
her for ever.

She paused for a moment. 'You know I see him from time to
time, yes, in Jakarta,' she answered. 'He is very sad. He is very
lonely.'

She has become even more mystic over the years and I couldn't
be sure of whom she was speaking. Who was sad? Her father's
spirit? Some long imprisoned friend?

'*He* is sad?' I asked. '*Who* is sad?'

She looked at me in surprise. 'Why Suharto is sad, of course.'
She paused. 'He feels betrayed by everyone. That's why I visit him.
We talk about the past when we meet, about when he and my father
were comrades. This makes him happier.

'You know,' she added, 'he never did all those things that people
say he did. It was his underlings, the people who manipulated him.
He is just a poor old man, now.'

Roger Adelson

WINSTON CHURCHILL AND THE
MIDDLE EAST, 1898–1922

No individual wielded more British power in the Middle East for more years during the twentieth century than Winston Churchill. If the inactive period following his retirement as Prime Minister in 1955 is excluded, Churchill held ministerial office for more than half his long parliamentary career from 1900 to 1964. Nor did any individual in the English-speaking world surpass Churchill's influence upon public opinion about the Middle East. His prolific publications, particularly the best-selling accounts of the First World War, the Second World War, and their aftermaths, defended British power in the Middle East. Yet, the vast region between Europe and India was only of strategic significance to Churchill. For him, as for most of his Cabinet colleagues and compatriots during the first half of the twentieth century, the Middle East was tied initially to the defence of India and the Suez Canal and then to British naval requirements for Persian oil. The Middle East mattered to Churchill because it helped secure British world power in relation to the other Great Powers, particularly the United States. This essay, reviewing Churchill's involvement with the Middle East, from 1898 to 1922, is part of a book that I am writing on the impact of his entire career on an area that, since Churchill's death, has remained strategically the most vital part of the world.

As noted in my book, *London and the Invention of the Middle East: Money, Power, and War, 1902–1922* (London, Yale University Press, 1995), the term 'Middle East' first appeared in a *National Review* article on the Persian Gulf, written by A.T. Mahan, a US naval officer known for his best-selling histories of the British Navy.

Mahan argued that Britain could rely on the Navy to defend its commerce and communications between the Suez Canal and the subcontinent of India, which countered Russia's Asiatic empire and Germany's proposed railway to Baghdad and beyond. The term 'Middle East', as distinct from the 'Near East' and 'Far East', was given some currency by Valentine Chirol, the Germanophobic head of the foreign department of *The Times*. By 1917, when the British had thousands of troops involved in the so-called Mesopotamia and Palestine campaigns, 'Middle East' began to be used more widely in Whitehall, Westminster, Fleet Street, and the City. And, by 1921, when Churchill became Colonial Secretary and established a Middle East Department, the post-war usage of the term encompassed Iraq, Palestine, the Sinai and Arabian peninsulas, as well as the Persian Gulf and the Suez Canal. For purposes of this paper, the Middle East also includes Egypt and Sudan, as well as the Turkish and Persian Empires, because the British linked all these areas together strategically.

Churchill was a year old in 1875 when Benjamin Disraeli negotiated the British Government's purchase of the largest number of shares in the Suez Canal Company. This action was very significant for the British, who sought to protect the sea routes to India and made the most use of the canal. As Churchill was growing up, the British occupied Cyprus in 1878 and Egypt in 1882. When General Gordon was killed by the Mahdi in 1885, the British believed that Egypt had to be held to protect the Suez Canal, and that the Nile made the Sudan essential to the defence of Egypt. Churchill, like his compatriots, presumed that neither Russia nor any other power should be allowed to threaten British paramountcy between Europe and India.

Churchill passed through the Suez Canal on his journeys to and from India, but he only became directly involved with the area in 1898. From India Churchill urged his mother to gain the Prime Minister's approval to be attached to the 21st Lancers and participate in the Anglo-Egyptian reconquest of Sudan, commanded by the sirdar, the future Lord Kitchener of Khartoum. After Churchill joined in the cavalry charge on Omdurman in this well-prepared and well-publicized campaign, he wrote a book, which appeared in 1899. *The River War* vividly recounted his experiences in the campaign in the context of Sudanese geography and demography, but with little interest in the area's religion and history apart from the rise of the Mahdi, the murder of General Gordon, and the 'Oriental' fanaticism and corruption that characterized the thirteen years that elapsed before the flags of Britain and Egypt once again waved over the upper Nile. The two-volume work was a critical and popular success that helped bring Churchill's name to the attention of London. His contemporaries, George Curzon and Mark Sykes, wrote books about the Persian and Ottoman Empires, whose shahs and sultans for decades had been identified with and indebted to Britain. While Curzon and Sykes travelled and published more extensively than Churchill, all three men used the Middle East to further their political ambitions at Westminster.

Churchill achieved fame in South Africa after he escaped from his Boer captors and publicized it. Elected to the House of Commons in 1900, he left the Conservatives to join the Liberals in 1904 and first held office as Parliamentary Under-Secretary for the Colonies from 1905 to 1908. He spoke for the Colonial Office in the House of Commons, where his Boer War fame enhanced his credibility with Liberals on South African questions. The post-war settlement there dominated Colonial Office business, but Churchill managed to take several months off late in 1907 to tour north-eastern Africa. He sent back reports to the *Strand* magazine that were republished in yet another book, *My African Journey*. Churchill enjoyed the advantages of travelling as a minister of state, stopping in Malta and Cyprus on his way out to Somalia and Kenya, and returning home via Sudan and Egypt. He was most impressed by the beauty and fertility of Kenya. He made many recommendations to the Colonial Secretary, Lord Elgin, who praised the junior minister's energy and exuberance. In 1908, the new Prime Minister, Herbert Asquith, appointed Churchill President of the Board of Trade, and in 1910, Home Secretary. In these positions, Churchill favoured limited defence and imperial expenditures, as did David Lloyd George, the most outspoken 'Little Englander' who served as Asquith's Chancellor of the Exchequer. With the Agadir Crisis in 1911, Churchill and Lloyd George closed ranks with hard-line 'Liberal Imperialists' until the outbreak of war in 1914.

When a German gunboat appeared off the coast of Agadir, within the French sphere of Morocco, Asquith's Cabinet took an anti-German stance that gained praise from Fleet Street. To reduce anxieties at home, David Lloyd George made a tough speech at Mansion House. Asquith then convened a meeting of the Committee of Imperial Defence, to which he invited Lloyd George and Churchill for the first time, along with officials from the Foreign Office, War Office, and Admiralty, as well as army and naval personnel. This meeting laid the foundations for the linking of British and French expeditionary forces in the event of war with Germany, and for the further build-up of the British Navy. For the Admiralty, Asquith selected Churchill, a figure who knew how to court public opinion, and announced the appointment in October.

The new First Lord of the Admiralty increased naval expenditures, accelerated ship construction, altered many procedures, and sought oil as the British Navy turned from coal to oil. In 1912 the Anglo-Persian Oil Company (APOC) needed £2 million because it had gone into debt to build a long pipeline from the oilfields of south-western Persia to Abadan, an uninhabited mudflat island in the Shatt-al-Arab waterway flowing into the Persian Gulf, where the company had also erected a huge refinery. Churchill purchased oil from APOC, and suggested that the British Government become the company's majority shareholder. Churchill's boldness shocked some officials in Whitehall, colleagues in the Cabinet, and naval officers. He made a case for the need to guarantee oil for the Navy by citing the precedent of the British Government's purchase of stock in the Suez Canal Company in 1875. Churchill gained enough support from Fleet Street and Westminster to pass a law purchasing the APOC stock for £2 million in 1913.

When Churchill came to the Admiralty, the British had already abandoned their nineteenth-century policy of backing the Shah of Qajar Persia and the Sultan of the Ottoman Empire. Russia's defeat by Japan and the outbreak of revolution in Persia led to the Anglo-Russian Convention of 1907, which divided Persia into a Russian sphere in the north, a neutral area in the middle, and a British sphere in the south. While turmoil persisted in Tehran, the British contented themselves with predominance in the south. The Turkish revolution in 1908 indicated weaknesses that prompted the Austro-Hungarian Empire immediately to annex Bosnia-Herzegovina, encouraged Italy to take Libya from the Turks, and precipitated two wars initiated by aggressive Bulgarian, Serbian, and Greek nationalists in the Balkans. The British accepted all these Turkish humiliations as the inevitable last gasps of 'the sick man of Europe'. While old Turks regretted the passing of their ties to London, young Turks looked to Berlin. British alienation of the increasingly militant Young Turks concerned Churchill no more than the Foreign Secretary, Edward Grey, and their Liberal colleagues.

The assassination of the heir to the Austro-Hungarian Empire at the end of June 1914, precipitated a further Balkan crisis that led to the outbreak of war throughout Europe in August. Britain did not declare war on the Turks until early November. During the preceding three months, Churchill's actions as First Lord of the Admiralty helped extend the European war to the eastern Mediterranean. At the end of July, he prevented the Turks from taking possession of two new battleships commissioned from a British shipyard. The Turks had paid £3.7 million for the two ships and had a crew of 500 ready to sail the already christened ships to Constantinople when Churchill ordered British sailors to board both vessels and prevent the hoisting of the Turkish flag. The Turks were offered no compensation for the Admiralty's requisitioning of the two ships. Churchill's rashness was matched in Constantinople by Enver Pasha, the pro-German Minister of War, who in early August signed a secret treaty with Germany by which Berlin agreed to support the Turks if they declared war against Russia. Another naval incident worsened Anglo-Ottoman relations in mid-August, after two German ships escaped into the Turkish Straits from pursuit by the British Mediterranean fleet. Under the conventions of war, enemy ships could not remain in neutral waters for more than 24 hours without giving cause for war, so the German Ambassador in Constantinople immediately announced that the ships had been 'sold' to the Turks. On hearing the news, Churchill ordered a British blockade of the Mediterranean entrance to the Dardanelles. In defiance, Enver gave the German ships Turkish names, designated the chief German officer 'Commander of the Ottoman Fleet', and ordered German sailors to don fezzes. Furious, Churchill wanted to send a torpedo flotilla through the Dardanelles, but Asquith's Cabinet avoided the appearance of Britain starting a war against the Islamic Empire.

While waiting for the Turks to start the war, Churchill embarked on some personal diplomacy with Enver Pasha that received no reply. Churchill's proposal to support a Greek military attack on the Dardanelles was tabled by Asquith, who endorsed the Foreign Office maintaining an uncompromising stance against Turkey while negotiating secretly with the Russian and French Ambassadors in London. In the meantime, Churchill secured the defence of the Suez Canal and Persian Gulf, and dispatched three ships to protect the oil refinery at Abadan. The Admiralty's efforts were soon followed by the Colonial Office, Foreign Office, India Office and War Office, which ordered preparations for war in Cyprus, Egypt, Sudan, and in the Persian Gulf. On 29 October the Turkish Navy bombarded the Russian port of Odessa. On 3 November Churchill ordered British and French battleships to fire on the outer forts of the Dardanelles in order to test the range of Turkish guns on the Gallipoli peninsula. On 5 November he was pleased by reports that British ships had forced their way past the only Turkish fort guarding the entrance to the Shatt-al-Arab, which prepared the way for a British expedition to capture Basra in only two days. On 6 November Britain formally declared war on Turkey.

Churchill would become so closely identified with the failure of the Dardanelles expedition and the disasters of the Gallipoli campaign in 1915 that his political career was very nearly ruined by them. His role must be seen in relation to Asquith's mismanaging war policy, Lord Kitchener being ill-suited to run the War Office, and John Fisher's unfortunate return as First Sea Lord after the outbreak of the war. Despite the favourable press Asquith gained in the short term from having Kitchener and Fisher as part of his war team, the performances of Asquith, Kitchener, and Fisher in 1915 were no better than Churchill's on the naval expedition at the Dardanelles and the warfare on the Gallipoli peninsula.

Frustration over the stalemate on the Western Front had mounted in Downing Street by the end of 1914, when several memos appeared recommending alternative strategies: Churchill reviewed the amphibious possibilities around Europe, including the Turkish Straits; Lloyd George favoured a military offensive in the Near East as a prelude to a Balkan confederation; Maurice Hankey, the naval officer who served as the secretary of the Committee of Imperial Defence, recommended joint naval and military operations at the Dardanelles, which was supported by Arthur Balfour, the former Conservative Prime Minister. Hankey's suggestion rekindled Churchill's enthusiasm for the Dardanelles. He discussed with Grey and Kitchener an appeal made early in 1915 by the Tsar for help in Russia's campaign against the Turks in the Caucasus. Given Kitchener's reluctance to commit troops, Churchill wired Admiral Sackville Carden, the commander then responsible for blocking the Mediterranean entrance to the Straits, to see if the British Navy itself could force the Dardanelles. Carden replied that the Straits could not be rushed, but might be forced by extended operations with many ships. After Churchill wired him for a detailed proposal, Carden called for bombarding the outer and inner forts of the Gallipoli peninsula and then, once the minesweepers had done their job, advancing through the narrows to the Sea of Marmara. Elated that the naval bombardment of the Gallipoli peninsula had been approved by Asquith's War Council in mid-January, Churchill soon heard Fisher expressing reservations about the naval expedition and Kitchener resenting all the operational interference coming from politicians.

Churchill became alarmed when two British ships were destroyed and another severely damaged in February. He pressed Kitchener to add more troops to the auxiliary force under the command of General Ian Hamilton, whose conduct of the military campaign at Gallipoli turned out to be even worse than Carden's expedition at the Dardanelles. Churchill's confidence persisted despite army casualties numbered in the thousands in the spring reaching the tens of thousands by summer. When *Goliath* and its crew of 600 men was sunk in mid-May, Asquith convened the War Council. At that meeting Fisher recalled the *Queen Elizabeth*, refused to send any more vessels, and left the meeting to make these arrangements at the Admiralty. The next morning, when the First Sea Lord discovered that Churchill had subsequently amended his orders to send more ships and supplies, the famous Admiral resigned. Fisher's fury soon spun round Tory circles in Westminster, which had been set spinning at the end of April by Fleet Street reports that a shortage of shells accounted for recent losses on the Western Front.

In May 1915 Churchill was replaced at the Admiralty when Asquith formed a coalition with the Conservatives over the crisis at the Admiralty in order to head off a full-scale attack on the Government. Churchill was demoted to Chancellor of the Duchy of Lancaster, but Asquith did allow him to serve on the Dardanelles

Committee. In this larger body with lots of Conservative members who loathed him, Churchill continued to call for a major summer offensive at Gallipoli, which would require more divisions than Kitchener was willing to send. Military casualties reaching nearly 100,000 by August, General Hamilton requested 40,000 more men to replace those lost in August and another 50,000 reinforcements. Downing Street, shaken out of its Gallipoli stupor by Bulgaria's mobilization, agreed to an Anglo-French landing at Salonika and an Anglo-Indian advance on Baghdad, neither of which turned out as expected. In November, when Asquith set up a small new war committee from which he excluded Churchill, he tendered his resignation before Gallipoli was evacuated at the end of 1915.

Churchill became Fleet Street's main scapegoat for the Dardanelles and Gallipoli, long after the Dardanelles Commission issued its report in 1917. The parliamentary investigation requested the minutes from Asquith's war policy committees, but Hankey's minutes had not been approved by committee members and he thought they should not be used as evidence. Asquith settled the matter by refusing to release the committee minutes on the grounds that this would compromise the principle of collective Cabinet responsibility. The Dardanelles Commission met only twenty times and called few witnesses, the commissioners readily accepting Hankey's carefully crafted explanation of the expedition, argument about the higher organization of the war, narrative of events, and account of British diplomacy. However, the Dardanelles Commission was more critical than Hankey of Churchill and Fisher. Although the horrors of Gallipoli were not included in the report of the Dardanelles Commission, John Masefield's highly critical *Gallipoli* was published in October 1916 and went through three printings by the end of that year. Churchill would devote nearly a third of *The World Crisis*, his war memoir published in five volumes between 1923 and 1931, to the Dardanelles and Gallipoli. His book, while selling well, did not absolve Churchill of his main responsibility for conceiving and initiating naval and military action at the Dardanelles, although he shared responsibility for the Gallipoli disaster with other members of Asquith's Cabinets.

Churchill joined Lloyd George's Coalition in July 1917, and served as Minister of Munitions until the end of the war. In the landslide victory Coalition candidates won in December 1918,

Churchill retained his formerly safe Liberal seat of Dundee mainly because he was so closely identified with Lloyd George, whose popularity peaked in the Armistice. The two men held diametrically opposite views on the strategic importance of Russia and the Middle East immediately after the war: Churchill had vigorously supported British and Allied intervention against the Bolsheviks in Russia and believed that it should continue, even if this meant military reductions in the Middle East. Lloyd George favoured withdrawing British and Allied troops from Russia better to secure British interests in the eastern Mediterranean and Middle East. Churchill had slight influence upon Lloyd George's handling of diplomacy with the Turks and negotiating League of Nations 'A' mandates for the former Ottoman provinces in Asia. Churchill often found himself carrying out policies in the Middle East with which he disagreed.

As Secretary of State for War and Air from January 1919 to February 1921, Churchill presided over the demobilization of millions of British troops, a process accelerated by post-war economic dislocation and reducing governmental expenditures. Churchill had the unenviable task of presenting the Army Estimates to the House of Commons. In February 1920 Churchill gave the Cabinet the following figures: 14,000 British and 46,000 Indian troops in Mesopotamia; 9,500 British at Constantinople and the Turkish Straits; 9,000 British in Palestine; and 6,000 British in Egypt. He estimated annual costs at £18 million in Mesopotamia and £9 million in Palestine. In May, when violence erupted in Mesopotamia, Churchill dispatched fewer reinforcements than had been requested, but made up some of the difference by relying on air power until troops could be transferred there from Constantinople and by endorsing the use of 'police bombing' against tribes in the south. By October the crisis in Mesopotamia had passed, but another one soon heightened in Turkey, when the Turks successfully retaliated against reckless Greek military advances in Anatolia and the Greeks demanded more British military support. Churchill pressed Lloyd George to end his anti-Turkish policies that were opposed by the United States, France and Italy. Also opposed were Conservatives and senior army officers, the latter's patience having been severely tested by Lloyd George's handling of the civil war then raging in Ireland. In December 1920 Churchill received a £40 million supplementary Army Estimate, including £9 million for Mesopotamia. Churchill argued that a vote against the Government would harm the situation there, which could then lead to more fighting and more expenditures. Lloyd George did not budge from his anti-Turkish stance, but he did ask Churchill to take over the Colonial Office and promised him latitude over civil as well as military affairs in Palestine and Mesopotamia.

As Colonial Secretary from February 1921 to October 1922, Churchill used a new Middle East Department to devise ways of cutting costs for Britain in the area. For the department's Permanent Under-Secretary, Churchill chose James Masterton Smith, whose Whitehall career had begun at the Admiralty in 1901 and who knew how his chief worked. Churchill appointed T.E. Lawrence as his political adviser. The 'Lawrence of Arabia' legend had been created the year before by Lowell Thomas, the American lecturer whose magic-lantern slide presentations on Lawrence and General Edmund Allenby had attracted capacity crowds in London through late 1919 and early 1920. Churchill preferred to have Lawrence with him rather than writing letters to *The Times* and criticizing the Government for surrendering Syria's Arabs to France. Churchill appointed Richard Meinertzhagen, a pro-Zionist, to be his military adviser. These individuals, along with representatives from the Indian Office, Treasury, Foreign Office, and War Office, made elaborate preparations for a secret conference that Churchill convened that spring in Cairo.

To the Semiramis Hotel came all the prominent British officers and officials who were involved with the Middle East. It took more than fifty participants almost fifty meetings to work their way through an agenda of administrative problems in Iraq, its Arabic name now having replaced the biblical Mesopotamia; Palestine, the Balfour Declaration to the Zionists in 1917 having been reinforced by the League of Nations mandate in 1920; and the Arabian peninsula, contested by Ibn Saud in the east, still subsidized by the British thanks to India's taxpayers, and Hussein in the west, heavily subsidized by the British through Egypt's budget. Churchill's main priority in Cairo was to cut British military costs without disrupting local situations that would require more armed interventions. British troops could leave once British officers had trained Arab armies, the costs of which were to be paid by the countries themselves. The Royal Air Force could back up land and police forces. The Arabs could be accommodated by instituting indirect British rule of Iraq and Transjordan, with Faisal to be king in the former and Abdullah to be prince of the latter. Faisal and Abdullah had become estranged from their father, Husayn, the Sharif of Mecca and King of Hejaz. Britain continued to pay the leader of western Arabia so long as he was co-operative. Britain had other collaborators in the eastern part of the peninsula, but only later were the provisions to Ibn Saud increased as he proved his military prowess. Cairo's arrangements were made prior to the discovery of oil in the eastern parts of the Arabian peninsula.

Following the Cairo conference, Churchill spent a week in Palestine, staying at the official residence of the High Commissioner in Jerusalem, Herbert Samuel, a Jewish Liberal pro-Zionist, with whom he discussed the conflicting aims of Arab and Zionist leaders. Churchill reminded a delegation of disgruntled Arabs that Palestine had been liberated by the British, not by the Arabs, and that thousands of British soldiers were buried there. Churchill found the Zionists' leadership more co-operative, but he had not yet told them that Palestine would be confined to the area west of the Jordan river. Churchill and Lawrence met four times in Jerusalem with Abdullah, who was promised financial and military support as long as he made no trouble for the French in Syria, the British in Iraq, or the Zionists in Palestine.

Churchill was back in London early in May, when Muslim-Jewish riots broke out in Jaffa. He supported High Commissioner Samuel's declaration that Jewish immigration would be limited to the 'economic capacity' of Palestine to absorb them. This historic announcement dismayed London's Zionists, whom Churchill sought to placate by instructing Samuel to deal more firmly with those Arabs who attacked Jews in Palestine. In mid-June Churchill ended the secrecy surrounding his new Middle East Department and the conference in Cairo. Speaking in the House of Commons, Churchill contrasted Turkish mistreatment of the Arabs with the British policy of building up an Arab state in Baghdad. As for the unrest in Palestine, he expected the Arabs to be satisfied with administrative autonomy in Transjordan and the Zionists to understand that Zionist immigration depended upon Palestine's economy being able to absorb them. In the meantime, the British had to maintain an adequate military presence in Palestine. Churchill's speech was very well received in Westminster and Fleet Street.

Churchill had to face some very difficult questions raised late in 1921 at Downing Street, Westminster and Fleet Street, as well as by Zionist and Arab leaders. In July Churchill tried to reassure Chaim Weizmann, head of the Zionist Executive Committee, at a meeting with Lloyd George and Hankey held at Balfour's house in Carlton Terrace. In August Churchill met with Muza-Kazim and other Arab representatives, who refused to agree to Churchill's suggestion that they meet with Weizmann. That autumn, when Lloyd George was so weighed down by Irish negotiations that some feared he might resign, Churchill knew that he had to help Lloyd George if the Coalition Government was to survive. In November, on the fourth anniversary of the Balfour Declaration, Arabs attacked the Jewish quarter. Pro-Zionists in London blamed Churchill, while right-wing newspapers in London became increasingly anti-Zionist, and the *Morning Press* barely suppressed its anti-Semitism.

By the summer of 1922, Churchill's policies for the mandates in Palestine and Iraq came under more attack. Balfour presented Britain's case to the League of Nations, which approved the Palestine mandate's incorporation of the British commitment to Zionism. The House of Lords, despite a strong maiden speech by Balfour, newly-created an earl, voted against the Balfour Declaration by sixty to twenty-nine. King Faisal demanded an Anglo-Iraqi treaty, but refused to sign it unless all references to the mandate were deleted so as to give him complete diplomatic autonomy. Exasperated, Churchill favoured an ultimatum until Lloyd George reminded him that the French and the Americans would move to exploit oil there. Leaving Iraq, Palestine, and some Arabian matters to Churchill, Lloyd George put the rest of the Middle East in the all-too willing hands of the Foreign Secretary, Lord Curzon. Regarding Churchill as an amateur, Curzon would perform no better in Persia and Egypt.

When Lloyd George mismanaged a Turkish crisis from August to October 1922, Churchill remained loyally at the premier's side. Turkish military forces were galvanized by Mustafa Kemal, who had proved himself at Gallipoli and later took the name of Ataturk, 'Father of the Turks'. In September Greek soldiers retreated to Smyrna, the port city that the Turks set aflame after more than three years of Greek occupation. Curzon urged Britain to make Greece sign an armistice with Turkey and vacate Asia Minor, but not to abandon any of Europe. Churchill agreed, but Lloyd George doubted if the Greek Army was finished. The British Navy evacuated tens of thousands of Greeks and Armenians from Smyrna's flames. Also outnumbered by Turkish troops were a few thousand British troops at Chanak, a port located on the Asiatic side of the narrows between Smyrna and Constantinople, across from the Gallipoli peninsula. Downing Street had to decide whether to evacuate its forces at Chanak or take military actions to keep Kemal's army from entering Constantinople and reasserting Turkish control in Europe.

An atmosphere of war crisis returned to Downing Street, where meetings took place from early morning to late at night and on weekends. Lloyd George deputed Churchill to communicate with dominion leaders, but only New Zealand and Newfoundland were willing to risk more bloodshed against the Turks. Curzon led two missions to Paris, but was unable to get the French to join with British military action. When Lloyd George asked Churchill to co-ordinate naval, military, and air positions, the *Daily Mail* demanded a stop to 'this new war' so that, 'Mr Winston Churchill may make a new Gallipoli'. Downing Street sent an ultimatum for Kemal, to be delivered by General Charles Harrington, Commander in Chief of British Forces in Constantinople. However, when Harrington met with Kemal, the two generals refused to join battle and agreed that British and Turkish representatives should meet to discuss the future of Chanak, the Straits, and Thrace. That meeting in early October would set the scene for the larger conference at Lausanne in Switzerland, where an enduring Anglo-Turkish treaty was concluded in 1923.

The political consequences of the Chanak crisis became clear in Britain when an independent Conservative announced that he would challenge Lloyd George's coalition candidate at the forthcoming Newport by-election. In mid-October, when the anti-coalition candidate won, Conservatives met at the Carlton Club and declared that Lloyd George would not destroy their party as he had already destroyed the Liberal Party. Lloyd George immediately resigned and Churchill was defeated at Dundee in the November 1922 General Election.

Churchill's career in the Middle East, from 1898 to 1922, was significant for him, for Britain, and for the Middle East. His shifting from the Conservative to the Liberal Parties before the outbreak of war in 1914 mattered little in the mostly bi-partisan and pragmatic British positioning in the Middle East. Churchill took big risks against the Turks when hostilities broke out in Europe in 1914, launched the Dardanelles expedition and persisted at Gallipoli in 1915, deployed British forces to the Middle East in 1919 and 1920, shaped the post-war administrations of Iraq, Palestine, and Transjordan in 1921, and supported another war against the Turks in 1922. While Churchill became the scapegoat for the Dardanelles and lost his parliamentary seat after Chanak, these were but two episodes in a long career involving British power in the Middle East. Churchill's strategic preoccupations were in step with the mainstream newspapers of Fleet Street before, during, and after the First World War. Yet, because of Churchill's visibility with the public, his experiences with the Middle East from 1898 to 1922 would affect the way he subsequently wrote about a region where he never hesitated to use force to protect what he and most of his compatriots believed to be in Britain's best interests.

D.R. Thorpe

ALEC DOUGLAS-HOME:
THE UNEXPECTED PRIME MINISTER

In retirement Alec Home was once travelling back to Berwick-upon-Tweed on the train when he was engaged in conversation by an elderly couple. 'My husband and I think it was a great tragedy that you were never Prime Minister,' said the lady, as they parted. 'As a matter of fact I was,' replied Home, with his customary politeness, before adding, 'but only for a very short time.'

If Bonar Law was, in Asquith's famous phrase, the unknown Prime Minister, Alec Home was the unexpected one in October 1963, the dark horse that saw off more heavily backed rivals. Few would have expected a scion of a great aristocratic family to have become Prime Minister in the febrile and modish 1960s, yet this was not the only unexpected thing about Alec Home, who was in so many ways an unconventional representative of the landowning political tradition. There are not many Foreign Secretaries, landed or otherwise, who would have taken a Soviet counterpart, Andrei Gromyko, to dine at that shrine of conservatism, the Carlton Club, or have been greeted by the strains of the Eton Boating Song in the Great Hall of the People's Republic of China. Few former prime ministers were so untarnished by fame, loyal to their successors or oblivious to station as Alec Home, who, on returning from the tense Rhodesian negotiations in November 1971 during his second spell as Foreign Secretary, received a letter – 'Thank you for coming to Rhodesia. We have a Union Jack curtain in our play room. We have 9 turkeys and they can fly. We have a baby jackal called Henry. I am six' – to which he found time to reply at once in his own hand, 'How very nice of you to write me such a good letter. Perhaps we

will meet one day when I next come to Rhodesia. I hope so.'* He
always had time for the young, as when – in less security-conscious
days – a group of Sea Scouts called at 10 Downing Street, seeking
the Prime Minister's autograph as part of an initiative test. Alec
Home invited them all in, gave them a tour of the Cabinet room
and a hastily arranged buffet lunch.

Perceptions and reality rarely coincide, and this was particularly
marked in the case of Alec Home, who was oblivious to image. He
did not 'market' himself in the way that has become obsessional
with later political generations. One evening during his tenure the
television was broadcasting a speech by Harold Wilson, in which
the then Leader of the Opposition asked rhetorically what Home
could possibly know about ordinary life and the concerns of families and their children. It was a much played tune at that time by
the 14th Mr Wilson. One of the duty secretaries had to go to the
upstairs flat with some urgent government business and found the
Prime Minister putting his first grandchild to bed in the spare room,
as the Wilson speech continued in the same vein on a flickering
portable set.

Unusually among twentieth-century Prime Ministers (Bonar Law
is the only real parallel), Alec Home's ultimate reputation will not
rest on his time in Downing Street. Few prime ministers have been
able to make a major impact without serving a full term. The inter-
war years may have been dubbed the Baldwin Age, but the 60s were
not Alec Home's. He did not, as Hegel demanded of great men,
'actualise' his age. Although he was not a Prime Minister of the first
rank, Alec Home was, however, a figure who did make a major
impact on the development of his party while leader, through the
organizational changes he instituted, notably the procedures for
the formal election of the leader.

The 'customary processes' of October 1963, by which Alec
Home became Prime Minister, cast a long shadow over the subsequent twentieth-century history of the Conservative Party, and it
was Alec Home who exorcized that past, purging its divisive
anguish. This was achieved by instituting a clearly codified elective
system, based on a form of alternative vote as the simplest, quickest
and fairest method of ensuring that when one man had to be chosen

---

* Correspondence of 27 November 1971. Home Papers.

out of three or four, the most acceptable leader emerged. Ironically, in the light of the furore caused in some circles by his emergence under 'the customary processes', Home could well have become leader under that alternative vote system had it been in operation in October 1963.

As Prime Minister, Home may not have been an innovator, changing the political landscape, like Margaret Thatcher; or a reformer, bringing about a major change of direction in policy, like Clement Attlee. He was certainly not an egoist, living for the adrenalin of office, like Lloyd George. He came in a different category of Prime Ministers, as a balancer chosen to bring differing wings together. Some thought him a 'conscript balancer' but that underestimated his steely determination to succeed to the office when his one opportunity presented itself. Such figures need the most sensitive political antennae, for their role is essentially a cohesive one, whether on the national stage or in the party committee rooms, a role that was second nature to Stanley Baldwin, or, more recently, James Callaghan. However, Alec Home's ultimate shortcoming as Conservative leader was not his failure to deliver victory in the 1964 General Election, but his inability in the face of significant internal party opposition to be the focus for that unity.

In the Cabinet room itself, Home was a formidable chairman, pushing the agenda onwards, being crisp in his summings-up and shrewd in his preparation of the agenda. He cut a swathe through the ever-burgeoning number of *ad hoc* Cabinet committees, many of which had now run their natural course. This reorganization was symptomatic of the pragmatic approach Home brought to his task as Cabinet Chairman. Indeed no less a distinguished mandarin than Sir Burke Trend, who was Cabinet Secretary under four Prime Ministers, believed that Alec Home was the most orderly and efficient of all in his conduct of Cabinet business.

All prime ministers need time and a modicum of luck. These were precisely the political assets that Home lacked. Harold Macmillan had the time in January 1957, coming to the Premiership only twenty months into a parliamentary term, and, like a favoured Napoleonic general, he made his own luck. James Callaghan also had over three years in 1976 before an election was due, but the political dice did not fall his way. Alec Home did not even have the time. An election was due within a year of his taking power, and at a time when one of the great political sea changes was coming over British society, he could not reverse that tide. After a long period of domination by one party or one leader, the successor faces special problems as the pendulum begins to swing, as Balfour found after Salisbury, and Callaghan after Wilson, both on the cusp of seismic upheaval. Yet Balfour and Callaghan were both to squander the position they inherited (admittedly in Callaghan's case not the strongest one), but in Home's case the drift was *towards* the Government in its last year, not against. It is often forgotten that the Conservatives were 11 percentage points behind Labour when Alec Home became Prime Minister; twelve months later they suffered defeat by only 0.7 per cent, indeed the Labour share of the vote (at 44.1 per cent) was only 0.3 per cent higher than in October 1959 when they had lost by 100 seats. Defeat in October 1964 remained the bitterest disappointment of Alec Home's political career, its narrowness (a four-seat Labour majority) adding to the intensity of the disappointment. But few incoming Prime Ministers had been delivered a more unpromising hand and he left Downing Street with his reputation enhanced, especially among non-Conservative voters, despite a sustained and vitriolic campaign against him by the Young Turks of the broadcasting world.

Only Bonar Law of twentieth-century Prime Ministers (with his seven months) had a shorter tenure in Downing Street than Alec Home, with his 362 days. History will remember Alec Home rather for his two spells as Foreign Secretary. These coincided with some of the most important events of the Cold War, and the rise of national consciousness in Africa, when his patience was of such value in negotiations. With Balfour in mind, Rosebery once said that to have an ex-Prime Minister in a Cabinet was 'a dangerous and fleeting luxury'. Alec Home, in his second spell as Foreign Secretary from 1970–4, was the undoubted exception, adding weight and experience to Edward Heath's team. Rosebery also said that in politics it was the 'character breathing through the sentences that counts', and Alec Home was a man of character, tempered in an adversity that would have defeated lesser men. During the Second World War spinal tuberculosis confined him to bed for almost two years in what he described as a plaster sarcophagus. His illness, one of great medical complexity, was one of the major turning points of his life, and from which he emerged with a deeper understanding of the kind of person he was. His spiritual side had always been strong, though he never paraded his religious nature. In the years of weary convalescence, he drew on these springs, which gave him the will to be what he was, through greater self-knowledge. In acquiring such identity Home never lost hope or his sense of humour. 'There are compensations about bed,' he wrote, 'especially the feeling of power when one's wife has to do up one's shoes.'* And of the operation, which involved scraping out the diseased hole in his spine and filling it with healthy fragments from his own shin to plug the gap, he would later say characteristically that he was the only politician to have had backbone put into him. As a result, he was determined to do something of value in any bonus years that were granted to him. He had always had the enviable characteristic of repose, with marriage to his beloved Elizabeth for fifty-four years the bedrock of his existence, but for the sake of those who did not survive, including his youngest brother George, killed on service with the RAF at the age of twenty-one, he now felt he had obligations he was even more determined to fulfil.

In the field of international relations, as his adversaries soon discovered, Alec Home proved to be a Foreign Secretary who was not easily deflected from the path he had set himself. Macmillan is often, mistakenly, portrayed as the 'unflappable' politician of the post-war period. In fact his personality sometimes led him to betray to his inner circle of confidants a nervous vulnerability that was masked from the public gaze. The loyal Sancho Panza to this mercurial Don Quixote varied over the years.

The most unsung episode in Alec Home's time as Macmillan's Foreign Secretary was during the long, sleepless hours of the Cuban Missile Crisis in October 1962. His role was not so much as President Kennedy's and Harold Macmillan's go-between, but as the link between No. 10 and Dean Rusk, the American Secretary of State. Whenever Macmillan rang Kennedy on the famous 'hot-line', Home was in the room for consultation. Alec Home always believed that Kennedy had made a mistake by meeting the Russian leader Khruschev in Vienna so soon after his inauguration as President in 1961. 'Khruschev, being a very shrewd man, probably summed the situation up fairly well, but his advisers almost certainly concluded

---

* Lord Dunglass to Mrs Walter Elliot, 1943. Baroness Elliot of Harwood papers.

that here was a young man around whom Khruschev could make rings. They found out they were wrong, but only after the most anxious months of trial and error and brinkmanship.' Home also played a significant part in influencing the Russian Diplomatic Corps in London during the Cuban Missile Crisis, as he made it plain that there were no 'ifs and buts' . The missiles had disturbed the balance. They were a new factor. Therefore they would have to go. The missiles in Turkey did not come into it. They already existed and were part of the status quo. Intelligence reports indicated how this message reached the Kremlin. The mood of dazed anxiety in those weeks reminded some of the period leading up to Munich, though Home's regular contacts with Sir Frank Roberts, the British Ambassador in Moscow, gave him insights into what the ordinary Russian people were thinking, which proved so different from those in Havana and London. When Kennedy's ultimatum about the missiles was made public Frank Roberts told Alec Home that there was no sign of panic buying in Moscow and that people were going about their business in an orderly manner. Roberts interpreted this, correctly, as a sign that in the end Khruschev would back off from full-scale nuclear confrontation. The atmosphere both men remembered in London before Munich was notably absent.

All great events in world history, it has been said, reappear in one fashion or another, the first time as tragedy, the second as farce: not, however, the Cuban Missile Crisis, the gravest event of which Home had direct experience since the days of Munich. Alec Home was able to trace the parallels better than most. Accompanying Neville Chamberlain to Germany in September 1938 had given him a lasting distrust of summitry (he first came to the Foreign Office in the immediate wake of the disastrous Paris summit in the summer of 1960) and a keen eye for the vanities and posturings of international figures. He never forgot how Göring at Munich had changed his uniform several times that day to intimidate the British party. 'He would have impressed Chamberlain far more if he had talked to him about scaup ducks' was Home's recollection of that visit. (Alec Home's father, a saintly man, who saw sermons in stones and good in everything, remarked of Hitler at this time, 'Poor fellow, surrounded by all those generals, and not one of them able to tell him he's got his Sam Browne on the wrong way round.')

Alec Home was never deflected by bluster or bravado, one of

the reasons that the Texan bullying of Lyndon Baines Johnson was so counter-productive in their talks of February 1964 in Washington. The issue that divided them was the seemingly Lilliputian one of the sale of British Leyland buses to Cuba. Johnson was incensed. Home stood firm. 'There is no question of dictation by the United States Government to this country over commercial relations with Cuba,' he said. 'This is a subject which is decided solely by the British Government.' Macmillan knew that Alec Home was a 'resolute character – iron painted to look like wood'. Had he been of another generation, Macmillan thought Home would have been of the Grenadiers and the 1914 heroes. 'He gives that impression by a curious mixture of great courtesy, and even of yielding to pressure, with underlying rigidity on matters of principle. It is interesting that he has proved himself so much liked by men like President Kennedy and Mr Rusk and Mr Gromyko.'*

Of all Alec Home's relationships, few were as complex as those with Andrei Gromyko, his Russian counterpart as Foreign Minister, whom he variously referred to in private as 'Old Grom' or 'the Abominable No-Man'. (This fondness for nicknames was a characteristic of British politics at that time, Macmillan alluding privately to Dean Rusk as 'the biscuit man'.) Over the years Gromyko's obstinacy by turns perplexed and infuriated British diplomats. Yet against all the odds, considering the very different personalities involved, their relationship was a fruitful one, surviving such traumas as the Cuban Missile Crisis and the expulsion from Britain by Alec Home of 105 Russian spies in 1971. There were two sides to Gromyko: the official and the personal, and Alec Home soon assessed that as long as one was aware which persona Gromyko was adopting, progress was possible. Gromyko could, of course, be formidably obstinate; the shutters could come down and then there was nothing but obdurate reiteration of the Kremlin line. But Home knew that 'Old Grom' could also be human and amusing on the private level. The relationship over the years between the two was fascinating to the informed observer, especially as some knew that Mrs Gromyko had taken a shine to the man she described as 'The English Lord', which Gromyko joked about with Alec Home in his

* Harold Macmillan to HM Queen Elizabeth II, 15 October 1963. PREM 11/ 5008. Public Record Office, Kew.

more informal moments. There were actually many points of contact between the two men. Both were professionally detached and hardened by experience. For Gromyko politics was like a game, which he played hard, but he could stand above the battle while arguing over detail. In private he spoke English, but when on business confined himself to Russian. Though knowing perfectly well what Home was saying, he waited for the interpreter to finish whilst he thought out his response, like an icon on a computer screen indicating that calculations were unfolding. He was tough and battle hardened, but he still found Home an elusive opponent. Home soon understood that Gromyko was fascinated by tradition. Shooting was one of Gromyko's main pastimes and he always sought Home's advice on his Purdey guns when he came to London, insisting that his son get the best that the London gunsmiths had to offer, as 'He, silly boy, waits for ducks to fly off lake before shooting them!' Home invited Gromyko one August to stay at his estate at Douglas for the shooting, but the old Russian instincts led Gromyko to ask first whether Douglas was private land and then he baulked at acceptance, though Home, tongue-in-cheek, suggested that he could lease the land to Lanark County Council for the day if that would assuage Gromyko's conscience. When Home expelled the Russian spies, Gromyko found it very difficult, despite his apoplectic reaction, in an appropriately padded room, deep in the bowels of the United Nations, to make any headway with his protest. Each knew the other too well and Alec Home had only to say that he thought Gromyko would be grateful, because otherwise people back home in Russia might believe that he was not in control of the KGB, for capitulation to follow.

Home's forthrightness was not a sign of inflexibility. He had an unusual combination of shrewdness and humility that enabled him to acknowledge his mistakes. He bitterly regretted, for instance, his remark in an interview with Kenneth Harris for the *Observer* in September 1962 that, 'when I have to read economic documents I have to have a box of matches and start moving them into position to simplify and illustrate the points to myself'. Although the prospect of Home's becoming Prime Minister did not then seem remotely possible, this remark was to be pure gold for his opponents, and the cartoonist Vicky had his defining image for Alec Home. The damage was to prove retrospective, and the Conservatives were to pay a heavy price for it. Alec Home was to admit privately that it was a prime example – along with Harold Wilson's 'pound in your pocket' and Edward Heath's 'cutting prices at a stroke' – of a remark becoming a hostage to fortune. Likewise his reference to pensions as 'donations' in an *Election Forum* in September 1964, which he knew at once to be ill-judged. One of his enduring memories was of Neville Chamberlain stepping back from the window at 10 Downing Street after his 'Peace in our time' remark. Chamberlain's eyes were full and both knew it was a fatal mistake.

Contrary to the convenient myths, many circulated by Iain Macleod, Alec Home was in fact sensitive to the demands of changing political realities. He knew that political choice was often a matter of the unpalatable or the disastrous, one of the reasons why he never joined in the bandwagon of hindsight over Neville Chamberlain and the Munich agreement, for which he remained an unashamed apologist, and for which one of the most convinced of the anti-Munichois, Anthony Eden, always respected him. Home was not always a politically correct figure; but he was invariably an honest one. He admired consistency from all sides of the political spectrum, whether in Julian Amery or Tony Benn, even if the views expressed were at odds with conventional political wisdom or awkward from the point of view of party expediency. He was prepared to ruffle political feathers when he held strong views himself, as over the Yalta Agreement in February 1945, which Winston Churchill described as 'an act of justice'. 'I could recognise it as a fact of power,' said Alec Home, on the occasion of Churchill's centenary, 'but repudiated any suggestion of an act of justice.'

Home's Scottish background helped in detaching him from metropolitan concerns and in viewing the hothouse of Westminster politics in a more dispassionate manner than some of his contemporaries. There was always for him a world elsewhere. 'The trouble with our party is that leaders are South East based,' wrote Selwyn Lloyd in 1968, adding, without any sense of pejorative irony, 'The only real provincials are Alec Douglas-Home and myself.'* Yet Alexander Frederick Douglas-Home, as he was christened, was London-born, on 2 July 1903, at 28 South Street in an age when a

---

* Selwyn Lloyd diary, 3 January 1968. SELO 124 (2). Selwyn Lloyd Papers (Churchill College, Cambridge).

London birthplace was considered a desirable, if not an essential, accompaniment to landed heirs as they embarked on life's journey. Among his contemporaries, he was thus six years younger than Anthony Eden, in whose Cabinet he first sat in 1955; a year older than Selwyn Lloyd, and seven months younger than Rab Butler, the two figures who preceded and succeeded him as Foreign Secretary. He was nine years younger than Harold Macmillan, whom he succeeded as Prime Minister in October 1963. His Eton contemporary Cyril Connolly famously observed that in the eighteenth century he would have been Prime Minister before he was thirty. Christ Church, his Oxford college, had already produced eleven prime ministers by the time he arrived in 1922, and he was to be the thirteenth Christ Church occupant of 10 Downing Street. The previous Christ Church Prime Minister, Anthony Eden, was acutely aware of how his own career had been passed almost exclusively in the foreign political domain.

This specialization in foreign affairs is often assumed to be the Achilles heel of Alec Home's outlook, but it is now forgotten that when Alec Home was appointed Commonwealth Secretary in 1955 by Eden, it was precisely because Eden wanted to *broaden* Home's experience. Thus he was given overseas responsibilities and not promoted to a domestic post such as Health or Housing. Furthermore, before the war he had worked at the Ministry of Labour and been greatly influenced by a now forgotten Scottish Conservative, Noel Skelton, who had first coined the resonating 'One Nation' phrase about a 'property owning democracy'. From 1951-5 he had worked in the Scottish Office, where his travels had taken him the length and breadth of the country on every conceivable political issue. He had been to the Island of Mull, to advise on reorganization of local government, and to the Turnberry Hotel to meet the Scottish Farmers' Union. He had been the conduit in Edinburgh for the expression of the views of the Educational Institute of Scotland; in transport matters, he had paved the way for the building of the Forth Road Bridge (opened in the last week of his Premiership in 1964); he had dealt with the problems of crofting and depopulation in the Highlands and Islands, walking in the summer months at midnight along the silver beaches of Bettyhill by the light of the aurora borealis. He could be very sharp on legal niceties: once the Agriculture Department submitted a draft proposal for changing arrangements for tied cottages 'by regulation'. The experienced parliamentarian soon had that changed to 'by legislation'. He had an alert eye for potential difficulties and he kept the proprieties with his civil servants. On one occasion, a secretary offered a conversational gambit about the problems Herbert Morrison was having as Labour's deputy leader. He was met with a stony stare.

His distaste for prevarication could have its amusing sidelines. When Bertrand Russell sent him a signed copy of his book *Has Man a Future?* in 1961, he wrote back, 'Many thanks. I hope your answer is Yes.' When the England cricket captain Colin Cowdrey, a renowned slip fielder, wrote to him as 'Sir Alec', he replied, 'You can drop the Sir, if you ever drop anything.' One August in the early 1970s his staff at the Foreign Office gave him a great bundle of papers on the origins of the Icelandic Cod War, in case he wished to study background material whilst on holiday. 'A kindly thought, but an erroneous one,' he minuted.

He was shrewd in his assessments of character. This comes over most clearly in the last of his three books, *Letters to a Grandson*, in which he covers his career from the time of the First World War. The early letters, with accounts of Sir Edward Grey and Rosebery, have the immediacy and vividness of Churchill's *Great Contemporaries*. Of Stanley Baldwin's appearances in the Commons, he observes that, 'Baldwin would "smack kisses on the Order Paper as though he were starved of affection!"' At memorial services, for which he was in great demand, he was especially successful. The acoustics of Westminster Abbey may have been, in his own words, 'like King's Cross Station during the rush hour', but he invariably made a telling assessment in his addresses, because he was able to speak the truth in a kindly way. At his own memorial services, held appropriately in his native Scotland at St Giles Cathedral, as well as in Westminster Abbey, he was recognized not only as a politician of decency and honesty but also as an exemplary countryman, and no impression of his life could be complete that omitted mention of his love of the Borders and the sport to be had in the gentle countryside around the Hirsel. Those who seek his picture in the National Portrait Gallery will find him, not behind some government desk, but by the Tweed, fishing rod in hand and black Labrador by his side.

Born into the Edwardian world with its illusory imperial certainties, Alec Home lived through all but seven years of the twentieth

century, and was witness to some of the most important transformations in history. His longevity was positively Gladstonian in its
range, stretching from the end of the Great War to the end of the
Cold War. He fought his first election in the 1920s, before entering
Parliament in 1931 as MP for the mining district of South Lanark
when Ramsay MacDonald was Prime Minister. He was still politically active sixty years later in the era of Margaret Thatcher, who
drew on his expertise from her first days as Conservative leader in
February 1975. He knew European monarchs from King George V
to King Juan Carlos. His friendships stretched back to Balfour, a
golfing partner at North Berwick, and Earl Haig, a frequent guest at
the Hirsel, who spoke with him as a schoolboy about the Great
War; his political dealings encompassed Mussolini and Mao Tse-
tung. He saw the League of Nations superceded by the United
Nations; he died in the much-changed world of European Union
with all its controversies. At his death on 9 October 1995 a distinct
era came to an end in British political life. He was described in the
obituaries as 'the quiet aristocrat of British politics' and the lesson
of his career that, 'politics and honour are by no means incompatible'. For Lady Thatcher, he was the wisest of men, and 'represented
all that was best in his generation'. Alec Home's own assessment,
some years earlier, was characteristically low-key and modest. He
felt that his own political epitaph would simply be 'an uncontrover-
sial man who was involved in controversial events'. Nevertheless
it is a verdict with which many politicans would be pleased, and
which could be applied to few other Prime Ministers, expected or
unexpected.

John Grigg

HERBERT GLADSTONE

The sons of great men who engage in the same line of business are easy targets for invidious comment. In October 1922 Herbert (Viscount) Gladstone, most political son of the great W.E. Gladstone, was memorably savaged by Lloyd George, who was fighting at the time for his political life. The enemies besetting him included fellow Liberals of the rival Asquithian faction, of whom Gladstone was one.

A few days after Gladstone had attacked him at the Manchester Reform Club, Lloyd George visited the same place and returned the compliment. Gladstone, he observed, had 'excommunicated' him and those Liberals who supported him, and he went on to say:

> Well, the Papacy is not an hereditary office, and Mr Gladstone in his most powerful moments never excommunicated Liberals who dared to disagree ... But Lord Gladstone excommunicated us. What service has he rendered Liberalism that gives him that right? I know of no service except one. He is the best living embodiment of the Liberal doctrine that quality is not hereditary ... There is no more ridiculous spectacle on the stage than a dwarf strutting before the footlights in garments he has inherited from a giant.[1]

In the circumstances Lloyd George could hardly have been expected to speak of Gladstone with scrupulous fairness, which is anyway not the commonest feature of political controversy. But in this case the degree of unfairness was extreme. Seventeen years earlier he and Gladstone had together become members of one of the greatest reforming ministries in British history. Lloyd George's contribution to it is well known; even people otherwise largely ignorant of history have a vague awareness of his activity as a social reformer before 1914. Herbert Gladstone's contribution, however, is almost entirely forgotten.

Yet up to 1910 his record as a reformer was second to none. As Home Secretary under Campbell-Bannerman and Asquith he put through a legislative programme of exceptional range and substance. Earlier he played a very significant part as Liberal Chief Whip between 1899 and 1905. And his role after 1910, as the first Governor-General of the Union of South Africa, was by no means negligible. Far from being a 'dwarf', or a conspicuous example of the non-transmissibility of talent, he is in fact the most impressive political son of a major British politician during the past century – with the one obvious exception of Winston Churchill. In solid achievement he has more to show than Loulou Harcourt, Austen or Neville Chamberlain, Lord Robert Cecil, Malcolm MacDonald – or Gwilym Lloyd George. Historians have given him much less attention than he deserves.

He was born in 1854, when his father was Chancellor of the Exchequer in Lord Aberdeen's Government, and he was the youngest of Gladstone's four sons. In many ways Herbert was a model of filial piety, entering politics as his father's private secretary and never deviating from his free trade principles, or from his later commitment to Irish Home Rule. He also shared his father's high Anglicanism. Until advanced middle age he remained within the orbit of his family, and married only in his late forties, when both his parents were dead. Towards the end of his life he and his brother Henry (to whom he was closest in age and sympathy) went to great lengths to vindicate the GOM's good name, when a book was published in which the worst construction was put on his nocturnal forays among prostitutes. Since the law of libel could not be invoked on a dead man's behalf, they denounced the author of the book as a liar and forced him to sue them for libel. The result was a triumph for their cause, the jury adding to its verdict in their favour an explicit vindication of 'the high moral character of the late Mr W.E. Gladstone'. As Roy Jenkins says, 'Rarely has a statesman been able to arouse a favourable public demonstration twenty-nine years after his death.'[2] (Had the jury been able to read the Gladstone diaries, as the brothers had, they would have seen that his motives were rather more complex than they thought.)

All this might suggest that Herbert was a mere acolyte, almost a clone, of his father (wearing only 'garments . . . inherited from a giant'). But he was nothing of the sort. In two very important respects his political outlook differed from Gladstone's. He did not take the minimalist view of the State's responsibility for social reform that was characteristic of Gladstonian liberalism. On the contrary, he believed strongly that the State should broaden its role in improving the condition of the people. This made him what was known a century ago as a 'New Liberal'. He was also unlike his father in being an advocate of women's suffrage. Gladstone felt that exercising the vote would 'trespass upon [women's] delicacy, their purity, their refinement, the elevation of their whole nature'.[3] Herbert had no such fear.

There were other differences. Herbert was less formidable intellectually than his father, and no classical scholar. But he proved that he could excel in his own line. At Oxford, after getting a third in Mods (classical texts) he turned to Modern History and got a first in it. He tried twice for All Souls, and for a short time – before he went into politics – was a lecturer at Keble College. His mind was more scholarly than he would ever admit, and he was also capable of working, when necessary, extremely hard. But he was not, like his father, a workaholic. He enjoyed recreation and sport (he was a good shot, and as a golfer had a low single-figure handicap), and he loved music. He was an easy companion, naturally gregarious.

Most important, perhaps, was his freedom from the casuistry, convolutions of language and agonies of conscience that people found so exasperating in his father. Herbert was a straightforward man; people knew where he stood, and where they stood with him. This difference was illustrated in the contrasting ways he and Gladstone approached the subject of Irish Home Rule. Herbert made his position clear in a speech to his Leeds constituents in 1883. Two years later his father was still keeping not only the public, but his principal colleagues – in particular, Lord Hartington and Joseph Chamberlain – in the dark about his intentions. Herbert then spoke to journalists with his usual candour, and reports appeared which are known to history as the 'Hawarden kite'. It is possible that Gladstone may have been using his son to signal the movement of his thought, but Herbert's own account leaves one in little doubt that the initiative, right or wrong, was his: 'The net result was the commitment of the party to Home Rule, led by Mr Gladstone. In short, I did what I thought and still think had to be done. No one else would, perhaps could, have made the venture.'[4]

In Gladstone's last Government (1892–4) Herbert was junior minister at the Home Office, with Asquith as his departmental chief, and in the brief Rosebery Government that followed he was First Commissioner of Works. In this post he just had time to show his flair for practical administration (averting a threat to the amenities of Richmond Park, raising the pay of his department's employees, and arranging for the Union Jack to fly over the Victoria Tower at Westminster). During a most difficult period in opposition he did a superb job as Chief Whip, in holding the Party formally together despite the internal conflicts generated by the Boer War. His warm and open temperament, allied to shrewdness, enabled him to command the trust of colleagues who were fighting each other. He also negotiated an historic deal with Ramsay MacDonald, whereby in a number of seats the Liberal Party and the Labour Representation Committee agreed to help each other by not running candidates in competition. The result was that twenty-nine Labour MPs were returned at the ensuing (1906) General Election. The Gladstone–MacDonald pact was not, as it turned out, necessary to ensure a change of government. After the Conservative Party began to tear itself apart over tariff reform its defeat was a certainty (since the same issue united the Liberals in defence of free trade), and the election produced, of course, a Liberal landslide. But in a longer perspective it was vital for the Liberal Party to cultivate good relations with the rising Labour movement, and Gladstone's approach was enlightened. Unfortunately not all Liberals shared his comradely and unsnobbish attitude.

In the Government formed by Campbell-Bannerman at the end of 1905 (when Balfour resigned instead of asking for a dissolution) Herbert Gladstone was appointed Home Secretary – though it seems that he would, rather surprisingly, have preferred to be First Lord of the Admiralty. At all events it was the right appointment, and when the Prime Minister left him free to pick his own under-secretary he made an excellent choice in Herbert Samuel.[5] Together these two worked most fruitfully until, in 1908, Asquith replaced Campbell-Bannerman as Prime Minister and appointed Samuel to the Cabinet. For his last year at the Home Office Gladstone's junior minister was Charles Masterman, another outstanding representative of New Liberalism.

In these days when every department of state has an establishment of at least four ministers, and in many cases more, it is hard to believe that Gladstone was able to run the Home Office – a department whose responsibilities were even wider then than now – with the assistance of only one ministerial colleague. But he did so, and nobody could say that his task was lighter than that of recent home secretaries. During his period of office thirty-four pieces of legislation, large and small, were enacted. The large ones included measures on workmen's compensation, coal mines regulation, trade boards, children, probation of offenders, criminal appeal and prevention of crime.

Gladstone had long been interested in prisons, and he understood the need for more humane methods of dealing with young offenders. Under his auspices probation was introduced as a substitute for prison in certain cases, and the borstal system was devised as a means of saving young people from a life of crime. Juvenile courts were brought in, and the imprisonment of delinquents under sixteen was abolished.

His Workmen's Compensation Act added many new categories of worker to those already covered in Joseph Chamberlain's pioneer measure (1897). Sailors and domestic servants were among the new categories, which amounted in all to 6 million people. The act also for the first time included industrial diseases as a subject for compensation. Gladstone's Coal Mines Regulation Act established the principle of an eight-hour-day underground. Some owners complained that it would reduce output by 25 million tons a year, but Gladstone disregarded the complaint and events proved him right. By 1914 output had *risen* by nearly that amount.

As well as legislation, Gladstone had more than his share of the 'banana skin' type of business for which the Home Office is notorious. In this respect by far the worst vexation, in his time, was the suffragettes' campaign. Acting against them was particularly odious to him, because he was convinced that women should have the vote. But it was his duty to uphold the law and to prevent self-victimization by the suffragettes, even at the price of forcible feeding. It was typical of him to have the process inflicted on himself, to make sure that it was neither dangerous nor intolerably painful.[6]

On top of all his other work it fell to him, when Parliament was sitting, to write every night a report to the King on the day's proceedings in the House of Commons. These letters were written in his own hand, often at the end of a fourteen- to sixteen-hour day.

His success as a minister owed much to his willingness to give credit to others, and to encourage their work. Samuel acknowledges, in his memoirs, what a considerate chief he was.[7] He knew how to get the best out of officials, listening to them, and often deferring to them, but never losing his own independence and authority.

As Home Secretary he lived, until 1908, in the house where he was born, No. 11 Downing Street (which was numbered 12 at the time of his birth). Asquith as Chancellor of the Exchequer preferred to stay in his own house in Cavendish Square, so the Chancellor's official residence was available for Gladstone. When Lloyd George succeeded Asquith at the Treasury, he wanted the house and the Gladstones moved out.

In 1910, on agreeing to become Governor-General of South Africa, Herbert was succeeded at the Home Office by Winston Churchill. He was upset when Churchill swiftly acted on his proposals to change prison rules for suffragettes, in such a way as to suggest that they were his own proposals – that he (Churchill) had 'done the obviously right thing' that Gladstone had failed to do 'from foolishness and inhumanity'. Replying, Churchill more or less said that incoming ministers normally took credit for measures that they inherited. Gladstone remained hurt, but did not pursue the correspondence: 'all this is a small matter & I am sorry to have troubled you'.[8] There is pathos in the incident. Churchill was a good Home Secretary, but no better than Gladstone. Of course he was, in general, a far bigger man, but he was also a relentless self-advertiser, while Gladstone was unpushy to a fault. Even before he earned immortal fame, Churchill made sure that his merits were fully recognized. Gladstone did not promote himself, with the result that his merits were insufficiently recognized even in his own time.

On his appointment to South Africa he left the House of Commons and accepted a peerage, as protocol then required for a governor-general. Some Liberals were sad that Mr Gladstone's son should permit himself to be tainted with nobility. (Lloyd George's uncle, Richard Lloyd, was one such, saying at the time that he was 'very sorry' Gladstone was allowing 'the title of lord to be attached to that famous old name'.[9]) Since the Gladstones had no children the title became extinct at Herbert's death.

His four years in South Africa were on the whole well spent. On arrival he had to appoint a prime minister of the new union – which comprised Cape Colony, Natal and the former Boer republics, Transvaal and the Orange Free State. The decision was his, and he made the bold choice of General Louis Botha rather than the highly qualified, but British, J.F.X. Merriman. Botha repaid his conciliatory gesture by unwavering loyalty to the Crown.

Gladstone's geniality and political experience, together with the prestige of his name, helped to reduce the mutual suspicion of two white communities so recently at war. As for the majority of the population that was not white, it cannot be said that his thoughts or actions in that regard were very far in advance of his time. There was no meeting of minds (or of any kind) between him and M.K. Gandhi, then developing in South Africa his technique of non-violent resistance. But in the high commission territories for which the Crown was directly responsible Gladstone upheld 'native' rights, and on one occasion incurred the odium of white settlers in Rhodesia, by commuting the death sentence imposed on an African for raping a white woman. (He was dissatisfied with the evidence and thought that a lesser charge would have been appropriate.) When he visited Rhodesia soon afterwards the settlers gave him, at first, a very hostile reception; but he spoke to them with frankness and tact, and so gradually won them round.

Towards the end of his time in South Africa there were rather menacing strikes by white workers on the Rand, but he stayed calm even when besieged in his office, withdrawing the guards and inviting a deputation to see him. At the same time he called out troops in sufficient strength to maintain order. Though the Government had the chief responsibility, he played his part in bringing a dangerous situation under control.

After South Africa his career was effectively at an end, though he occupied himself in many useful ways. During the Great War he was very active on behalf of Belgian refugees, and after the war he undertook many worthy chores. He and his wife also travelled a lot, and their most memorable trip was to Bulgaria, where his father's name was – and still is – venerated. In Sofia they drove through streets 'strewn with flowers' and found that in the city's largest college, where the walls were hung with paintings of Bulgarians who had fought for freedom from the Turks, 'alone, above them all, presided the portrait of Mr Gladstone'. Before they left a crowd of 'fifty or sixty thousand people' marched past their hotel.[10] The visit is described (actually by his wife) in the book of memoirs, *After Thirty Years*, which he published in 1928. This is more readable than anything written by his father, and enjoyed a modest success. But, as the title implies, the book is mainly about his father and his own early years. There is nothing about his work as Chief Whip or at the Home Office.

Good-natured though he was, he did not avoid controversy in the last phase of his life. He entered into Liberal Party arguments (so attracting the broadside from Lloyd George). He was always ready to defend his father's honour. Apart from the libel action mentioned, he had a 'violent' row in print with George Buckle over the latter's edition of Queen Victoria's correspondence. He suspected that the editor (Disraeli's co-biographer) had left out letters helpful to Gladstone's cause, but eventually 'had to accept' Buckle's denials.[11]

For the last fifteen years of his life he lived at Dane End in Hertfordshire, a charming house rented from his wife's family. She was Dorothy (Dolly) Paget before their marriage. Music was one of many bonds between them, and gardening was another. In 1930 he died at Dane End and was buried in a nearby churchyard. There was a well-attended memorial service in Westminster Abbey, at which the Prime Minister of the day, Ramsay MacDonald was present. He had reason to remember Gladstone.

History should remember him too, and it is time for a proper life of him to be written. Soon after his death a very bland biography by Sir Charles Mallet appeared, but since then nothing, though books have been written about many politicians of less importance and also, for that matter, less human interest. He deserves to be rediscovered.

* * *

NOTES

1. 15 October 1922 (report next day in *The Times*).
2. Roy Jenkins, *Gladstone*, p. 106.

3. W.E. Gladstone to Samuel Smith MP, using his influence to bring about the defeat of Sir Albert Rollit's suffrage bill in 1892. (It was nevertheless defeated by only twenty-three votes, and thereafter no women's suffrage bill was defeated in the House of Commons.)

4. Herbert Gladstone, *After Thirty Years*, p. 314.

5. The reasons he gave for choosing Samuel were that he 'had written a good deal about Factory Legislation' and 'was interested in Home Office subjects'. (Walter Runciman to Winston Churchill, 13 December 1905, quoted in the official life of Churchill, Companion vol. II, part 1, p. 414.) Runciman was disappointed at not getting the job.

6. Sir Charles Mallet, *Herbert Gladstone*, p. 222.

7. Herbert Samuel, *Memoirs*, p. 50.

8. Exchange of letters between Herbert Gladstone and Winston Churchill, 16–18 March 1910. (Official life of Churchill, Companion vol. II, part 2, pp. 1157–8.)

9. D.R. Daniel, unpublished memoir.

10. Herbert Gladstone, *After Thirty Years*, pp. 154–8 (recollection by Dorothy Gladstone of 'Three Days in Sofia').

11. *Dictionary of National Biography*, Supplement 1922–30, entry on Herbert Gladstone by W.V. Cooper.

Alex Danchev

BASIL LIDDELL HART

Captain Sir Basil Liddell Hart (1895–1970), military historian, critic, journalist, propagandist, controversialist, archivist, and god-father, was not the Clausewitz of the twentieth century, as he and others were wont to claim; but he was perhaps the next best thing. A war poet in prose – his inter-war writing carried a comparable charge – he wrote no great book, no timeless synthesis, like the unfinished masterpiece *On War*. It was Clausewitz's ambition to write something 'that would not be forgotten after two or three years, and that possibly might be picked up more than once by those who are interested in the subject'. It was Liddell Hart's too. *Thoughts on War* (1944) is the skeleton of such a work, *The Revolution in Warfare* (1946) the sketch, *Strategy: The Indirect Approach* (4th revised edition, 1967) the simulacrum. His output is staggering – dozens of books, hundreds of articles, thousands of letters – but his oeuvre is not so much an oeuvre as an aggregation, and very often (too often) a repetition. Yet his influence was and is enormous. There is hardly a military writer of repute in the Western world (including Alistair Horne himself) who was not touched in some way by this indomitable lighthouse of a man. Goethe says that the true sign of genius is a posthumous productivity. On that criterion Liddell Hart would certainly qualify. He lived as a fron-deur, a thrower of stones, and later as an exemplar. He survived, and survives still, as a climate of ideas. Liddell Hart is the Bertrand Russell of his field: he is all-pervasive.

*

He described himself as 'border', meaning something more than geography, and always felt a certain distance from the social and intellectual heartland of England, a distance he worked uncommonly hard to close. He was born in Paris, where his father was Minister of the Methodist Church. He had a conventional upbringing, peripatetic on the Methodist circuit. A series of prep schools led eventually to St Paul's in London. His school career was undistinguished. He rose laboriously through the Pauline ranks more by the passage of time in each form than by any sign of intellectual distinction. In 1913, after some frantic cramming, he went up to Corpus Christi College, Cambridge, to read for the History Tripos. His university career was, if anything, even more undistinguished. Many years later, when asked to contribute to a survey on 'What I Owe to Cambridge', he put first a taste in food and wine. In the examinations at the end of his first year he recorded a dismal Third. At the same time he drew up a list of his own dominant characteristics: a pen picture or self-portrait, at once revealing and discerning, in both its flattering and its unflattering aspects. Young Liddell Hart was a patent prig, but an unusually reflective one.

> Logical, self-love [cancelled], too egotism [sic], affectionate but not demonstrative, large brain-power, tactful and diplomatic, conventional, certain amt [amount] of individuality of thought, rather too methodical or even fussy, inclined to be philosophical not practical, head and heart fairly evenly balanced, too much love of detail, may fail to grasp whole.
>
> No insanity, no suicide, no ermine, fairly long-lived, work out own destiny, fortunate and successful, know what I want, not influenced by other people, simple life, not travel mind[ed], extremely jealous in affections concerning Mary [identity unknown], opposite in tastes and temperament, not flirtatious by nature, health good, cultivate will, art and poetry not great influences but may incline towards them, not nervy, but sensitive, well-balanced mentally, slightly indolent.

When war was declared in 1914 Liddell Hart was one of the young men unconscionably eager for action. On a temporary commission in the King's Own Yorkshire Light Infantry (KOYLI), he went to this war three times, a persistence of which he was very proud. 'On going to the front for a third time,' he wrote to his parents, 'I desire to say that in any notice or memorial the fact of my going a third time be emphasized.' These were short stints, abruptly curtailed by injury; in each case a certain ambiguity surrounds the curtailment. The first was for about three weeks, in September–October 1915, in a quiet sector near Albert. The second was for a few beleaguered days in November 1915, very much in the thick of things, in the water-logged lines of the Ypres Salient. The third was again for about three weeks, in June–July 1916, for the Big Push on the Somme, in the Fricourt sector, where he was gassed and traumatized in Mametz Wood. That was enough, but that was all.

Officially 50 per cent disabled from gas poisoning, he was relegated to the half-pay list in 1924. He left the Army, sorrowfully, three years later, bearing his galling, eternal rank. With the passage of time that lowly station became a kind of inverted status symbol, epitomized in Yigal Allon's graceful tribute to 'The Captain Who Teaches Generals'. Henceforth he lived by his pen, and he lived well. He was first a sports correspondent, producing in short order four different accounts of the same match for four different outlets – the *Manchester Guardian*, the *Observer*, the *Westminster Gazette*, and *American Lawn Tennis* – and an early *succès d'estime*, *The Lawn Tennis Masters Unveiled* (1926), 'an introduction to all the famous lawn tennis players, showing how far their play is affected by their personality, and what are the secrets of their strokes and their strategy on the court', an intriguing anticipation of the famous *Great Captains Unveiled* (1927), which swiftly followed.

He was also a leading authority on fashion – women's fashion – in particular tight-lacing. For Liddell Hart, as for Franz Kafka, that realm of the senses so anaemically labelled 'fashion' or 'costume' was of indissoluble significance. It was instinct in his thinking and writing, in his way of life, and in his mode of work. The affinity with Kafka is no less striking than the original orientation. Like Kafka, Liddell Hart was an overgrown young man plagued by poor health – influenza in 1918, tonsillitis in 1919, 'soldier's heart' in 1921 and 1922 – and a hypochondriac awareness of his own constitutional inadequacy for the life he wanted to lead, or the man he wanted to be; not only for fighting but even for writing. In his unveiling of General James Wolfe he wrote empathetically that, 'Wolfe seems ever conscious that his life was a race between achievement and disease.' Like Kafka, as a student he self-consciously played at being a dandy and a boulevardier. 'I wore my new blazer and scarf and caused quite a sensation in this drab place called

Derby. Everyone in the streets stopped and stared. It was quite amusing.' In later life traces of dandification persisted, most spectacularly the made-to-measure silk waistcoats from S. Fisher in the Burlington Arcade, or the linen handkerchief protruding roguishly from an immaculate left cuff, or on occasion something a little more unusual. 'Fancy dress ball at Onslow Court Hotel. Jessie [his first wife] took first prize as a Venetian lady – in orange taffeta hooped dress [her waist was 19″]. I took first prize for men, as an Elizabethan. Everyone suggested I should wear a beard permanently!' Liddell Hart was much attracted by the rigour of elegance; and not averse to the riot of display. He wanted to be seen *and* heard. For his tailor, Welsh & Jefferies, of Duke Street, St James's, the rigour of elegance was demanding indeed.

> We found on returning from Cambridge yesterday that the two light-weight suits and the new green-brown one had arrived. I am glad to say that they all fit excellently. But, most unfortunately, they do not have enough pockets. Although I had particularly reminded you at the last fitting that they should have the usual fifteen pockets – six on the jacket, four on the waistcoat, and five on the trousers – they have only eleven in all.
>
> The small inside ticket pocket on the left side of the jacket [for small address book and reserve paper clips] is missing, while there are no hip pockets nor front fob pocket on the trousers. Moreover, the side pockets on the jacket are a little more shallow than usual, so that the cover of my cheque book sticks out.

Like Kafka, also, Liddell Hart was adept at literary cross-dressing. He had a sophisticated appreciation of *l'artillerie de nuit*. He wrote strategic accounts of lawn tennis, fashion-conscious accounts of strategy, and games-playing accounts of war. 'The Western Front idea of attacking the enemy at his strongest point and giving him every chance to develop his heaviest armament was not war, nor is it tennis.' 'It is a proverb of fashion that simplicity is costly' (of the French Plan XVII, for an all-out offensive in 1914). 'So far as any impression of the American Civil War penetrated the consciousness of the General Staffs of Europe it was that of the battledore and shuttlecock tournament in Virginia – which they faithfully imitated with even greater lavishness and ineffectiveness on the battlefields of France from 1914 to 1918.'

Like all great artists, his best ideas were other people's, made matchlessly his own. He had a gift for the expressive phrase – he called them parables – and an unshakeable humanity. He was in general an unsympathetic reader of Clausewitz ('the Mahdi of mass and mutual massacre'), but his reading of the Mahdi's most famous dictum was very acute. For Liddell Hart, 'the object in war is to obtain a better peace – even if only from your own point of view. Hence it is essential to conduct war with constant regard to the peace you desire. This is the truth underlying Clausewitz's definition of war as "a continuation of policy by others means" – the prolongation of that policy through the war into the subsequent peace must always be borne in mind'. The moral he drew was as bold as it was unpopular in its time. 'It is wiser to run [the] risks *of* war for the sake of preserving peace than to run the risks *in* war for the sake of finishing with victory . . . Perseverance in war is only justifiable if there is a good chance of a good end – the prospect of a peace that will balance the sum of human misery incurred in the struggle.' A secure peace, thought Liddell Hart, is better than a pyramid of skulls.

Progressively, the vainglory of 'victory' became one of his most fervent teachings. The inverted commas were more tragic than ironic. All through the low dishonest decade preceding the Second World War, Liddell Hart found himself in a fateful double bind. As he was attaining guru status, so he was losing his faith. While the barbarians sharpened their teeth in the wings, he embarked on an agonizing reappraisal of the moral and intellectual foundations of his calling.

Around the middle of the decade, the guru and the apostate collided. 'War is a monstrous fraud,' he recorded blackly in 1936. 'The more I reflect on the experience of history the more I come to see the instability of solutions achieved by force, and to suspect even those instances where force has had the appearance of resolving difficulties.'

Any reasonable man must hope that war will have no future . . . But for this we must understand the conditions we are attempting to treat. Rational pacifism must be based on a new maxim – 'if you wish for peace, understand war'. Ignorance means the disarmament of the peace-lover, rendering him impotent either to check war or to control its course. History has ample evidence of how often a move to preserve peace, or to restore it, has been paralysed by so-called 'military reasons' that were no more than a rationalization of unreasonable impulses. There lies the tragedy, a tragedy which pacifism of the proverbial ostrich variety has always invited, and still invites. Hence we need to understand not only the causes but also the conduct of war.

If you wish for peace, understand war was an adaptation of the Roman authority Vegetius: 'Let him who desires peace, prepare for war.' For Liddell Hart, the coinage was peculiarly apt to the coiner. It became his motto and his epitaph.

Rational pacifism was something even more personal. In many obvious ways, not least his eternal rank, Liddell Hart was not a pacifist. His writings of the 1920s are sprinkled with slighting references to ignorant or deluded members of that unhappy breed; and in principle he never gave up on organized violence. In practice, however, he came very close. 'There is a streak of pacifism in every intelligent European soldier whose character was shaped by the Western Front in the First World War,' wrote Richard Crossman on 'The Strange Case of Liddell Hart' in 1950. It was a shrewd observation. In Liddell Hart the pacifist streak was ineradicable. As time went on his unbelief yawned wider. By the mid-1930s he was convinced that war was an abhorrence (and total war a nonsense), victory a semblance, and battle an excrescence. During the Second World War – he called it 'the war of Chamberlain's face' – he had grave practical and ethical doubts about almost every aspect of Allied strategy, especially the area bombing campaign, against which he joined with the courageous Bishop Bell in testing the moral significance of the Establishment to the utmost, as Donald Mackinnon expressed it. He deplored the use of the atomic bomb in 1945, and was from the outset an atomic sceptic, supporting the campaign for nuclear disarmament long before there was a Campaign for Nuclear Disarmament, and giving intellectual aid and comfort to the non-violent resistance of the Committee of 100. 'Whatever the value of nuclear weapons as a *deterrent* they are not a *defence*, as their actual use would be suicidal.' Liddell Hart was always a crushing unbeliever.

Shortly before he died he told Bernard Levin, smilingly, that he was and always had been a pacifist. Whatever lay behind the smile, this was a paradoxical position for the world's leading military writer, and a far cry from the philosophy of 1914. By the mid-1960s, at annual reunions with his fellow KOYLIs, the toast to the regiment was drunk to the strains of 'Oh What a Lovely War' on the gramophone. The scene had a cabaret bizarrerie worthy of the original production, yet it was somehow appropriate. 'Anti-war' is a crude slogan – who, after all, is pro-war? – but it is a badge of commitment. Liddell Hart was expertly anti-war.

To be more exact, he was anti-massacre. It was Robert Lowell, a conscientious objector and not a pacifist, who appreciated that 'the one thing worse than war is massacre'. Once a conscientious warrior, Liddell Hart became an equally conscientious objector. If Clausewitz was the Mahdi of massacre, he would be the Lama of limitation. 'Strategy has for its purpose the reduction of fighting to its slenderest possible proportions,' he argued heretically. 'The perfection of strategy would be, therefore, to produce a decision without any serious fighting.' This was the thinking behind his biggest idea: the Indirect Approach.

The Indirect Approach became his signature tune. Announced in 1927, first developed in book form in 1929, it was four times further elaborated by its restless author, in 1941, 1946, 1954, and 1967, sales mushrooming gratifyingly with every new edition. Used as a vade-mecum by various statespersons (Brandt and Nehru), number-less strategists (armchair and armipotent), and the militarily curious of many lands – a Chinese edition came out in 1994 – it continues to live an active and inspirational life to this day, not least in the 'manoeuvrist approach' of official British defence doctrine.

It is more an attitude of mind than an arrow on the map. 'Throughout the ages, effective results in war have rarely been attained unless the approach has had such indirectness as to ensure the opponent's readiness to meet it. The indirectness has usually been physical, and always psychological.' It may even have been unintentional. Indirectness is multiform. As a strategy it is both devious and vaporous. Normally, though not necessarily, it is a manoeuvre directed at the enemy's rear: an eccentric manoeuvre, literally and figuratively. Robert Graves suggested *The Art of Out-Flanking* as a catchpenny title. 'In strategy,' averred Liddell Hart, 'the longest way round is often the shortest way home.'

The business of war, therefore, was not position and attrition and mutual exhaustion (as on the Western Front), but analysis and paralysis and maximal preservation. Liddell Hart prescribed frugality, not prodigality. He also prescribed another parable. His earliest theoretical figure was resurrected. The man-in-the-dark, his original metaphor for personal combat, became the man-in-the-ring. Here he faced a new predicament. He had moves to make, and maxims to follow. War was not milling; it was wrestling, or better yet ju-jitsu. 'In war, as in wrestling, the attempt to throw the opponent without loosening his foothold and upsetting his balance results in self-exhaustion . . . The most effective indirect approach is one that lures or startles the opponent into a false move – so that, as in ju-jitsu, his own effort is turned into the lever of his overthrow.' The enemy had to be unhinged before being unmanned.

Liddell Hart's object was to dethrone what Clausewitz had called the destructive principle, with the decisive battle its apotheosis, in favour of the preservative one: less glorious, perhaps, but more decent and more efficient. Just as Clausewitz overreacted to the antiseptic idea of making war geometrically – the pseudo-science of oblique movements at acute angles expounded by Pfuel, Tolstoy's monstrous theorist-general – so Liddell Hart overreacted to the *Schlacht* and *Schweinerei* of war, the bloodlust of Napoleon the Corsican vampire, and the bloodletting of 1914–18. 'Philanthropists might of course think that there was some ingenious way to disarm or defeat an enemy without too much bloodshed, and might imagine that this is the true goal of the art of war,' wrote Clausewitz scathingly. In these terms Liddell Hart was a philanthropist. Could he be brought to battle even in principle? Eventually he would define away the thing itself. He defined strategy as 'the art of distributing and applying military means to fulfil the ends of policy'. This has become the canonical text in the literature of war. He himself pointed the contrast with Clausewitz ('the use of the engagement for the purpose of the war'). In the meantime he wriggled. His preference was clear: no battle, if possible. The Indirect Approach was to obviate the need for it. 'A surfeit of the "hit" school brings on an attack of the "run" method; and then the pendulum swings back,' his friend T.E. Lawrence remarked cannily in 1928. 'You, at present, are trying . . . to put the balance straight after the orgy of the late war. When you succeed (about 1945) your sheep will pass your bounds of discretion, and have to be chivvied back by some later strategist. Back and forward we go.'

Not coincidentally, Liddell Hart's strategic precept harmonized
with Britain's 'historic practice'. What he called the British Way in
Warfare functioned as a magnificent demonstration of the Grand
Strategy of Indirect Approach. In the conduct of war – according to
Liddell Hart – Britishness was indirectness nationalized.

The two concepts were developed in parallel. He unveiled the
British Way in Warfare in a lecture in 1931. Its title was 'Economic
Pressure or Continental Victories'. Its thesis was Baconian and
Swiftian. 'Thus much is certain,' Bacon had asserted in a famous
essay, 'he that commands the sea may take as much or as little
of the war as he will. Whereas those that be strongest by land
are many times nevertheless in great straits.' And in his scathing
demolitionist tract on 'The Conduct of the Allies' in the wars
against Louis XIV of France, Jonathan Swift had mordantly regretted 'that the Sea was not the Duke of Marlborough's Element,
otherwise the whole Force of the War would infallibly have been
bestowed there, infinitely to the Advantage of his Country, which
would have gone hand in hand with his own'. Two hundred years
later, Liddell Hart took up where Swift left off. He argued that the
British Way in Warfare was essentially businesslike. Finding that
by happy chance she did indeed command the sea, Britannia had
almost instinctively evolved an historic practice based on economic
pressure exercised through sea power. 'This naval body had two
arms: one financial, which embraced the subsidising and military
provisioning of allies; the other military, which embraced sea-borne
expeditions against the enemy's vulnerable extremities.' So far as
Britain was concerned, the war on land (wherever it might be) was
prosecuted by proxy, by the artful dodge of 'lending sovereigns to
sovereigns', and not by sending an expeditionary force. That is
to say, not a *British* expeditionary force. Hessian mercenaries were
another matter. This practice was continued over three centuries,
from the sixteenth to the nineteenth, achieving its ultimate
expression in the epic imbroglio that was the Seven Years' War
(1756–63).

The British Way was to enlist others. It was at the same time a
strategic orientation – maritime rather than continental, periphery-
pecking rather than ironmongering – and a politic disposition:
auxiliary rather than principal in Swift's parlance, conservative
rather than acquisitive in Liddell Hart's. In each instance it was

suitable, flexible, and, above all, profitable. Britain, 'Ever-Greater Britain', had baled out and waxed fat.

Like the wearing of a kilt, like the Indirect Approach itself, the British Way in Warfare is a classic example of an invented tradition. Like many such inventions (including the kilt) it continues to be the object of extraordinary fascination. This has taken several forms. The most arresting is a series of vigorous refutations offered ritually every decade by the cream of commentators from George Orwell to Michael Howard. '"Limited aims" strategy is not likely to be successful unless you are willing to betray your allies whenever it pays you to do so,' wrote Orwell feelingly in the midst of the Second World War. 'Disgusted by the spectacle of Passchendaele, Captain Liddell Hart seems to have ended by believing that wars can be won on the defensive or without fighting – and even indeed that a war is better half-won than won outright. That holds good only when your enemy thinks likewise, a state of affairs which disappeared when Europe ceased to be ruled by an aristocracy.'

The British Way has taken many beatings. But it has also been adapted to many purposes, most recently a swelling interest in 'strategic culture' – the values, beliefs, customs and conditions that combine to influence the use of force, or the consideration of the use of force. The subject is still in its infancy, but one thing is readily apparent. In any assessment of British strategic culture the salience of history and tradition (invented or otherwise) would be difficult to overestimate. Here at least Liddell Hart and his historic practice find complete acceptance, and a rare tribute, apropos yet ironic. The tradition he invented is now part of the culture it purported to explain.

*

Liddell Hart eventually gained admission to some of the places he had always wanted to go. He redeemed his border beginnings. In 1964 he was awarded the honorary degree of Doctor of Letters at Oxford. A large audience relished the Public Orator's ingenuity in finding some Latin for the anachronistic tank: *clibanus*, an iron cooking vessel or oven. A few months later he was offered an honorary fellowship of his Cambridge college. His seventieth birthday was celebrated by the publication of two stout volumes of memoirs, setting the record straight down to the Panzer spring of

1940; and a *Festschrift, The Theory and Practice of War*, with admiring contributions from a decorated company of scholars and soldiers from all over the world. 'What a marvellous life you have – what is the word I want? – *sculptured* for yourself,' wrote Storm Jameson, on reading the former. 'It really is like a sculptor working in stone or marble, needing as much patience, and strength, and vision, vision above all. Intensely hard but – surely? – intensely satisfying.' Guy Chapman's conclusion was brief and to the point. 'I suppose we should shoot you and bury you with the OM.' In the New Year's Honours List of 1966, Liddell Hart finally received a knighthood for services to military history, thirty years after John Buchan had first proposed it. In spite of his public protestations – 'a man has gone far towards attaining a philosophy of life when he realizes, reflectively or instinctively, that honour is more satisfying than honours' – there was nothing he desired more; though until the very end he played hard to get. He refused to consider a CH ('manifestly a second-level honour') and lobbied instead for Chapman's second suggestion. 'A number of people have suggested that the only fitting award now, commensurate with my standing in other countries, would be an OM. . . . If you are inclined to share that view, a word from you to the PM might be very helpful.' When it became clear that it was a knighthood or nothing, he took it with both hands, protesting to the last. 'Personally, I value it only for such practical utility as it may have as a kind of *laisser passer* with minor officials and bureaucratic impediments. I appreciate far more . . . the *Festschrift* . . . the Oxford Hon. D. Litt., and the Cambridge honorary fellowship at Corpus.'

He was usually twenty years ahead of his time. His close-range prophecy was relatively poor, spoiled by passionate advocacy. Long range, however, he came into his own. This foresight was not confined to armoured warfare, where his parable of 'the expanding torrent' foretold the *Blitzkrieg* with brilliant clarity and devastating personal consequences. His writings on the potential of air warfare in the 1920s have the unmistakable flavour of nuclear deterrence. 'Though in Europe an air blow would be decisive, its achievement would probably depend on one side being superior in the air, either in numbers of aircraft or by the possession of some surprise device. Where air equality existed among rival nations, and each was as industrially and politically vulnerable, it is possible that either would hesitate to employ the air attack for fear of instant retaliation.' The Lama of limitation was not fazed by the nuclear revolution.

In the suggestive final chapter of his *Deterrent or Defence* (1960) is a passage much quoted by President John F. Kennedy and his circle in the days before the Cuban Missile Crisis, and by many others since: at once an amplification of his famous maxim – if you wish for peace, understand war – and an illustration of the analects that are his quintessential literary legacy.

> There is no panacea for peace that can be written out in a formula like a doctor's prescription. But one can set down a series of practical points – elementary principles drawn from the sum of human experience at all times. Study war, and learn from its history. Keep strong, if possible. In any case, keep cool. Have unlimited patience. Never corner an opponent, and always assist him to save his face. Put yourself in his shoes – so as to see things through his eyes. Avoid self-righteousness like the devil – nothing is so self-blinding. Cure yourself of two commonly fatal delusions – the idea of victory and the idea that war cannot be limited.

The style is the man. Liddell Hart marked a meaningful reflection in the memoirs of his writer friend Osbert Sitwell: 'Had I been content, as the prudent advise, to live within my pay and my allowance, I should have learned to pare and prune and scrape, it may be, but I should never have won renown. I should have remained a mute, inglorious Osbert Sitwell. But my blood did not lean in that direction. I heard from far off, in many directions, the drumming and singing of the exuberant in life and art. I was of their race, and their faults were mine.' Liddell Hart's blood did not lean in that direction either. He too could hear the drumming and the singing. He was not a mute, inglorious Liddell Hart, but a self-made one. He was the Liddell Hart of the twentieth century.

For this there was a price to be paid. 'One can't be angry with one's own time without damage to oneself.' Liddell Hart was very angry, 'flame-hot', as Lawrence said, 'on his pet subject, which is the deficiency of thinking in the British Army. He lives for the avoidance of battle and murder, and for winning campaigns by wise dispositions . . . I think he is really interested in generals of individuality, and his books on Sherman and Scipio were excellent: really excellent. And one chapter of his study of war-from-the-British-angle was almost the only bit of abstract military philosophy in English. Yet he is not a philosopher: all his knowledge applies itself.' If ever a writer was engaged, it was Liddell Hart. Victory was a delusion; but he wrote to win. He set out to make a difference, and he did. Not everyone was grateful. He had enemies, and jealousies, and callouses, and pain. 'We make out the quarrel with others, rhetoric, but of the quarrel with ourselves, poetry.' It was said of Churchill that he mobilized the English language and sent it into battle. It could be said of Liddell Hart that he mobilized battle and sent it into the English language. Much of his output was rushed. He seemed incapable of working slowly even when he had the means. What was not rushed was too long-delayed. He quarrelled more with others than with himself: the rhetoric outstrips the poetry. Yet his colossal achievement cannot be gainsaid. 'A man produces so many words,' mused Elias Canetti, 'and creates so few.' Basil Liddell Hart created more than most.

*   *   *

All quotations by Liddell Hart as in The Alchemist of War *by Alex Danchev (Weidenfeld & Nicholson, 1998).*

Victor Bonham-Carter

WULLY ROBERTSON:
FROM FOOTMAN TO FIELD-MARSHAL

In 1915 died Lady Cardigan, widow of the 7th Earl of Cardigan, hero of the Charge of the Light Brigade at the Battle of Balaclava in October 1854. At the time of her death, the Chief of Staff of the British Expeditionary Force (BEF) in France happened to be Sir William Robertson who – forty years earlier – had been a footman in the service of the Cardigan family at Deene Park, Northamptonshire. Will – as he was known at home – or Wully, as he was covertly called by fellow officers – must have had some curious memories.

Son of Thomas Robertson, village tailor-cum-postmaster at Welbourn in Lincolnshire, and of Ann Dexter Beet, a woman of strong character and firm religious faith, his was a modest but secure upbringing. He attended the church primary school and did well. He liked learning, was an avid reader, could draw, and showed much interest in geography and maps. Clearly he was a bright boy. After leaving school, he got a job as a garden hand at the rectory, where the incumbent arranged for him to have extra lessons with his daughters, learning French with a Mademoiselle.

After four years' domestic service Wully volunteered for the Army in 1877. His action horrified his family, who subscribed to the popular view that all soldiers were lewd and licentious. His mother, particularly, was distraught. She wrote:

> My very dear Boy
> you never could mean what you put in your Letter on Sunday
> . . . what cause have you for such a Low Life . . . you have as good

> Home as any one else in our Station ... you know you are the
> Great Hope of the Family ... the Army is a refuge for all idle
> people ... I would rather Bury you than see you in a red coat.

Wully was not to be dissuaded, however. 'I was seventeen and three-
quarters old when ... I took the Queen's Shilling from a recruiting
sergeant in the city of Worcester on the 13th of November 1877.
The minimum age for enlistment was eighteen, but as I was tall for
my years the sergeant said that the deficient three months would
involve no difficulty, and he promptly wrote me down as eighteen
years and two months, so as to be on the safe side.'

From Worcester Wully was posted to G Troop, 16th Lancers,
then stationed at Aldershot where he was advised to deposit his
watch with the sergeant major, as it was unsafe to leave it lying
about. In 1877 the Army was still a social anachronism, for which
the system of purchase had been largely responsible: whereby an
intending officer had to buy his commission and in effect his
promotion as well. However, in 1871 purchase had been abolished
by Royal Warrant, and £7 million paid by way of compensation to
serving officers. Changes, however, came slowly.

Wully spent ten and a half years in the ranks, during which time
he gained quick and regular promotion, becoming Troop Sergeant
Major in March 1885, at the age of twenty-five. He had got on by
hard work, keen intelligence, and dogged determination. Only one
higher non-commissioned rank, that of Regimental Sergeant Major,
remained open to him, but that was a matter of waiting for dead
man's shoes – inconceivable for a young man of Wully's calibre.

The obvious move was to apply for commission; but for the
ranker there were formidable difficulties – educational, financial,
and social. Educational was the least of these. As an NCO Wully
had probably acquired more knowledge than most junior officers.
He was already an instructor in musketry, signalling and elementary
intelligence duties. Otherwise all he lacked was a First-Class Certificate in Education, which he duly obtained in 1883. Finance was
more serious, but at least it was tangible. A subaltern was paid over
£100 a year, a captain less than £200. That meant that a cavalry
officer needed a private income of not less than £300 a year – a
conservative figure. Social barriers were the real crux. A ranker
could never disguise his origin. He was continually being given away

by his accent, tastes, habits, jokes, relations, friends (or lack of them), and enforced parsimony. In the fashionable regiments, a social misfit was got rid of at once.

However, Wully refused to admit defeat. He read all the books on tactics, strategy, and military history that he could find: so that finally – encouraged by a sympathetic commanding officer – he seized the chance to take a commission in India, where pay was higher and expenses proportionately less. In June 1888 he was gazetted Second-Lieutenant in the 3rd Dragoon Guards, then stationed at Muttra. Before leaving he wrote a letter to his mother, long reconciled to his choice of career, who replied:

> My dear William,
>   Goodbye and May God bless you and Keep you is the constant
> Prayer of your Loving Mother Ann Robertson.
>   Deuteronomy Ch4 Verse 9.

Wully was kindly received by brother officers in his new regiment, and his work was neither difficult nor strenuous. However, he needed all his powers of self-denial to keep his end up in the mess. 'Water was the only drink I could afford ... not altogether agreeable when others were drinking champagne; and I had to be content with a fixed amount of tobacco and cheroots at two shillings a hundred.'

He also had to exert will power to adapt himself to the Indian climate. Instead of resting in the heat of the day like everyone else, he spent his afternoons learning Hindustani, to the disgust of his *munshi* or 'teacher'. By the end of two years he had qualified as an interpreter in five Indian languages, adding a sixth (Gurkhali) later. The other way he got on was by making himself indispensable in the regimental office, standing in for the adjutant when ill, organizing events, and negotiating with contractors – besides playing a full part in training and regimental duties. But it was a hard row and a lonely one. To his father, he wrote: 'It is miserable out here ... how often I feel cut off from all friendship ... not once has any one taken offence at being in my company; but there is much difference between this and sincere mutual interest; this cannot naturally be between a born gentleman and one who is only now beginning to try to become one.'

The worst, however, was almost over. Within just a few

years he was to gain immensely in self-confidence and content-
ment, through marriage, promotion and official recognition of his
abilities.

In 1891 Wully had his first experience of active service, as
Railway Transport Officer to a mixed force sent to deal with
tribesmen raiding the frontier near Kohat. Next year he was posted
to Simla to work in the Intelligence Branch, concerned with territories adjoining northern India, and in June 1894 he started on a
three months' journey to the Pamirs at the foot of the Himalayas. In
the following year he was attached to a force sent to quell disorders
in Chitral and rescue an army unit under siege in the capital. Soon
afterwards he fought a contest of his own, when suddenly attacked
by a couple of local 'guides', one of whom slashed him with his own
sword. He was lucky to escape with his life, but duly recovered from
his wound before rejoining the Intelligence staff at Simla and being
promoted Captain.

In late 1894 he married Mildred Palin, daughter of an Indian
Army general. The marriage was lasting and harmonious, producing
a family of two sons and two daughters. Brian, the eldest, was a
distinguished soldier in his own right, becoming chief administrative
officer of the Eighth Army in the Second World War and the first
British High Commissioner to the Federal Republic of Germany in
1949.

Mildred gave her husband much practical help in preparing for
the entrance examination to the Staff College, for which he was
awarded a special nomination. He was the first ranker officer ever
to enter the College, and in 1896 he left for England, after eight and
a half years in India – and nineteen since he took the Queen's
Shilling at Worcester in 1877.

Wully joined the Staff College at Camberley in January 1897
and graduated at the end of December 1898. He could hardly have
timed it better, for he emerged at the moment when there was an
urgent need for trained staff officers, ready to ride the tide of war
and reform. Once dubbed 'a haven for shirkers', the College was
now attracting some of the best young brains in the Army, men like
Haig and Allenby who were to rise to prominence in the First World
War. Within a very few years, Wully rose from being a diffident
ranker Captain to that of Lieut-Colonel of high professional ability,
confident of his powers, bothered no longer about his social origins.

One of his teachers at Camberley was Colonel G.F.R. Henderson, a military historian, who became Director of Intelligence to Lord Roberts in the Boer War and sent for Wully to join his staff. After nine months in South Africa, Wully returned to his previous job at the Colonial Section at the War Office and stayed there until September 1901, when the entire Intelligence Division was reorganized. Wully was put in charge of the Foreign Section, with the rank of Brevet Lieutenant-Colonel, having four subsections and nine officers under him, some of them his seniors. In 1904 Intelligence was expanded, Wully's appointment confirmed and his term of office extended, so that he did not leave the War Office until 1907. In a little over five years he had transformed the Section and left his mark upon it. There was a great need for accurate information: so handbooks were produced, one for each foreign power, and a wide circulation given to military and technical journals. Wully also secured grants for his officers to visit the countries they were studying, while he himself travelled widely to look at past or potential battlefields. It might be thought that his insistence on detail clouded overall interpretation. Not so. In his view proven facts were the foundation of broader understanding. As to the next war, Germany – he felt – was the real enemy, thanks to the massive growth of German industry and aggressive foreign policy, sharpened by the Kaiser's genius for *faux pas*.

In 1907, for the first time in his life, Wully was not given a fresh appointment straightaway and found himself 'unemployed'. It was an unpalatable experience. His pay – so-called half-pay – fell from £800 to £300 a year. With a wife and children, the outlook was bleak. However, he refused to be idle. With the help of his wife, he set about translating German manuals sent him by the War Office. Mildred outlined a literal version, which Wully then converted into appropriate jargon. A by-product was the insight the work gave him into German military technique and armament.

Although half-pay only lasted four months, Wully fully expected to command troops – something he had not done since leaving India. The irony was that his excellent record as a staff officer got in the way. By nature he was a born commander of men, and he was long overdue for a command for the advancement of his career. However, instead of the brigade he had hoped for, he felt obliged on purely practical grounds to accept yet another staff post, that of

Assistant Quarter-Master General (AQMG) at Aldershot Command
– with the proviso that he be given a command at the next
opportunity. It never came.

In the summer of 1910 Wully was appointed Commandant of
the Staff College, in succession to Henry Wilson, who then became
Director of Military Operations (DMO) at the War Office. Of Wully
a student wrote:

> He was a great Commandant, very severe but at the same time
> human and encouraging. We were all frightened to death of him,
> yet admired him greatly and were fond of him. On one occasion
> he roused the students at 2.00 am to conduct a picket exercise. We
> all started off in a bad temper, but luckily I had marked on the
> map where I had put the pickets and, by the Grace of God, and
> after the devil of a climb in the dark, we arrived at the top of the
> right mountain (in Wales), half-an-hour before dawn. We were
> then told to go home independently. Breakfast at 8.00 am. Start
> work at 9.00 am as usual.

Britain declared war on Germany on 4 August 1914, and by
the 20th the BEF had taken station – just in time – on the left of the
French Fifth Army under Lanrezac. Due to a last-minute reshuffle
Sir John French, Commander in Chief (C-in-C), picked Archibald
Murray as Chief of Staff (CGS), which allowed Wully to replace
Murray as Quarter-Master General (QMG) in France. Henry Wilson, who spoke the language fluently, in due course became Chief
Liaison Officer with the French. Wully crossed to France on 14
August and devoted the first few days to reconnoitring areas through
which the British troops were moving. He had few doubts about
the immediate future. At the Staff College he had lectured on the
technique of retreat and practised it in exercises. Realism indeed, as
the tiny BEF (six divisions at most at the outset) stood plumb in the
path of the German onslaught through Belgium, and was forced
back – between 24 August and 5 September – from Mons to the
River Marne, but survived as a fighting force. Wully was responsible
for supplies of every sort, and rose superbly to the occasion. 'In the
retreat, a large amount of clothing and equipment were either lost,
captured, or thrown away . . . and it was my duty to see that they
were immediately replaced . . . the expedient was also adopted of
dumping supplies – flitches of bacon, sides of beef, cheese, boxes

of biscuits, etc., alongside the road, so that the troops might help themselves as they passed.'

Wully's brilliant improvisations saved the day for the BEF. Moreover, the immediate agony was nearing its end. Sir John French was persuaded (somewhat reluctantly on his part) to advance into the gap left by the German right wing (under von Kluck) swinging to the south-east away from Paris. The BEF was thus prodded into the counter-stroke that took the Allied forces back to the river Aisne, an advance of 70 miles. On 14 September, however, with the arrival of German reserves, the advance was halted and, quite soon, trench warfare set in, all the way from near the Channel coast, down almost as far as the Alps in the south.

Wully's chief worry was that industrial production at home nowhere near met the needs in France. Moreover, the First Battle of Ypres (19 October–14 November) put an enormous strain on supply and communications. Stocks of ammunition visibly vanished: so that at one moment the 18-pounder guns and 4.5 howitzers – the staple field artillery – were reduced to a ration of 3 rounds per day. Wully sent a constant stream of demands to the War Office for practically everything a soldier needed for survival in the bitter Flanders weather, and for the prosecution of the war.

In most quarters false optimism temporarily infected the conduct of operations. The outstanding exception was Lord Kitchener – or 'K' as he was known – who forecast that the war would *not* be over by Christmas, but would last several years, and involve millions of men. In other respects his judgement was at fault. Long absence from Britain had cut him off from the major army reforms introduced by Haldane under the Liberal Government. He thought the Regular Army far too small and the Territorial Army beneath contempt: an entirely erroneous opinion based on preconceived notions about part-time soldiering. However, his reputation with Parliament and the public was so high that Asquith had decided, at the very last moment, to haul him off a cross-Channel steamer and appoint him Secretary of State for War – the first time a serving soldier had held the post for almost a century. Kitchener suffered from an inability to delegate. When he gave advice, it usually took the form of an order or pronouncement, which led him to use subordinates unable to stand up to him. Kitchener was sixty-four, but thanks to his national reputation as a military commander who

had never lost a battle, he never admitted that the 1914–18 war
was incapable of being directed by one man. His death by drowning
– en route to Russia in June 1916 – was a deliverance.

In January 1915 Wully accepted the invitation to become CGS
in place of Murray. He had hesitated because he knew that Sir John
French was inadequate as C-in-C, was touchy and impulsive and
unable to control large formations, nor was he on good terms with
Joffre who all during 1915 was conducting a series of disastrous
offensives in Artois, Champagne, and the Verdun-Nancy area –
driven by a burning desire to rid France of the enemy, at whatever
cost.

What part should or could the BEF play? Morally it was under
obligation to assist the French offensives; and Wully was convinced
that the war could only be won or lost in France. All the other
fronts that surfaced in the course of the war – Salonika, Italy, Egypt,
etc. – were peripheral and could only weaken the main effort in the
west. The one exception was the Dardanelles campaign, which lasted
all through 1915, but which failed – basically – owing to incompetence and bad planning.

Wully and Douglas Haig (who succeeded Sir John French) were
both 'Westerners'; but they were also aware that the BEF would not
be ready for a major effort before 1916. Yet, something had to be
done right away to assist the French. Thus the BEF was engaged
in five operations during 1915 – Neuve Chapelle (10–15 March),
Second Battle of Ypres (22 April–5 May), Aubers Ridge (9 May),
Festubert (15–25 May), and Loos-Lens (25 September–16 October):
all were costly in casualties, and virtually nothing was gained other
than expensive experience. Second Ypres – a ferocious battle that
had to be won to prevent a breakthrough and was the first time that
the Germans used gas – left the British with a constricted salient
which Sir Horace Smith-Dorrien (commanding the BEF Second
Army) wanted to evacuate. Sir John French promptly sacked him,
but ordered Wully to break the news in a tactful manner. Wully
drove up in his car, pulled Smith-Dorrien aside, saying, ''Orace,
you're for 'ome.'

Towards the end of 1915 Wully found himself in an extraordinary position, for he was being privately consulted by Haig (commanding the BEF First Army), Kitchener and the Prime Minister, no
less; and was attending meetings of the Cabinet. At Kitchener's

request he was submitting memoranda of military policy – essentially that the Secretary of State should be separate from the Chief of the Imperial General Staff (CIGS); and that the latter, backed by a general staff of trained officers, should be the 'one authoritative channel' to advise a war council (or committee) for the conduct of the war. Kitchener then offered to resign, but Asquith persuaded him to remain with modified powers. In December Wully was appointed CIGS and Kitchener never interfered with strategy again. However, the two men got on well together and agreed a modus vivendi whereby the CIGS issued (his own!) orders 'under the authority' of the Secretary of State. Kitchener called this arrangement 'Our Bargain' and stuck to it faithfully until his death. On 8 December Sir John French resigned and Sir Douglas Haig became C-in-C of the BEF. The two Westerners were now in charge.

Wully's first task was to establish the authority of the General Staff beyond all doubt as the supreme planning organism of the Army. He split the Operations Directorate into two – Operations and Intelligence – appointing Sir Frederick Maurice as DMO and Sir George Macdonogh as DMI; both had held corresponding posts in France. With Sir Robert Whigham as Deputy CIGS and others in subordinate posts who knew his ways, he assembled a team of professionals, but there were two sources of friction. The first related to personalities. Wully was by no means an easy man himself, yet he needed all the support he could get to master the fearful problems that beset him every day. So long as Kitchener stuck by the Bargain as he did, and Asquith remained Prime Minister, Wully felt reasonably secure. However, when Lloyd George succeeded Kitchener as Secretary of State in July 1916 and became Prime Minister of the Coalition Government in December 1916, antagonism and stress developed.

The second source of friction was the lack of any permanent body for co-operation between the Allies before the Inter-Allied Supreme War Council was set up at the end of 1917. Hitherto, action had depended on ad hoc meetings with Joffre for the prosecution of the campaign in France, while at home the Cabinet relied on the succession of advisory committees, e.g. the Dardanelles Committee, and on ministers dealing direct with service chiefs. As Wully said sardonically, since the Navy was a technical service, naval officers were adept at taking cover behind technical jargon;

but anyone, it seemed, could lay down the law about military strategy. It told him on him heavily.

> At 11.00 am every day of the week except Sunday, I was required to attend the meeting of the Cabinet . . . in order to report events of the past 24 hours; to predict, when required, what they might be during the next 24; and to elucidate or justify such General Staff recommendations as awaited Government sanction . . . Thus I seldom left the meetings before 1.30 pm and serious encroachments were made upon the time available for other work.

Sir Maurice Hankey, Secretary of the War Committee, said that Wully was a tower of strength. His policy, if not very inspired, was always definite, and his advice therefore always consistent. He was an admirable administrator and, once a decision was taken, the Committee could rely on him to carry it out. However, like Haig, he suffered from one drawback – he had no fluency in speech. Hankey added: 'In speech he was slow and deliberate. He never uttered an opinion he had not thought out. He would address an international conference in correct French (carefully written out as a rule) and with an English accent.'

It was this characteristic that aggravated Lloyd George, an instinctive man of action, who thought and felt fast. Wully was baffled by the quick unpredictable shifts of debate, and on such occasions would take refuge in silence and scowls, or in a series of grunts, fearsome disapproving sounds, which were the armour of a deliberate mind, but never a stupid one.

Hankey concluded: 'Perhaps the greatest quality, transcending his great powers of work, his austerity of principle, his organising ability, and his judgement of men, was "character". His was a dominating personality.'

Five days after his appointment as CIGS, Wully's plea to regard France and Flanders as the main theatre of operations was approved by the War Committee. That meant he was free to salve what he could from the five other fronts outside France. The Dardanelles had recently been evacuated, but the other four – Salonika, Egypt, Mesopotamia, and East Africa – were not capable of dissolution, and locked up large forces until the end of the war. Although all contributed to final victory, they were liabilities so far as the Western Front was concerned.

The principal British effort in France during 1916 took place on the Somme, the first full-scale offensive launched by the British Army. The loss of nearly 60,000 men (one third killed) on the very first day – 1 July – has gone down in the black annals of history. Most of the casualties were volunteers (from Kitchener's New Armies), for compulsory military service was not enacted till 25 May – far too late for the Somme. It is not possible to evaluate the battle here except to say that it was launched earlier than planned in order to relieve the French Army bleeding to death at Verdun. The Somme lasted four months and gained relatively little ground. For Wully, as for Haig, it represented the first great test of Western strategy, but its appalling cost did not devalue the strategic concept, for the fundamental weakness lay in the inability of tactics to validate the strategy; that came later as the war progressed.

Wully and Haig had much in common, though their social backgrounds were in glaring contrast. They were both regular soldiers at the top of their profession, disliking politics and mistrusting most of the politicians. On the other hand, while Haig had the support of fellow officers on the spot, Wully was in a truly lonely situation, for he had to grapple with vast and various problems of manpower, material, movement, communications, etc. and answer for the progress, or lack of it, on *all* the fronts.

Inasmuch as this was part of the job of the CIGS, Wully did not complain. What he found hard to bear was the unending struggle to secure government support, the amateurishness of ministers, and their ignorance of logistics. 'They regard me,' he told Haig, 'as an optimistic ass, when not as a stupid soldier. They think and many say – that all soldiers are stupid.'

In London the Somme was the sombre background that darkened every official meeting. No one knew exactly what was happening, except that the cost in casualties was colossal, and expected Wully to come up with the news. He couldn't do so as, for what seemed a long time, Haig told him nothing. Eventually he did render a report that satisfied the War Committee for the time being. Lloyd George had another complaint. As Secretary of State, he rejected the Bargain (with Kitchener) and insisted, on constitutional grounds, on being fully apprised before Wully communicated with the War Committee. He had his way, and quite rightly so.

One of Lloyd George's first acts as Prime Minister was to replace

the War Committee with a War Cabinet of five men which, thanks
to the efficiency of the Secretariat headed by Hankey, resulted in a
marked improvement in the momentum of government. In France
Joffre was at last displaced, his successor being General Nivelle who
had made a big reputation at Verdun by a system of limited attacks
backed by creeping barrages. Nivelle impressed Haig, not least by
his ability to speak English (he had an English mother); and Lloyd
George likewise sang his praises. Wully's comment was 'I've 'eard
different.'

Nivelle combined personal ambition with a belief in the mathematical certainty of his formula attack, and he was determined to
apply it in the next offensive, a predominantly French affair, not a
process of attrition but a massive knockout blow that would ensure
success in a matter of hours at minimum cost. However, events
combined to disrupt Nivelle's plans. In the early spring of 1917 the
Germans had retired to a fortified position of great strength, known
as the Hindenburg Line, and awaited events. In April the British
Army launched an offensive to the east of Arras, designed to capture
the northern hinge of the Line and break into open country beyond.
After initial success and an advance of up to 5 miles on a front of
40 miles, the attack petered out by the end of May. Nivelle's
offensive on the Aisne likewise made some progress by the standards
of the time, but at such a crippling cost that it destroyed the morale
of the French troops and generated outbreaks of mutiny, exacerbated also by unrest behind the lines and war fatigue. Pétain, the
real hero of Verdun, had to be called in to suppress the disorders
but also to humanize the conditions of service and restore confidence. For many months the French were in an acutely precarious
situation, and this had an important bearing on Haig's subsequent
operations.

The Nivelle episode had horrified Wully from the start: for
instance, his criminal carelessness about security. He wrote to Haig:
'Nivelle very stupidly sent to the French Government his whole plan
which he had previously given you. This was sent to our Foreign
Office and was hektographed off in the usual manner, and I suppose
there are now dozens of copies of the paper about London to say
nothing of Paris. I myself did not intend to send it even to the War
Cabinet.'

Wully simply never believed that Nivelle's successes at Verdun could automatically be repeated on a large scale – German defences this time were too deep and the fronts too wide; and he also felt that another failure in France would endanger the British plan to clear the Belgian coast in the next year (Third Ypres). But the most serious trouble arose out of a secret plot hatched by Lloyd George and Nivelle to place the latter in supreme command of both Armies. Neither Haig nor Wully knew anything of this until all was revealed in a document passed to them at a conference in Calais on 26 February. The scene has been described by Sir Edward Spears: 'General Robertson dined with General Maurice. As he finished he was handed a translation of the Nivelle proposals. As a stimulus to good digestion they were a failure. Wully's face went the colour of mahogany, his eyes became perfectly round, his eyebrows slanted outwards like a forest of bayonets held at the charge – in fact he showed every sign of having a fit. "Get 'Aig," he bawled.'

Haig arrived and, like Wully, was stunned by what he read but reacted differently, retreating within his armour of well-bred reserve, lest anything he said might savour of his 'saving his skin' as C-in-C. Wully, in a fury, marched along to see the Prime Minister. A stormy scene ensued. Lloyd George said that the War Cabinet had already agreed to the principle of unified command, and showed him the door. Wully did not sleep well and at 6 a.m. next morning demanded to see Nivelle, who expressed pained surprise. Did not General Robertson know? The idea had not come from him, but had been agreed by the two Governments before the conference and had instructed him to work out the details. This he had done.

It transpired that this was a barefaced lie.

However, the hostile exchanges continued; and even when Lloyd George threatened to close down the conference, Wully refused to budge. Hankey and Maurice then acted as mediators, Maurice recalling the precedent when Gouraud, commander of the French troops in Gallipoli, had conformed to the orders of Ian Hamilton, the C-in-C, but retained the right to appeal to his own government. This proved to be the solution accepted by both parties at Calais although Nivelle – a small man intoxicated by personal ambition – continued to try to treat Haig as a subordinate. But events settled the issue in the end.

Plans for Third Ypres (Passchendaele) were being debated in detail in the spring of 1917, and gathered momentum as the French

Army mutiny developed. It became clear that the British would have to bear the burden of attack, with some French support, if available. Haig's plan was to break the enemy defences north and east of Ypres, capture Roulers and Thourout (an important railway junction) and advance north-east to Ostend and Zeebrugge. There were bonuses: to clear the U-boat bases on the Channel coast, offset the Russian collapse before the Germans transferred divisions to the west, and generally to maintain pressure on the Western Front. In June the capture of the Messines Ridge, a fortified area just south of the Ypres salient, was a good omen.

At that moment Wully stood at the summit of his career. He had been proved right about Nivelle and the ignoble subterfuge for unified command connived at by Lloyd George, and he was regarded by the nation, as well as by those in the know, as a father figure of resolution and common sense. However, Wully had disturbing reservations about Third Ypres. He did not believe that the British should fight unsupported by the French, or that the Germans would be unable to stand further battering. He knew that the terrain in Flanders was vulnerable, with a high water table, criss-crossed by land drains and subject to flooding; and he doubted Haig's contention that each objective should be secured by a fully mounted assault in a continuous offensive – what happened if one or more of these components failed? And he knew that Britain was running short of manpower. However, as a Westerner, and out of loyalty to Haig, he deliberately backed Third Ypres which, after preliminaries, was launched on 31 July 1917.

It is not proposed to analyse Third Ypres beyond saying that it finished on 10 November at a cost of a quarter of a million casualties for an average gain of four miles, and yielded an aftermath of suffering that has never been forgotten. Surprisingly the French contribution of four divisions under General Anthoine did remarkably well, helped indirectly by Pétain's limited operations elsewhere. The Germans suffered heavily, but were never overwhelmed and made good their losses by transfers from the Eastern Front. In October the Italians were routed at Caporetto, and had to be rescued by the dispatch of six British and five French divisions, before the line was held on the River Piave. Wully visited General Cadorna's HQ at Treviso in the Udine on 31 October. His visit confirmed his worst fears about peripheral fronts and, on hearing of the fall of

Cividale, commented sourly, 'Shittydale'. Hardly had he returned home when, on 20 November, a bold and initially successful attack by British tanks at Cambrai ended in deep disappointment. Three hundred tanks suddenly shot out of the mist and took the defenders by surprise, breaching a gap on a 6-mile front, a brilliant stroke. However, the supporting infantry could not follow up fast enough when the tanks had reached their limit, and a powerful enemy counter-attack recovered all the ground lost and gained some more.

These failures in the latter part of 1917 fell right into Lloyd George's lap, and accelerated the creation of the Inter-Allied Supreme War Council, by now accepted as essential for the coordination of the Allied war effort, with HQ at Versailles. On 2 November the scheme was approved by the War Cabinet and Henry Wilson appointed Permanent British Military Representative (PMR). Foch was nominated for France. Wully disapproved and on 7 November, when the powers of the new Council were being discussed by the War Cabinet, he walked ostentatiously out of the room. In fact he did not object to the principle but deeply distrusted Lloyd George.

The declared object of the Supreme War Council was to 'watch over the general conduct of the war'. For this purpose the PMRs were appointed as 'technical advisers'. Ostensibly an advisory body, the new Council incorporated a dualism, for any advice on military matters would either duplicate or controvert the advice and actions of the General Staffs of the participant governments – in short, what happened if Wully and Henry Wilson disagreed? The orthodox solution was to fuse the function of the CIGS and the PRM; but Lloyd George would not have Wully at Versailles, and Wully thought that the whole concept would not work in practice.

Although this seemed principally a conflict between personalities and a dispute about procedure, the reality resided in the fact that the war was fast approaching its final and critical stage. Russia was in the throes of revolution, and the German Army was transferring troops from the Eastern to the Western Front, in preparation for the massive offensive of March 1918. This was delivered against the British Fifth Army and, once again, came within striking distance of Paris, before the Allied counter-strokes drove the Germans back to defeat in November 1918.

Wully and Haig were both aware of the German threat and of

the contraction of manpower affecting the British and French Armies by early 1918. Wully in particular pressed General Pershing, C-in-C of the American troops, now slowly arriving in France, to provide the reserves that the Allies so desperately needed. The matter was discussed at a meeting of the Supreme War Council at Versailles at the end of January 1918, but Lloyd George demanded more positive statistics regarding combat strengths, reserves and casualties, besides favouring an offensive against Turkey in the Middle East – since the Western Front in France had proved so costly for so long and yielded such meagre results. Wully stuck to his guns and proposed once again that the Chiefs of Staff should collectively direct Allied strategy.

The arguments continued with one important change: namely that the PMRs, hitherto only advisers, be given executive authority; further, that the strength, composition and employment of a general reserve for all the fronts be controlled by a committee of the PMRs – to be known as the Executive War Board – with General Foch in the chair – and have the power to transmit orders to the armies concerned: in short an embryonic form of Inter-Allied High Command. Here was the crux. As Wully pointed out, the Board now had all the powers reserved only to the chiefs of staff and ministers of war: in short a rival authority to the constitutional arrangements of the countries concerned. This was something that Wully could not accept and it led to his resignation as CIGS on 16 February 1918.

This really is the end of the story, other than to record Wully's subsequent appointments as C-in-C Home Forces, C-in-C British Army of the Rhine, and promotion to the rank of Field-Marshal. All were in effect consolation prizes for a man who had begun life as Will Robertson and ended it in 1933 as Field-Marshal Sir William Robert Robertson, GCB, GCMG, GCVO, DSO, DCL, LLD.

John Whittam

MUSSOLINI

'It is useless for anyone to attempt my life. It has been foretold that I shall not die a violent death. That is a prophecy in which I believe.' Benito Mussolini was talking to a British Embassy official just minutes after the anarchist Lucetti's bombs had failed to kill him. This was in September 1926, the third out of four attempted assassinations within a year; only the deranged Violet Gibson drew blood when her bullet grazed the bridge of his nose. On 28 April 1945 the more accurate fire of communist partisans brought an end to his charmed life. Mussolini had survived so many crises in the past thirty years that his failure to reach the Swiss border and fulfil the prophecy seems almost an affront. It is easy to see why Mussolini has attracted so many biographers and why, for most of this century, he has become the best known Italian since Julius Caesar. Mussolini's life was not only an Italian version of the American dream – instead of log cabin to White House, rustic cottage to Palazzo Venezia – but seemed to be the embodiment of a new ideology called Fascism. Interpretations of this phenomenon and its significance for Italy and the rest of Europe have been endlessly debated from the 1920s to the present. Mussolini proclaimed that the twentieth century would be the century of fascism. It would, in fact, have been closer to the truth to call it instead, the century of fascist historiography.

*

Mussolini was born on 29 July 1883. Unlike 20 April in Hitler's Third Reich, the Italian dictator sternly discouraged any celebration of his birthday as this would attract attention to his age. He was less reticent about his birthplace, which was Dovia near Predappio in the Romagna. This obscure settlement, difficult to locate on the map, later became a place of pilgrimage for devotees of the Duce. His father Alessandro was a blacksmith, a prominent left-wing anti-clerical and revolutionary activist. An exponent of the politics of confrontation, he taught his son to act as well as to think and thereby instinctively anticipated the philosopher Giovanni Gentile's insistence that no value could be attached 'to any thought which had not already been translated into action'. It was fitting, therefore, that Gentile became Mussolini's first education minister and co-author of the official definition of fascism. Education at a lower level was his mother's profession and as an elementary schoolteacher she watched anxiously as her rebellious son went from school to school, acquiring a reputation for disobedience, anti-clericalism and embittered class-consciousness. He was undoubtedly talented and she encouraged him to study for a teaching certificate. He obtained one and began a brief, inglorious career as a teacher. It was rumoured that he frequently lost control of his class and of himself when in the company of his colleagues' wives. To avoid various complications, including military service, he left for Switzerland in the summer of 1902.

Mussolini's two years in Switzerland marked the first important turning-point in his life and, for the historiography of the future, it is not without significance. This is because it launched his career as a revolutionary socialist. He met international socialists like Angelica Balabanov who vainly struggled to teach him the finer points of Marxism, and the Italian leader Giacinto Serrati who provided him with valuable contacts in the socialist movement. They did succeed in transforming this visceral radical into an unorthodox socialist. They had to admit, however, that he still looked like a *teppista*, a shady gangster, and that is what his critics claimed he was and would remain. In between odd jobs, where he became aware of the contempt felt by many foreigners for 'inferior' Italians, he began to read more widely and became exposed to the ideas of Georges Sorel, Friedrich Nietzsche, Vilfredo Pareto and Gustave Le Bon. Myths, supermen and the will to power, elites and the nature of 'the crowd' in the new age of the masses, all began to play a part in Mussolini's thinking.

After returning to Italy in 1904 to undertake his military training, he decided to resume teaching, but once again this was a disaster and he spent much of his time organizing socialist meetings and writing for newspapers.

He had, at last, found his vocation. He was proving to be an effective agitator, a forceful orator and an exceptionally talented journalist and editor. In 1909 he once again crossed the border, this time to edit a newspaper in the Austrian Trentino. When the Austrian authorities expelled him, he became something of a hero and not only in socialist circles because he had begun to attract the attention of nationalist intellectuals in Florence. His identification as a nationalist and an irredentist was decidedly premature – the Austrians had objected to his attacks on the Church – but this did not prevent a man like Giuseppe Prezzolini from corresponding with Mussolini and later on, in publishing his account of the Trentino in his prestigious journal, *La Voce*.

Back in his native Romagna, Mussolini edited *La Lotta di Classe* and soon became recognized as one of the most influential leaders of the revolutionary Left. This was confirmed by his violent opposition to the Libyan War in 1911. He had already bitterly attacked Prime Minister Giovanni Giolitti's political system and those reformist socialists who sought compromise with the liberals. He now denounced this imperialist war, and the man who later made the trains run on time incited his followers to tear up railway lines and sabotage mobilization. It earned him a spell in prison but this episode had made him a national figure and impelled him towards the leadership of the Socialist Party. His dynamic personality became apparent at the socialist congress in Reggio Emilia in 1912, when he helped to expel the reformists and secure victory for the revolutionary wing of the Party. As a reward, he was elected to the directorate and appointed editor of the party newspaper *Avanti!*. This required residence in Milan, in many ways the industrial, cultural and socialist capital of Italy. In his new setting, the provincial rabble-rouser had to be taken more seriously. Mussolini himself certainly thought so, firmly convinced that he was a man with a mission, a predestined leader who must seize power, violently overthrow the existing system and emerge as the saviour of Italy. He had chosen the socialist route to power but he was destined never to tread it. Within two years Mussolini had broken with the Party. The circumstances are well known but still controversial. When war broke out in August 1914, Italy declared its

neutrality, a decision warmly supported not only by Giolitti's liberals and most Catholics, but also by Mussolini and the socialists.
Within two months, however, Mussolini became convinced that
Italy should enter the war on the side of the Entente, and
announced this in *Avanti!*. The party that he had hoped to lead
promptly dismissed him as editor and after he had founded his own
newspaper, *Il Popolo d'Italia*, in November 1914, he was expelled
from the Party. His critics denounced this betrayal and accused him
of accepting bribes from the French and big industrialists. It was
true that his newspaper received funds from these sources, but he
became an interventionist for other reasons. Like many left-wing
activists, he was disillusioned by the events of Red Week in the
previous June when strikes and disorder had failed to produce a
nationwide revolution. Even more disturbing was the collapse of
the Second International in August. Mussolini not only found the
socialists' lack of dynamism totally frustrating, he regarded the
prospect of Italy remaining as a passive onlooker, while the rest of
Europe was at war, as intolerably humiliating. If the socialists
rejected his views he would find a new route to power. He still had
a mission to fulfil and the faith that he alone could accomplish it.
As he had written in 1912: 'We want to believe, we have to believe;
mankind needs a credo. Faith moves mountains because it gives us
the illusion that mountains do move. This illusion is perhaps the
only real thing in life.' Such a statement lends credence to Denis
Mack Smith's claim that Mussolini consistently mistook illusion for
reality.

Mussolini's 'first life' as a socialist effectively ended in the
autumn of 1914. It is important in the historiography of European
fascism because it seems to reinforce the arguments of historians
who assert that it was essentially a left-wing phenomenon. The
careers of Sir Oswald Mosley, Jacques Doriot and many others
could also be cited. This approach, however, excludes the not
insubstantial figure of Adolf Hitler, a dilemma that can only be
resolved by defining National Socialism as a distinct ideology. Since
the 1970s, A. James Gregor has been rehabilitating Mussolini,
analysing his 'developmental dictatorship', and drawing the conclusion that fascism was a variant of Marxism. Noel Sullivan's general
book on fascism in the early 1980s supports this interpretation.
Zeev Sternhell, whose detailed study of French fascist ideology bore

the significant title *Neither Right nor Left*, published his controversial *The Birth of Fascist Ideology* in 1989, with a translation from the French appearing in 1994. Placing perhaps undue emphasis on revolutionary syndicalism in Italy, he interprets fascism as a revision of Marxism, a revision so drastic that it developed into anti-Marxism! All this is in stark contrast to Mack Smith's description of Mussolini as less like a socialist than a 'Romagnol tyrant, a petty Renaissance despot in modern dress'.

*

Il Popolo d'Italia became one of the leading interventionist newspapers. Its masthead declared it to be socialist and this was only altered by the editor in July 1918 to read 'for combatants and producers'. This brief but crucial period of less than four years marked Mussolini's transition from socialism to fascism. Despised by the Left and regarded with suspicion by the Right, he emerged from isolation by joining the groups or *fasci* calling for Italy's entry into the war. These interventionists were a small but very influential minority. They included the nationalists who later joined Mussolini in 1923 and played a key role in consolidating his regime. One of their leaders, Enrico Corradini, had propounded the idea of replacing class war with international war, 'proletarian nations' like Italy pitting themselves against the plutocratic powers, a theory that Mussolini adopted once in power. Like the nationalists, Filippo Marinetti's frenetic Futurists glorified war and imperial ventures and they also played their part in the rise of fascism. Revolutionary syndicalists, now transformed into national syndicalists following the pattern described by Corradini, joined the interventionists along with irredentists and a scattering of republicans and democrats. Presiding over all these groups was Gabriele D'Annunzio, the 'Poet as Hero', the future inventor of *lo stile fascista*. Most interventionists despised the materialism of both liberalism and socialism, condemned democracy and the parliamentary system. They advocated the politics of violence and the diplomacy of force, the virtues of heroism and sacrifice. Only by these means could the aspiration of the *Risorgimento* be fulfilled, the creation of a truly united and strong Italy.

In April 1915 King Victor Emmanuel III and Prime Minister Salandra joined the Entente and in 'Radiant May' street demonstrations by the interventionists compelled a reluctant Parliament to support Italy's entry into the war. Ignoring the palace intrigue that had preceded it, Mussolini often dated the rise of fascism from May 1915. He joined his unit in August and spent six months on the Austrian Front where he witnessed 'the spirit of the trenches', which he and many other combatants attempted to revive after the end of the war. Wounded in a training accident in February 1917, Corporal Mussolini was soon back at his editorial desk, attacking liberals, socialists and Catholics for defeatism, especially after the Italian defeat at Caporetto. As the Habsburg monarchy collapsed in 1918, the Italian Army was able to take the offensive, winning the battle of Vittorio Veneto just a few days before signing the Armistice on 4 November.

Although Italy emerged a victor, there was widespread disillusionment. The war had not produced a 'Second *Risorgimento*'. Existing divisions were wider than ever and new ones had been created, especially that between neutralists and interventionists. In addition, the Bolsheviks' success in Russia increased fears of the Left, intensified class hatred, and was soon to split the Socialist Party. The Government's performance at the Paris Peace Conference in 1919 was universally deplored. It was true that Italy had acquired territory stretching from Trieste to the Brenner, incorporating over half a million Germans and Slavs, but her allies had reneged on their promises in the Adriatic, Asia Minor and Africa so that Italians referred bitterly to the 'mutilated victory'. The old ruling class had proved ineffective both in waging war and making peace. In the post-war crisis, it seemed equally incapable of resolving not only the crucial economic and political problems confronting the country but also the basic issue of the maintenance of law and order. There was a growing demand for firm leadership, for some form of 'new order' whether of the Left or the Right, for a rebirth or what Roger Griffin has called 'palingenesis'. In the event, it was Mussolini who answered this call.

*

Even his most severe critics admit that Mussolini was an outstanding journalist and a forceful orator, but in the post-war years he demonstrated an awesome ability as a manipulator of men, ideas and events. Italy was in disarray, there was a looming power vacuum and there was a man determined to fill it, to seize power and regenerate his country.

Summoned through the pages of his newspaper, the first *fascio italiano di combattimento* assembled in Milan on 23 March 1919. It was the birth of a movement that first its enemies and then its supporters called Fascism. Its Latin root *fasces*, the bundle of rods containing an axe carried by the lictor as a symbol of authority, was later emphasized and became the emblem of a regime claiming continuity with the Roman Empire. Mussolini drew support from many of the interventions of 1914–15 but the first *fasci* were spearheaded by ex-combatants and especially the *arditi*, the daredevil commandos in their black uniforms with their daggers, their '*me ne frego*' motto and their marching song '*Giovinezza*'. Mussolini sought to attract the disaffected by formulating a radical programme that was republican, anti-clerical, advocated a forty-hour week and votes for women, and attacked various aspects of capitalism. 'We declare war on socialism,' he said, 'not because it is socialist but because it has opposed nationalism.' Patriotism was the password and syndicalists were welcomed into the movement if they had supported the war.

Fasci were created in many centres outside Milan, and despite his contempt for parliamentary democracy Mussolini, perhaps unwisely, decided to test his popularity in the elections of November 1919. It was a fiasco and in their stronghold of Milan, Mussolini won only 5,000 votes compared to the 70,000 for the Catholic *popolari* and 168,000 for the socialists. As in October 1914, his political career appeared over. Even more alarming for his future prospects, D'Annunzio had seized the disputed port of Fiume and became the undisputed hero of Italy. With his legions, his balcony speeches, blackshirted followers with outstretched arms, the promulgation of charters and colourful nationalistic rituals, D'Annunzio had provided the scenario that Mussolini ruthlessly plagiarized for his own movement. At first, Mussolini had supported the Fiume enterprise but soon resented his junior status and began to distance himself from the man whom one historian has called 'the first Duce'. D'Annunzio's expulsion from Fiume in December 1920 was a relief for Mussolini. It removed a strong contender for the leadership of Italy who had seriously spoken of a planned march on Rome.

By this time, fascism was recovering from the debacle of late

1919. Parliament was deadlocked as the two mass parties of socialists and Catholics opposed each other, leaving government in the
hands of ephemeral liberal ministries. Peasant leagues occupied
landed estates and industrial workers took over factories in Turin
and Milan. Giolitti and the old political class seemed unwilling or
unable to maintain order or protect property. Independently of
Mussolini, local fascist leaders known as *ras* organized *squadre
d'azione* who attacked socialists, communists and Catholics in Tus-
cany and the Po valley. Industrialists and landowners who felt
abandoned by the State's authorities turned to these *squadristi* for
help and provided them with money, weapons and lorries. Fire-
power and mobility allowed the squads to conquer large tracts of
central and northern Italy. The Army, the police and the prefects
made no serious attempts to intervene; even the Church failed to
protest as, after all, this was a crusade against the red peril. The
success and spontaneity of *squadrismo* took Mussolini by surprise.
Always an advocate of violence, he praised their use of the club –
the *sacro manganello* – of castor oil and of more lethal weapons to
purge Italy of its ills. As the number of *fasci* rose dramatically, he
realized how indispensable the squads had become. His problem
was to make them aware of how indispensable he was to them. For
Mussolini had determined upon a two-pronged attack on the citadel
of power. While the blackshirts in their paramilitary formations
'converted' *Italia reale* to the cause, he would use more conventional
methods to penetrate *Italia legale*. He was helped by Giolitti who
called for elections in May 1921 and invited the fascists to join his
National Bloc. Thirty-five, including Mussolini, were elected. Fascism was becoming respectable. Some left-wing fascists left the
movement in disgust but their places were more than filled by an
influx of middle-class elements and students.

   There was a crisis, however, in August 1921 when Mussolini
signed a Pact of Pacification with the socialists as the escalating
civil war was alarming the middle classes and hampering his negotiations. Italo Balbo, Dino Grandi, Roberto Farinacci and other
ras were furious and refused to suspend their operations. They
spoke of asking D'Annunzio to lead them. Mussolini resigned from
the national executive. 'Fascism can do without me?' he asked.
'Doubtless, but I too can do very well without fascism.' The crisis
ended when Mussolini gave way and the *ras* agreed to support

his decision to convert the movement into a party at the Rome congress in November 1921. The National Fascist Party, the PNF, was born and, increasingly, its members greeted him as their Duce.

By 1922 the Duce had abandoned the radicalism of 1919 with its anti-clericalism and anti-capitalism, and in his Udine speech in September he dropped his republicanism. The armed forces owed allegiance to the King and Mussolini had no intention of pitting his blackshirts against the Army. In the summer of 1922 these black-shirts numbered over a quarter of a million and party membership was approaching half a million. Fascist columns occupied entire towns and regions while the Duce negotiated with a series of divided and bewildered political leaders. In October Mussolini concentrated his forces around the capital and threatened a march on Rome. To avoid bloodshed the King gave way and by the end of the month Mussolini was formally appointed as the twenty-seventh Prime Minister. At thirty-nine, he was also the youngest. Like all his predecessors he formed a coalition government. The following day, his blackshirts finally entered Rome.

The significance of these events was disputed at the time and has been ever since. For some it was the Fascist Revolution and the beginning of a new era; for others it was just another coalition government. Parliament granted him full powers to resolve the financial and administrative crisis. The Duce found it easier to manipulate liberals and conservatives than to control his own party. For this reason he established the Fascist Grand Council and incor-porated the blackshirts into a National Militia, but it took several more years to achieve his aim. The more radical fascists deplored the Duce's compromises with the Establishment and particularly the fusion between the PNF and the nationalists, which took place in 1923. Men like Luigi Federzoni and Alfredo Rocco took over key ministries and it was they who constructed the authoritarian state that became the fascist regime after 1925. It was they who virtually imposed their version of corporativism and helped to sideline Edmondo Rossoni's fascist syndicates. Non-Fascists like Arturo Bocchini controlled the police and the key administrators of the peninsula, the prefects, acted as state officials superior to the Party's federal secretaries. Mussolini's 'everything within the state, nothing outside the state, nothing against the state' was an accurate summary of these developments. As the political power of the PNF was eroded in the late 1920s, the Duce encouraged it to exert ever increasing social control over the population.

*

The event, however, which had led to the creation of an authoritarian regime and Mussolini's personal dictatorship was the Matteotti crisis of June 1924. Giacomo Matteotti, a socialist who had attacked fascist terrorism during the April elections, went missing on 10 June and was later found murdered. Suspicion centred on the Duce and there was widespread revulsion. If opposition deputies had taken a stronger line instead of boycotting the chamber and if the King had been prepared to dismiss him, the Duce would have found it hard to survive. As it was, he felt increasingly vulnerable but, as in 1914, 1919 and 1921, he managed to extricate himself. He kept the support of the Right by promising to rely more upon the conventional state power and then threatened to unleash his blackshirts to silence the moderates and the Left. In reality, the only alternative to rule by Mussolini seemed to be a return to civil disorder and a renewal of the Bolshevik threat. His more extreme followers challenged him to act as the true Duce of fascism or else to step aside. The result was his notorious speech of 3 January 1925 when he accepted responsibility for all the crimes of fascism and pledged to establish an authoritarian regime.

Over the next two years, influenced no doubt by four assassination attempts, he fulfilled his pledge. Repressive legislation was passed, strict censorship imposed and all political parties other than the PNF were outlawed. More imaginatively, he launched a series of campaigns to enhance the power of the State and to change the character of Italians, to create the *uomo fascista*. The 'battle for births', the 'battle for wheat' and the 'battle for the lira' were attempts to make Italy self-sufficient and demographically strong. The *Dopolavoro* was set up as a vast leisure organization intended to introduce Italians to sport, travel, the cinema, the theatre and art. The Age of the Masses required this mass mobilization, a theme that historians like Philip Cannistraro, Victoria De Grazia and D. Thompson have explored most effectively. Education and youth movements were obviously a top priority for the regime and a plethora of party organizations sprang up to enrol youngsters, teenagers and young adults. Teachers in schools and universities took an oath of loyalty and were expected to instil the values of fascism. This involved introducing the cult of the Duce, that, 'Mussolini is always right' and that it was necessary to 'believe, obey and fight'. Their leader was a Messiah bringing spiritual rebirth and an Augustus destined to revive and surpass the glory of ancient Rome.

This made Roman Catholics uneasy. After all, they had their own Duce in the Vatican, their own creed, organization and propaganda apparatus. Pius XI, however was in no position to condemn Mussolini. He had been sympathetic to Fascism even before his election in 1922, he shared the Duce's anti-socialism, anti-liberalism, and anti-feminism; like the Duce he detested Masons and deplored the activities of Luigi Sturzo's *popolari*. Above all, he welcomed Mussolini's determination to reconcile Church and State. When this was accomplished by the signing of the Lateran Pacts in February 1929 he hailed Mussolini as 'a man sent from Providence'. Mussolini had never been so popular, but it came with a price. Despite some shared characteristics, Christianity and Fascism were basically antithetical. The independence of the Church, if only in spiritual matters, made the fascistization of Italians virtually impossible. Add to this the largely non-fascist royal court, the Army and the industrial establishment, and the Duce's determination to create the *uomo fascista* and 'a society permanently mobilized for war' appeared unrealistic.

*

If, instead of elevating himself above Party and State and cultivating his cult status, Mussolini had paid more attention to the problems of the armed forces and the economy, he might have pursued a more successful foreign policy. Fascism was designed to eradicate political and class divisions and the regime's propaganda strove to raise national consciousness so that, for the first time, there would be mass involvement in Italy's quest for greatness. Italians must become a nation of warriors, respected, feared and even hated.

Even when Grandi and Ciano were designated Foreign Minister, Mussolini remained in charge of foreign policy. He had clear goals but in the 1920s had scant opportunity to pursue them. His priority had to be internal consolidation, the vicious colonial war in Libya had to be won and, after the Corfu incident of 1923, he needed to be wary of Anglo-French obstructionism. Weimar Germany was too weak to counterbalance Britain and France, which is why he had to appear 'statesmanlike' and pursue his revisionist schemes in secret. His aims were threefold: to make Italy the dominant Mediterranean power, to preserve a sphere of influence in Austria and the Balkans, and to enlarge the African empire. The impact of the Great Depression and the arrvial of Hitler seemed to present the Duce with the opportunity to take the initiative. Perhaps for a fleeting moment Mussolini had the chance to convince the economically destabilized Western democracies and a dynamic new Germany that they should follow his lead and implement his revisionist schemes. However, the Four Power Pact of 1933 was stillborn, his support for 'universal fascism' quickly waned, Hitler rearmed too rapidly and the Austrian question divided the two dictators. He then moved closer to the 'degenerate democracies' to force Germany to be more compliant. At the same time he expected the Nazi threat to force Britain and France to make concessions in order to retain Italian friendship. This explains his talks with Laval in January 1935 leading to the Franco-Italian military agreements in the summer and his participation in the Stresa Front. These cynical tactics were ruined by his decision to invade Ethiopia in October 1935.

This was the most popular war in Italian history, which Renzo De Felice has called 'Mussolini's masterpiece' and the crowning point of the 'years of consensus'. It proved to be a disaster. The League of Nations, headed by Britain and France, imposed economic sanctions. It was an important factor in Hitler's decision to remilitarize the Rhineland. It also drew the Duce closer to the Third Reich, a process hastened by the two dictators' intervention in the Spanish Civil War in support of General Franco. This, in turn, led to the Rome–Berlin Axis, Italian acquiescence in the *Anschluss* and the signing of the Pact of Steel in May 1939. De Felice, Richard Lamb and Rosaria Quartararo have claimed that Mussolini sought to pursue a policy of equidistance between Germany and the Western powers and that it was only the misguided diplomacy of Britain and France that caused it to fail. They could cite the mediatory role of the Duce at Munich, but this was a false assessment as he was acting as Hitler's auxiliary. Indeed, as Sir William Deakin and, more recently, MacGregor Knox have correctly pointed out, Mussolini's Grand Design conceived in the 1920s involved the reduction or elimination of British and French power in the Mediterranean either by diplomatic pressure or by war. The Duce's speech on 4 February 1939 revealed his geopolitical vision of an Italy that could only be truly independent if it ceased to be a 'prisoner in the Mediterranean'. This required a 'march to the oceans' through French North Africa to the Atlantic and through Egypt and Suez to the Indian Ocean and the creation of a *spazio vitale* for the Italian race. Knox has described this as a Mussolini *Mein Kampf*. The revisionist approach of De Felice and others is further discredited by the diplomatic record, the refusal to pull Italian troops out of Spain, the signing of the anti-Comintern Pact in 1937, the demand for French territories in November 1938, the invasion of Albania in April 1939 and the Pact of Steel the following month. Criticism of 'missed opportunities' for detaching Mussolini from the Axis is decidedly misplaced.

The irony is that in seeking to break out of Anglo-French tutelage, Mussolini became Hitler's vassal. Achille Starace, general secretary of the PNF in the 1930s, who put the Italians into uniform, enforced the fascist salute and encouraged the *passo romano* or goose-step, made the regime appear identical to the Nazis. The racial laws of 1938 sanctioning anti-Semitism enhanced this impression. It also led to growing opposition to the Party, the regime and eventually Mussolini himself. His decision to declare non-belligerence when Hitler went to war in September 1939 was well received by Italians but Mussolini felt humiliated. When he finally went to war in June 1940, he suffered a series of disastrous defeats. His 'parallel war' revealed the military and economic deficiencies of a regime that glorified war and autarchy. His 'hollow legions' met with defeat in North Africa and Greece and only the contemptuous support of the Germans kept Italy in the war. By the end of 1941, it was no longer just a war against Britain but also the Soviet Union and the United States. After the successful Allied invasion of Sicily and the bombing of Rome and other cities, there were increasing calls for peace. Hypnotized by Hitler, Mussolini refused to listen so, on 25 July 1943, his own Grand Council voted to transfer his powers to the King, who then had him arrested. Once again his career seemed to be finally over. There was, however, a brief but even more humiliating reprieve. Released from captivity by German forces, he was installed as leader of the Italian Social Republic on the shores of Lake Garda. Physically and mentally a broken man, his attempts to revive the radicalism of 1919 were a grotesque caricature that failed to disguise the fact that the Republic was merely a tiny satellite state of Germany. Resistance groups and the advancing Allies closed in during April 1945. Captured and shot by partisans, his body was transported to Milan and strung up to be reviled by the mob. Emilio Gentile has written eloquently about the 'sacralization of politics' in Fascist Italy and there has been great emphasis on the cult of the Duce so it was perhaps fitting that a failed Messiah should have been treated in this fashion.

It is equally understandable that myths and legends, debates and controversies would arise after his death, that De Felice's eight-volume biography would launch a series of historiographical wars between those representing the 'anti-Fascist consensus' and their awkwardly named 'anti-anti-Fascist' opponents. Thirty years after his death, an interview between Michael Ledeen and De Felice became a best-seller. On 28 April 1976 Mack Smith and De Felice crossed swords on the anniversary of his death on prime-time RAI television. The controversy has continued up to and beyond De Felice's death in 1996, reflecting the political developments of contemporary Italy and, as Richard Bosworth points out in *The Italian Dictatorship*, the factionalism among Italian historians and historians of Italy.

*   *   *

WORKS CITED

R. Bosworth, *The Italian Dictatorship* (London, 1998).

P. Cannistraro, *La Fabbrica del Consenso* (Bari, 1975).

F. W. Deakin, *The Brutal Friendship* (London, 1962).

R. De Felice, *Mussolini* (8 volumes, Turin, 1965–97).

V. De Grazia, *The Culture of Consent* (Cambridge, 1981).

E. Gentile, *The Sacralization of Politics in Fascist Italy* (Harvard, 1996).

A.J. Gregor, *Italian Fascism and Developmental Dictatorship* (Princeton, 1979).

R. Griffin, *The Nature of Fascism* (London, 1991).

M. Knox, *Mussolini Unleashed 1939–41* (Cambridge, 1982).

R. Lamb, *Mussolini and the British* (London, 1997).

M. Ledeen, *Universal Fascism* (New York, 1972).

D. Mack Smith, *Mussolini* (London, 1981).

R. Quartararo, *Roma tra Londra e Berlino* (Rome, 1980).

Z. Sternhell, *The Birth of Fascist Ideology* (Princeton, 1994).

D. Thompson, *State Control in Fascist Italy* (Manchester, 1991).

Alistair Horne

AXEL VON DEM BUSSCHE

In the thirty years of the Fellowship's existence, I only once resorted to a droit de seigneur – or what might now be called 'cronyism' – in the proposal of candidates. And unashamedly. This was in 1984–5, when inviting our one Fellow from Germany, Axel von dem Bussche, to write his own autobiography. Axel was one of the few survivors among the plotters against Hitler in the Second World War, and a close personal friend. Sadly, he proved to be one of the handful to fail to complete his book. It was a bitterly sad disappointment to me – but it was much, much harder for Axel. I never cease to blame myself, because his story was so remarkable, so much a part of our century just ended. I have requested droit de seigneur once again – in order to tell a small part of what he was himself unable to write.

*   *   *

I was a young foreign correspondent for the *Daily Telegraph* in Bonn when I first met Axel von dem Bussche. It was November 1952; an upheaval had occurred within the so-called *Amt Blank*, the shadow defence ministry where the shape of the future West German *Bundeswehr* was currently being hammered out. The upheaval shook parochial Bonn in no uncertain manner. At the same time it brought von dem Bussche before the eyes of the foreign press for the first time. It would, perhaps, all have been no more than a storm in a teacup, a domestic matter within four walls, had it not been for the dramatic resignation of two distinguished former *Wehrmacht* officers. One of them was Axel. The two feared that the school of *Kommiss*, of hard-line Prussian discipline, might be gaining ground among those charged with this historically responsible task of developing the structure and philosophy of the new *Bundeswehr*. That was what we foreign journalists first heard. Understandably, the direction the new West German forces, only seven years after that cataclysmic day of May 1945, would be likely to assume was of paramount concern to us and to our newspapers. It was, of course, the background of Freiherr von dem Bussche that brought the dispute far greater publicity than it would otherwise have had. Hitherto only a small group of people in Germany, and in England (through the writings of the historian, John Wheeler-Bennett, in his remarkable book about the German Army, *Nemesis of Power*) had known the details of twenty-four-year-old von dem Bussche's mad, one-man suicide plot to kill Hitler, with grenades in the pocket of a demonstration overcoat. Suddenly they became public property.

In the aftermath of 1945 and the early years of the Federal Republic, Axel, together with Count Baudissin, ex-Generals Speidel and Heusinger, Herr Oster (the son of another executed leading Julyist), and ex-Colonel Count Kielmannsegg, a close personal friend of Colonel Claus von Stauffenberg's, had become founder members of the Blank Office. All had been to a greater or lesser degree associated with the Resistance. They were also staunch supporters of Count Baudissin's distinctly liberal reform plans. In 1952 these plans had collided with the seemingly more traditionalist viewpoint of former Colonel Bogislav von Bonin, a Prussian, Potsdam-trained officer of the old school with a brilliantly rational mind, former staff officer on the Army Command (OKH). 'Dream-dancing' was how he contemptuously dismissed the ideas of the 'reformers'; and by November it must have appeared to Axel that the Bonin 'school' was winning the day.

Consequently Axel resigned amid a blaze of publicity. Had he stayed on, almost certainly a distinguished career in government would have lain ahead of him. In the light of later events, it seems that his act of resignation from the Blank Office may have been somewhat precipitate – something that was perhaps not altogether untypical of so passionate a personality. Herr Blank made it at once clear that Bonin's proposals would not receive his support, and their author was sidetracked shortly thereafter to a position of minor importance.

Axel held a press conference to explain the principles lying behind his resignation to the outside world. I wrote in a dispatch shortly afterwards:

> His tall, distinguished figure with its heavy limp became a familiar and impressive sight in Bonn. There was something about his almost quixotic idealism that made him strike one as the very epitome of Hölderlin's 'inwardly torn' German. He seemed an anachronistic survivor of a breed nearly extinct as a result of two wars and the massacre which followed the '20th of July',* the best of the German nobility that opposed Hitler.

In the context of the times, it brought home to me powerfully then that:

> Von dem Bussche's resignation had perhaps an even more significant aspect, for it drew outside attention to the existence in the Blank Office of a much deeper split than the Bonin–Baudissin controversy: the psychological rift between the ex-officers who had taken part in the resistance movement which culminated in the '20th of July', and the 'loyalists', or those who had not.

Now that it lies so far in the distant past, one has to remind oneself what were the salient facts of the '20th of July' plot. Led by Colonel Claus Schenck von Stauffenberg, the officer who planted the bomb that narrowly failed to kill Hitler at his headquarters on 20 July 1944, most of the conspirators were rounded up and brutally executed. Unlike them, however, Major Axel von dem Bussche knew in advance that his earlier one-man, suicide mission would, had it succeeded, inevitably have led to his own death.

In 1943, therefore almost a year before the Stauffenberg plot, Axel, then a highly-decorated Regular Army officer aged twenty-four, volunteered to 'model' a new army overcoat before the Führer. In the pockets of the coat were hand grenades that he would detonate, thereby killing both himself and Hitler. With his extraordinary sixth sense, Hitler cancelled the demonstration; nevertheless twice Axel screwed up his courage agonizingly for yet another attempt. His self-dedication must have been little short of superhuman, and such a willingness to sacrifice all for an ideal remained a motivating force all his life.

What *had* motivated him?

---

* The date of the (failed) Stauffenberg bomb plot against Hitler, of 20 July 1944.

Though his mother was Danish, Axel came of an old Saxon family. His was a German generation that grew up in the aftermath of the bitterness of the Versailles Treaty. Briefly he joined the Hitler Youth, in 1934, then quit – 'out of boredom'; four years later, though even in those early years he had little respect for Hitler, with enthusiasm he joined the *Wehrmacht* as a regular officer. His regiment, the 9th Infantry, stationed at Potsdam, was an elitist and patrician body comparable to Britain's Brigade of Guards, with a long and honourable tradition. An old Prussian unit just celebrating its 250th anniversary, '9 IR' had a low regard for Nazism (more members of the Resistance came from its ranks than any other *Wehrmacht* regiment, nineteen were executed after 20 July); however, when war had come in 1939 they marched for the '*Vaterland*' with few qualms, and fought with great courage. 'We were', Axel once observed, 'determined to prove to ourselves and the world that we were as good as the boys of 1914–18.'

On the first day of the war in Poland, one of the first of Axel's comrades to be killed, a few yards from him, was the brother of Richard Weizsäcker, later to become President of Germany, who remained his closest friend. It was the brutalities he witnessed during the Polish campaign in September 1939 that first began to shake Axel's nationalist convictions. However, the following May, with scores to settle against the French, for twenty-one-year-old Axel the fast-moving *Blitzkrieg* seemed like a 'jolly picnic', with his footsore men wheeling their weapons along through the Ardennes in commandeered prams – and minimal casualties. One of the first officers to cross the River Meuse, Lieutenant von dem Bussche saw a frightened French colonial soldier take aim at close range: it cost him his right thumb.

For his role in the 1940 campaign, he was awarded the German equivalent of the British VC – which was to grant him his special access to the Führer. In June 1941 his regiment was in the vanguard of the attack on Leningrad. It was while recuperating at Dubno in the Ukraine (he had been wounded once more, this time shot through the lung), in the following year that Axel had first-hand experience of what the 'Final Solution', or what Winston Churchill during the war defined as the 'Crime without a Name', really meant.

On an unused airfield, his unit was ordered to take part in a 'special operation'. With some intuition of what was afoot, the

Commanding Officer, Colonel Utsch, refused, and a renegade unit of Ukrainians was employed instead. Many years later, Axel recalled:

> There in the beautiful autumn sunshine, was a queue about a mile long of old men, women, children, babies – all naked. Large trucks were driving away with their clothes. It was the Jewish population, they were waiting to lie down in these enormous holes – graves that they had themselves been forced to dig – and be shot by the SS.

A woman fell on her knees and begged Axel for his life. 'I was unable to help her.' He urged Colonel Utsch, in vain, to do something. The other officers were left in a state of shock, but that was the moment when he resolved to assassinate Hitler – whatever the cost.

In November 1943 all was set for yet another attempt on Hitler – Axel's second – via the overcoat demonstration; then, by a million-to-one chance, the overcoat was destroyed in an RAF air raid. The raid was, ironically, to save both Hitler's and Axel's lives. The demonstration was now fixed to take place at Christmas; but before this Axel was suddenly recalled to his regiment on the Russian Front, which had flared up. A few days later he was severely wounded, resulting in the amputation of his leg. Although under constant suspicion from the Nazi staff (with the utmost difficulty, he had to dispose of the bombs, which went with him into the hospital), the long hospitalization that followed isolated Axel from the conspirators in the Stauffenberg plot – thereby undoubtedly saving his life.

Meanwhile, through a combination of bad luck and poor co-ordination, on 20 July 1944 Stauffenberg failed disastrously. He and most of the other members of the German Resistance, including Axel's closest friend, Fritz-Dietlof von der Schulenburg, were all killed in barbaric circumstances. When giving evidence in the Nazi court that sentenced him to death, von der Schulenburg declared fearlessly: 'We took upon ourselves this deed, in order to save Germany from an unspeakable misery.'

*

Back in 1952, very possibly we all exaggerated the *Amt Blank* episode – but that was how it appeared to a British correspondent in Germany of those early 1950s – tensely nervous as it was. Eighteen months later, at the emotive tenth anniversary commemoration, in 1954, of the '20th of July', President Heuss's pointed quotation from Schiller's 'William Tell' brought home to us foreign correspondents once again the significance of Axel, and what he stood for – and had been prepared to die for.

> There is a limit to the tyrant's power.
> When justice is denied to the oppressed,
> When insupportable becomes his burden – then
> He reaches upwards, confident, to heaven,
> And fetches down his everlasting rights . . .
> And if all other means shall fail his need
> One last resource remains – his own good sword.

Axel would have been thirty-two when I first set eyes on him, at that press conference in Bonn. I shall never forget the first impression; to anybody, his presence was, all his life, simply unforgettable – and, at first sight, rather overpowering. His god-daughter, Adelheid ('Neiti') von der Schulenburg Gowrie, once described him as being like a 'wounded lion'. Exactly. But he was not a smiling lion, then; perhaps the date, and the place, were still too close to the events of only eight years previously. I became friends with Axel and his Irish wife Camilla over the next two years while I was in Bonn; yet it was not an easy friendship. Perhaps, though only six years his junior, I was too young. Also I could not help viewing him with considerable awe. Memories of the war were still close at hand for both of us, and I was to him as a junior captain to a most distinguished battalion commander. There inevitably stretched a chasm of achievement that neither I nor any of us could ever cross. It was not just his immense presence, his heavy limp and wounds were a constant reminder of how the deed he had planned would have demanded his own life.

He used to remark, 'Our only fault is to have survived.' Through surviving he had somehow crossed over a frontier into a land of which the rest of us could have no conception. It was, I often used to fear in later years, this unbridgeable frontier, this inevitable setting of himself aside from the rest of the world, which never ceased to mark, and torment Axel.

When I next met Axel, in 1956, I found him a man totally changed. It was in Washington, where – after his stormy resignation from the *Amt Blank* – he had become press officer in the Federal German Embassy (1954–8). I could hardly believe my eyes. In Bonn, just three years previously, he had been so heavily weighted down by *Weltschmerz*, wanting to take the whole responsibility for Germany's past, present and future upon his own shoulders. Now, in discovering America for the first time, a new carefree gaiety seemed to have come over him. He was bursting with almost kittenish good humour, and kept us in fits of mirth with an endless flow of funny stories and anecdotes about his life in Washington. 'I love the Americans,' he declared without reservation. 'Particularly, I love their innocence – and I *don't* mean *innocence* in a derogatory sense.' Then, with great seriousness: 'Since I have been living here, for the first time I feel free from all that has happened in Europe over the past twenty years. Can you understand what I mean?'

Yes, I thought I could. Some of Axel's most comic stories concerned his own initial experiences with 'segregation' in Washington – which in the mid-50s – was becoming a major issue. Coming from a country that was then unique among the Western Powers in not having either colonies or an indigenous black population (except for a few scattered mementoes of the American Occupation), Axel's discovery of Black America was both humorous and affectionate. His affection for America was immediately reciprocated; he became an immense success in Washington. He was one of the few Germans who really understood the essence of America, which for him unswervingly remained the land of hope and strength. Suddenly, that time in Washington, I discovered I had a new friend – whom I not only admired, but with whom I could laugh, and a man with a quite unique, and sadly irreplaceable sense of humour.

The von dem Bussches moved back to Europe, to live in Switzerland, where I visited them regularly. Axel had just resigned, with regrets, from being headmaster of the prestigious Salem School on Lake Constance – Germany's nearest equivalent to Eton. There he had made a powerful impact on the young German teenagers, but, in 1960, he had suffered a mild heart attack. It was yet another setback in his career, but of course he made light of it. Girls had been brought into the traditionally male ambiance of Salem, to make it a co-educational school, while he was there. 'Now,' explained Axel, 'if you have to combine boys and girls in the same institution, there are only two possible ways of doing it; either they must be right inside the dormitories, each guarded by a dragon; or else they must be sixteen kilometres apart.'

'Why sixteen kilometres, precisely?'

'Well, because fifteen kilometres is the maximum distance a boy of seventeen can run – there, and back, in an afternoon. At Salem they were only a couple of kilometres apart – and that was why I had a heart attack!'

Axel never seemed at ease in post-war Germany, but at En Menthon Camilla made a marvellously cheerful and comfortable home for them, their two young daughters, Nicola and Jane-O, and her four older sons from her previous marriage to a Stauffenberg. For all the years she had lived in Germany, married to a German, she always retained a remarkable quality of Irishness. The house was an extraordinary meeting place for writers like Han Suyin, for history professors from Germany, and diplomats from Geneva. As his friend President Richard Weizsäcker observed, with them 'there was always cheerfulness and no single second of boredom'. The conversation was rich and varied, ranging over every subject, and every part of the world; often it would descend to the Rabelaisian. Camilla would pretend not to hear as Axel would produce old barrack-room anecdotes. ('Is it true, did the troops in the British Army, too, really think they were given "bromide-in-the-beans" to calm their sexual urges?') Camilla's special quality of gentleness provided a unique foil to the rather rough, sometimes crude, but never tough side of Axel.

From En Menthon for a while Axel worked on the secretariat of the World Council of Churches in Geneva – supported by his old regimental comrade, Richard Weizsäcker, then the President of the *Kirchentag*. But, happy as these times were, I often sensed a deep restlessness in Axel, frustrated by the limitations his war wound imposed on him, but never admitting defeat. His constant changes of job suggested a deep inner disquiet. Where was his true home? That was also the problem. He had his Danish mother, and always spoke with special affection for his heroic Danish cousin, Andy Lassen; who – in an extraordinary interplay of destiny – won the

Victoria Cross (the only foreigner ever to do so), fighting on the 'other side' in the British Army. It was a posthumous decoration; he was tragically killed within hours of the end of the war, in Venice. But Axel was, basically, so very German, so Hanoverian; yet, on occasions when we met in Germany, such as at the annual Anglo-German Königswinter Conference, he never seemed totally '*bien dans sa peau*' – as that marvellously untranslatable French expression has it. He was not at home in the new Germany, and it was alien to him. One felt he always saw things from a certain distance; in the opinion of one German friend: 'The dead represented his world. With them he was at home. The past was the present, the present was alien . . .' He was a man from another star.

We came to talk a great deal about the past, the war, with increasing openness on Axel's part, but usually with a certain reticence when it came to his attempts against Hitler. Through his eyes, I began to understand how, outraged by the unfairness of the *Versailles Diktat*, a normally patriotic young German like him could have joined the new *Wehrmacht* as a career soldier – and yet utterly despise the man who had made possible the rebuilding of the German Army, Adolf Hitler. I could also understand something of the exhilaration that he, as a twenty-one-year-old, could feel about the triumphantly successful campaign against France of May 1940; I would have shared it. But that was the end of what a young German officer of his age might be excused for thinking was 'the good war'. Then, in 1941, had come Russia with all its horrors, its appalling losses on both sides – and the outrageous and unforgivable war crimes against humanity.

Perhaps, after all, America was Axel's natural habitat. We met there again in 1980–1. I was working for eight months in Washington at the Woodrow Wilson Centre. They had just bought nearby a ravishing, seventeenth-century farmhouse out on a promontory of Maryland's Chesapeake Bay. For me, it was a particularly good time, to be able to see so much of them. I discovered a thing that we both shared – a love of things American; Axel had a special sensitivity in seeing things in the United States that others do not. Then, out at Haddon Farm one night, very late, after a great deal of Danish *schnapps*, Axel, for the first time, began talking about the nightmare experience that had really pushed him over the edge from being a 'loyal' *Wehrmacht* officer to deciding to kill Hitler.

All the terrible details of what he had witnessed on the airfield at Dubno in the Ukraine in 1942, the herding and stripping of the Jewish civilians, women and children, and their massacre by the SS in front of his impotent and disgusted regiment, came out that night. He described to me how the officers had all discussed, in deep shock, what they had seen, and of their differing reactions. Some had been totally revulsed, others felt it was 'none of their business'. The CO, Colonel Utsch, a much-respected career officer who had lost an arm, was shattered. Against such wickedness, it was clear that neither he, nor the division, nor the Army, could do anything. To Axel, Colonel Utsch made a remark that clearly affected him the rest of his life: 'Now he [Hitler] has taken away even our honour.'

Here was a highly honourable regiment, in what its officers still held to be an honourable army commanded by an honourable man – yet totally powerless to prevent such an appalling atrocity, other than make this one pathetic utterance. Axel alone decided from that moment that there was only one choice now open to him. But before resolving to assassinate Hitler, Axel had a serious psychological problem to overcome: all German officers were bound by oath to Hitler, as Commander-in-Chief. By old Prussian tradition, the *Eid*, or 'Oath', held a solemn significance that is not easy for us Anglo-Saxons to comprehend – nor, thank Heavens, is it a dilemma that any British or American officer has ever yet had to confront. To break it meant a breach with all Axel's past training, and inherited beliefs, to become – in effect – a terrorist. Finally he, and his fellow conspirators, resolved it by the acceptance that – in initiating the Holocaust – Hitler had broken his reciprocal oath of commitment to the German people. Therefore they were liberated from theirs. But it was a decision that never rested easy with the men of 20 July – certainly not with Axel.

I reflected on that conversation repeatedly. After nearly thirty years of close friendship, I thought it was extraordinary that it should all have come out now, on Chesapeake Bay, in America, and wondered whether, perhaps, at last the time had come when something in Axel made him want to get it off his conscience. I asked him if he would not consider, now, writing it all down; if not in the form of a book, then as a kind of testament that would never be lost. He said no, he simply could not write; it was all too difficult, too difficult to organize his thoughts. Too painful. I discussed it

with his close American friend, David Atcheson; he agreed that
Axel's story was something that absolutely had to be set down, and
preserved. Would I not act as a ghostwriter, get him to talk out the
story of his life – then write it up? Reluctantly, I had to refuse; I was
myself then working against the clock on a mammoth biography*
of my own and simply could not take the time off. Anyway, was I
the right person? Preferably it should be a German.

I returned to England. Axel came over, partly to get a new
artificial leg. I could sense he had been suffering new torments,
though he said nothing. While in the driver's seat of a small rented
car in London, he found that he could not drive with the new leg.
Unable to remove the prosthesis with his trousers still on, he had
been forced to take them off just outside the Dorchester Hotel, and
expected to be arrested for exposure. He made a great joke of it all,
and dropped hints as to how much he and Camilla would relish a
spell of living in England, her homeland. Suddenly an idea occurred
to me, and I resumed the attack; it was some years previously that I
had started the Fellowship at St Antony's. Could we somehow entice
Axel and Camilla there? After a great deal of subtle manipulation,
the eminent British publisher, Lord Weidenfeld, expressed considerable interest in the idea. He would commission Axel to write the
book; would provide the services of a most talented German-
speaking editor, Miriam Gross, to 'ghost' the book with Axel, by
means of extensive tape interviews. Axel would be spared the pain
of actually having to put his thoughts together in print. And he and
Camilla would be given a year of tranquility at Oxford, within the
stimulating environment of St Antony's.

Axel and I went to see George Weidenfeld. In his later years, the
more the Holocaust preoccupied Axel – perhaps because of Dubno
– the more he felt inhibited in his relationships with the Jews.
However, George and he took to each other at once. A memorable
dialogue ensued, with Axel expressing the view that Germany would
never be forgiven for the crimes committed under Hitler, 'not for a
thousand years'; George, the Viennese Jew, a passionate Zionist,
saying, no, the time was more than ripe now for Germany to be
forgiven. It was a curious reversal of roles, upside-down – and

---

* A two-volume political biography of Prime Minister Harold Macmillan; published in 1988–9.

deeply moving. George and I both stressed to Axel that the story he had to tell should emphatically *not* be just the war and his experiences, but much deeper – recounting his upbringing in post-Versailles Germany, and exploring the motivations that led him to the bomb plot. George felt, rightly, that the major part of the book should be narrative prior to July 1944, and then continue to his relationship with post-war, contemporary Germany.

It was a hugely important story of our times, which no one but Axel could write. Axel was persuaded and accepted, with reservations – could he actually do it? Camilla was delighted.

The new term at Oxford began. It seemed full of promise. But it started badly. Axel's injuries played up, the stump of his amputated leg causing painful sores. However, he was a huge success in the College, giving lectures to enthusiastic groups of postgraduates. Camilla was blissfully happy; they found a pleasant and convenient apartment in north Oxford, near the College. Then all the inhibitions, all the nightmares, came swarming back upon Axel. He wrote me several anguished letters, concerned that he was letting me down. I tried to reassure him, telling him that the deal had always been that, even if no book resulted, he would more than requite the terms of the Fellowship by just his presence at St Antony's – which he did.

Finally, no book did emerge; to my great sadness, more than disappointment. He tried to explain, wryly, that the German Resistance 'was an overcrowded ship'. And, whenever he saw his name in print, 'I throw up!' I couldn't bear Axel feeling that he had let me down in any way; rather, I have always felt that it was I who had let *him* down. I had failed him as a friend. I felt sure that if only I had been able to manage the time, had dropped everything else, working with him myself and knowing him as well as I did, understanding his moods, and quite a lot of the background, we could have succeeded together. It would have been a majestic endeavour; but above all, I always felt, it might have purged Axel of those black hobgoblins of the past. I never cease to blame myself. Perhaps I was wrong ever to have pushed him so hard. On the other hand, I never regretted getting them over to Oxford; Camilla loved her year there, and started busily to write her own memoirs – in lively competition with Axel. For a moment I thought we might have two books!

They left England, and the unimaginable happened. Camilla, the strong one on whom Axel had leaned for support for all those years, died of a sudden stroke. It was heartbreaking. Axel never really recovered. En Menthon suddenly seemed cold and empty. He couldn't quite make up his mind where he wanted to live, aged seventy and increasingly troubled by his many wounds. Eventually he settled for a small ground-floor apartment in Bad Godesberg, back in Germany at last. There he was at least tended and cosseted by adoring young women who lived nearby, and comforted by the proximity of his old friend, President Richard Weizsäcker. There were distractions. Through the special intervention of Weizsäcker, when the Berlin Wall fell Axel was able to be one of the first visitors inside East Germany. Typically he made a highly comic tale out of what must have been an emotional return, after forty-five years, to his old home at Quedlinburg, left by the war tantalizingly close to the inter-zonal frontier, but on the wrong side. Axel found that it had been turned into a Marxist seminary. Nervously the incumbents told him that two-thirds of the instructors had unaccountably gone missing; the remainder were now learning English! Did he wish to reclaim his old property? they asked anxiously. No, he assured them; he had no such intent, he just wished occasionally to be able to return, to walk in the woods of his childhood. Sadly, he never would.

The letters continued, the spidery writing as indecipherable and rambling as ever, but always so full of original thoughts. I would visit him regularly; the conversation, the huge breadth of interests never flagged; nor did the hospitality, or the laughter. But one felt the laughter died away as soon as his visitors left him alone. He was dogged by pessimism about the future of Germany, following Reunification, and frustrated that he seemed unable to get himself across to young East Germans. The last time I saw him, in September 1992, he was obviously suffering more and more discomfort; there were the frequent 'phantom' pains from the lost leg and thumb; then he had fallen over the small wall outside his house, painfully chipping a vertebra. The painkillers were never far away; the heavy drinking was an indication. I took my travelling companion, David Montgomery, son of the Field-Marshal, to have dinner with him – at the restaurant of his old admirer, Frau Maternus. It was a cheerful, boozy evening. Yet I left Germany feeling that my old friend, the old hero, had had enough ('*hatte die Nase voll*' – as he would put it), and that I would never see him again.

I didn't. On 26 January 1993, just four months later, came the news that he had died.

The obituaries were predictably moving, but hardly managed to give a sense of the man – of his breadth of interest, of his warmth as a human being, or his extraordinarily powerful effect on people. But how could they? Writing in *The Times* there was little I could add – except perhaps to say what I felt so strongly: 'To his many friends across the world he stood for more than just the conscience of Germany . . .'

He was also, quite simply, in so many ways, the bravest man I ever knew – and one of the noblest. To borrow the words of the old German soldier's farewell: '*Ich hatte einen Kameraden: einen besseren findst du nicht!*'

All special friends leave a hole when they die, which is hard to fill. Axel, because of the size of the man in every sense, left an enormous hole in my life – which will never be filled. He left me with many things I wished we could have talked about. I revisited Axel's and Camilla's magical Chesapeake in the glorious fall of 1993, the geese and ducks were just flying in and, with a great lump in my throat, I thought of them at their precious Haddon Farm just across the way. Perhaps it was one of the few places where Axel had truly managed to escape from the burden of the Hitler years; where he had at last felt free of the European past. Whenever the issue of Britain's reluctance to commit herself to Europe comes up, I think of Axel and all he stood for and suffered. Often I wonder what sort of career he would have had, if it had not been for Hitler and the war. I feel it, and he, would have been outstanding.

John Campbell

'THE EYES OF CALIGULA, THE MOUTH OF MARILYN MONROE' – THE FEMININITY OF MARGARET THATCHER

Whatever view historians eventually take of the achievements or failures of Margaret Thatcher's Government, one thing can never be taken away from her. She was Britain's first woman Prime Minister. She was also one of the first female leaders anywhere in the world to reach the highest office by her own efforts, in competition with male rivals, rather than as the widow or daughter of a former leader, like Mrs Bandaranaike in Ceylon or Indira Gandhi in India. The only precedent, in fact, was Golda Meir in Israel; but she was a grandmotherly figure who did not enter politics until she was over fifty – a very different career pattern from Mrs Thatcher, who first stood for Parliament at the age of twenty-four, won a safe seat when her children were still only six, and was the first mother of young children to hold government office. These were all remarkable achievements: Margaret Thatcher was a true pioneer and trailblazer, not only for women politicians, but for women in all professions who have learned to juggle work and family responsibilities: she won the Tory leadership, appropriately, the year that Shirley Conran published *Superwoman*. Such successors as she has had in other major countries (Edith Cresson in France, Kim Campbell in Canada) have so far been short-lived and unconvincing. Though there are more women in British and world politics today than there were in the 1960s and 1970s, when Mrs Thatcher and Barbara Castle first locked hairdos across the Commons chamber, Mrs Thatcher's sex remains her most immediately distinctive characteristic in the still predominantly grey-suited world of Westminster and Whitehall, Washington and Brussels.

One has only to look back at those formal Cabinet photographs, with the Prime Minister seated in the centre, flanked by her male colleagues – she only ever had one other woman in her Cabinet, Lady Young, for less than two years – to be reminded that she was quite simply different. Over eleven years we got so used to her difference that it came to seem quite natural. There were stories of young children asking their parents 'Can a man be a prime minister?', and the parents almost having to think twice before replying. Once we had got used to the novelty – which happened very quickly – it made a sort of natural sense for the prime minister to be a woman and all her colleagues men. The way the office has developed in this century, the British prime minister is a different order of being from his colleagues, no longer *primus inter pares* but much more the spider at the centre of the web, or the queen bee served by her workers. Mrs Thatcher's commanding occupation of the premiership mirrored on the 'efficient' side of the Constitution the Queen's position on the 'dignified' side, and tapped into a whole range of historical and mythic echoes from Boadicea and Britannia to Elizabeth I.

In short, once she had attained the premiership her sex was an almost unqualified source of strength to Mrs Thatcher, which she consciously and skilfully exploited. On the way up it was arguably a different story. As an undergraduate politician she was excluded from the Oxford Union. As an aspiring candidate she faced the reluctance of Conservative Associations in the 1950s to adopt a young mother for a winnable seat; and once at Westminster she suffered the patronizing gallantry of men who took it for granted that a woman could only hope to rise so far. On the other hand none of these held her back for very long. She still became President of the Oxford University Conservative Association; she won adoption for Finchley in time for the 1959 election; and she was the first member of that Tory intake to win promotion. She then benefited from the perceived need to have a token woman in the Shadow Cabinet, and later the Cabinet. On balance such prejudice as she encountered did her more good than harm. If she had to work twice as hard as male rivals to put herself in a position to challenge them, it was precisely that experience that made her so formidable when she did challenge them.

There were at least three clear advantages in being a woman Prime Minister that Mrs Thatcher was able to exploit. First, the mere fact of being the only woman, particularly on the world stage, made her the star of every summit she attended – the G7, European councils, bilateral meetings with kings and presidents. (The only exception was Commonwealth conferences, where she had competition from the Queen and sometimes Mrs Gandhi.) She enjoyed immediate recognition all over the world, and was an object of fascination and wonder in countries where they had never seen a woman politician before. Mrs Thatcher loved being the star. She claims in her memoirs that she did some amateur acting as a girl, but there is no record of her taking part in plays at school and it was not the sort of thing they did at Finkin Street Methodist Church: the truth is rather that she was a latent but frustrated actress who found her stage in politics. The playwright Ronald Millar not only helped to write her speeches, but directed her delivery of them: much of his success with her was that he treated her like the temperamental stars he was used to dealing with in his professional life. Though her own taste in clothes was conservative, not to say dowdy, Mrs Thatcher understood their iconographic power and was willing to be advised and moulded by her image makers – notably Gordon Reece – in a way that no man at that period would have tolerated for a moment. One need only think of Harold Wilson's rumpled suits, Ted Heath's ghastly casual clothes, or Michael Foot's notorious duffel coat. Mrs Thatcher lent herself to Reece's makeover with enthusiasm because she was a woman. She was used to being judged on her appearance, as a man was not, and she made an asset of it.

Second, being a woman gave her a wider range of possible roles than is open to a man, to suit the political need of the moment. All politicians play roles, but the repertoire of female stereotypes is far more varied, sharper and more resonant than comparable male images. Mrs Thatcher's repertoire comprised, with variations, five basic roles. In perhaps ascending order of importance, one can distinguish: first, the mother; second, the sexual woman; third, the housewife; fourth, the woman in authority – a broad category comprising the headmistress, nurse, nanny and other professional women; and fifth, the queen – particularly the warrior queen.

She was not very good at playing mother – the 'milk snatcher' image established when she was Education Secretary was always stronger, and as Prime Minister she deliberately refused demands that she should show 'compassion' for the poor, the homeless and the unemployed. No one who saw her television interview with David Dimbleby in 1987 will ever forget her contempt for those who 'drool and drivel that they care'. Nevertheless she could play the role occasionally, when required – notably when her son Mark was lost in the Sahara; when 'our boys' were at risk in the Falklands; when visiting the victims of terrorist attacks or other disasters; and perhaps most famously when 'we' became a grandmother.

Moreover she was genuinely good at it in private. When members of her staff or colleagues had family difficulties or bereavements they always found her extraordinarily sympathetic and caring. 'Whatever the demands of the diary,' Ronald Millar wrote, 'when some disaster, national or personal, struck she would ignore, cancel or postpone her commitments and rush to the side of whoever was in distress.'

She could play the mother in more everyday situations as well. When working late in the upstairs flat at No. 10, she would not send out for food but take a feminine pride in knocking up baked beans, scrambled eggs or cups of coffee herself for colleagues and aides. She would mother her ministers in little, fussy ways, telling Nigel Lawson or Kenneth Clarke to get their hair cut, tidying up their papers or insisting that Ferdie Mount take Alka-Seltzer when he had a fit of sneezing. (Alka-Seltzer was her remedy for everything.) David Steel recalls travelling with her to state funerals, along with other opposition leaders and ex-prime ministers. 'She tended to fuss round us like a clucking hen . . . brushing people's collars and seeing ties were straight . . . which I found rather endearing . . . I think in these ways she is genuinely kind and motherly.'

Likewise the flirtatious sexual woman was very definitely not part of her public image; but she could turn it on in private with devastating effect on susceptible male colleagues. People who met her for the first time, knowing only her public persona, were frequently surprised at how fragile, feminine and even sexy she could appear. Several of her colleagues and courtiers have admitted to finding her disturbingly attractive – not only self-conscious Lotharios like Alan Clark and Woodrow Wyatt, but others too. It is perhaps hard to believe John Junor's story – told him by Jim Prior – that 'one or two ministers had . . . tried unsuccessfully to get a leg over'. But at least one of her Cabinet ministers has confessed that he used to sit on the front bench wondering what sort of underwear she was wearing.

Perhaps the underwear is the point. She was unquestionably an attractive woman – more so in her fifties than in her twenties or thirties – but armour-plated and very definitely unavailable, like a nun. Although she was a wife and mother, her severity, wholesomeness and air of chastity conveyed an almost virginal appeal. Norman St John Stevas called her 'the Blessed Margaret'; other idolators idealized her as a sort of fairy princess.

She was a notably untactile person, before it became compulsory to kiss practically everyone on meeting and parting. Ronnie Millar once told her that the famous phrase that he adapted for her use, 'The Lady's not for Burning', had previously been adapted to almost every verb imaginable, including 'The lady's not for kissing'. She told him firmly: 'The last is certainly true.' She once embarrassed Willie Whitelaw by planting a smacker on him for the benefit of the cameras just before she beat him in the 1975 leadership contest. But the only person she regularly kissed in public was Ronald Reagan (leading to Ted Heath's memorable comment that he did not approve of heads of government kissing 'even if they are of different sex').

But she was responsive to handsome men. She liked tall smooth men with film star looks like Cecil Parkinson and Humphrey Atkins, and would often pick out young civil servants with these looks to come and brief her. She was susceptible to aristocratic charm as deployed by people like Peter Carrington and Lord Gowrie; even Ian Gilmour was forgiven a lot for being tall and charming. She did like gallantry – at least some of the time, which was what was so confusing for her male colleagues. Part of the problem between her and Heath, long before 1974, she told John Junor, was that he did not look at her the way most men look at a woman. Conversely one of the secrets of Tim Bell's influence with her was that he did treat her as a woman. So did Ian Gow who, according to Alan Clark, 'actually loved her . . . in every sense but the physical'. Marina

Warner pointed out in 1985 that Mrs Thatcher, by being conventionally feminine in dress and manner, exacted chivalry from men 'in a way that a woman more contemporary in style, like Shirley Williams, fails to do'. She also enjoyed old-fashioned ballroom dancing – and was good at it – whenever she got the opportunity, at her annual constituency dinner dance or, more privately, after dinner at the Washington Embassy.

There was just one group of her most ardent admirers who saw her in an explicitly sexual way: the armed forces. For soldiers in the Falklands War, according to John Keegan, Mrs Thatcher was 'far and away the favourite object of sexual fantasy'. But even the *Sun* never dared to put her on Page Three.

Much more central to her repertoire was the practical housewife. To the despair of feminists, she positively embraced and exploited this image both in speeches and in interviews with women's magazines, as she had done from her first days in politics as a candidate in Dartford and Finchley. Knowing that it would otherwise be turned to her disadvantage, she early on decided to make it an asset, pretending to be much more of an ordinary housewife than she really was, emphasizing, first, that she, as a woman, knew about prices in the shops (unlike a man) and knew from personal experience how economic policies affected people in their daily lives; second, that she would run the national budget like a household budget, thriftily and efficiently, spending only what the country could afford and being sure to get value for money from public spending; third, that she could clean up the mess left by previous governments (evoking images of spring cleaning, or cleaning the Augean Stables); and finally that she, as a housewife and mother (as well as running a full-time career), was used to juggling her time and doing six things at once (unlike a poor one-dimensional man). In 1982 she specifically compared running the Falklands War with running a household, boasting that 'every woman is a manager twenty-four hours a day'.

The homely imagery of housewife economics was a brilliant way of making the harsh and theoretical doctrine of monetarism politically acceptable: no man could have made controlling the money supply sound so much like common sense. Another way of administering nasty medicine to the electorate was by playing Nurse or Doctor Thatcher. 'After any major operation,' she told the country in a party political broadcast in 1980 as both inflation and unemployment soared, 'you feel worse before you get better. But you don't refuse the operation when you know that without it you won't survive.' Or again, a few months later: 'Which is better, the nurse who smothers the patient in sympathy and coddling, or the one who says, "Now come on, shake out of it." Which is the one more likely to get results? The one who says, "Come on, you can do it." That's me.'

This image did not have to be popular to be effective. The novelist Julian Barnes shifted it subtly from nurse to nanny in looking forward gloomily, after the 1983 election, to another four years of 'cold showers, compulsory cod liver oil, the fingernail inspection and the doling out of those vicious little pills which make you go when you don't want to'. But all these images of professional women – often in uniform – helped reinforce Mrs Thatcher's authority by associating her with figures whom men – with memories of childhood – were used to obeying. The headmistress or governess was another, accustomed to exercising authority by a mixture of precept – Mrs Thatcher always had a strong didactic streak – and punishment: enforcing good behaviour on disobedient or anti-social children for their own good. These were on the one hand moralistic images, drawing on a woman's authority in matters of right behaviour – women are traditionally expected to behave 'better' than men, and to keep weak and irresponsible men from moral backsliding; but they were also disciplinarian images, associated with women in uniform – which also merged into images of spanking, bondage and torture, the dominant woman disciplining her willing male slaves. The amateur Freudian Labour MP Leo Abse wrote of public school educated Tory MPs voting for the cane in 1975 and devoted a whole chapter to what he saw as the 'sado-masochistic affair' between Mrs Thatcher and the electors; while Denis Healey doubted her economic policy 'sado-monetarism'. Consciously or unconsciously, the image of Miss Whiplash played its part in Mrs Thatcher's hold on the imagination of at least half the nation.

Finally there are the regal images, both historical and mythical. First there were the ancient or mythical warrior queens like Britannia and Boadicea (for all practical purposes indistinguishable). This was an image that took hold particularly during the Falklands

War. Marina Warner in her book *Monuments and Maidens: The Allegory of the Female Form* has shown how a particular front page of the *Sun* in June 1983 – a few days before the re-conquest of Port Stanley – helped to establish Mrs Thatcher's identification with Britannia, and how she then moved on to adopt an existing iconography of female patriotic heroines, notably Elizabeth I and (less often) Queen Victoria. (The Victorian heroine she was best identified with was Florence Nightingale rather than the Queen.) Other writers invoked more exotic mythical females: Paul Johnson, one of her most ardent supporters – whose allegedly masochistic predilictions subsequently became known – saw her in 1987 as Kali – 'the grim Indian goddess of destruction'. She was compared with the Red Queen in *Alice in Wonderland*, forever shouting, 'Off with his head!'; and with Rider Haggard's terrifying *She* – the original 'She Who Must Be Obeyed'. Julian Critchley irreverently dubbed her 'the Great She-Elephant'; and *Private Eye* called her 'the Supreme Ruler of the Universe'. These epithets all evoked a powerful combination of wilful, quixotic femininity with absolute power, which helped to lend Mrs Thatcher an authority and a capacity to inspire fear that is not available to a male prime minister, however large his majority. Archetypal male tyrants – Stalin, Caligula, Idi Amin – are simply loathed, without the element of admiration that a powerful woman inspires in both sexes.

Unfortunately there was little she could do to act these mythical roles. She did not mind playing the warrior in a modern context – think of the famous picture of her in a tank, wearing a headscarf – and it is easy to believe her daughter Carol's word that at the height of the Falklands War, 'she would have preferred to be charging around Goose Green with a gun rather than sitting at Number Ten waiting for news'. But she had the good sense not to try dressing up in military uniform like Churchill.

The historical image she could play up to was Queen Elizabeth – the Virgin Queen, presiding over England's greatest period of mercantile expansion and confidence, surrounded by her court of flatterers and buccaneers, all ready to do her bidding, all dependent on her favour. She encouraged this identification by her susceptibility to handsome protégés like Cecil Parkinson and John Moore, flatterers like Woodrow Wyatt and Lord Young, favourite businessmen like Lord Hanson and Lord King; and self-consciously adopted the chilling phrase, when one of her servants displeased her, 'Shall we withdraw our love?' In her memoirs she explicitly – or maybe unconsciously? – echoed Elizabeth by writing that in taking it for granted (wrongly, as it turned out) that all her ministers by 1990 broadly shared her goals, 'I did not believe I had to open windows into men's souls on these matters'. It was a textbook demonstration of hubris when she appeared at the Lord Mayor's Banquet in November 1990 wearing an amazingly regal, high-collared Elizabethan dress, looking like Judi Dench in *Shakespeare in Love*.

Until very near the end this was all good myth-making propaganda, which she exploited brilliantly. But in the real world she also usurped Elizabeth II's role as the anointed embodiment of Britain, especially on her foreign tours. Being the same age and sex, but with real power and better dress sense, she easily eclipsed the Queen at her own game, so that children and foreigners came naturally to believe she was the Queen. Even within Britain she took to visiting the injured in hospital after disasters (and was invariably quicker off the mark than the Palace); and her visits to places of work – for instance to the *Glasgow Herald* in 1983 a few weeks before the Queen – were 'more regal than that of the Queen'. She took to using the royal plural, not only when it could be explained as a proper sharing of credit with her ministers, but when she was talking solely about herself. 'When I first walked through that door,' she said in 1988, 'I little thought that we would become the longest-serving Prime Minister of this century.' And of course, unforgettably, 'We are a grandmother.'

Of course there are hostile images of powerful women too: bossy, strident battleaxes and tweedy harridans, the nagging wife, or scold – was it Healey or Critchley who called her 'Attila the Hen'?; the wicked witch. But these were somehow rendered harmless by being hallowed stereotypes. All these images of strong women, both positive and negative, had the effect of diminishing the men around her, so that they all appeared as wets, wimps, vegetables and creeps. This started as early as the second Tory leadership ballot in 1975, when Willie Whitelaw, Jim Prior and Geoffrey Howe crept out of the woodwork to challenge her, after she had defeated Heath, and were widely derided as cowardly latecomers putting their heads above the parapet only when the dirty work had already been done. None of them could ever compete with her relentless disparagement of them all – assiduously fed to the press by Bernard Ingham – as mere men. As a woman, she was shamelessly able to boast of the superiority of women and the general uselessness of men, in a way that would have been quite unacceptable the other way round. 'If you want someone weak you don't want me,' she told Jimmy Young in 1986. 'There are plenty of others to choose from.' 'I just think that women have a special ability to cope,' she told Michael Aspel in 1984. Or again, to Miriam Stoppard in 1985: 'So often women are left having to cope . . . and women, always somehow, if they are left to cope, can cope . . . You do just keep going. There is a difference between men and women in that way.' All this praise of women, however, was essentially self-praise. She found very few others of her own sex worthy of promotion either within government or in the wider public service. Janet Young, the only other woman to sit briefly in her Cabinet and supposedly one of her oldest women friends, is duly disparaged in *The Downing Street Years* as not up to the job ('too consistent an advocate of caution on all occasions'). The truth is that Mrs Thatcher frankly did not like other women, and was jealous of any rival who might steal her limelight.

Although in so many ways Mrs Thatcher liked to present herself as stronger, tougher, more 'masculine' than most men, however, she also used her femininity shamelessly to manipulate and wrongfoot men to get her way. François Mitterrand was not the only one to be confused by her unsettling combination of 'the eyes of Caligula and the mouth of Marilyn Monroe'. In negotiation she could play the 'hard cop, soft cop' routine expertly, playing both roles herself. Either way, she could deploy techniques of argument not open to a man. On the one hand she could be more rude, brutal and bullyingly aggressive than a man, and get away with it because men felt unable to respond to a woman in the same way as they would to another man. But she could also be very emotional, illogical and 'feminine', which was equally hard to handle. Almost all her ministers have recorded how maddening she could be, in what they regarded as a specifically feminine way – 'unbelievably discursive', shifting her ground, jumping from point to point, full of something her hairdresser or driver had told her that morning. 'She could, on occasions,' Cecil Parkinson has written, 'seize unreasonably on an unimportant secondary point and flog it to death, while ignoring

much more important . . . issues.' Very often she would change the
subject if she was losing on the main argument, picking on something minor in order to win on that. Alan Clark characteristically
describes an argument about the labelling of Canadian fur imports
in 1984. 'As the Prime Minister developed her case she, as it were,
auto-fed her own indignation. It was a prototypical example of an
argument with a woman – no rational sequence, associative, lateral
thinking, jumping rails the whole time.' Men simply found her very
difficult to deal with.

From her own point of view, then, Mrs Thatcher's sex was
almost pure advantage, which she exploited brilliantly to establish
and maintain her political authority. But what of the country? How
did the fact of being a woman affect her attitudes and performance
as Prime Minister. What distinctive qualities did Margaret Thatcher
bring, *as a woman*, to the government of the country? Here the
verdict is more ambiguous.

First, it has to be said that she did not bring to politics that gift
for human sympathy that is generally – perhaps sentimentally – held
to be specifically feminine when demonstrated by the likes of Shirley
Williams or Mo Mowlam. If this was one hope that many women –
and indeed men – entertained of a woman prime minister, they were
disappointed. Mrs Thatcher did not in any way feminize politics.
She promoted few other women in public life. She did nothing,
except by example, to assist or attract other women into politics
(for instance by changing the hours of the House of Commons); nor
did she do much specifically to improve the lot of women in general,
for example by increasing childcare provision for working mothers.
On the contrary, she increasingly told women – contrary to her own
example – that their first duty was to stay at home and look after
their children. She positively denied the possibility of a softer, more
feminine style of politics by the way she prided herself on beating
the men at their own game, being tougher and stronger than them,
sending out the message that a woman could only get to the top by
being thoroughly masculine, hard-headed and hard-hearted. One of
her less appealing role models sometimes appeared to be Lady
Macbeth. ('Come, you spirits, unsex me here . . . Fill me from the
crown to the toe with direst cruelty.') She was happy to use
specifically male language. As late as 1989 she treated her party
conference to her vision of 'Freedom that gives a man room to

breathe ... to make his own decisions and chart his own course.'
She had no truck with political correctness or equal opportunities.
'What has Women's Lib ever done for me?' she once demanded; and
she nursed a particular loathing for Elspeth Howe of the Equal
Opportunities Commission.

The question of her sex was thrown into sharpest focus by the
Falklands War. On the face of it, waging war is the last thing a
woman prime minister should be fitted for. In fact, either because a
woman has to be extra-strong to prove that she is not weak or just
because it was her temperament, Mrs Thatcher was actually a more
ruthless and bellicose war leader than most men would have been –
certainly than any of the possible alternative prime ministers around
her. Her colleagues are almost unanimous – admiringly so – that no
male prime minister, except perhaps Churchill, would have reacted
to the Argentine invasion of the islands as unhesitatingly as she did,
or resisted American and United Nations efforts to find a solution
short of war so determinedly as she did. Precisely because she had
no military experience – and little imagination – she was less
inhibited than her male colleagues by the horror of war. Willie
Whitelaw, Peter Carrington, Francis Pym and most of her other
senior ministers had all been in the Second World War; John Nott
had been a regular soldier in Malaya; even the Archbishop of
Canterbury, Robert Runcie, who enraged her by praying for the
Argentine war dead, had won the Military Cross. The American
Secretary of State, Al Haig, who equally infuriated her by his
peacemaking diplomacy, was haunted by the memory of the body
bags in Vietnam. Mrs Thatcher had none of these inhibitions.
Certainly she wept for the British casualties and wrote handwritten
letters of sympathy to their grieving mothers. But she saw a military
job to be done and did not know what Britain maintained armed
forces for unless to do it. But also because she had no military
experience, she let the professionals get on with it, without political
interference, to a greater extent than most male prime ministers
would have done, and as she herself would have done with no other
group of professionals (economists, teachers, lawyers, or even the
police). So if it was right to fight the Falklands War at all, her sex
actually made her an exceptionally good war leader.

But there is a wider aspect to Mrs Thatcher's lack of military
experience, which goes to the heart of her political uniqueness in

her generation. Her experience of the Second World War was fundamentally different from that of any of her male contemporaries. While they were in Europe, or North Africa or the Far East fighting, she was at school in Grantham and then at Oxford – doing her homework under the kitchen table while sheltering from air raids, listening to Churchill's famous broadcasts, following the war with little flags on maps, listening to the sound of American bombers flying from Lincolnshire air bases and witnessing the invasion of American airmen spending their leave and their dollars in Grantham. It is striking that this very patriotic girl chose not to join one of the women's services on leaving school, like many of her contemporaries, but seized her chance to go straight to Oxford. She had no brothers or friends fighting in the war, either; her father had not even fought in the First World War, having been medically unfit. Moreover she never went abroad until her honeymoon (to Madeira) in 1952, and thereafter only on annual skiing holidays until she began to travel as a front-bench spokesman in the 1960s.

This sheltered experience of the war still fundamentally shaped her view of international relations forty years later. First, it shaped her negative view of the continental Europeans: they were all either wicked, intrinsically aggressive Germans who had to be stood up to and defeated; or else feeble and corrupt French, Italians and Belgians who had needed to be rescued by Britain and America in the war and could not be relied on now. These are crude stereotypes; but there is plentiful evidence that her private conversation was full of such scornful generalizations. Second, it shaped her positive view of the Americans as the generous soldiers of freedom and the leaders of the free world, the great ally from whom Britain should never be parted. Finally it gave her an essentially romantic and heroic view of war, derived from such influental books of her adolescence as Richard Hillary's *The Last Enemy*, Barbara Cartland's life of her fighter pilot brother, and Herbert Agar's *A Time for Greatness*. All her life she retained a more positive view of war as a means of defending moral causes than most of her contemporaries – or the National Service generation that came after her – could often bring themselves to feel. Not until Tony Blair did another leader emerge so much at ease with the righteousness of waging war.

The ideals and prejudices of her Grantham youth still formed Margaret Thatcher's geopolitical world view after 1979 – instinctively pro-American and anti-European (particularly anti-German); firmly anti-Soviet (taking an unusually positive view of the Cold War as an ideological conflict that could be won by the assertion of military strength); and aggressively patriotic. This world view was based on an experience of the world quite different from that of any male politician of her own age or indeed younger: not until Malcolm Rifkind, Chris Patten and John Major did a generation of ministers begin to reach the Cabinet who had never worn uniform. This was the big difference between Mrs Thatcher and all the men around her, beside which other differences are trivial. It was a huge difference of political outlook, and one that was specifically attributable to her sex.

Norman Davies

ADAM MICKIEWICZ AND HIS TIMES

Everyone knows the archetype of the national bard from Central or Eastern Europe. In the hour of the nation's greatest need, surrounded by alien oppressors without and by traitors within, he calls the patriots to arms. Standing symbolically on the steps of the nation's most treasured cultural monument, with fiery eyes and flowing locks and flamboyant gestures, he pronounces the seductive lines that shame the cowards and urge the heroes to battle (I quote):

> [Patriots] arise! It is the country's call!
> The time has come, say one and all:
> Shall we be slaves, shall we be free?
> These are the questions. Now answer me!
>> For by [our country's] God above
>> We truly swear,
>> We truly swear the tyrant's yoke
>> No more to bear!
>
> . . .
>
> A miserable wretch is he
> Who fears to die, my land, for thee.
> His life is worthless who thinks to be
> Worth more than thou, sweet liberty!
>> Now by [our country's] God above
>> We truly swear,
>> We truly swear the tyrant's yoke
>> No more to bear!
>
> The sword is nobler than the chain.
> Men cannot nobler gems attain:
> And yet the chain we wore, O Shame!
> Unsheathe the sword of ancient fame!

> For by [our country's] God above
> We truly swear,
> We truly swear the tyrant's yoke
> No more to bear!
>
> And where our graves in verdure rise
> Our children's children to the skies
> Shall speak the grateful joy they feel
> And bless our names the while they kneel.
> For by [our country's] God above
> We truly swear,
> We truly swear the tyrant's yoke
> No more to bear![1]

And then, from word to deed. Regretting his role as a pen-pusher during the War of National Liberation, when other men were dying, he enlisted in the army that had been inspired by his words, and died a martyr's death. Donning a white silken shirt, the ill prepared but ever stylish bard rushes onto the field of battle, falls transfixed by a Cossack lance, and disappears for ever under the heap of unidentified dead.

My Hungarian friends will forgive the caricature (or perhaps not). For that was *not* Adam Mickiewicz. With a couple of minor changes, it was Centaur Petrowicz (Petöfi), Hungary's national bard, reciting the lines of *Talpra Magyar*, or 'Magyar Arise' on the steps of the National Museum in Budapest on 15 March 1848 and dying on the field of Segésvar on 31 July 1849. The important thing to realize is that Adam Mickiewicz, despite some similarities, was *not* that sort of poet.

It is also important that Mickiewicz had a full-fledged literary language at his disposal. Unlike many European languages in the early nineteenth century, unlike Petöfi's Hungarian or Russian before Pushkin, Polish possessed a thorough literary pedigree going back to the Renaissance and beyond. It was in a similar state of maturity to that of English or French. In this regard, one may contrast the favourable position of Mickiewicz with the predicament of his exact contemporary Dionysios Solomos (1798–1857), the 'national poet' of modern Greece, whose early works were written not in Greek but in Italian.

*

There can be few people in the world with Polish connections who do not know that Adam Mickiewicz is universally accepted as 'the greatest of Polish poets', and that 1998 saw the bicentenary of his birth. It was very difficult that year to visit Poland without encountering Mickiewicz at every turn. There were a torrent of learned conferences, of popular TV programmes, of publications, and of other celebrations. One of the savoured moments of my own family's summer vacation, whilst staying at a house in the park at Natolin, was to watch the film director, Andrzej Wajda, working on some of the hunting scenes from his forthcoming production of *Pan Tadeusz*. When Wajda announced earlier this year that he was holding auditions for the role of Zosia, Pan Tadeusz's sweetheart, he ended up by making his selection from 1,500 budding actresses. For *Pan Tadeusz* is a work that every Polish child must read at school, and which many have learned by heart.

Despite the fame of Mickiewicz, however, especially in Poland, I don't think I am risking much by saying that in some ways he is doubly unknown. He is largely unknown abroad, except perhaps among tiny groups of Polonists, Polonophiles and literati. And arguably, he and his works are not so well known in Poland as his popular standing suggests. I was particularly struck by a report in the theatre column of *Le Monde*. The newspaper was reporting the first ever production in France of Mickiewicz's drama *Dziady*, which is generally known in English as 'Forefather's Eve'. The producer was the well-known Polish actor, Andrzej Seweryn. What caught my eye, however, was the journalist's statement, after interviewing the French cast, that not a single one of those professional French actors had ever heard of Mickiewicz prior to that pioneering production.

*

Incidentally, the first ever production of *Dziady III* in England took place at the Aldwych Theatre in 1974. It was part of a successful international series using simultaneous translation, which enabled the Aldwych to make a wholesale importation of the late Konrad Swinarski's production from the Stary Teatr in Kraków. On that occasion, the London *Times* was so hard-pressed to find anyone who knew anything at all about Mickiewicz that they initiated the one-night career of an obscure drama critic called Norman

Davies. I spoke briefly to Swinarski before the performance. I remember him being extremely anxious about the possibility that the British press would pick up on the 'anti-Russian' aspects of the play and thereby cause him political trouble at home. That anxiety, I suggest, speaks worlds about the cultural politics. Cultural politics has a lot to answer for. I would be very curious to know, for example, how many of the International Slavists, who recently held their congress in Kraków, had ever read a line of Mickiewicz for themselves.

As for the Poles, I think it was my wife's mentor, the distinguished Cracovian critic, Kazimierz Wyka, who chanced the paradoxical view that the famous Mickiewicz was not really known even in Poland. I suppose Wyka was pointing to the obvious fact that a great deal of superficial knowledge about Mickiewicz circulates. Once a poet reaches the status of national bard, everyone repeats the equivalent of 'To be or not to be' without ever progressing beyond the clichés. Everyone knows a little; few know enough. For Mickiewicz is a poet who needs to be placed very firmly in the appropriate context of Time and Space. And that context is very unfamiliar to most Poles of today's post-war generation.

Adam Mickiewicz was born on 24 December 1798 in the small country town of Nowogródek. Both '1798' and 'Nowogródek' require an extensive gloss.

In 1798 there was no place on the map of Europe called 'Poland'. The ancient *Rzeczpospolita* or 'Commonwealth of Poland-Lithuania', still one of Europe's largest states, had been abolished three years previously; and the three partitioning powers – Prussia, Russia, and Austria – had just signed a treaty agreeing never to revive the name of 'Poland' in any of their territories. Neither the French-run Duchy of Warsaw, nor the Russian-controlled Congress Kingdom of Poland had yet been created. The noble citizens of the late Commonwealth had seen their Constitution suppressed by an invading Russian army. Then, having supported the National Rising called to oppose those oppressions, they had watched as Warsaw was stormed by General Suvorov amidst a general massacre and their country declared 'not to exist'. Now, three years on; the last king of Poland, stripped of his throne, had expired on his deathbed in Russian exile; General Suvorov was campaigning against Napoleon in Northern Italy; and thousands of Polish volunteers were

enlisting in Napoleon's Army, eager to join his fight against the
reactionary emperors and monarchs. Mickiewicz was born in Lithuania exactly at the time that Napoleon's early victories were
reviving hopes for a restoration of the Polish state. He would be fed
throughout his childhood on news of Napoleon's Wars and of the
numerous Polish regiments fighting under French command. This
was the glorious era of the Chevaux Légèrs, the Polish Lancers of
Napoleon's Imperial Guard, and of General Dąbrowski's Legions,
whose magnificently rhythmic *mazurek* was to become Poland's
national anthem, *Jeszcze Polska nie zginęła* ('Poland has not perished yet'):

> Poland has not perished yet, so long as we still live.
> That which alien power has seized, we shall yet revive.
> March, March Dąbrowski! Under your command
> We shall march from Italy to God's own Polish land.[2]

As a thirteen-year old schoolboy, Mickiewicz was to see the soldiers
of the Grande Armée tramping through his home town on their way
to Borodino and central Russia. And he would see them again, in
their great distress, during the fatal winter retreat from Moscow.
For British audiences, who are taught to think of Napoleon as the
enemy and of the Russian Empire as a brave ally, the retreat from
Moscow is generally regarded as a wonderful triumph, a step
towards Europe's liberation. For Mickiewicz, and for almost all the
population of Lithuania, it was the great disaster, the shattering of
dreams, *the* return of enslavement to tsardom and of alien Russian
tyranny.

Today, Nowogródek – or rather Novohorodok – lies in western
Belarus, 80 miles from Minsk and 100 miles from the present Polish
border. It is surrounded by the lush meadows and dense forests of
the valley of the Niemen. In 1798, following the Third Partition, it
had just been annexed to the Russian Empire and would soon be
assigned to the new *gubernia* of Grodno. Yet for centuries before
1795, it had formed part of the Grand Duchy of Lithuania and had
no close Russian connections. Founded according to tradition either
by the Ruthenian Prince Jaroslav in the eleventh century, or by a
Lithuanian prince after the Mongol invasion of 1241, it had developed as a fortress and a market town in a region where Lithuanian,
Ruthenian and Polish influences overlapped. Historically, the district

was variously known as *Ruś litewska* (Lithuanian Ruthenie) or as
Czarna Ruś (Black Ruthenia). At the time when Mickiewicz knew
it, after 250 years of Polish supremacy, the ethnic make-up of the
town contrasted sharply with that of the surrounding countryside.
The local custom was to count people by religion; and a highly
colourful and detailed nineteenth-century source states that in a
town of some 12,000 souls, there were 470 Orthodox Christians,
2,200 Roman Catholics, 1,160 Muslims, and 8,170 Jews. Prior to
1839, when all Slavic rite Christians were forcibly converted to the
Russian branch of Orthodoxy, the 470 'Orthodox' (4 per cent)
would have been Ruthenian-speaking, Greek-Catholic Uniates. The
2,200 Roman Catholics (18 per cent) would have formed an overwhelmingly Polish, educated, and propertied class. The Muslims (9
per cent) were of military Tartar origin; but by that time they only
spoke Polish among themselves and cultivated highly patriotic Polish
attitudes. The Jews (69 per cent) spoke Yiddish. In that part of the
former Commonwealth they would have been divided into a Chas-
sidic minority and a majority group practising Orthodox rabbinical
Judaism. In Mickiewicz's day, the number of Jews assimilated into
Polish culture, still less into the Russian culture of the new regime,
would have been minimal. The town contained six places of Jewish
worship, where Hebrew was used. There were two stone Uniate
churches, where the services were held in Old Church Slavonic, two
less impressive Catholic churches, where Latin was used: and one
wooden mosque, where the holy texts were written in Arabic. This
multilingual, multi-religious, multicultural environment is crucial.
Poland's national bard was brought up in a typical small town
of the eastern borders where Poles formed one of several ethnic
minorities, and where Jews formed an absolute and overwhelming
majority.

The ethnic composition of the countryside showed a rather
different balance. Statistics from c.1880 put the total population of
the *powiat* or district of Nowogródek at 185,000. Of these, 9,400
(5 per cent) were counted as Lithuanians, c.18,000 (9 per cent) as
Poles including Catholics, Muslims and Protestants; 25,000 (13 per
cent) were Jews; and 141,200 (76 per cent) were classed as *Rusini*,
'Ruthenians', partly Uniate, mainly Orthodox. Again in 1880, after
nearly ninety years of tsarist rule, 507 out of 680 major landowners
were Polish, holding 88 per cent of all non-State and non-Church

land. In a changeless rural setting, the social and economic supremacy of those Polish landowners was unrivalled.

Mickiewicz, whose father had a legal practice in Nowogródek, belonged to the urban sector of that dominant Polish group. He loved the countryside, and would write stunning poetic sketches of its natural beauties. But he never forgot the sights, sounds and smells of his much-loved birthplace. Writing to a friend from Istanbul in 1855, a few days before his death, he still had Nowogródek in mind. 'Many parts of this city,' he mused with pleasure, 'are exactly like my own little town in my native Lithuania. Please imagine a market place covered in a thick layer of feathers and manure, over which chickens, turkeys and all sorts of other creatures wander, surrounded by the usual crowd of sleepy dogs.' To those who habitually deride Eastern Europe as culturally primitive because it was undoubtedly economically retarded, Mickiewicz was brought up in Europe's ultimate Styx.

*

The life of Adam Mickiewicz, from Nowogródek in 1798 to Istanbul in 1855, falls into three clear periods – the Lithuanian, the Russian, and the French. I shall briefly characterize each of them. After that, I shall try to extract three of the most prominent themes that run through his life and work. Finally, I shall offer a few reflections on how we might remember Mickiewicz together with that inimitable, romantic and long-lost part of Europe from which he came.

*

After the years of infancy, Mickiewicz's Lithuanian period was almost entirely absorbed with education; and it is the phenomenally high quality of that education, in one of Europe's supposed backwaters, that strikes one today as most remarkable. He studied at the district school in Nowogródek (1807–15), pursued higher studies at the University of Wilno (1815–19), and served as a teacher in the secondary school at Kowno (Kaunas) (1819–23). He could not have been better educated had he attended the most famous schools and colleges in London, Paris or Berlin. His school was one of those reformed by the Polish National Education Commission in the last decades of the Commonwealth. It gave him a command of Latin and Greek that a quarter of a century later sufficed for a professorial chair in Classics in Switzerland: and a knowledge of modern languages that enabled him to work in French, German, English, Italian and Russian as a matter of course. His alma mater at Wilno, now the University of Vilnius, had been founded in 1584 by King Stefan Bathóry as a Jesuit college. Thanks to the patronage of Prince Adam Czartoryski, Alexander I's leading minister, it enjoyed the protection of the Tsar and for a brief period was the top Polish university of its day. There, Mickiewicz followed courses in classical philology, history under Joachim Lelewel, literary theory, philosophy and, for one term, mathematics. He was also an active member and co-founder of the secret student society of 'Philomaths', which, like so many of the fashionable *Burschenschaften* in Germany engaged in a heady mixture of self-improvement, nationalist politics and anti-authoritarian demonstrations. This, after all, was the era of the Congress System, when the Tsar competed with Metternich in policing the rebellious youth of Europe and suppressing the continuing vogue for revolutionary ideas. As a young teacher in Kowno, Mickiewicz experienced both the salutary discipline of ordering one's knowledge for the benefit of others and the damaging shock of an unrequited love affair. He was already writing serious poetry. In 1820 he composed a manifestatory *Ode to Youth* rejecting the sclerotic world of rationalism and the Enlightenment:

> Bez serc, bez ducha, to szkieletów ludy;
> Młodości! dodaj mi skrzydła!
> Niech nad martwym wzlecą światem
> W rajską dziedzinę ułudy:
> Kędy zapał tworzy cudy,
> Nowości potrząsa kwiatem
> I obleka w nadziei złote malowidła.

> *Heartless, spiritless – these are the people of old bones;*
> *Oh Youth! Give me wings!*
> > *May I soar above the dead world*
> *Into the paradise of illusions,*
> > *Where enthusiasm creates miracles*
> *Brandishes the flower of novelty,*
> > *And covers the golden paintings with hope.*[3]

Two years later, 1822, the publication by Mickiewicz of his first volume of collected verse is generally seen as the starting point of Polish literary Romanticism.

Mickiewicz's Russian period began on 4 November 1823, when he was arrested with several colleagues on suspicion of subversive activity. After a few months' incarceration, he was leniently treated, receiving only an administrative order for compulsory residence in the Russian *gubernias* of the Empire 'with pedagogical duties'. He was never given the requisite pedagogical duties. But he spent four formative years in Russia, initially in St Petersburg, later in the south, in Odessa and Crimea, and from 1826–9 in Moscow. He was free to meet the cream of Russia's liberal and artistic intelligentsia. This was a rich opportunity. In Petersburg, he met Ryleyev and Byestuzhev, soon to be Decembrists; and, according to some reports, he stood under the same coat with Alexander Pushkin, sheltering from the rain in front of the statue of the Bronze Horseman. (In the era of photography, that would have made a famous snapshot.) In Odessa – as you can read in a chapter of Neal Ascherson's magnificent book *Black Sea* – he mixed in the high society of the new city and conducted a romance with the sister of the great collaborator, Henryk Rzewuski. In Moscow, apart from Pushkin, he met Polevoi, Wiazemski, Volkonska, Zhukovsky. Above all, he was free both to write and to publish. 1826 saw the publication of his superlative *Sonnets*, 1828 his formidable psycho-political study, *Konrad Wallenrod*; and 1829 two more volumes of verse. *Konrad Wallenrod*, which explores the dilemmas of resistance and collaboration, is set in the historical surroundings of the Teutonic Knights. Yet it was a thinly veiled allegory of Polish-Russian relations.

The sojourn in the south, particularly in Crimea, bore rich fruit. He was there in 1825, at the time that the accession of the autocratic and markedly anti-Polish Nicholas I was bringing Russia and Poland onto a collision course. He knew nothing of what was going on at home. Impressed and attracted by the beauties and harshness of the landscape, he was repelled by the remoteness. His sonnet *Stepy Akarmańskie*, 'The Steppes of Akkerman' was written after a day on the open plains of southern Ukraine near the old Turkish port of Akkerman, when his thoughts turned to distant Lithuania:

Wpłynąłem na suchego przestwór oceanu,
Wóz nurza się w zieloność i jak łódka brodzi,
śród fali łąk szumiących, śród kwiatów powodzi,
Omijam kolarowe ostrowy burzanu.

Ju mrok zapada, nigdzie drogi ni kurhanu;
Patrzę w niebo, gwiazd szukam, przewodniczek łodzi;
Tam z dala błyszczy obłok – tam jutrzenka wschodzi;
To błyszczy Dniestr, to weszła lampa Akermanu.

Stójmy! – jak cicho! – słyszę ciągnące żurawie,
Których by nie dościgły źrenice sokoła;
Słyszę, kędy się motyl kołysa na trawie,

Kędy wąż śliską piersią dotyka się zioła.
W takiej ciszy – tak ucho natężam ciekawie,
że słyszałbym głos z Litwy. – Jedźmy, nikt nie woła!

I have sailed on the expanse of a dry ocean.
The wagon is submerged in greenery, and like a boat, wanders
Through the rustling waves of the prairie, and glides among the flowers.
I pass coral islets of rank vegetation

Already dusk is falling. No road here, no dolmen.
I look up, seeking the stars, my ship's couriers.
There, afar, a cloud gleams in the sky. The morning star glimmers.
There lies the glistening Dniester! There, the pharos of Akkerman.

Halt! How still! I can hear the flight of cranes
Which are invisible, even to the falcon's stare.
I listen to a butterfly snuggling in the grassy lanes,

And to a smooth breasted snake nestling in the clover.
In such silence, my curious ear strains
To catch a voice from Lithuania. . . . Drive on! No one's there.[4]

The view of Russia, which Mickiewicz portrayed, combined cultural
sympathy with revulsion for the political system. This strikes me as
a rather healthy formula. But it does not prevent Mickiewicz, like
most of his compatriots, often being classed as 'anti-Russian'. There
is a profound misunderstanding here; and the general tendency of
many Russicists and academic Slavicists to turn their backs on the
Polish sources of their subject is, in my view, misguided.

Mickiewicz sailed from Petersburg in April 1829, after which he
embarked on a long and leisurely continental tour from Bohemia to
Sicily. He listened to Hegel's lectures in Berlin; visited Goethe in
Weimar; talked to the future Napoleon III in Rome. This meant that
he missed the outbreak and excitement of the November Rising in
Warsaw. A none too determined attempt to enter the rebel-bound

Congress Kingdom from Prussian Poland left him stranded in Dres-
den, where he completed an intensive phase of creative work including the supreme masterpiece, *Dziady III*. As fate decreed, Poland's
national poet would never set foot either in Warsaw or Kraków.

Mickiewicz's French period occupied, with intervals, more than
half of his adult life. He himself was not really a refugee, though it
would have been senseless to return home; but he arrived in Paris in
1832 in the company of thousands of Poles of the 'Great Emigration'
fleeing the defeated November Rising. He lived there throughout the
reign of Louis-Philippe, the 'Citizen-King'; saw his fellow poet,
Lamartine, reach the front of the political stage in 'the Springtime
of Nations'; and witnessed the creation of the Second Empire. As in
Russia, he quickly made the acquaintance of liberal and literary
circles. But whereas in Moscow, he had been a minor provincial
youth, in Paris he was already an established man of letters, recognized as such by his French friends like the Abbé Lamennais, or
Georges Sand, and adored by the Polish émigrés. He was married
(1834) to Celina Szymanowska. Their son Władysław (1838–1926)
became in later life the guardian of his father's papers and the
director of the Bibliothèque Polonaise on the Île St Louis.

Yet life was not comfortable. Mickiewicz found his métier
neither with the Polish émigrés, whose political squabbles distressed
him, nor with the French intellectual elite, for whom he remained
no more than a respected outsider. He joined no political party. He
continued to write in Polish; and spoke French with a heavy accent;
he found no success with his various forays into writing in French.
He could never rival his younger compatriot, Frédéric Chopin,
who was the darling of the salons. In the background, the mental
and physical frailties of his wife, and a household of six children,
strained his nerves to the utmost.

Mickiewicz went through three distinct phases in Paris. In the
1830s he was at the height of his literary powers, publishing
regularly, writing sometimes feverishly. These were the years of a
third collection of verse: of the quasi-biblical *Books of the Polish
Nation and Pilgrimage* (1833) and of his nostalgic epic about life
among the petty Polish nobility of Lithuania; *Pan Tadeusz* (1834).
In the 1840s Mickiewicz embarked on two contradictory and, as it
proved, incompatible enterprises. On the one hand, he accepted an
academic post at the prestigious Collège de France, where he lec-

tured on Slavonic literature. On the other hand, tempted by promises of a cure for his wife's mental breakdown, he joined a radical
and mystical sect, the Circle of the Divine Cause of Andrzej Towiański. As the obsession with the sect increased and the quality of his
lectures deteriorated, he worked his way into an impasse. Eventually, he lost both his job and his faith in the sect. In the 1850s,
having rejected the poetic muse and working as a minor librarian,
he turned himself into a full-time, one-man activist for the sinking
Polish cause.

The Parisian decades were interrupted on three occasions by
extended absences in other countries. The stay in Lausanne, in
1839–40, when he taught Classics at the local francophone Academy, was occasioned exclusively by his wife's ill health. The
expedition to Italy in 1848–9 was inspired by the revolutionary
events in Paris and elsewhere and by hopes of persuading the Pope
to support them. Mickiewicz organized the core of a Polish legion,
which fought for the Roman Republic; edited a radical international
journal, *La Tribune des Peuples*. Back in Paris, he found that the
regime of Napoleon III had put him under police surveillance.
The departure for Constantinople-Istanbul in November 1855 was
caused by the outbreak of the Crimean War. Mickiewicz had long
held that Europe's misfortunes resulted partly from Russia's insatiable ambition and partly from the hypocritical cowardice of the
Western Powers. So the open conflict in Crimea between Russia and
the Franco-British-Ottoman coalition must have seemed to him a
godsend. He hoped to find funds and followers for the Ottoman
Cossack Brigade, whose Polish General, Michał Czajkowski, held
similar views to his own. But cholera intervened. The body of the
man who no longer regarded himself a poet was shipped back to
France, and buried in the cemetery of Montmorency.

*

In the year that Mickiewicz died, 1855, the causes that he held most
dear did not appear to have advanced one inch. The Russian Empire
still ruled over Nowogródek. No move had been made in over fifty
years to restore the Grand Duchy of Lithuania, and the world was
beginning to think of Lithuania (quite wrongly) as an historic and
integral part of Russia. Though the serfs had recently been emancipated in Prussia and Austria, their subjection still lingered on under

Russian rule. The Constitution of the Congress Kingdom of Poland had been suspended for a quarter of a century; and even the advent of a so-called 'liberal Tsar', Alexander II, offered few rays of hope. In the event, it was to lead to an even longer and more desperate Polish Rising than that of 1830. The Austrians had recently suppressed the independent Republic of Kraków, and were busy germanizing the Jagiellonian University. The Prussians had terminated the autonomy of the Grand Duchy of Posen (Poznań), which in the coming period would be subjected to still fiercer germanization. Polish culture was being pushed through the political grinder. None of Mickiewicz's works could pass the official censorship in any part of partitioned Poland. The University of Wilno, which he attended, and which had carried the torch for a generation, was closed and had not yet found a successor. The University of Warsaw would be replaced by an Imperial (Russian) University of Warsaw. The great University of Lwów, like Kraków, had not yet lived to see the glorious days of Galician autonomy. To get a higher education, Polish students had to forego their own language. Even the Polish Catholic Church was succumbing. Bishoprics lay vacant: seminaries stayed half-empty: the loyalty of Catholics was in doubt. In 1855 the Vatican signed a Concordat with St Petersburg, effectively abandoning its Polish clergy to the dictates of a state-run, not-so-Holy Synod, and recommending its faithful to the mercies of a merciless Tsar.

Most disturbing perhaps, the long-lasting solidarity of the peoples of the former Commonwealth of Poland-Lithuania was beginning to break up. Although the Polish Rising of 1863–4 would receive a significant measure of armed support in Lithuania, new trends were afoot. At the instigation of the Polish bishops of Wilno, the Lithuanian language was now being taught to ethnic Lithuanian children in church schools in order to prevent them falling for Russian Orthodoxy. The experiment developed rather differently than intended. Henceforth, despite the common Catholicity, those Lithuanians would think of Polish-speakers, like Mickiewicz, as the cultural enemy, no less dangerous than their Russian Government. National feelings were being similarly fanned among the Ruthenians. Whilst the tsarist authorities insisted that all Ruthenians were Russians, anti-tsarist activists were beginning to persuade the Ruthenian peasants that they were either Ukrainians or, in the north and with more delay, Byelorussians. Taras Shevchenko (1814–61), who would gain a similar position among Ukrainians to that of Mickiewicz among Poles, was highly active at this time. The Jews, too, who to date had formed a community defined essentially by religious criteria, were laying the foundations of a separate secular identity. Political Zionism was still some way off. But the Hebrew Revival was under way, as was cultural Zionism. The first poet of stature writing in modern Hebrew, Jehudah Gordon (1830–92), author of *Hakkitsah Ammi*, 'Arise My People' was born in Wilno, shortly after Mickiewicz left.

Mickiewicz, I think, would not have thought ill of these national and cultural revivals. But the idea that the new nationalisms would have turned his neighbours in Nowogródek into sworn enemies would surely have broken his heart.

*

Adam Mickiewicz led a rich, restless and, in some regards, tragic life. To have consciously rejected the God-given talent, which must have provided so much spiritual fulfilment, both for him and his readers, might seem to have been a capital mistake. And to have done so, first in favour of a dead-end, pseudo-religious sect and then in favour of nineteenth-century Europe's greatest Lost Cause, could have been doubly embarrassing. As he lay dying on the banks of the Bosphorus, Mickiewicz could have had little inkling of the scale of his posthumous triumph. He must have died wondering whether Poland, like himself, was lost beyond recall.

The principal problem for the biographer, therefore, as for the biographical sketcher, is to establish a convincing link between the oeuvre and the actions, between word and deed. In this, one cannot reach a conclusion through some sort of mechanical calculation. One has to identify the dynamic, to show the constantly changing interplay between what he wrote and what he did. Here, I am sure, one has to concentrate on the very obvious contrast between the early years, when poetry had absolute priority, and the later years, when action was supposedly all. As a youthful poet, Mickiewicz was entirely absorbed with his creative self. The student Philomath supposedly took to poetry as a means of coping with the loss of his idyllic childhood. He called it his *wiersz-płacz*, his 'rhyming and weeping'. This sounds somewhat contrived, but the tendency was undoubtedly strengthened by his involuntary exile in Russia and by his subsequent emigration. There was always a definite predisposition to spiritual and religious rumination, frequently reflected in the nature of his heroes, like Konrad Wallenrod or Gustaw-Konrad in *Dziady*, who are more interesting for their moral dilemmas than for their derring-do. Many readers have been disappointed by the fact that Konrad Wallenrod did not openly rebel against the Teutonic Order. In the poet's life, the key moment came in Wielkopolska in the summer and autumn of 1831, when with a false passport in his pocket he nevertheless failed to cross the frontier and participate in the national rising. Had he really tried, he could easily have slipped into Poland; he could have joined the Army like Petöfi, or the nearest partisan band, and have fought in the patriotic ranks. Instead, he held back. That decision, or lack of it, haunted him for the rest of his life. Once, at a public meeting in Paris, when he expressed the view that the insurrectionaries should never have surrendered, one of the émigré veterans added, 'And you would have sat on the ruins to write your poems.' A guilty conscience opened the way for the blandishments of Towiański's sect, where he hoped to gain a new inner purpose. Mickiewicz had already parted company with the sect before embarking on his political ventures in Italy and in Turkey. On the eve of his departure on the final journey, to Constantinople, his son watched him burning papers in the grate. Critics have speculated that they contained the final, unknown parts of *Pan Tadeusz*. If so, for a poet, it was a desperate act of self-immolation. It also meant that, despite his public silence, he had not stopped writing. Full acceptance of his chosen role as the 'wandering knight of Freedom's Revolution' only came at the very end.

*

Mickiewicz, like Poland itself, spanned the space between Europe's East and West. He belonged to the part of Europe that has been regularly excluded from most schemes of Western civilization and which in the eyes of many contemporary scholars continues to brim with all manner of negative stereotypes. A Slav, and a citizen of the Russian Empire, he was nonetheless steeped in classical, Catholic and Western civilization. In Russia, he was a Westerner. In France, he was an Easterner. His works are saturated with an inimitable fusion of occidental and oriental motifs.

In his mature years, however, Mickiewicz undertook an extended and systematic mission to expound a large slice of the culture of Eastern Europe to West. For his *Cours de la littérature slave*, presented at the Collège de France over the four academic years 1840–44 amounted to exactly that – a pioneering mission. One of the entrances to the Collège de France still bears a tablet dedicated to '*Mickiewicz, Michelet, Quinet – leurs auditeurs reconnaissants*'.

As an academic exercise, those lectures are seriously flawed, certainly by today's standards. They are unusually opinionated, shamelessly speculative and, in the later parts, they openly propagate the sectarian ideology of Towianism. Their factual information was not even up to date by the standards of the 1840s. The dismissive section on Finnish folklore, for example, was penned in ignorance of the fact that the *Kalevala* had already been published.

On the other hand, amateur philosophizing was very much à la mode and Michelet was equally given to it. Even the brazen Messianism, which tried to establish a providential role both for Poland among the Slavs and for the Napoleonic tradition in France, was tolerable until it became the one and only message. The grand survey of Russian, Polish, Czech and Serbian language and literature undoubtedly had its weaknesses. Not everyone will accept the judgement that the Czech language is the ideal medium for poetry, and Polish for government documents. Yet it provided one of the launch pads for the whole discipline of Slavonic Studies.

I sometimes think that Mickiewicz lecturing in Paris in the 1840s should be compared to Czesław Miłosz lecturing at Berkeley in California in the 1960s and 70s – the bard of Nowogródek reincarnated as 'the Bard of Grizzly Peak'. A Pole from Lithuania born a subject of the Tsar, a philosopher and poet, an émigré who long feared that he was a voice crying in the wilderness, he shared the Master's world-view. But his immediate task was to expound Slavonic Studies. In California, few people know that Slavonic Studies is not equivalent to Russian Studies. (In the Californian university where I taught, the Slavic Department consisted of five professors of Russian language and five specializing in Dostoyevsky.) So Miłosz lectured on Dostoyevsky, with more insight, I imagine, than most, but as a step to putting Russian literature into the wider context. Unlike Mickiewicz, Miłosz has lived to see his full reward.

The position of Mickiewicz as 'national bard' inevitably emits overtones of parochialism, even chauvinism. National standing can limit a poet's universal standing: and invention and elaboration by Mickiewicz of the metaphor that others labelled 'Poland, the Christ of Nations' has disturbing implications, and not only for Catholics. Yet the linking of national sentiments with biblical images and biblical language was quite deliberate, not least in *Books of the Polish Nation and Pilgrimage*:

> In the beginning, there was belief in one God, and there was Freedom in the world ... But later the people turned aside from the Lord their God, and made themselves graven images, and bowed down ... Thus God, sent upon them the greatest punishment which is Slavery. ...
>
> But the Polish Nation alone did not bow down ... And finally Poland said 'Whosoever will come to me shall be free and equal, for I am FREEDOM'. But the Kings when they heard were frightened in their hearts and said: 'Come let us slay this nation.' And they conspired together ... And they crucified the Polish Nation, and laid it in its grave, and cried out: 'We have slain and buried Freedom.' But they cried out foolishly ...
>
> For the Polish Nation did not die. Its body lieth in the grave; but its spirit has descended into the abyss, that is, into the private lives of people who suffer slavery in their country. ... But on the third day, the soul shall return to the body, and the Nation shall arise, and free the peoples of Europe from slavery.[5]

'The Polish Nation alone', 'the third day' and crucifixion – these are not mere allusions. They form an unambiguous metaphor – Poland as the Redeemer.

Unease of a different sort can be expressed about *Pan Tadeusz*. The rural idyll of the old Polish *szlachta*, in which Mickiewicz sets the inhabitants of the fictional Soplicowo, has been seen as expressing approval for the backward-looking, narrow-minded, classridden, self-satisfied Sarmatism that was old Poland's undoing. Mickiewicz, in other words, was fuelling national megalomania. Following these lines of thought, it is not hard to reach the conclusion that the works of Mickiewicz underpinned the ugly, obscurantist and exclusive brand of integral Polish nationalism that caused so much hurt in later times. In short, *Pan Adam-Polakatolik*.

But hold on! People with very different outlooks from Mickiewicz

have been able to highlight selective extracts from the poet's works
and to claim him as their own. For in very real ways, Mickiewicz
was neither a Pole, nor a Catholic. He was exactly the sort of
complicated creature that the nationalists, the *Polakatolicy*, abhor.
Mickiewicz, like Marshal Piłsudski who came from the same part
of the world, would never call himself 'a Pole'. On his visiting
card, he would write 'A.M. – Litwin' (Adam Mickiewicz-Lithuanian)
or 'A.M. Nowogrodzianin'. Nothing in the world can overcome the
fact that the most famous line in Polish literature – the patriotic invocation in the opening line of *Pan Tadeusz* – invokes
not Poland, but Lithuania. *Litwo, Ojczyzno moja! Ty jesteś jak
zdrowie* (O Lithuania, my fatherland. You are like health.) Not
Polsko! But *Litwo*! The only way to explain this to a British
audience is to imagine Mickiewicz as a Scot from the New Town
in Edinburgh – New Town – Nowogródek? – or as an Irishman
from Newtown (Co. Cork), whose native language was English, but
who would never, never, never have thought of himself as an
Englishman.

And as for his faith, Mickiewicz was indeed baptized in the
parish church at Nowogródek; and he remained a highly religious,
mystical person throughout his life. Yet one cannot deny that he
deviated seriously from the strict Catholic path. In devout Catholic
eyes his metaphor of the 'Christ of Nations' was blasphemous; his
lectures on *L'Eglise officielle et le Messie* were heretical; and his
membership of the Circle of the Divine Cause was a form of
apostasy. Mickiewicz was a patriot at the most for the old *Rzeczpospolita*; and he was only a catholic with a small 'c'.

Innumerable examples could be found to prove that the poet's
national concerns formed part of his wider concerns for universal
justice and freedom. The aims of the Legion that he led in Italy in
1848–9 and which are enshrined in his fifteen-point *Skład Zasad* or
'List of Principles' are anything but narrow or nationalistic. They
followed closely the ideas of the Polish legions of his youth whose
uniforms carried the slogan: *Gli uomini sono fratelli*, 'Men are
brothers'. Point 10 affirmed civil liberties for the Jews. Point 11
called for emancipation and equality of women. Point 13 contested
the absolute right of private property, bringing all communes in the
country under the care of the nation. This was revolutionary.
Mickiewicz must be identified with that most noble of Polish slogans

from that era, which read: *Za waszą i naszą wolność!* 'For Your Freedom as well as Ours!'

Which makes one wonder how he ever attained the status of 'a national bard'. The main answer to that obviously lies in the sheer power of his language. But there are other factors. His Messianism, for example, gave the image of a *wieszcz* or 'prophet', which he cultivated. His near-martyr's death in distant exile did him no harm. And his extraordinary emotional range, from lyrical tranquillity to fierce polemics, appeals to all. Polish opinion was deeply divided in the nineteenth century between hot-blooded romantic insurrectionaries and the dour, practical positivists who opposed all open resistance. The prominence that Mickiewicz gave to the *rząd dusz*, 'the mastery of souls' as a preliminary to politicking decisions appealed to all parties in the debate. Crucial, too, was the fact that Mickiewicz staked out his claim in the formative period of national consciousness and literacy. Even Słowacki, who died before him but whose impact came later, was too late. If the works stayed banned in Russia till the Revolution, they were freely published in Austrian Kraków and Lwów from the 70s onwards. By the time the bard's body was brought from Paris in 1890, to lie with the Polish kings on Wawel Hill, his unique place was assured. By the time of Polish independence in 1918, when all Polish schoolchildren could for the first time study the works without hindrance, he had no rival.

*

Two hundred years on, the world into which Mickiewicz was born, has vanished. The Grand Duchy of Lithuania, which he so loved, was never restored; its colourful multinational culture and society has not survived either. The Russian Empire, which destroyed the Grand Duchy, was itself destroyed in 1917; and the Soviet Union, whose empire was built on the ruins of tsarism, has risen and fallen in its turn. After the German Occupation of the First World War, Nowogródek passed for twenty years under the rule of Poland's Second Republic. But in 1939, as a result of the Nazi–Soviet Pact, it was captured by the Red Army; most of the descendants of Mickiewicz's Polish neighbours, together with many of the educated Byelorussians from the surrounding countryside, who had attended its Polish schools, were deported, never to be seen again. In June 1941 it was in the eye of the storm in the immediate front line of

Operation Barbarossa. After the Nazi hordes had crossed into the Soviet Union – not, incidentally into Russia – most of the descendants of Mickiewicz's Jewish neighbours were killed in the Holocaust. After such a double scathing, there were few townsfolk alive, few buildings intact. Like most towns in the region Nowogródek emerged from war an empty shell. Fifty years on the outer Soviet fringe brought few improvements. Sullen collectivized peasants, mixed with resentful Russian migrants, could not easily forge new traditions or a new identity. Today, as Novohorodok, its main claim to fame is a statue to the great Byelorussian poet (Adam Mickievič is Byelorussian) which surely looks more out of place than its counterpart in the Place de l'Alma.

Mickiewicz's Wilno has also ceased to exist. Heavily russified in the tsarist period, it was disputed in the inter-war years between the Poles, who still formed an absolute majority of the population, and by the Lithuanian Republic, which claimed it for its capital. Scourged first by the Soviets in 1940 and then by the Nazi Occupation, it was liberated from the Nazi rule in July 1944 by the Polish Home Army units, which, having held a joint victory parade with advancing elements of the Red Army, were promptly arrested en masse by the NKVD. After that, with the remaining Poles largely expelled, it was set up, as Vilnius, as the capital of the Lithuanian SSR and since 1991 of independent Lithuania. Its physical beauties surprisingly, intact, it was repopulated under Soviet auspices by ethnic Lithuanians. This is not easy to explain to British listeners. But it is rather like an American army of occupation in Scotland, giving absolute priority to the Highland Gaels, expelling all English-speaking Scots to England, renaming Edinburgh Dunedin, and pronouncing Robbie Burns to be a great Irish poet. There is only a handful of Poles in modern Vilnius; and virtually no Jews. There is, of course, a statue to the great Lithuanian poet Adomas Mickievičius.

Poetry itself has changed out of all recognition. National bards are no longer in fashion. All manner of trends have come and gone. Even so, the Romantic poets have not lost their popular appeal as one can see from today's *Times* leader about the bicentenary of Wordsworth and Coleridge's *Lyrical Ballads*. In the English-speaking world, it is Wordsworth and Tennyson, Keats and Shelley, whose poems are most widely remembered. And if Mickiewicz still tops the list in Poland, in Lithuania it is probably his contemporary and imitator, A. Baranauskas (1835–1902). In 1859, Baranauskas, a peasant who became a bishop, composed a poem called *The Forests of Anykščiai*, which was consciously modelled on the scenes describing the primeval woods of Lithuania in *Pan Tadeusz*. Its lines evoke not only the wonders of nature but equally the communion of the common people with their native soil. They are well known to present-day Lithuanians as are the lines of *Pan Tadeusz* to present-day Poles:

> Kalnai kelmuoti, pakalnės nuplikę!
> Kas jūsų grožei senobinei tiki?
> Kur toj puikybė jūsų pasidėjo?
> Kur ramus jūsų ūžimas nuo vėjo,
> Kai balto miško lapeliai šlamėjo
> Ir senos pušys siūravo, braškėjo?
> Kur jūsų paukščiai, paukšteliai, paukštytės,
> Katrų čiulbančių taip ramu klausytis?
> Kur jūsų žvėrys, gyvuliai, žvėreliai?
> Kur žvėrių olos, laužai ir urveliai?
> Visa prapuolę; tik ant lauko pliko
> Kelios pušelės apykreivės liko! . . .
> Skujom, šakelėm ir šiškom nuklotą
> Kepina saulė nenaudingą plotą,
> Į kurį žiūrint taip neramu regis:
> Lyg tartum rūmas suiręs, nudegęs,
> Lyg kokio miesto išgriuvus pūstynė,
> Lyg kokio raisto apsvilus kemsynė! . . .

> *Stump-littered hillocks, desolate and bare,*
> *Can anyone believe you once were fair?*
> *Where are your former charms? Where did they go?*
> *Where is your humming when the wind would blow*
> *And toss the white-wood foliage to and fro*
> *And rock your pines, as centuries ago?*
> *Where are your birds and nestlings to be found*
> *Whose chirping such contentment spread all round?*
> *Where are your living creatures large and small,*
> *The burrows and the lairs that housed them all?*
> *All, all has gone: in the deserted plain*
> *A few disfigured pines alone remain.*
> *With needle, cone and twig the earth is strewn –*

A barren waste the sun baked hard in June,
A sight the soul views with as much distress
As ruined palaces rank weeds possess,
Or heaps of rubble where a town once teemed,
Or bone-dry moss where marshland softly gleamed.[6]

Nowadays, therefore, celebrating 'Pan Adam' is not a simple matter. (I doubt if there are quite such problems surrounding Sandor Petöfi.) Sometime in the future, perhaps, Mickiewicz may be seen as a great European poet, a voice bridging East and West. In which case, we can expect a new line of parodies starting with *Europo, ojczyzno moja,* 'O Europe, my homeland'. In the meantime we can either join the Poles, who seem to think that Mickiewicz belongs to them, or, as I would prefer, we can place him firmly in the pantheon of great universal poets. One part of the poet's greatness is forever locked into the particular language of the original, accessible only to those possessing the linguistic key. In the case of Mickiewicz and of other Polish Romantics, the linguistic lock is especially hard to pick. At one level, he writes with breathtaking clarity, framing Romantic themes in a poetic style marked by classical restraint, economy and precision. At another level, his purposes are dependent on a shared familiarity with the political, social and cultural environment. Readers master the syntax and the vocabulary, but who cannot break the code of imagery and allusion, can be left in the dark.

On the universal front, Mickiewicz is surely a prime exemplar of the supremacy of culture in human affairs. All can be lost – the political game, material welfare, even life itself. But culture remains. Mankind is, above all, a cultural animal. Our being is most deeply affected by cultural phenomena – by reflection on our present condition, by hopes of eternity, by thoughts and feelings expressed in pictures, music and above all words. Notwithstanding his anxieties about the vanity of just talking, Mickiewicz, like Petöfi, knew very well that no action was more powerful than the forging of great words, since the words can subsequently inspire millions to great deeds. The 'Mastery of Souls' leads to the mastery of everything else in life. Konrad in the 'Improvisation' of *Dziady III* says it all:

(259–61) Ja i ojczyzna to jedno.
          Nazywam się Milijon – bo za milijony
          Kocham i cierpię katusze.

I and the Fatherland are one.
My name is million, since it is for millions
That I love and suffer torment.

or again,

(50–4)   Boga, natury godne takie pienie!
Pieśń to wielka, pieśń-tworzenie,
Taka pieśń jest siła, dzielność
Taka pieśń jest nieśmiertelność!

Such singing is worthy of God and of Nature,
Such a great song, is a song of creation,
It is power, action, courage.
Such a song is immortality![7]

Through Time and Politics, and Man's Inhumanity to Man, the world of Mickiewicz has passed away. Yet his voice, his near-immortal song, lives on.

* * *

NOTES

1. Alexander Petöfi, 'National Song' in *Magyar Poetry. Selection from Hungarian Poets*, tr. William N. Loew (1899).
2. Juliusz Willaume, 'Jeszcze Polska' in S. Sussocki, S.K. Kuczyński, et al., *Godło, Barwy i Hymn Rzeczpospolitej: Zarys dziejów* (Warszawa, 1970).
3. Adam Mickiewicz, 'Oda do młodości,' in *Pisma poetyckie* (London, 1956), p. 9.
4. Adam Mickiewicz, 'Stepy Akermańskie', *Dzieła poetyckie* (Warszawa, 1965), p. 259.
5. S. Pigoń (ed.), *Księgi narodu polskiego i pielgrzymstwa polskiego* (Kraków, 1922), 53 ff.
6. A. Baranauskas, *The Forests of Anykščiai*, tr. Peter Tempest (Vilnus, 1981).
7. Adam Mickiewicz, *Dziady III* in *Pisma poetyckie* (London, 1956), p. 603.

Roy Foster

THE DANCER AND THE DANCE:
THE PERFORMANCE OF YEATS'S LIFE

Before he was fifty, W. B. Yeats knew how important it was to have your biography written: over and over again, he warned friends and collaborators that the way their lives were accounted for would affect posterity's view of their place in Irish history. 'The power of our epoch on Ireland in the next generation will greatly depend upon the way its personal history is written.' In a significant late poem, 'The Municipal Gallery Revisited', he describes his feelings on seeing the portraits of his generation staring down from the walls of a modern art gallery in independent Ireland: and in one of those ringing invocations and instructions that resound through his work, he tells his readers to come to 'this hallowed place' and 'trace Ireland's history' in the faces of his friends. For all Yeats's hatred of Carlyle, as representative of the Victorian bombast and rhetoric that he wanted to expel from his own work, he could still claim – like Carlyle – that certain individuals at once made history, and epitomized it.

And this was the role that he was determined to play, from an astonishingly young age – from, in fact, his latter schooldays in Dublin during the early 1880s. He played it with such panache that his magnificent personality became – on occasion – inseparable from the historical artefact that he was preparing himself to incarnate. There are those who may say it served him right. His hieratic assumption of a mask is central to the performance that was his public life, and this led easily to accusations of insincerity and pomposity. During his lifetime, such accusations came from people who thought themselves slighted or ignored by him, as he ascended to Olympus; after his death, this attitude affected some of his biographers too. Breathless reverence was always one danger, and Yeats has attracted more than his share of sentimental gush; but the vast corpus of Yeats studies is also remarkable for regular bursts of censorious irritation. Sometimes these issue from critics annoyed by the direction the work has taken, the way an apparently straight-forward poem may swerve into an occult conclusion flourished like a supernatural rabbit out of a magician's hat. Sometimes the censure comes from biographers fixated upon the trivial: Yeats is never going to answer to an approach founded on breezy superficiality, or on vulgarized Freudianism, though he has had more than his share of both. Auden's much-quoted elegy written immediately after Yeats's death in 1939 presents him as someone whose magnificent gift had to survive much that was merely 'silly' in his personality and attitudes, but this is, from a biographer's point of view, insufficient. If he is to be understood and appreciated, it must be by scraping off the accretions of varnish that were assiduously applied to his portrait from very early in his own lifetime, and by placing him rigorously in relation to the history of his times. Both processes involve interrogating very closely the performance that his public life became. But this does not mean reducing either the scale of his achievement or the seriousness of his art: rather, the reverse.

Yeats's own autobiographies, which he began constructing before the age of fifty, appeared irregularly from 1916 to 1935, and only dealt with his life up to the late 1890s. They are deliberately impressionistic and ostensibly disjointed: shafts of light play selectively on remembered scenes and characterizations, clear in outline but oddly distanced, and the life of the mind is discussed with an intensity and emotion not always accorded to his treatment of family and friends. In a sense, his preoccupation seems to be with spiritual autobiography; he had been introduced to the writings of Jung and Freud (characteristically, through the *Journal of the Society for Psychical Research*), but his method may have been more directly affected by Joyce's *Portrait of the Artist*, which he had been reading in pre-publication extracts just before he began writing *Reveries over Childhood and Youth* in 1914.

Like Joyce, Yeats tempered artistic honesty with disingenuousness. His early life, shuttled between his mother's family in Sligo and the Bohemian world embraced by his improvident portrait-

painter father in late-Victorian Bedford Park, is marvellously conveyed in the autobiographies: so is his own apprenticeship to poetry
and politics, and the agenda that he constructed to bring them
together. He would work on these interlacing patterns all his life,
drawing them out on occasions such as his speech accepting the
Nobel Prize in 1923, and creating a poetry of personal recollection
in the elegies he wrote to Augusta Gregory from the late 1920s. The
theme is continued through to his very late verse. The scene is set
early on: coming from the declining Protestant gentry of Ireland, he
discovers a certain genius of place in his almost-native Sligo: folk
wisdoms, peasant tradition, the inherent nobility of a mythologized
Ireland is posited against the materialism of nineteenth-century
England. The disillusionment of Irish politics after Parnell's fall in
1891, with the collapse of the Home Rule enterprise, allows a
vacuum in intellectual life, filled by the cultural revival for which
Yeats and his friends act as brokers. By the turn of the century he
has not only made a start on creating a viable national literature for
Ireland, which can (fortunately for Yeats, who could never learn
Irish) be in the English language. He is also on the edge of mounting
a theatrical movement with the objective of creating a common
cultural identity among its audience. 'In the theatre,' Victor Hugo
had said, 'the mob becomes a people.'

Yeats could not learn French either, but he had a fondness for
ringing phrases from the arbiters of late nineteenth-century French
literary culture, fed to him by his friend Arthur Symons. One such
mantra came from the archpriest of symbolism and decadent languor, Villiers de l'Isle-Adam: 'As for living, our servants will do that
for us.' As uttered by the hero of *Axel*, this refers to suicide: Yeats
apparently interpreted it as leaving aside the everyday and concen-
trating upon the otherworldly, in true fin-de-siècle mode. And his
autobiographies contain an important implication for his biography,
not often enough realized: he was intellectually formed in the 1890s,
and remained in many ways a product of that potent decade. The
'Rhymers Club', a loose association of poetic talents such as Ernest
Dowson, Lionel Johnson, and John Davidson, gave him the sort of
support-group he always craved. Through Bedford Park he had
known Wilde and Morris as well as Shaw and Chesterton; the taste
for Japanese aesthetics that would flower in his Noh-inspired plays
from 1914 dated back to the governing modes of the 90s, along

with most of the most important relationships of his life, except his marriage. Through his obsessive love for Maud Gonne, a beautiful English ex-debutante turned Valkyrie who had embarked on a lifelong identification with the most uncompromising kind of Irish nationalism, he became embroiled in Fenian politics, and literary-political controversies, which are retailed in his autobiographies with a considerable amount of deliberate confusion. At the same time he continued his education in the founding texts of Irish nationalism, through the circle of the venerable (and venerated) patriot John O'Leary. In 1896 Yeats also met the writer whose work would become a touchstone of artistic value for him, and whose reputation he would, in a sense, annex – the playwright John Millington Synge. And the 90s also brought him his closest friend and collaborator, Augusta Gregory. Her house Coole Park became Yeats's second home for nearly every summer over almost thirty years; and she would provide a driving force behind the organization and sustenance of a national theatre. And at the very start of the decade, 7 March 1890, Yeats was initiated into the Order of the Golden Dawn – the occult society that would provide him with metaphors, insights, language and relationships directly traceable through his work for the rest of his life.

Thus it is apposite that his own autobiographies got no further than 1900: so many lines had been laid down then that they required careful disentangling. It was also a period of his life when, as Richard Ellmann has put it, Yeats resembled a man lost in a strange hotel late at night, opening the door to one room after another. It is a revealing metaphor. Ellmann wrote a consummately constructed biography of Yeats half a century ago, which follows the poet's own method of dealing with this confused period: each hotel room is entered, inspected, inventoried as a separate experience. The politics occupy one chapter, occult matters another, love affairs another; and the appropriate poetry attaches, so to speak, to each. But life does not actually happen like that: the hotel rooms in fact intercon-nect, wiring and pipes running back and forth, fire escapes creating surreptitious bridges from one window to another. Love and politics are intertwined in the confusion Gonne brought in her wake; in February 1898, for instance, they spilt over into the world of Coole Park, when Yeats told an appalled Lady Gregory that Gonne was inciting the peasantry of Kerry to rise up against their landlords' property, and Gregory swiftly talked him out of endorsing it. Occultist agendas dictated the content of poems like 'To Ireland in the Coming Times', making the point that you could be an occultist from a Protestant ascendancy background, but a radical Irish nationalist none the less:

> *Know, that I would accounted be*
> *True brother of a company*
> *That sang, to sweeten Ireland's wrong,*
> *Ballad and story, rann and song;*
> *Nor be I any less of them,*
> *Because the red-rose-bordered hem*
> *Of her, whose history began*
> *Before God made the angelic clan,*
> *Trails all about the written page.*
> *When Time began to rant and rage*
> *The measure of her flying feet*
> *Made Ireland's heart begin to beat;*
> *And Time bade all his candles flare*
> *To light a measure here and there;*
> *And may the thoughts of Ireland brood*
> *Upon a measured quietude.*

But it is simultaneously a love poem to Gonne:

> *I cast my heart into my rhymes,*
> *That you, in the dim coming times,*
> *May know how my heart went with them*
> *After the red-rose-bordered hem.*

Joint supernatural and psychic researches always affected the course of his relationships with the women who meant most to him – with Gonne and her daughter, with his first lover Olivia Shakespear, with the fascinating actress Florence Farr, eventually with his wife. It was a sphere in which he could assert control. And it was a fellow initiate and ally in the Order of the Golden Dawn, Annie Horniman, who provided the money to start the Abbey Theatre – and whose obsessive love for Yeats nearly brought the whole enterprise crashing down in dissension. The complexity of these cross-currents must be traced and restored, often illuminating a crisis or change of direction that is otherwise inexplicable. Yeats's biography, like all biographies, must be a process of disaggregation as well as accumulation.

In the process his own priorities often have to be discounted. The awkward figure of Horniman does not feature in his own memoirs; nor do the more agonizing features of his relationship with Gonne, and his own manifest sense of inadequacy faced with the challenges she brought him, both sexual and political. He turned her impact upon his life into a magnificent assertion: she brought depth, resonance, 'the middle of the tint, a sound as of a Burmese gong, an over-powering tumult'. It is initially tempting for the biographer to assume that Yeats revelled in the poetic appositeness of enslavement to a figure who might have come out of a Shelley romance, and also possessed the kind of dramatic and uncontrollable character that always magnetized him. But it was far more than a convenient inspiration for poetry about spreading the cloths of heaven under his beloved's feet, or becoming white birds together on the foam of the sea. His notebooks, drafts, astrological calculations demonstrate the pathos of an obsessive relationship whose reality could never approach the fantasy that held him. A draft that never became a poem is perhaps most revealing of all: he compares their association to children playing at marriage, with images she shows to him but will never allow him to possess. And her sudden and ill-advised marriage to an unmystical republican activist in 1903 was one of the greatest blows of Yeats's life.

His own version of his part in events, while it could appear disarmingly frank, was always well defended. His use of dates is apparently cavalier, but often hides an actual change of sequence, in order to build up his own pattern, and mislead the reader by a flattering air of confidential collusion (he endearingly asks us 'Was it in' such-and-such a year that this or that happened – well, was it?). His inflections of language can subtly but radically impose an interpretation (his mother's family are cast in a deliberately archaic pose, as 'merchants' and 'sea-captains', rather than the hard-headed property-developing town-councillor Victorian bourgeois that they were). 'Glamour' was a favourite word of the Celticists with whom he was associated in his youth, signifying the eerie light of some Scottish or Irish half-world: in Yeats's case, it could be applied in its modern sense too. Much as he looked like the ideal figure of the poet (haunted, dreamy, dark, exotic), the self-conceived and self-created style of his life had to mirror a world of occult inspiration and romantic languor and longing. There was little room for admitting his other existences as Stakhanovite literary journalist and reviewer, consummate committee manipulator, or dictatorial theatre manager. It may be a biographer's *déformation professionnelle* to overemphasize these personae, as an act of compensation, but still a worthwhile reclamation is being made.

From about 1900, Yeats once wrote, everybody came down off their stilts; the modern age had arrived. Living could no longer be delegated to the servants. Tracing his own life from this point provides its own challenges. His autobiographical reflections are scattered, in essays on Synge's significance, or episodic diaries, or his vast correspondence; he was beginning to be so famous that his slightest statements were preserved and conned for significance. This has its disadvantages too. That patina was beginning to develop; and he was simultaneously embarked upon a retreat from the politics of his youth, as well as a decade-long obsession with the theatre. There are love affairs kept concealed from his friends, and quarrels with old associates. He was also tired of confinement in the 'Celticist' mode, and impatient with the imitators already springing up around him. He was in search of a new diction, an unadorned style, a harsh edge to his work, which confused old admirers: it comes intermittently through his poetry from the early 1900s, but announced itself to the world in his landmark collection of 1914, *Responsibilities*. Much of this was presented as an unmaking of what had gone before, but many of the old themes and relationships persisted below the surface.

> I made my song a coat
> Covered with embroideries
> Out of old mythologies
> From heel to throat;
> But the fools caught it,
> Wore it in the world's eyes
> As though they'd wrought it.
> Song, let them take it,
> For there's more enterprise
> In walking naked.

In 1916–17 a series of seismic upheavals convulsed the landscape of his life, and when the dust settled he had to subtly alter his view of his own history. The Easter Rising of 1916 was as unexpected to Yeats as to everyone else. It came at a time when he was spending far more time in England than Ireland, and had ostentatiously declared his disillusionment with much that characterized modern Ireland. Fifty years old and increasingly conservative, he was by now a constitutionalist Home Ruler rather than a Fenian revolutionary, and had even expressed sympathy for the fears of the Ulster Protestants, unfounded though he believed them to be. He was, indeed, prepared to call on his own chastening experience at the hands of Catholic zealots who had attacked his early plays; this sometimes made him look uncomfortably like a traditional Irish Protestant, invoking the caste whence he came. He was in receipt of a civil list pension, and had recently refused a knighthood. The extreme Republicans who made the Rising were very often people he had quarrelled with over the previous ten years or so: he had declared a commitment to artistic freedom and an openness to the ideals of the European avant-garde, which some guardians of nationalist probity (notably the Sinn Féin founder Arthur Griffith) found suspect on both counts. Yeats's reaction to this shattering event was, at first, cautious: but he rapidly decided it was time to return to Ireland and 'begin building again'. He also expressed his feelings about the Rising, and the transformation it effected in Irish nationalist politics, in poetry: the quintessentially ambiguous poem 'Easter 1916', where the idea of a 'terrible beauty' born again was counterpointed by an appeal to the humane values of everyday life, and a plea against fanaticism. It is, in many ways, a reprise of his great essay 'J. M. Synge and the Ireland of his Time', published six years before, where he had written prophetically of nationalists whose 'patriotism was great enough to carry them to the scaffold', but who limited themselves with the 'morbid persistence of minds unsettled by some fixed idea'.

> Hearts with one purpose alone
> Through summer and winter seem
> Enchanted to a stone
> To trouble the living stream.
> The horse that comes from the road,
> The rider, the birds that range
> From cloud to tumbling cloud,
> Minute by minute they change;

A shadow of cloud on the stream
Changes minute by minute;
A horse-hoof slides on the brim,
And a horse plashes within it;
The long-legged moor-hens dive,
And hens to moor-cocks call;
Minute by minute they live:
The stone's in the midst of all.

Too long a sacrifice
Can make a stone of the heart.
O when may it suffice?
That is Heaven's part, our part
To murmur name upon name,
As a mother names her child
When sleep at last has come
On limbs that had run wild.
What is it but nightfall?
No, no, not night but death;
Was it needless death after all?
For England may keep faith
For all that is done and said.
We know their dream; enough
To know they dreamed and are dead;
And what if excess of love
Bewildered them till they died?
I write it out in a verse –
MacDonagh and MacBride
And Connolly and Pearse
Now and in time to be,
Wherever green is worn,
Are changed, changed utterly:
A terrible beauty is born.

The poem is also – yet again – an implicit love poem to Maud Gonne, but she did not like it: astutely spotting the ambiguity that lies at its centre and somehow infuses it with complexity rather than decisiveness. Her long-estranged husband John MacBride had been executed in the Rising, and Yeats wrote much of 'Easter 1916' at her Normandy house in the summer of 1916 – where he proposed to her once more, and was finally refused. But he finished the poem at Coole, and Augusta Gregory was a strong influence in fixing his ideas about the Rising as a possible rebirth. Gregory was, all the same, a more convinced republican than he was. He kept the poem unpublished for four years, but the intervening period saw a series of increasingly nationalist poems and plays, keeping pace with the polarization of nationalist politics in Ireland and the increasingly desperate and draconian nature of British rule. Thus Yeats emerged in 1922 as a founding father of the new State set up by the 1921 Treaty that ended the Anglo-Irish War. Significantly, over the same period he was writing the next instalment of his autobiographies, which would place the actions of his youth, and the achievement of his generation, as the essential preparation for the Irish revolution. It required some strategic amnesia about the position he had occupied vis-à-vis Irish nationalism since the turn of the century; it also required a careful publishing strategy, and some rather disingenuous dating of poems. For instance, his apocalyptic poem-sequence 'Thoughts on the Present State of the World', written in 1921, was re-titled 'Nineteen Hundred and Nineteen' (the year of the outbreak of the Anglo-Irish War) in order to shift the focus onto Ireland rather than the world at large. The alteration also changes the implications of dates within the poem. ('We who seven years ago / Talked of honour and of truth', as originally written, referred to the outbreak of war in 1914; with the change of title, it became 1912, the year of the Home Rule crisis.) It is just one of many instances where the historian's sleuthing instinct is as necessary as the literary critic's analysis, in uncovering the pattern Yeats was determined to present in his own life.

By 1922 his life had changed direction in other ways too: he was married with two children. His rather dutiful last proposal to Gonne had been succeeded by an overpowering obsession with her fascinating and beautiful daughter Iseult: she, too, refused to marry Yeats, who was twenty-nine years her senior, but he was still deeply and traumatically preoccupied by Iseult when he rapidly married Georgie Hyde-Lees in 1917, to everyone's astonishment, including his own. The marriage was unexpectedly successful: famously, because of collaboration in supernatural experiments through 'automatic writing'. His own commentary on the process is half-concealed in several poems, and fully revealed in *A Vision*, the peculiar philosophy of history and astrology that he published in 1925 (and drastically revised twelve years later). As philosophy, it is

Benito Mussolini (1883–1945)

Axel von dem Bussche (1920–93)
in his *Wehrmacht* uniform *(left)*
and in 1992 *(below)*.

Right:
Margaret Thatcher (1925–)

Adam Mickiewicz (1798–1855)

W. B. Yeats (1865–1939)

Carole Lombard (1908–42)

Clement Greenberg (1909–94)

Humphry Davy (1778–1829)

Michael Faraday (1791–1867)

J. M. W. Turner (1775–1851)

Charles Babbage (1791–1871)

Aimé Thomé de Gamond (1807–76)

Richard Cobb (1917–96)

Isaiah Berlin (1909–97)

well-nigh incomprehensible; for biographical purposes, it is vital. The same holds true for the reams of automatic script recorded over the five years following his marriage, which have been published and annotated by scholars and read more like transactional psycho-analysis than voices from the void.

What *A Vision* shows is not only someone determined to make sense of the world, through the insights of the otherworld; it is also a gallery of archetypes, since Yeats not only believed in astrology but subdivided his acquaintance into people of certain 'phases', identified by specific great historical personages. His wife always maintained that he had no interest in people as such, but was deeply interested in what they said or did: an interesting distinction, which might explain the strangely Martian way he views so many of his acquaintanceship in his autobiographies. But his wife also said that the thing that always surprised her about her husband was his uncanny ability to know exactly how things would seem to people afterwards. He was brilliantly adept at emerging on the right side of history – and, indeed, at aligning allies and isolating enemies. All his life he remembered what Madame Blavatsky said to him in his days as an apprentice (and rather unsatisfactory) Theosophist. 'I used to wonder at and pity the people who sell their souls to the devil, but now I only pity them. They do it to have somebody on their side.'

By the 1930s, which spanned the last decade of his life, the world might be supposed to have come over to his side. He was internationally famous, assured, uniquely grand: a great institution of Irish life as well as of world literature. But he was never complacent, and always embattled. From early on in the history of the new Irish State, he was a flag-bearer against literary censorship, and determined to form a group of writers who would stand both for artistic freedom, and a distinctively Irish literary tradition. Now, however, he found his antecedents in eighteenth-century precursors like Swift and Berkeley, and his politics became increasingly author-itarian; his early support for an Irish proto-fascist movement is well recorded, but so is the fact that he withdrew it early on. (Nor was he the only respectable personage to follow this path.) At the same time in his own poetry he continued to pursue the hardness, economy and clarity that he had sought since abandoning the 'decorated' style that had made his name in the 1890s. In fact, he sometimes turned back to the ballad metres of his youth, but put them to aggressively modern use in his sequence of poems featuring 'Crazy Jane'; and the archetypal philosophical and world-historical insights (if that is what they were) of *A Vision* were still being explored in poems like 'Long-legged Fly'.

> That civilisation may not sink,
> Its great battle lost,
> Quiet the dog, tether the pony
> To a distant post;
> Our master Caesar is in the tent
> Where the maps are spread,
> His eyes fixed upon nothing,
> A hand under his head.
> *Like a long-legged fly upon the stream*
> *His mind moves upon silence.*
>
> That the topless towers be burnt
> And men recall that face,
> Move most gently if move you must
> In this lonely place.
> She thinks, part woman, three parts a child,
> That nobody looks; her feet
> Practise a tinker shuffle
> Picked up on a street.
> *Like a long-legged fly upon the stream*
> *Her mind moves upon silence.*
>
> That girls at puberty may find
> The first Adam in their thought,
> Shut the door of the Pope's chapel,
> Keep those children out.
> There on that scaffolding reclines
> Michael Angelo.
> With no more sound than the mice make
> His hand moves to and fro.
> *Like a long-legged fly upon the stream*
> *His mind moves upon silence.*

Themes from neo-Platonism and classical antiquity still accompany his enduring interest in Irish mythology. It is a strong mixture. Not all his late experiments were happy, and he fell into odd company in literature as well as politics: but poems like these, uniting complex thought to simple language, are near the summit of his achievement.

It is significant – certainly for the biographer – that in this last phase he was still inventing personae: some new, like 'Crazy Jane', some revisited, like 'Michael Robartes' and 'Owen Aherne', originally created for his underrated supernatural fiction of the 1890s, and resurrected to form a framework for *A Vision*. He had always dealt in alter egos: a man of the 90s still, Yeats liked to summon up doppelgängers, invent histories, surround himself with people and give them assigned characters as well as characteristics. His own personality was in some ways another invention: conceived in his youthful shyness and insecurity, and consummated in the glamour with which he was invested from his first great success. A young schoolteacher who sat at his feet not long before his death was struck by the reverence of another of the guests, who breathed approbation at every pronouncement given out by the sage, no matter how bizarre: finally, the visitor was delighted when the poet snapped back with: 'Madam, I was not entirely serious.'

Was he always entirely serious? How far does the carapace of reputation imprison greatness? Yeats somehow transcends the process, because of the deliberateness with which he controlled it. But the preoccupation with masks and self-creation, important in his life, is also central to his work – notably in his plays, which are often biographically revealing in an exactly inverse proportion to their literary merit. *Where There Is Nothing* and *The King's Threshold* are about the position of the artist in conventional society. *The Countess Cathleen* is, in its successive versions, invaded by his relationship with Maud Gonne. The *Only Jealousy of Emer* is a coded treatment of upheavals in his personal life around the time of his marriage. *The Player Queen* is an extended reflection on the assumption of masks, and the sexual tension underlying the performance of life. Finally the mythic hero Cuchulainn, subject of a play and poems at the very end of his life, supplies his last alter ego. As with Wordsworth, Yeats's life is a subject for his art; the ever-present danger of assuming that a first-person reference in a poem refers to the poet 'himself' is a less hazardous supposition with Yeats than with most other poets, even if other sleights of hand are being simultaneously practised. Another magnificent late poem, 'The Circus Animals' Desertion', is a case in point.

Those masterful images because complete
Grew in pure mind, but out of what began?
A mound of refuse or the sweepings of a street,
Old kettles, old bottles and a broken can,
Old iron, old bones, old rags, that raving slut
Who keeps the till. Now that my ladder's gone,
I must lie down where all the ladders start,
In the foul rag-and-bone shop of the heart.

In the end, we must rely upon the simple but towering fact of chronology to unite the process of creation with the life as lived. Yeats did not live his life in compartments, even if that is how he wanted to interpret it; the contingent and unforeseen had to be coped with, no matter how much retrospective effort he devoted to proving that his fate – and everyone's – had been written in the stars all along. To reconstruct his existence week by week is a liberating as well as a humbling experience. For one thing, it shows just how many levels he lived at: a single day may include plunges into theatrical activity, journalism, social life and writing, and be ended by dashing off several letters to different correspondents giving different constructions on the several involvements. But more importantly, restoring the 'thick' texture rather than simply admiring the gleaming chiaroscuro helps show how a reverse in one sphere galvanized an advance elsewhere, how the pattern may re-form in one circle just as it breaks up in another, and how what might have been an astonishingly disparate life is unified by the steely will of someone who knew that his greatest challenge was to finish what he had begun.

Here, as ever, the clues lie in his own beginnings: the man whose artist father was psychologically incapable of declaring a painting finished became the poet whose sense of closure was both dramatic and inimitable. Even when a Yeats poem ends (as they often do) with a question, it is the unanswerably right ending. Perhaps his most famous final interrogation – 'How can we know the dancer from the dance?' – might profitably be applied to reconstructing the story of his own life. Much of his own writing became a kind of retrospective choreography, shaping the structure of the great drama that ended on 28 January 1939. The biographer's work is neither simply to accept this presentation, nor to reject it completely, but to build it in as part of the overall creation (or performance): and at the same time to follow through each step and turn in the order it happened, always conscious that a change of direction is rarely premeditated, even if carried off with the combination of apparently inevitable logic and dramatic effect that marks the consummate artist.

Alan Davidson

TO BE OR NOT TO BE:
CAROLE LOMBARD

> Her entry on a set often occasions so many greetings from prop-
> men, mechanics, assistant directors and electricians on the rafters
> far above the set that the uproar sounds like a reunion between
> Tarzan and his monkeys.

This was written about the film star Carole Lombard by Noel F.
Busch, author of the article on her in *Life* magazine of 17 October
1938. She was on the cover of that issue and at the height of her
career. Busch's description provides a good keynote to this essay
about her, because it gives a very vivid impression of how much fun
she got out of life, and how much she communicated to others –
plus the fact that she was class-blind, everyone's friend.

In a career marked by Californian sunshine and constant laughter, there were nonetheless dark moments. 'To be or not to be?'
Hamlet's words have been repeated countless times since Shakespeare penned them, but never with more poignant effect than when
used as the title of Carole Lombard's last film.

Fate determined that for her the answer would be negative. She
did not live to see the premiere of the film in February 1942. On 16
January of that year, an aircraft carrying her and her mother home
to California crashed into a mountain near Las Vegas. All aboard
were killed instantly.

Thus ended her career and her life when she was only thirty-
three. Her image remains, and will always remain, that of a young
woman at a peak of beauty and a peak of accomplishment. In an
era when the ambitions of many young American women were to

become a star in Hollywood and, more specifically, to marry Clark Gable, she had done both. It was Gable who flew to Nevada and joined in the sad search for remains. It was to Gable that President Franklin Roosevelt sent his moving tribute:

> She brought great joy to all who knew her and to millions who knew her only as a great artist. She gave unselfishly of time and talent to serve her government in peace and war. She loved her country. She is and always will be a star, one we shall never forget, nor cease to be grateful to.

Roosevelt's choice of words touched twice on an important point. Millions knew her as a 'great artist' (and millions more would so know her after her death). She 'always will be a star'. The future tense could be used here in a literal way that only became possible in the twentieth century, when the cinema came into being and its stars were given eternal life on film.

Carole Lombard was by no means the only beautiful and well-known young woman to die young. But she was one of the first such who not only lived in the Cinema Age but was a creative part of it. This was important. In earlier times, one could speak of a person being 'immortalized' in a painting, or even by a sculpture or a poem. But in none of the media could a person 'live on' in the same way as someone captured on many hours of film, someone who could be seen from here to eternity moving, talking, eating, loving, joking, fighting . . . whatever.

That was a big difference; and there were certain circumstances that set Carole Lombard apart from the few among her contemporaries who could be compared with her in respect of beauty, fame and early death. Of these others, Jean Harlow and Marilyn Monroe were the most famous. Both died young, but in each instance there was an element of mystery involved, and not an attractive sort of mystery. In contrast, the instant and accidental death that ended Carole Lombard's life was a completely 'clean' final curtain and left her potential as a twentieth-century icon unclouded.

This potential was buttressed by many other factors. Her enormous likeability and her gift for generating laughter were important. The laughter matched a need of the time when she made her best films; the historical context in which she operated included the Depression and the outbreak of the Second World War. In this essay

I consider how the conjunction of these and other factors contributed to a result of unique brilliance, ensuring that, in Roosevelt's words, she 'always will be a star, one we shall never forget' – and one of the brightest in our rear-view mirror as we forge ahead out of the twentieth century.

Jane Peters was born in Fort Wayne, Indiana, in October 1908. Her parents, of the upper middle class, had already produced two older brothers for her. She referred later to the difficulty that she had in keeping up with them. When her mother and the greater part of the family (but not her father) migrated to California in 1914 and settled in the Los Angeles area, this element of striving was already apparent. Her bio-bibliographer, Robert D. Matzen (1988), has drawn a deft picture of the tomboy character that Jane Peters developed and of how her combat skills were enhanced by boxing lessons from Benny Leonard, who was for a time lightweight boxing champion of the world. Many suppose that her use of bad language – not just the occasional swear word, but frequent use of what then seemed strong stuff – had its roots in this part of her life, when prowess in fist-fighting, self-protection, and keeping up with the brothers were important preoccupations. Others think that the habit was acquired later, as a defensive mechanism against predators who tried (unsuccessfully, it seems) to push her onto the notorious 'casting couch'. The photographer John Engstead, whose book of reminiscences (1978) includes much about Carole, took the latter view and also remarked that Carole had no difficulty in turning off the profanity when in the company of her mother (or, he adds, either of her husbands, neither of whom liked it).

A girl might benefit from having a pretty-but-tough image. Leonard Maltin (1976), another Lombard biographer and one who is well known for his knowledge of the cinema world of the 1930s, relates that Jane Peters was given her first film part (as the hero's tomboy little sister in *A Perfect Crime*) because she had been observed looking cute and 'knocking hell out of the other kids' in a back street. This assignment led to nothing further for the time being, but helped to mould ambitions, as did her environment. As a teenager, very pretty, great at sports, showing a flair for drama, she lived and attended school in the heartland of the film community. Charlie Chaplin's agent took an interest in her. Turning sixteen, she left school and changed her name; first to Carol Lombard (Carol for a tennis-playing friend and Lombard for a banker friend of her mother) and then some years later (when the name was misspelt on a poster, and judged to look better that way) to Carole Lombard. (I refer to her from now on as Carole, anticipating this change.)

Ups and downs as a budding starlet followed. The famous actor John Barrymore gave her a hand up. But then a car accident, sustained while she was joyriding with a friend in his roadster, seemed likely to stop her in her tracks. The worse of two gashes was halfway up the cheek, ending not far from nostril and lip. It was deep. She was told that the only hope of avoiding permanent disfigurement was to have the necessary surgery done without anaesthetic; if the facial muscles were allowed to relax for any length of time, they would never recover. The plucky patient, still determined to succeed, accepted the doctor's advice. Even so, when the bandages were removed weeks later, the effect was discouraging. Much more time was needed before the scar would fade to the just perceptible mark that may be seen in some of her films.

Fortunately, after many months of vainly seeking parts, she was taken on by Mack Sennett, king of the crazy comedy shorts that enjoyed a vogue during the 1920s. The scar did not bother him, and he was pleased by the way Carole took to slapstick as one of his Bathing Beauties. Hilarity came naturally to her. Now, amid the flying custard pies and slipped-on bananas, she developed in addition a sense of comedy timing, which underpinned her later success in the genre with which she is identified: screwball comedy.

However, she did not progress straight from slapstick to screwball. Even while working mainly for Sennett (until his enterprise collapsed in 1929), she was able to take on some work for other studios. During the years 1928–34, she played many roles, of various kinds, and was developing into an experienced and competent actress. A lifelong friend and long-term secretary whom she acquired in the Sennett studio, Madalynne Fields ('Fieldsie'), helped keep the flame of her ambition alight, and she was sustained in her efforts by her mother, with whom she had a close and easy relationship. She also had some lucky breaks. At one point, Joseph P. Kennedy, father of the future US President, gave her a Pathé contract. He is said to have advised her to lose some weight, and to have relished her quick response, that he should do the same.

In one of her first non-Sennett films, *Man of the World*, she played opposite William Powell, who was indeed a real man of the world, charming and sophisticated, one of Hollywood's most eligible bachelors. By the time they did a second film together, a mutual courtship of high intensity was under way. Larry Swindell, author of the most polished of the biographies of Carole (1975), has described wittily how far apart the couple were, not only in age (nearly twenty years) but also in their tastes and attitudes (he was moody, intellectual, sardonic, accustomed to fine wines, limousines, servants and all the social graces, while she was casual, spontaneous, fun-loving, prankish, impatient of etiquette); and how each professed a desire to be more like the other, while actually planning 'to remake the other in his or her own image'.

It may be that each did in fact have a beneficial effect on the other, but the differences were too great. Powell must have blanched at some of Carole's practical jokes, and Carole no doubt was increasingly oppressed by her husband's stuffiness, although continuing to be very fond of him. Besides, professional commitments tended to keep them apart. Carole obtained an uncontested divorce in August 1933. The couple remained friends, even resumed going out together for a while, and subsequently co-starred in one brilliant film (*My Man Godfrey*, 1936). But the relationship never achieved, for Carole, the emotional intensity of what she would later describe as the great love of her life. This was her affair with Russ Columbo, a rival of the young Bing Crosby. They may have planned to marry, but he was sent for ever offstage by a bizarre and fatal accident with an antique firearm, in September 1934.

This tragedy occurred several months after the release of the 1934 film *Twentieth Century*, which inaugurated the climactic phase of her career. The part she played opposite John Barrymore was not meant for her, but other plans went awry and it eventually fell into her lap. Barrymore, not yet too far gone in his downward spiral of depression and alcoholism, enthused. To him, and to Howard Hawks, the director, must go much of the credit for Carole's fiery and uninhibited performance, which brought her, at true star level, into the mixture of farce and satire with surreal elements that would soon be dubbed 'screwball'. This term, with which Carole became so closely identified that Swindell's biography of her is simply entitled *Screwball*, deserves some explanation. Apart from its use in baseball, it does not go far back. In a cinema context, the *Oxford English Dictionary* (2nd edn) offers this definition:

> Used, chiefly *attrib.* or as *adj.* (esp. as *screwball comedy*) of a kind of fast-moving, irreverent comedy film produced in the US in the 1930s, of which eccentric characters were the chief feature, or of persons, etc., connected with such films.

Neither *Merriam Webster's Collegiate Dictionary* (1993, 10th edn) nor the *Random House Dictionary of the English Language* (2nd edn, unabridged, 1987) makes a mention of the word in a cinema context. Their definitions centre on such phrases as 'crazily eccentric or whimsical' and 'whimsically eccentric'.

Use of the word in a cinema context is attested in the *OED* by citations that come mainly from the late 1930s; a reference to 'another of those screwball comedies' occurred in the *New York Times* in 1938. The retrospective application of the word to particular films extends as far back as films released in 1934 (e.g. *It Happened One Night, Twentieth Century*); but there were some earlier films with similar characteristics (e.g. *Love Me Tonight*, 1932).

Regular features of the screwball genre included echoes of the medieval tradition of the Lord of Misrule, when someone normally at the bottom of the power ladder suddenly emerges on top – witness the proto-screwball film *We're Not Dressing* (1933), in which Carole, the wealthy playgirl yacht-owner, heartlessly bosses Bing Crosby, a sailor, around, only to find that when they are shipwrecked she and the others all depend on him. Other 'upside down' effects, role-reversals and role manipulations were common.

Stock characters included the wilful young heiress; the uncomprehending millionaire father; the reckless young reporter; and the gambler – compare Clark Gable in *No Man of Her Own* (1932, directed by Wesley Ruggles), who lets the toss of a coin determine whether he will marry Carole (playing a small-town librarian with revolutionary instincts), although he only met her a couple of days before. The wise old-timer (of either gender, sometimes even a couple of them) with a heart of gold, abetting the conquest of wealth and power by love and stubbornness, also figured.

James Harvey (1987) is probably the author who has given the most thoughtful analysis of the screwball comedies, setting them in the broader context of romantic comedies of his book's title, and

relating them to the social conditions of their time (caused by the
Great Depression and then by the outbreak of the Second World
War). It was certainly a period when people felt a need for laughter.
Harvey calls 1934 'the screwball year', when the genre first flowered
fully; and he demonstrates clearly how, once seen to be successful,
it grew by imitation. Just about all the female stars, and many of
the finest directors, had a go at it. But the screwball pantheon
harbours a limited number of superstars, most notably Carole
herself, Irene Dunne, Jean Arthur, and (occasionally) Claudette
Colbert and Katharine Hepburn. The career of Gingеt Rogers was
pleasantly infected but not dominated by the genre. Barbara Stan-
wyck, supremely versatile, had at least two more or less screwball
roles (*The Lady Eve* was the outstanding one). Cary Grant and
Rosalind Russell abandoned their more usual kinds of performance
to go splendidly screwball in *His Girl Friday*.

One comes back to the conclusion that – no disrespect to the
others – the two greatest practitioners were Carole and Irene Dunne;
and that, as between these two, Carole may be said to have deserved
first place. The reasoning behind this judgement takes one back to,
and beyond, the question of definition already discussed. Do the
greatest screwball performances require something over and above
the stock ingredients? Does there have to be a recognition that
underneath the comedy lies something more serious, perhaps tragic?
This of course depends on the script and on the direction to a large
extent. But the deportment of the screwball heroine is also crucial.
Carole, in my view, had a special gift for somehow getting across to
the audience the existence of this additional element. Cavorting with
abandon on the tip of the iceberg, she somehow implied the dark
and mysterious mass below the surface.

Needless to say, not all her films after *Twentieth Century* had
a screwball character, and, of the ones that did, not all had this
additional depth. Thus *Hands Across the Table* (1935) and *The
Princess Comes Across* (1936) were effective comedies, with pleas-
ingly mad episodes, but could hardly qualify as true screwball.
However, *My Man Godfrey* (1936) certainly could. At one level it
is a crazy-go-round of dotty antics in a wealthy household, with
Carole playing the younger daughter Irene Bullock, and William
Powell (her former husband in real life, her discovery as a 'forgotten man' living on a city dump in the film) providing single-handed

the necessary contrast of common sense and competence. At another level, it is a satire that could be, and was at the time, compared to acknowledged masterpieces. The London *Times* critic wrote that: 'The exuberance of the idle rich is turned into a spectacle of pure imbecility, with much charmingly inconsequent dialogue, and with a pleasing demonstration of the theory that the irresponsible possession of wealth produces characters that strongly resemble those of Chekhov.' Graham Greene, in the *Spectator*, thought that the early sequences well conveyed the atmosphere of *The Cherry Orchard*, 'of a class with little of the grace and all the futility and some of the innocence of its Russian counterpart'. That he then deplored the happy ending suggests to me that he missed the point. He was evidently thinking that if you start off like Chekhov then you should finish likewise. But not if you are Gregory La Cava (the director), Carole, and William Powell. They tell a different tale, with a different moral. The intensity of Carole's infatuation for Godfrey, of her emotions generally, of her romantic attitude of the world – these were bound to transform everyone and everything within range. To complain that they do not lead to frustration and tragedy reflects a failure to understand that in the American screwball world, unlike Chekhov's world, the sheer incandescence, purity and dottiness of Carole's love would be enough to burn away like fluff any ephemeral obstacles. Yes, it is amazing that the shanties on the city dump are transformed into gleaming new buildings. Yes, it is astonishing that the derelicts are turned into busy happy workers, and the previously reluctant Godfrey into the contented spouse of the radiant young woman who has at last snared him. But would it not have been even more amazing if these things had not happened?

Nothing Sacred (1937, directed by William Wellman) was a worthy successor. For some, it represents Carole's greatest achievement in screwball. The part of Hazel Flagg, the girl in a small town in Vermont who is thought to be dying of radium poisoning and who, even when the preposterous local doctor reveals that he made a mistake and that she is perfectly healthy, goes along with the plan of a reporter (Fredric March) to fly her to New York for a civic welcome and salute, a final flourish to a doomed life, suits her perfectly. Never has an essentially incredible part seemed more credible. Certain surreal touches heighten the incredibility and the credibility alike. When March, already disconcerted by the taciturnity of the inhabitants of the Vermont town (Yep and Nope seem to be the full extent of their vocabulary, and when even the most basic courtesy would demand a Yep they go Nope), is walking along the street towards the doctor's house, a gate suddenly opens behind him and a small boy scuttles out, like a dog, catches up with him, bites him in the leg and scuttles back. It's all over in seconds, indeed some people who watch the film don't realize what has happened.

In this film, Carole acts to perfection, so much so that it does not seem like acting. One has the feeling that if the 'real' Carole had somehow gotten into a situation like that of Hazel Flagg – thrust into a limelight of extreme intensity on the basis of a colossal misunderstanding – this is how she would have behaved. Those almost imperceptible flutters of the tiny muscles under her chin, signalling panic or elation or both, would have been taking place just as in the film. She would have risen to the absurd occasions confronting her, acquiesced in crazy schemes for concealing the truth, even jumped into the river to fake suicide, and almost certainly started to fall in love with Fredric March. Doing all these things, and much more besides, in front of the cameras cannot have been a problem for her. She *was* Hazel Flagg.

This film, her first to use colour, was photographed by W. Howard Greene, not by Ted Tetzlaff, her favourite photographer and one who was most skilful in bringing out her distinctive beauty. However, she never looked more beautiful. There is a shot of her wearing a fireman's helmet after she has been pulled, bedraggled, by March from the river, and then pulled, still bedraggled, from the improvised shelter in which she and March had taken refuge and (so we can tell from the antics of their protruding feet) finally discovered their mutual love, and taken onto the firetruck that had come to rescue her from the river. This is a shot of ineffable beauty. Would that in that moment she could have sat for some Antonello da Messina paint-alike, as the Madonna of the Firetruck!

Carole's beauty was distinctive, in that no one else looked quite like her, but it was not static. She had very fine blonde hair, of which she would have wished a greater abundance, but of which there was quite enough to enable her hairdresser, Loretta, to achieve numerous transformations. In the early 1930s Carole wore her hair in such a way as to leave her prominent forehead fully exposed. This could create an effect of marmoreal, even glacial, aloofness when viewed from the front. Viewed from the side, it achieved a stunning effect of classical beauty, just right to be painted by one of the fifteenth-century Florentine masters who specialized in that kind of portrait. Later she softened the effect by having a cloud of curls on her forehead; the transition can be seen in *Twentieth Century*. But this risked making her seem top-heavy; and later still she moved on to what became her trademark style for the 1930s, with a curl jutting forward over her right forehead (and often another on the left forehead).

This was how she looked in 1937, with everything going her way. Professionally, she had become the highest-paid woman in Hollywood. On the personal plane, she had developed, since the famous White Ball of 1936 (at which she arrived in a white ambulance, to be carried in on a stretcher – there was no limit to her 'gags'), a relationship with Clark Gable, which was to dominate the remainder of her life. Gable, who had hitherto made a habit of marrying older women, was stuck with his then wife, Rhea Langham, and it was not until early March 1939 that he achieved a divorce. After that he and Carole were married at Kingman in Arizona and soon afterwards they settled in a new home, in fact a whole estate, in the San Fernando Valley, two dozen miles from Los Angeles. The couple were portrayed as taking to 'ranch' life with great enthusiasm; Carole looked after the barnyard animals and improved her already good shooting so as to become the perfect 'buddy' for Gable on the 'hunting' expeditions he loved. 'She can handle a shotgun as easily as lipstick,' wrote one reporter at this time.

Carole's slim, almost boyish figure was fine for life on the ranch, and it was also fine for the very glamorous clothes that were designed for her, especially by Travis Banton, and which she wore with a delightful and natural grace. The easy way in which she could switch between outdoors mode and the chic appropriate for films and for Hollywood occasions must have delighted Gable. Her own attitude to him was full of love and affection, but she never pretended to think him perfect. She confided in friends, without any trace of malice, that his technique as a lover needed improvement, an idea that would have seemed heretical and incredible to any of Gable's countless female fans. And there is a story, passed on to me by Alistair Horne, that Carole was once asked by someone what it was like being married to Gable, and replied, 'Well, he's no Clark

Gable.' Even if the story is apocryphal, this is just the sort of thing she would have said – but always with affection.

Although allowances were made for the ups and downs of marital life, and for Gable's notorious susceptibility (it was said that, filming with the young Lana Turner, he had to be monitored by Carole) the pairing worked well. Evenings were spent at the ranch, not in nightclubs or at glitzy social events. Carole read a lot. Asked by her husband whether she had everything in life that she wanted, she is said to have replied yes, except that she could do with some manure for the fruit trees in the orchard. However, there was something more important that she wanted and apparently could not have: a baby. Evidence from people who knew her well at this time suggests that she was deeply disappointed and that, had her wish been fulfilled, she would probably have retired from films.

The non-screwball films with which Carole had followed *Nothing Sacred* were not great successes. Fortunately for her reputation, she returned from a series of dramatic roles to comedy with *Mr and Mrs Smith* in 1941. This film was directed by Hitchcock, whose memoirs record a practical joke played on him by Carole (one of the scores recorded in the literature, but better attested than some of the others). Before leaving England for Hollywood, he had been heard to say something on the lines of 'actors should be treated like cattle'. So, he found one day that Carole had had a small corral built on the sound stage of *Mr and Mrs Smith*, in which she installed three young cows bearing her name and those of Robert Montgomery and Gene Raymond. This was taken in good part, as were most (but not all) of Carole's gags.

Carole's last film, *To Be Or Not To Be*, is a masterpiece, yet difficult to describe. Imagine a Polish theatre company putting on a performance of Hamlet in Warsaw while the Germans were invading Poland in 1939. Embroider with espionage and romance. Give Jack Benny a part and involve Hitler himself. The director, Ernest Lubitsch, himself declared that the mixture was unclassifiable – tragic farce, farcical tragedy, pathos mixed with lunacy, satire and drama.

The brew was partly stirred by Carole, playing Maria Tura. She had essayed on at least one previous occasion to take part in the direction of a film, *True Confession*, but her efforts had been skewed by an excess of devotion to John Barrymore, he who had helped her so much at an earlier stage in her career. This time, there was no such problem. Lubitsch himself said that he had invited her to be an unofficial co-director, and clearly valued what he called her 'cerebral contribution'. Indeed, as Swindell has put it: '*To Be Or Not To Be* was the happiest experience of her career – the one, she said, when everything began right, stayed right, and ended right.'

The film was still being made when the Japanese attacked the US fleet at Pearl Harbour. Carole's reaction was as one would expect. She wanted to take her gun and fight the Japanese. Next best would be if Gable, despite his age, could get into the war (as he did eventually). But for the time being, something less dramatic had to suffice. Gable, sitting on a victory committee in Hollywood, received a request that he go to Indianapolis for a major event to promote the sale of war bonds. He couldn't or wouldn't go himself, but thought that Carole, whose home state was Indiana, would be the perfect person to take this on, and that she might take her mother with her.

Carole bought new clothes for the occasion and went, rejoicing that she had something to do to aid the war effort. In fact what she was doing was more important than it might seem. The war bonds campaign was taken very seriously by the President and the Government, and they had determined that it should be inaugurated in the Midwest, America's heartland. Thus Carole's role was to launch the whole campaign, not just give a boost to a local effort. She succeeded magnificently. In a vivid description of the events at the state capital on 15 January, Swindell wrote:

> That night she donned a strapless, black velvet formal and made her final pitch before 12,000 persons crowded into the auditorium at the Cadle Tabernacle. It was a stately occasion, more sentimental than frenzied, and some of Carole's relatives were among the assembly ... Carole said she was proud to be an American, and more grateful than she'd ever been that Indiana had bred her. They had sung 'The Star-spangled Banner' at the start of the programme, before Indiana's Governor Henry Schricker introduced the glowing star; but at the end of the festivities Carole decided she wanted to sing it again. She led the throng in an *a capella* rendering of the national anthem, while dignitaries from every corner of the state ... made bond pledges.

Carole was delighted by the success of her visit, but showed herself eager, almost desperate, to get back home as soon as possible. Her mother feared flying and tried to persuade her to take the train, but Carole's feeling of urgency prevailed, and at Indianapolis airport they joined a multiple-stop flight from New York to Los Angeles. The aircraft, a twenty-one passenger TWA 'Skyclub', was fine. The weather that night was fine. What was not fine, according to the official report (reproduced by Matzen) of the Civil Aeronautics Board on the accident, was the conduct of the flight on leaving Las Vegas, where it had made an unscheduled but authorized stop for fuel. The pilot seems to have set a course that would have been correct if he had been leaving Boulder City (on the route most commonly taken) rather than Las Vegas. Hence his flying head-on into a mountainside, at nearly 8,000 feet, just fifteen minutes after take-off from Las Vegas. Hence the end of Carole's life as a person, and the beginning of her existence as a cherished public memory, a kind of icon.

*

The proximate cause of Carole becoming an icon can only be public perceptions of her. Going one step further back, what was most influential in forming these perceptions? The 'real' Carole? The Carole who emerges from a conflation of her best-known parts in films? Or the Carole portrayed in the whole massive apparatus of publicity and public relations that formed a kind of filter through which, the studios hoped, people would view their various stars? To ask such questions accomplishes little more than to point up a difficulty that confronts biographers who seek to describe famous actors or actresses, whether of stage or cinema. But it does raise one other interesting question. To what extent is an actress likely to grow to be like the characters she portrays? Or is it more likely that the reverse will apply, and that the actress will be given certain parts because she really does possess the characteristics required? There is no telling in this instance. One can only say that in some respects there was remarkable congruity between Carole, Irene Bullock, Hazel Flagg and Maria Tura.

That said, what were the elements that conspired to make an icon of Carole?

I would rather separate the list of elements into a set of preconditions on the one hand and a set of precipitating factors on the other.

I see two preconditions. First, she was an archetypal all-American girl, bred in the American heartland. Second, she was extraordinarily beautiful, by which I mean beautiful in an extraordinary way. No one forgets that face.

Delete either of these factors, and she would never have gained her place as an icon. But of course much more was required. The following list, set out in two groups, contains the most important factors.

She died tragically young; her death instantaneous, 'clean' and accidental. The fact that she was returning from an official mission permitted saying that 'she died on active service', and was 'the first woman casualty' of the Second World War. The bereaved husband was none other than Clark Gable, exerting polar attraction to so many American women.

Further, of the many films she made, enough were so brilliant and memorable to ensure that 'she always will be a star'. Her personality was of the kind that people like to remember; she was tomboy, buddy, sportswoman, warm-hearted friend, glamourpuss, etc., all rolled into one. By her independence of spirit and demeanour she anticipated the emotions and attitudes that post-war feminism would bring into prominence.

So, there is an analysis. Supposing it to be more or less correct, it is interesting to look back on the various phases of her life and reflect how often and in how many different ways her development and career could have taken a divergent course. The supreme example is of course this: suppose Beth Peters had had her way about the return journey to Los Angeles. How would we now perceive and remember Carole? It is hard to imagine. In this connection I note that Carole herself said that she could not imagine herself as an older person. Becoming even more specific, she said that she could imagine herself with a baby, but not with an older child. It seemed as though there was some sort of threshold looming ahead of her in her early thirties that she could not imagine crossing, and which she did not cross.

* * *

SELECT BIBLIOGRAPHY

Noel F. Busch, 'A Loud Cheer for the Screwball Girl', in *Life* magazine, 17
      October, 1938.
John Engstead, *Star Shorts* (New York, E.P. Dutton, 1978).
Warren G. Harris, *Gable and Lombard* (New York, Simon and Schuster, 1974).
James Harvey, *Romantic Comedy* (New York, Alfred A. Knopf, 1987).
Leonard Maltin, *Carole Lombard* (New York, Pyramid, 1976).
Robert D. Matzen, *Carole Lombard, A Bio-Bibliography* (New York and
      Westport CT, Greenwood Press, 1988).
Frederick W. Ott, *The Films of Carole Lombard* (Secaucus NJ, Citadel Press,
      1972).
Larry Swindell, *Screwball, The Life of Carole Lombard* (New York, William
      Morrow, 1975).

Tim Hilton

CLEMENT GREENBERG

Most of us can remember, or imagine, the occasions when one took a hasty or otherwise unsatisfactory essay to a demanding tutor. I did not have too much trouble of this sort at Balliol; and at the Courtauld Institute of Art, where I was a postgraduate student in the mid-1960s, a number of people were kind enough to say that they thought there was some promise in my writing. I was privileged to gain the friendship of my supervisor, the late Michael Kitson, who in later years helped me to find my way to St Antony's. He was an old friend of Alistair Horne's and had served with him in MI5. All of my fellow contributors know of Alistair's interest in learning and letters. Michael Kitson was almost by nature an art historian, and he was devoted to a discipline that has little recognition in Oxford.

Michael was a shrewd and often challenging man, despite the quiet demeanour that he had inherited from his father, a scholarly East Anglian vicar. 'Tim, do you think that Sir Anthony is essentially an architectural historian, as some people say? Have you looked at his Poussin book recently?' Or, 'Tim, I think you have forgotten when Claude died.' 'Not at all,' I replied, with all the confidence of my twenty-three years of life. 'It was in 1682 and his last recorded painting is that big canvas in the Ashmolean. I think it is a totally autograph work. It must have been cleaned quite recently, if you look at those perfect greys and greenish blues. Have you talked to its restorer . . . ?'

You will see that I was a competent lad, at least in conversation. I used to talk for hours with Michael Kitson, in his study at the Courtauld Institute or in the public houses of its area, which was just north of Oxford Street. But now I go back to the problem of taking essays to my real subject, a tutor of ferocious kindness, or dismissiveness, Clement Greenberg. Uncle Clem was wary of the Courtauld, and I think never passed through its doors. Many members of the Courtauld teaching body, I know for a fact, were terrified of him. So a visit to our little academic community might not have been a success. Clem would have found more kindred spirits in the Warburg Institute, whose parent language is German rather than French, and where no undergraduates are taught. He disliked universities. There were many alarming aspects of Clem's attitude to education. I found out what they were when, for some years, he required me to present myself, with my recent writings and thoughts on culture and taste, at his temporary London head-quarters, which was usually the bar of the Dorchester Hotel.

I was always there first, being a respectful student. Our hour of rendezvous was at 11 in the morning, when the bar opened. Clem would come down from his suite and immediately energize the Dorchester staff. 'A triple vodka on the rocks! Not too many rocks! And the same for this Limey pansy!'

Many of us who loved him thought that the only topic on which Clem could possibly be uninteresting was the relative values of different brands of vodka. He would discuss vodka with the Dorch-ester barmen, or indeed with anyone who happened to be passing. The names of these strangers would be entered in a little book he carried, a part of his still unpublished diaries. Like many people who seek purity in art, Clem much preferred drinking to eating. In the twenty-five years of our rocky friendship I do not think I once saw him eat. The last time we met, in New York, we thought for a second or two about going somewhere for dinner, but never got ourselves off the sofas.

His apartment, I sometimes thought, was the fitting theatre for Clem's despair. In some ways it resembled the bar of the Dorchester Hotel. The carpets were deep, the furniture expensive but not good enough ('Not good enough' was a phrase often on Clem's noticeably sensuous lips, which he used to lick when he saw a painting he liked). From the windows one looked out over Central Park. As in the Dorchester, someone would come round every five minutes to bring more vodka and empty the ashtrays. In Central Park West this was Clem himself. He was a very tidy person.

There were paintings by Morris Louis, Jules Olitski, Alfred

Wallis, Kenneth Noland and Friedel Dzubas on the walls, and many other paintings too. On a table were some pre-Columbian sculptures. An exceptionally good small sculpture by Anthony Caro lay among the tufts of the carpet, like a fallen bird. Greenberg would keep reciting poetry to me, dozens of lines that he knew by heart. 'Who is that, kid?' I could never say. It was Browning, who, as anyone may discover, sounds either Jacobean or modern when read aloud (especially by a man with a Brooklyn Jewish accent). He laughed at having beaten me, the young English writer.

I jestingly said to Clem one day that, with his attention to ashtrays, his passion for differentiating between different styles of vodka, his (sometimes) courteous manner and his interest in remembering strangers' names, he might become a good barman, since it was obvious that no one wished to read his art criticism. That one halted him. 'You have me there, kid.' Our disputes were often of this ridiculous sort. Letters would come. 'Tim, I was unforgivably rude to you last night . . .' Then I would reply, 'You've forgotten, it was *me* who was rude to you . . .'

In the bathroom of the apartment on Central Park West was a Jackson Pollock, carefully glazed. It was from Pollock's best period, 1947–9. I believe that Pollock was influenced by Greenberg at that time. Pollock's work on paper was then most close to his painting on canvas. The pen drawing was exquisite, the painting exquisite too, and also balletic, because he walked round the canvas on the studio floor as he was painting on it. Clem said that he wanted to sell the lovely work in his bathroom. He would have gained a million dollars or so. But he couldn't put it on the market because all the world would know about the sale and thus find yet another reason for criticizing him. At the bottom of the sheet it says 'Clem from Jackson', and it had been a birthday present.

*

Clement Greenberg was born in 1909, so his parents belonged to the nineteenth century. It was a Yiddish-speaking family, originally from the Lithuanian Jewish enclave. They were socialists and discussed socialism. Clem grew up in Brooklyn and the Bronx. The father wanted the son to become an intellectual – which of course he did – but Clem as a child had a precocious artistic talent. He could draw 'photographically', to use the popular and misleading expression, and thought that he might become an artist. In his teens he attended the Arts Students League. Then he got himself to Syracuse University, graduating in 1930. At that period most other institutions of higher education did not admit Jews or were hostile to them. My interest is in the three years of Greenberg's 'self-education', as he called it, when he studied by himself while employed by the US Customs Service in some shed down by the Hudson waterfront. This was in the mid-1930s, in the Depression.

Self-education is never to be condemned but totally self-educated people, as Greenberg used to remark, are often egotistical and boring. He had met many folk of that sort in the world of art. To their own annoyance, Greenberg was always annoyed by artists who read too many books, or thought that they could write books. Of his bookish abstract expressionist contemporaries, he loved Barnett Newman but did not wish to talk to him about theories of anarchism. The self-proclaimed intellectual Robert Motherwell he found empty, absurd. 'Get away from me, you cripple!' (not the expression of one of nature's barmen) Greenberg shouted when David Hockney spoke to him at a party about his plans for a volume of his thoughts. Bewildered, Hockney did not realize that Greenberg thought him an intellectual rather than a physical cripple. Clem made many enemies with remarks of this sort. I think that this trait in Greenberg's character came from the memory of his own self-education, of which he seldom spoke. But he must have taught himself in a dedicated and disciplined way, while also finding some joyful freedom of thought. I asked him once whether Jews were better at self-education than other people. 'Of course, you've got it, kid.'

What is the nature, and the history, of self-education? We can easily imagine what is most often read: politics, philosophy, Marx. Self-educating people are attracted to such topics because of their efforts to become wise. But on the whole they do not study languages. Greenberg was an exception. Sitting in his customs shed, he applied himself to German, Latin, Italian and French. Thus he approached books through different tongues. Despite his enormous, demanding personality he always had the selflessness that we find in dedicated linguists; and I believe that this is a clue to the rarefied and even humble appreciation that he gave to art. It is significant that Greenberg always wrote least about the paintings and sculptures that he loved best, especially if their artists were his friends.

Politically, the young Greenberg belonged to the leftward side of humanity and in particular to American 'cultural Trotskyism'. This cast of mind led him to the group of intellectuals behind *Partisan Review*. Trotsky, apparently, thought that the people of *Partisan Review* were more interested in culture than in the forthcoming socialist revolution. That may well have been so, for they were writers. The group included William Phillips, Philip Rahv, Dwight Macdonald, Mary McCarthy, Lionel Trilling and Delmore Schwarz. Greenberg and the crazy Schwarz amused each other in various ways. They were friends rather than comrades. When Greenberg joined *Partisan Review* as an editor in 1939 (at a period when he was making some of the first English translations from Brecht and Kafka) he stood a little apart from the people who were nominally his comrades and colleagues. First, he was the only one of them who was truly interested in the visual arts. Secondly, Greenberg was obsessed with the idea that high culture could only be achieved within the context of American socialism. No one else at *Partisan Review* had such a utopian and futile vision.

We should think of this emphasis on culture in a worldwide context. It became part of the desire to rebuild global society after Hitler's war. The desire for culture may be glimpsed in the operations of UNESCO and such books as UNESCO's *Reflections on our Age* (n.d., but 1946), which consists of a predictable foreword by Stephen Spender, then the texts of papers read at a conference at the Sorbonne by, among many others, Jean-Paul Sartre ('The Responsibility of the Writer'), André Malraux ('Man and Artistic Culture'), Louis Aragon ('The Many and the Few'), Maurice Bowra ('International Aspects of Education'), and Herbert Read ('The Plight of the Visual Arts'). Nearly half a century later, this lecture still enraged Greenberg. These generally amiable statements are quite unlike Greenberg's contemporary writing, especially his famous first essay 'Avant-garde and Kitsch', in which he contrasted true and elevated culture, which he believed to belong to the avant garde (as he understood the term) with the meretricious and second-hand, the pseudo-art of the new capitalism. It is an essay of immense power and ambition. Put beside Greenberg's urgent reflections, the addresses contained within *Reflections on our Age* are meaningless. Greenberg travelled to Europe and presented himself to such figures as Jean-Paul Sartre (he wrote an essay on modern American art for

Les Temps modernes, which has still not been translated into English) and Ignazio Silone, but nothing much came from these encounters. The great benefit of his European expeditions was his study of painting in classic museums. Greenberg regarded Rennaissance artists as though they were his younger contemporaries. I found his conversation on old-master painting quite as thrilling as his discussion of new art.

By 1948 Greenberg was describing himself as a 'disabused former Marxist'. He was mixing with the painters and sculptors who were his comrades in the abstract expressionist school; and he realized that his future role in life was to be an art critic. Greenberg had no model to emulate within the field of art criticism. Instead he turned to T.S. Eliot. I have no doubt (for he told me so himself) that Greenberg wished to write about art with the perception and authority that Eliot had brought to literature. It happened that in this year, 1948, Eliot issued a book whose title, *Notes towards the Definition of Culture*, would have immediately seized Greenberg's attention. The preface to the first edition (dated January 1948) is uneasy. It states that parts of the book had appeared elsewhere, in periodical, but omits to mention that *Partisan Review* had been among these reviews. I like to think of the narrowed eyes of the 'PR crowd', with their cigars and tumblers of bourbon, as Eliot's prim formulations arrived in the New York office.

Thoughts of Eliot haunted Greenberg for many years after he had rejected his ideas about society, had absorbed his criticism and – because he knew his poetry by heart – could not come freshly to his creative work. This is a common experience, I believe, among Eliot's admirers. A vital part of Greenberg's character was his apparently insatiable desire for the fresh experience of art. He always said that he learned most about innovation, and how to use his eyes to discriminate, from the German painter Hans Hofmann, who ran a little painting school in downtown Manhattan. Many painters of the abstract expressionist school went to his classes, and Hofmann's influence extended beyond his academy. The school was experimental in nature, but Hofmann had many theories that derived from his former acquaintance with Kandinsky and other European artists. It is clear that he was an immensely gifted teacher. However, as is often the case with great teachers (especially in the field of modern art), it is hard to say of what that teaching consisted.

This problem is the more difficult to approach because Hofmann's English was so limited. Many of his pupils could not understand what he was saying. But Greenberg knew German, so he could assess Hofmann's ideas. He also saw the point of his art. Hofmann was producing the most splendidly unorthodox paintings of the mid-century. Proof of Greenberg's understanding of Hofmann is to be found in his cerebral little monograph on the painter, published in Paris in 1961. I am fortunate to have it on my shelves, but have never even seen another copy.

Greenberg's publishing record – as far as books are concerned – was disastrous. He never had a sensible relationship with a book publisher. He worked on some books that were never completed or, if they were finished, were never issued. Probably the most important of them was an account of Jackson Pollock, who died in 1956. Greenberg allowed it to be known that he was writing this book until as lately as 1961. Then nothing more was heard of the work. In the 1970s he was compiling, rather than composing, a book he called 'my home-made aesthetics'. From the parts one saw, it consisted of brief, wonderful rumination on all aspects of art. In 1948 he had published a book on Miró. It is excellent, but Greenberg didn't like it (partly, perhaps, because of its preface by Ernest Hemingway) and made sure that it was suppressed. Even close artist friends were unaware that such a book had ever existed.

*

Clement Greenberg's reputation as an art critic ought to rest on his *Art and Culture* (1961). Alas, this beautiful book, always rare, has been unavailable for the last quarter of a century. For some years it was my task to find a publisher who might be prepared to reissue the slender but extremely potent volume. I kept trying and my literary agent – from a large and old-established firm – was enlisted in the search. No publisher would touch the book. Most of them wouldn't even read it. When I finally reported failure to Clem he said that he didn't care. This was not the complete truth, for (privately, never publicly) he was proud of his writing. *Art and Culture* is composed of a series of essays, originally printed in *Partisan Review*, *The Nation*, *Commentary*, *Arts*, and *The New Leader*. 'Avant-garde and Kitsch' was too much of its time and place to be revised, but practically everything else in the book had been rewritten. Greenberg's intention was perfectly clear. He wished his book to be a classic. And so it is. *Art and Culture* is the best single work of modern art criticism; and since art criticism belongs specifically to the age of the avant garde, it may well be the best book of art criticism ever written.

In writing this, I of course do not mean that Greenberg was in competition with Ruskin or Baudelaire, both of whom he revered. But he thought that they were writing nineteenth-century literature. Greenberg became the leading art critic of the twentieth century and of the period of high modern art that has now closed. It does seem that intellectual Jewish New York in the later 1940s was an excellent vantage point from which to survey the development of artistic modernism. *Art and Culture* proves as much. There has never been a decent art critic who has not been in the first place an excellent art historian. Greenberg was indeed an historian, though he did not often cite dates, or even the titles of pictures. *Art and Culture* is filled not so much with art-historical knowledge, which is seldom displayed as such, but with art-historical wisdom, which is to be found on every page.

Greenberg read, looked and wrote all the time. In his later years few people realized the extent of his erudition. Some people who appreciated him – artists, on the whole – regarded him as an oracle, mainly because of the vigour and certainty of his talk. But he wasn't an oracle. He was human. The whole point about oracles, and thus their lack of value, is that they do not read and discuss books. Greenberg did; but often one had to dig the knowledge out of him while you were being abused for being young, or for being a Limey, or for not smoking big cigars, or for not understanding Kant. This was one reason why the tutorials in the Dorchester bar were so thrilling and could easily become quarrelsome. I often thought that if he had been less hostile to universities, Greenberg might have had a proper following among learned people, and might have been less reviled by the theorists of modern art. What a teacher he might have been! But a university environment would not have suited him, and he would not have suited a university. He was too 'difficult', whatever that means.

I once tried to get him out of the Dorchester to visit an exhibition. 'I wouldn't go to see an interesting young artist even if I were living in fifteenth-century Florence!' Such a remark was typical of one side of Clem. He just felt like being contradictory. The fact is that he went all over the world looking for interesting art, new as well as old, and was never more alive than when he was in exhibitions or in artists' studios. I have presented Greenberg as a tough, contrary man, which he was. Yet with artists he liked, and there were many of them, he was as gentle as a sister.

I briefly mention just some of these artists. It is important that Greenberg belonged to the generation that produced Abstract Expressionism. Seen from afar, Abstract Expressionism now appears as a movement that had long, slow, and often uncertain beginnings, all too brief a period of supreme achievement, then a rapid descent into mannerism and fashionableness. Greenberg realized that this was the pattern, even as it was happening. His first period of self-education corresponds with the efforts of contemporary artists to find a genuine American idiom that would break with the School of Paris. And then, as in the art of his friend Jackson Pollock, there was an especial new confidence, even majesty, in Greenberg's mind at the end of the 1940s. This was the time when he had given up Trotskyism and the exhausted, ingrown world of *Partisan Review* and fully devoted himself to art.

There is no doubt that Pollock meant more to him than any other artist. He wouldn't talk much about 'Jackson'. Perhaps it was too painful. In Pollock's personal tragedy he saw a metaphor for the disasters of American art and life, and also his own life. Greenberg was usually drunk when I heard him say such things. Pollock drank because he desired oblivion. 'He was an alcoholic *in excelsis*,' Clem used to say. Greenberg drank because he was unhappy: being so intelligent, oblivion was the last thing he wanted. Pollock never allowed anyone else in the studio when he was painting (and he never painted when he was drunk), but Greenberg was probably the first person – after Lee Krasner, Pollock's wife – to see any new set of paintings. I think Greenberg urged Pollock in some directions and tried to hold him back from other paths. In any case, anyone who knew Greenberg will be certain that he did not keep his reactions to himself.

In the aftermath of Abstract Expressionism Greenberg favoured clear, open, abstract painting with an emphasis on colour and bold shapes. It was the leading painterly (and sculptural) style of the 60s. Now there was a new group of artists, all of whom were just as indebted to Greenberg, the active and directing critic in the studio, as they were to each other. They included the painters Morris Louis, Kenneth Noland and Jules Olitski, with the sculptors David Smith (an old friend from abstract expressionist days) and Anthony Caro, who, in the 60s, was just as much an American as an English artist. All of these people in the 'Greenberg family' made art of a very high order, work that went immediately into museums and the most prestigious American collections. The artists suddenly found that they were rich, and Greenberg, too, became a wealthy man.

I don't know that lots of money is always good for artists, but wealth certainly suited Clem. Physically, he wasn't large (but this hadn't stopped him from being a fist-fighter at parties in his earlier days) and he was as thin as a refugee. His clothes were American or sometimes curiously English. I think he even had a jacket with oval leather patches on the elbows. But somehow, in an American way, wealth shone from Clem and seemed to add stature and weight to his frame. He had a very Jewish face. A remarkable feature was the immense bald dome of his head. The cranium was just like those portraits of Shakespeare. I've heard it said that he was the original 'egghead', an American term that came into widespread use in the years when he was most active in the world of American highbrow magazines. 'Highbrow' was one of his words, often used in a combative way. 'I'm a highbrow. What are you?'

A problem with the aura of wealth was that it obscured Greenberg's intellectualism. It was resented by young people in the art world, who tend to be radicals. The wealth – that Dorchester bar sort of wealth – concealed Greenberg's intellect and artistic taste. Nor were his views popular in the new artistic climate of the late 60s and early 70s. He said that Pop Art was no good. He wrote that Joseph Beuys and Andy Warhol were bad artists. He had no time for conceptual art. Greenberg claimed that all types of 'novelty art', to use his phrase, were more threatening to culture than the middlebrow art he had criticized in the years after the war. The next artistic movement of any value, he predicted, would come from 'the middle ground', not from youngsters whose only desire was to be 'far out'. These are not unreasonable opinions, and they are shared by very many cultivated people. But Greenberg was labelled a reactionary, a tyrant, a would-be manipulator of the art market, a simpleton, and probably an agent of the CIA, for had he not contributed to *Encounter* and broadcast on the *Voice of America*?

All these things, and more, are said and printed by people who have not read Greenberg's writing. There was something like a vendetta – which still goes on, years after his death in 1994 – and it is a discredit to the art world. Some of the attacks were deliberately disgusting. In one famous London art school a tutor persuaded students to rip pages from their library's copy of *Art and Culture*, chew them, then expectorate the chewed paper into a bowl of acid. I knew a couple of the students concerned. They told me that they had been so full of drugs that they did not know what the book was, or what they were doing. But their tutor knew, and he kept the results of their exercise, claiming that it was part of his oeuvre. The chewed-up book was respectfully displayed in an exhibition at the Museum of Modern Art in Oxford in 1991–2. The curator of the show claimed that it was 'a major piece of conceptual art'.

I mention this episode, and the Oxford exhibition, for two reasons. First, it ought to be known that Clem had many troubles of this sort in his later years, when he was often ill, was not sober at occasions when he should have been dignified, and suffered periods when he could only lie on his bed and read, not being able to write or converse. He died penniless, swindled by a 'financial advisor'. It is true that Clem's manner often invited hostilities, and he quarrelled with people who were his friends as well as with people who were not his friends. He was none the less a person to be treasured. Secondly, Greenberg believed that our new museums of contemporary art have no true commitment to aesthetic values or liberal knowledge. Indeed, from about the mid-1970s he feared that art itself was in decline. This foreboding does not prove that he was a reactionary; quite the contrary, in my view. A transcript of some things he said in a radio broadcast for the United States Information Service is worth quoting because it clearly outlines his belief about art as a minor part of life. I wish he himself had known more happiness.

I say that if you have to choose between life and happiness or art, remember always to choose life and happiness. Art solves nothing, either for the artist himself or for those who receive his art. Art shouldn't be overrated. It started to be in the latter eighteenth

century, and definitely was in the nineteenth. The Germans started
the business of assessing the worth of a society by the quality of
art it produced. But the quality of art produced in a society does
not necessarily – or maybe seldom – reflect the degree of well-being
enjoyed by most of its members. And well-being comes first. I
deplore the tendency to over-value art.

Wise words from an art critic – and, you notice, not at all utopian.
One of the things that annoyed Greenberg about the nineteenth
century was its tendency to have utopian ideas. He himself was a
realist, a personally miserable realist.

James Hamilton

DAVY, FARADAY AND TURNER

FATHER, SON AND BROTHER ARTIST

This essay is based on 'Art, Science and Song: Researching across bound-aries in nineteenth-century British culture', a lecture given by the author of St Antony's College, Oxford, in March 1999.

* * *

In the first five decades of the nineteenth century, artists, scientists and writers talked to each other, respected each other's achievements and felt they understood each other as perhaps never before or since. It was a golden moment in the history of ideas, when the beams converged and the light flashed. After those years, from 1801 when Humphry Davy was appointed to experiment and teach at the Royal Institution, until around 1851, the year Turner died and the year of the Great Exhibition, specializations, particularly in science, and what in art are called movements and '-isms', became so elaborate and complex and demanding to their followers that no amount of clever talk could weave them into a single strand.

Humphry Davy was the presiding genius in natural philosophy – the word 'science' had not yet been fully assimilated. He had come to London trailing clouds of glory from a successful period of two years as a lecturer on scientific matters in Bristol. Before that he had come from even further west, practically off the map both socially and geographically, as the son of a woodcarver from Penzance. Davy was charming, charismatic, ambitious and young – twenty-two years old – a breath of fresh air amongst the aristocrats and sophisticates who ran and patronized science in London at this time.

His originality of approach and presentation surprised and delighted his audiences at the newly-formed Royal Institution, where he gave lectures on the principles of chemistry, the art of tanning leather, on geology and agriculture. On one memorable occasion in 1811 he exploded a model volcano in the lecture theatre, and on others he gave entertaining public demonstrations of the effects of a new gas that he had synthesized and analysed, nitrous oxide, or 'laughing gas'.

Davy loved a party, was forever entertaining and being entertained at the best houses in town and country. Through the force of his own personality and eloquence he gave natural philosophy in London – and that meant the world – the sort of social platform it had never had before. The Royal Institution had been founded in Albemarle Street in 1799 by a group of benefactors and moneymen to be a centre for the teaching of the 'application of Science to the common Purposes of Life' – in other words to act as a conduit for the conversion of scientific discovery into practical improvements for all. Hence the lectures on the art of tanning and on agricultural improvement. Davy was what we now call a star – imagine Chris Evans and David Attenborough rolled together, and that would be about the mark.

London in the Napoleonic Wars, before Nelson turned the tide at Trafalgar, was ripe for the kind of clear-thinking, charismatic sensation that was Humphry Davy, and they flocked to hear him in their hundreds, causing serious traffic jams in Albemarle Street and Bond Street and fainting fits in the crush in the lecture theatre. Davy's outlook was positive and uplifting, he thirsted to enlighten, and in 1802 drew his introduction to a series of chemistry lectures to a close with the words: ' . . . we reason by analogy from simple facts. We consider only a state of human progression arising out of its present condition. We look for a time that we may reasonably expect, for a bright day of which we already behold the dawn.'[1]

The wonderful image that Davy draws there is somehow familiar. He probably did not know William Blake's coloured print *Glad Day* of the mid 1790s – very few people did, Blake was reclusive and his art had a limited audience – but the brightness of Davy's promise of change almost amounting to revolution takes an echo from the radical ideas behind Blake's vision of a resurrected Albion.

The fuel that drove Davy was a high-octane mix of social and professional ambition, technical insight, manipulative skill in the laboratory, and bravery in the face of unstable substances and exploding retorts. He was also brave in the field. When studying the eruption of Vesuvius in 1819 he was nearly burnt and suffocated by standing too long near the lava flows, for as he graphically put it, 'I . . . remained too long in that magnificent but dangerous situation . . . within five or six feet of a stream of red hot matter, fluid as water, of nearly three feet in diameter and falling as a cataract of fire.'[2]

Davy was the right stuff, the kind of glamorous intellectual athlete who might have gone on an Apollo moonshot in the 1960s, or who in the 1990s would be in earthquake, flood or other natural disaster zones taking scientific measurements and reporting back. Humphry Davy was always at the front.

Alongside lucid explanations of chemical activity that he gave in his lectures, Davy also wrote clearly on the role of art and poetry in civilization. He found close analogies between fine art and the truths of natural sciences, and evoked one by one the names of Newton, Shakespeare, Michelangelo and Handel when he wrote that, 'The perception of truth is almost as simple a feeling as the perception of beauty.'[3] By carefully selecting examples of scientist, writer, artist and musician of genius, Davy is placing science as part of an integrated system of knowledge built up, repaired and rebuilt from antiquity. He described knowledge as being 'like a river, which, unless its springs are constantly supplied, soon becomes exhausted, and ceases to flow on, and to fertilize.'[4]

In seeking truth and knowledge through his chemical experiments, Davy saw himself as a member of a team working across the known world and time: 'the philosopher who has made a discovery in natural science, or the author of a work of genius in art or in literature, is a benefactor, not only to the present generation, but likewise to future ages.'[5]

Thoughts of this kind, expressed from so influential a platform as the Royal Institution, are a classic expression of the way civilization was seen to have advanced in the latter years of the reign of George III. It is an uncomplicated picture, the river of knowledge taking its waters from incoming tributaries, supplied in buckets by philosophers of one kind or another. There is no thought of how the manner of flow further downstream might change.

But the landscape through which the river was flowing was itself changing radically, by influences both within and without science and the arts. Although the roots of this change are social and political, it developed its particular kind of motion in the following wind of specialization in science, the professionalization of scientists, and the sheer quantity and wonder of the knowledge and understanding then being obtained through scientific endeavour. Although Davy was the central commanding figure in English science, working around him were his brilliant contemporaries William Wollaston, David Brewster, Thomas Young, and Davy's own pupil Michael Faraday. Among artists, John and Cornelius Varley, John Martin and above all Constable and Turner responded specifically and intentionally to scientific advance, and in their different ways changed the public perception of nature by a new visual and intellectual expression of its vastness and interconnection. Looking across an Italian landscape in 1805, Samuel Taylor Coleridge spoke for all when he considered the endowment of nature:

> Imagination; honourable aims;
> Free commune with the choir that cannot die;
> Science and song; delight in little things,
> The buoyant child surviving in the man;
> Fields, forests, ancient mountains, ocean, sky,
> With all their voices – O dare I accuse
> My earthly lot as guilty of my spleen,
> Or call my destiny niggard! Oh no! no!
> It is her largeness, and her overflow,
> Which being incomplete, disquieteth me so.[6]

Davy and Faraday had the closest professional relationship. What began in 1813 as a master and pupil arrangement, evolved through an uncomfortable master/valet stage, to what became akin to father and son. Davy was inordinately proud of Faraday, the son he never had, and nurtured the young man's eagerness and potential as a natural philosopher. He took him to France and Italy (ostensibly as a valet) and at the Royal Institution taught him laboratory practice through leading him to the unsteady edges of his own knowledge. In his turn, Faraday listened to what Davy taught and showed him, and revealed a quickness of mind and a natural ability to understand and interpret complicated scientific notions. Through observing Davy at work – the chaos Davy created in the laboratory became legendary – Faraday developed his own patient and methodical practice, which remained with him all his life, and which set a standard for future generations of scientists.

J.M.W. Turner was just three years older than Davy, so when they met, as is likely, in Rome in November 1819, they were both at the height of their powers and maturity. For more than twenty years Turner had been startling artists and exhibition visitors with his radical evocations of ancient and contemporary landscape. He was in Rome in 1819 on his long-awaited first trip to Italy to see the light, landscape and antiquity of the place for himself. Davy was there to try to discover, among other things, ways of eliminating iron oxide spots that disfigured Carrara marble, and to inspect the frescoes by Raphael in the Vatican. These had become heavily damaged and were rapidly decaying, and Davy's job was to find what could be done urgently to preserve them. Thus, central among Davy's purposes in Rome was the cause of placing science at the service of art. High also among Turner's purposes was the study of Raphael's work, and indeed from early on he had in mind the gathering of ideas for a large composition in which Raphael and his works were to be the central figure. This became the painting *Rome, from the Vatican* (exh. 1820; London, Tate Gallery).

Turner and Davy had both friends and interests in common. They had both risen to justified fame through natural genius, accomplishment and hard work. Both had come from humble origins and had learned early on how to play the patronage game, and foster networks of rich and influential supporters. Both were keen fishermen and amateur poets, skills that seem naturally intertwined, like rod and line, and prompted by riverbank reflection. Both, too, had a love of the ancient world and a mission to record, express, preserve and reinterpret it. And both were visionaries. Turner had always had his feet on the ground in the early decades of his career: his landscapes in the 1810s and early 20s were based on how things were, and on his intense observation and indefatigable travel. In the later 1820s and 30s, however, his visions of landscape grew increasingly chromatic, and although the sense of real life is always close at hand in his work, Turner's use of glowing yellows and reds in many of his exhibited oil paintings came to strike his contemporaries as eccentric – 'All is yellow, yellow, nothing but yellow, violently contrasted with blue,' wrote one critic.[7]

If Davy had had his feet on the ground in his laboratory in the 1800s and 1810s, his mind rose gradually to other realms when he experienced landscape, particularly antique Italian landscape. Imagining himself sitting alone in the Colosseum in Rome one night in 1819, Davy wrote of visions of intense colour, and felt himself to be streaming through the cosmos, a one-man interplanetary voyager:

> From what appeared to me to be analogous to masses of bright blue ice, streams of the richest tints of rose-colour or purple burst forth and flowed into basins, forming lakes or seas of the same colour. Looking through the atmosphere towards the heavens I saw brilliant opaque clouds of an azure colour that reflected the light of the sun . . . I saw moving round me globes which appeared composed of different kinds of flame but of various colours. In some of these globes I recognised figures which put me in mind of the human countenance, but the resemblance was so awful & unnatural that I endeavoured to withdraw my view from them.[8]

Visionary language of this kind anticipates Turner's chromatic oil paintings and watercolours, and prefigures also much of the symbolism of the inhabited globes and bubbles that are found in Turner's later art.

We are hampered in studying Turner's life by patchy documentation. Although Turner could write lucid prose, and expressed himself clearly and lightly in letters, comparatively little of his correspondence survives.[9] This is due in great part to the unfortunate but deliberate destruction, independently, of four major collections of letters that would undoubtedly have been rich in Turner material.[10] As a result, our knowledge of many of Turner's friendships is vague. An entry in Thomas Moore's journal, in which Turner is reported to have attended, with others, a musical evening given in Rome by Lady Davy, is the sole piece of direct evidence of an association with Davy.[11] Was Sir Humphry himself present that evening? Probably, for he was in Rome then, but who can say for certain? No clue, either, has yet emerged proving that Turner knew Davy in London, but they had many friends and enemies in common, they lived no more than half a mile apart, and they were both part of the common culture of society, art and science in London that lived the metaphor of the river of knowledge. The parallels in their lives, accomplishments and realized ambitions are, however, so compelling, that they must be seen as interrelated, if not interacting, figures in the same piece of townscape.[12]

The crucial catalyst between Turner and Davy in Rome was, I suspect, their close mutual friend the sculptor Antonio Canova. They had both met Canova in November 1815, when the sculptor was in London – Turner had invited him to his studio, and was present at a Royal Academy dinner in his honour; Davy took him to a Royal Society meeting, where he also met Faraday and Charles Babbage. Canova was papal emissary to London at that time, and entertainment by the leaders of London cultural society was among the very many treats laid out for him.[13] In Rome four years later Canova was in a position to repay something of the friendship and hospitality he had received in London, and as entries in Thomas Moore's journal indicate, he was an attentive and sympathetic host.[14]

Artists and scientists had many opportunities to meet professionally and socially in the early decades of the nineteenth century. We know of gatherings at every hour of the day and night, from breakfast parties in the morning to soirées in the evening held in London in the ten or fifteen years before and after Waterloo. Notable hosts and hostesses, who mixed politics, fashion, science, literature and art, included Lord and Lady Holland, Lord Spencer, Lord Essex, the poet-banker Samuel Rogers, the surgeon-antiquary Thomas Pettigrew and the publisher John Murray. Among the scientists and artists who entertained each other regularly and professionally were Humphry Davy, Charles Babbage, William and Mary Somerville, Francis Chantrey and the architect Sir John Soane. There were private viewings at the Royal Academy and the British Institution, receptions at the Royal Society, lectures at the Royal Institution and *conversazioni* at the Athenaeum Club (founded 1824), and so on. And all this does not include the society of the court, which was something else altogether. This social activity took place in a very narrow geographical area, bounded by Regent's Park in the north, the river in the south, and on the east and west Blackfriars and Hyde Park respectively. If you played your cards right – if you *had* the right cards – you could be out every night of the week during the season.

There are dozens of specific instances of social meetings between artists and scientists, both set up so that they would mingle and meet at random, and brought together on purpose. In March 1825, for example, Sir John Soane held a three-day party in Lincoln's Inn to show off his extraordinary house and art and antiquities collection to his friends. He invited aristocrats and senior politicians, artists, scientists, writers and others to mingle at will. The sculptor Francis Chantrey was a regular and generous host to patrons and friends alike. In April 1832 he invited Charles Babbage to 'eat roast beef' with the artists Turner, George Jones, Augustus Callcott and Charles Landseer. He threw the stockbroker and amateur geologist Charles Stokes into the party for good measure.[15] Charles Babbage's weekly soirées in which he demonstrated his Difference Engine, were famous. He started them to entertain his ageing mother, but discontinued them in the 1840s when so many of his friends asked to bring their friends that, he said, 'At last I hardly knew more than half of the guests in my room.'[16]

And so they went on, with people variously meeting each other, avoiding each other, and losing and finding things. After one party at Samuel Rogers's house, Charles Babbage took the wrong umbrella, and when he got it home he found it had a two-feet-long dagger concealed in the handle – it was Turner's, one he used to keep bandits off in Italy.[17] The highlight of Francis Chantrey's evening parties came after supper when the guests looked at his specimens of minerals and fossils, and 'the instructive allurements of the microscope filled every moment; conversation never failed'.[18] One of Chantrey's good friends was the scientist William Wollaston. The pair were members of the same fishing club in Stockbridge, Hampshire, and would travel down there regularly to spend days sitting side by side on the banks of the River Test.

Humphry Davy was largely absent from the Royal Institution after about 1818, and the work there was led by Michael Faraday. Faraday had a different view of society from Davy. He was no socialite, but a devout and committed member of a small Christian sect, the Sandemanians. In pursuing his work in science he considered himself to be 'reading God's Book of Nature'. Faraday had a wide circle of friends and correspondents amongst artists and scientists, and drew many of them into the life of the Royal Institution. He became the driving force of a renewed and reinvigorated Royal Institution, devising the teaching programmes, and selecting and introducing speakers for the Friday Evening Discourses. He had instituted the Discourse series in 1826, to bring to a wide public news and information about scientific knowledge and advance, and gave many of the lectures himself. To broaden their appeal he took upon himself the task of gathering together objects of art and science for display on the table in the Royal Institution Library, to be the focus of discussion before and after the meeting. Among the objects displayed week by week were model steam engines, early German illustrated bibles, Eskimo carvings, insects from Brazil, the latest engravings by John Martin, paintings by Constable, daguerreotypes and all kinds of miscellanea to prompt intelligent and constructive talk. It was a catholic and random selection, which depended for material on the interest of the members and speakers, and Faraday regularly appealed for and encouraged contributions.

The Library Table was the living museum of the Royal Institution. It was always interesting, always a honeypot for the curious eyes of the audiences at the Friday Evening Discourses. Sometimes its contents were thought to be too much for unprotected eyes – when Faraday was sent two large Etruscan vases for display in 1839 he was advised to cover up the erotic decoration on one of them because it was 'too *free* to be publicly exposed'.[19] Earlier that same year it was the place where the very newest and most controversial development in art and science was put on public view in Britain for the first time. Six days before Henry Fox Talbot gave his paper on 'photogenic drawings' at the Royal Society, Michael Faraday displayed examples of these early photographs on the Royal Institution Library Table.[20]

There is considerable direct evidence of an active and constructive friendship between Turner and Faraday. They had good mutual friends in the amateur painter Harriet Moore, the scientist Mary Somerville and the lithographer Charles Hullmandel. Faraday's nineteenth-century biographer, Henry Bence Jones, writes that Faraday and Turner first met at a *conversazione* given by Hullmandel, and that Faraday 'afterwards often had application from [Turner] for chemical information about pigments'. Bence Jones goes on to tell us that Faraday always impressed upon Turner, and other artists, the importance of experimenting for themselves, 'putting washes and tints of all their pigments in the bright sunlight, covering up one half, and noticing the effect of light and gases on the other'.[21] These passages suggest that contact between Turner and Faraday was extensive over time, and in an apparently throwaway remark another early Faraday biographer, Sylvanus Thompson, records that of the few public dinners Faraday attended, 'he enjoyed most the annual banquet of the Royal Academy of Arts'.[22] That was where the 'brother artists', as Turner called them, and Turner himself, had a roistering time.

Ample opportunity to talk with Turner, clearly, and there is direct evidence within some of Turner's paintings that whatever it was that he and Faraday discussed had a distinct bearing on Turner's attitude to the way he saw, perceived and interpreted landscape. One work, *Snow Storm, Avalanche and Inundation, a Scene in the Upper Part of the Val d'Aosta, Piedmont* (exh. 1837; Chicago, Art Institute), suggests that Turner was well aware of what went on at the Friday Evening Discourses at the Royal Institution. There had been a terrible storm in the Alps in August 1834 – vast inundations of torrents of water, debris filling valleys, people and villages washed away. A friend and sometime travelling companion of Turner's, William Brockedon, was a well-known Alpiniste who may have witnessed the storm. Brockedon gave an emotional and rousing lecture 'On the dreadful storms of August 1834 in the Alps' at the Royal Institution in 1835, and in the summer of 1836 Turner himself visited the Val d'Aosta. Though the storm had long passed when Turner was in the valley, memories of it were fresh in local people's memories, and Turner need not have looked far for descriptions or evidence of the destruction.

Another storm painting, *Snow Storm – Steam Boat off a Harbour's Mouth* (exh. 1842; London, Tate Gallery), shows an intrepid little steamer battling against fierce seas to reach the safety of harbour. Turner has formalized the waves, cloud, smoke and wind into linear patterns, points and curves that have a controlled two-dimensional surface presence, despite the fury of the storm. This is a far cry from the chaos Turner depicted in earlier sea-storm paintings such as *The Shipwreck* of 1805 (London, Tate Gallery). One particular area of scientific exploration that was in the air in the 1830s was the phenomenon of magnetism, particularly the magnetism of the earth. Voyages of exploration went out under naval and government auspices to find the north and south magnetic poles; scientists, notably Faraday, were making experiments about it; and scientific writers, of whom Mary Somerville was one of the most widely read, wrote about terrestrial magnetism lucidly for an extensive lay and professional audience. Somerville, one of the rare, trusted individuals allowed into Turner's inner sanctum, wrote in her memoirs that she was a frequent visitor to Turner's studio, 'and was always welcomed'.[23]

So what did they talk about? Art, certainly; Mary Somerville was a talented amateur painter whose landscape paintings had Turnerian qualities. More than once, on looking at a sunset or sky effect, she shook her head and said that only Turner could paint that adequately. And they talked about science too, surely. Somerville, an eloquent popularizer of science, discusses in her book *On the Connexion of the Physical Sciences* (1834) the effect of the motion of the sea and ships on the earth's magnetism. What she is outlining is a form of electro-magnetic induction: 'Even a ship passing over the surface of the water, in northern or southern latitudes, ought to have electric currents running directly across the path of her motion. Mr Faraday observes that such is the facility with which electricity is evolved by the earth's magnetism, that scarcely any piece of metal can be moved in contact with others without a development of it.'[24] Somerville's thrilling image of a ship crossing lines of force has a Turnerian ring to it. And when we look at the patterns iron filings make when in the presence of a bar magnet, we can see a clear visual correspondence between Somerville's words, Faraday's experiment and Turner's *Snow Storm*.[25]

There are many other paintings in Turner's output that suggest that rather than following in the footsteps of scientific discovery, he is taking modern life and modern scientific thought together, head on. One in particular is *Staffa – Fingal's Cave* (exh. 1832; New Haven, Mellon Center for British Art), painted two years after Turner had taken the potentially dangerous trip round the Island of Mull to see the famous sparkling basaltic cave, the legendary home of the giant Finn McCoul, on the island of Staffa.

Turner takes a lowering, realist view in this picture. The lines of his brushstrokes echo the form of the island's basaltic columns; waves on the left transform themselves into basalt; the colours are sombre. Turner also shows us a meteorological clue, well known to sailors, of the nimbus round the sun, which foretells rain. The hero of the painting, like the hero of *Snow Storm – Steam Boat off a Harbour's Mouth*, is, however, the truculent little steamer that carried the party to the island and took them home safely again, despite worsening weather. In revealing a unity between nature and the works of man, Turner creates through art a vision of the world of science and technology in a tense co-existence with the powers of the living earth. In *Staffa* and *Snow Storm* Turner sets his own agenda, chooses his own path, and demonstrates and restates the power of art's voice during a period in which science was becoming a dominant cultural force.

From his diaries and letters, we know that Faraday had a more than particular interest in storms and the sky, how lightning worked, how it illuminated the cloudscape and landscape beneath. He wrote a number of passages in the 1830s and 40s about the aurora borealis, which he believed to be electrical in origin. Bence Jones tells us that Faraday had a particular admiration for Turner's paintings of skies, the truthfulness of their effect, their clarity. Turner's storms showed a control and understanding of the uncontrollability of the natural power unleashed by a storm, and it was this innate understanding in Turner for which Faraday had so much time.

There is such a communion between these two giants that it suggests that they knew they were on parallel tracks in the 1830s. In the decade in which Faraday was writing and publishing his *Experimental Researches in Electricity*, Turner was carrying out further explorations of his own. He did not claim them as experiments, as Constable had done for his paintings, but rather he exhibited them silently, sold them, or put them away in his studio. These are his paintings of the sun, its light, its creative and destructive power, such as *Mortlake Terrace* (exh. 1827; Washington DC, National Gallery), in which the sun's light exhibits the effect of appearing to eat away at solid structures that came years later to be known by photographers as 'halation'; or *Sun Setting over a Lake* (c1840; London, Tate Gallery), where both the sun and the landscape it illuminates are, simply, light.

To artists, the sun is the great unknowable, the source of all light, that thing in the sky that enables them to see, but at which they look directly at their peril. For Turner the sun had a quasi-religious significance. It had been his subject throughout his life; he had studied it in all its manifestations. He told the truth about it, and he has led us to a clearer understanding of what light is. He was reported by Ruskin as having said on his deathbed 'the sun is God'; but Ruskin may have reported that incorrectly.

There was nothing 'quasi' about Faraday's religious feelings. Sandemanians took the teaching of the Bible literally. In describing what he did as 'reading God's Book of Nature', Faraday was referring to his explorations of natural and physical phenomena to reveal the unity of purpose behind them, and to define their laws. He preached the Bible in his chapel on Sundays, and the 'Book of Nature' at the Royal Institution the rest of the week. Where Turner explored the nature of light, Faraday experimented with it, searching for, and finding, relationships between magnetism and polarized light. Faraday's work on electricity was his greatest achievement – in his view, electricity was the highest power known to man, the most potent physical force God had created. 'The beauty of electricity,' he wrote, 'is that it is under *law*.'[26] We should compare this with an observation Turner made in a Perspective Lecture, 'On Vision', first given to RA students in the 1810s: '. . . such should be the joint concordance of Rules and Nature: that whatever is depicted should appear *true*. Rules are the means, Nature the end'.

Here is a deep-running common foundation between Turner and Faraday, of a different kind to the airy connection between Davy and Turner. But both connections may be strong enough to build upon them a new critical and interpretative structure for the understanding of nineteenth-century culture. Sharing a sense of purpose, morality and respect for natural laws, Davy, Faraday and Turner represent the three piers that carry a bridge of understanding over the rapidly-breaking river of knowledge. Each saw his work as part of a wider context, in which science took cognizance of art, and art took advice from science. Each looked penetratingly at nature and uncovered some of her secrets. And all would be with Coleridge, when he exclaimed of nature with awe:

> It is her largeness, and her overflow,
> Which being incomplete, disquieteth me so.

NOTES

1. Humphry Davy, 'A Discourse Introductory to a Course of Lectures on Chemistry', Royal Institution, 21 January 1802. John Davy (ed.), *The Collected Works of Sir Humphry Davy, Bart* (London, Smith, Elder and Co., 1839), vol. 2, p. 323.

2. Letter Humphry Davy to Michael Faraday, 10 December 1819, Frank A.J.L. James (ed.), *The Correspondence of Michael Faraday* (Institution of Electrical Engineers, 1991), vol. 1, no. 108.

3. From *The Director*, no. 19, 30 May 1807. The essay is unsigned, but is reprinted as Davy's work in Davy, *The Collected Works*, vol. 8, pp. 306–8.

4. From Davy's introductory lecture for the courses of 1805; Davy, *The Collected Works*, vol. 8, p. 163.

5. Ibid.

6. Richard Holmes (ed.), *Coleridge: Selected Poems* (HarperCollins, 1996), p. 242.

7. Probably Richard Balmanno, in a cutting dated 30 April 1826 from the *British Press*. Balmanno sent the cutting to Turner. See John Gage (ed.), *Collected Correspondence of J.M.W. Turner* (OUP, 1980), no. 115.

8. Humphry Davy, *Consolations in Travel, or the Last Days of a Philosopher* (1830), Dialogue the First.

9. There are 342 letters to and from Turner in Gage, *Collected Correspondence*, compared to the 4,000+ letters to and from Faraday that will be revealed when all the volumes of Frank James's collected correspondence of Faraday are published.

10. I discuss this in my *Turner – A Life* (Hodder and Stoughton, 1997), Appendix 1, pp. 333–8.

11. W.S. Dowden (ed.), *The Journal of Thomas Moore* (University of Delaware, 1983), vol. I, p. 257, (15 November 1819).

12. For more on this, see my *Turner and the Scientists* (Tate Publications, 1998).

13. For the circumstances of Canova's important mission to London, November–December 1815, see Katharine Eustace, '"*Questa Scabrosa Missione*" – Canova in Paris and London in 1815', *Canova Ideal Heads*, ed. Katharine Eustace (Ashmolean Museum, Oxford, 1997), pp. 9–38.

14. Dowden, *The Journal of Thomas Moore*, vol. 1, pp. 243–319.

15. British Library, Add. MS 37186, fo. 331.

16. M.L. [Mary Lloyd], 'Charles Babbage', in *Sunny Memories*, (1879), part 1, p. 50.

17. Gage, *Collected Correspondence*, p. 280.

18. George Jones, *Sir Francis Chantrey, Recollections* (1849), pp. 98 et seq.

19. Letter Edmund Storr Halswell to Michael Faraday, 15 March 1839. James, *The Correspondence of Michael Faraday*, vol. 2, no. 1150.

20. During the Discourse on 25 January 1839.

21. Henry Bence Jones, *Life and Letters of Faraday* (1870), vol. 1, p. 378.

22. Sylvanus Thompson, *Michael Faraday – His Life and Work* (1898), p. 246.

23. Martha Somerville (ed.), *Personal Recollections from Early Life to Old Age of Mary Somerville, with Selections of her Correspondence* (1873), p. 269.

24. Mary Somerville, *On the Connexion of the Physical Sciences* (1834), pp. 352–3.

25. Both illustrated in my *Turner and the Scientists*, figs. 128 and 129.

26. Michael Faraday, 'Observations on Mental Education', *Experimental Researches in Chemistry and Physics* (1859), pp. 463–91.

Anthony Hyman

REFORMER MILITANT:
A MINIATURE OF CHARLES BABBAGE

Charles Babbage was an unusual figure in British history. One could hardly call him eccentric as he was most businesslike. He was a good mathematician, but so were others, though Babbage made real contributions to algebra, the theory of functions, and cryptography. Babbage was creative and inventive in a wide range of subjects, but again so were others, although Babbage's scope was remarkable. Babbage was a militant Reformer, but then this was the era of Reform. Babbage was, it is true, equally at ease in a particularly wide range of circles: academics, country clergy, working men, at court, or at the dining tables of the aristocracy. However, what was altogether unusual for British society was that Charles Babbage was a superb engineer.

Babbage was born on 26 December 1791 in London, near the famous hostelry of the Elephant and Castle. His forebears came from Totnes in South Devon, a family of goldsmiths turned bankers. It is a banker's work to put all considerations in quantitative terms, and in these family occupations we find two of Babbage's principal interests combined: mechanical construction, and a quantitative approach to economic and social subjects. In 1810 Babbage went up to Trinity College, Cambridge in the comfort of a generous allowance. He was interested neither in achieving university honours nor in securing a fellowship. Unencumbered with such distractions he was free to read widely in mathematics, economics, and a comprehensive range of scientific subjects.

Babbage and his mathematical friends were concerned that Cambridge, unswervingly loyal to the Newtonian tradition, had retained Newton's 'dot' notation for the calculus while on the Continent mathematicians were using Leibnitz's more powerful 'd' notation. Thus English mathematics, which at that time languished, was isolated from the main stream of Continental work. Babbage and his friends formed the Analytical Society to remedy the situation and to introduce the Leibnitz notation to the Cambridge exams, and hence to all England. After a few years their campaign was successful, and thus laid a crucial foundation stone for the development of nineteenth-century British science. The Analytical Society was the precursor to the Cambridge Philosophical Society.

While at Cambridge Babbage became engaged to Georgiana Whitmore of a good Shropshire family, the Whitmores of Dudmaston. Through Georgiana's half brother Wolryche, the MP who rose in the Commons year after year during the 1820s to propose repeal of the Corn Laws, Babbage met and became well acquainted with Lucien Bonaparte, then in exile in England after a violent quarrel with his brother Napoleon. Lucien lived in high style and his personality was formidable. He had a profound influence on the young Babbage, who gained a revolutionary approach to the development of science and its application to improve society. This background was to give Babbage's entire approach to science a Continental sweep and sharp cutting edge quite foreign to the English scientific milieu.

After coming down Babbage married Georgiana and settled in Marylebone, London. Georgiana was an excellent wife, and filled his house with children, of whom three boys lived to maturity. They had a moderate but adequate private income, lived comfortably, and often spent the summer in Devon, or visiting Georgiana's relatives. These were Babbage's happiest years. He continued to work at algebra and the theory of functions, and guided by the Herschels, the leading astronomers of the period, gave a remarkable series of popular lectures on astronomy at the Royal Institution. Babbage was elected to fellowship of the Royal Society, then to the elite Royal Society dining club. Babbage had enormous energy and great personal charm, and societies seemed to arise almost spontaneously wherever he moved. The Astronomical Club that Babbage and his friends established at this time was later to become the Royal Astronomical Society.

In 1822 Babbage launched an ambitious project to construct a machine, a 'Difference Engine', to calculate and print numerical tables such as tables of logarithms automatically: the manufacture of number. Particularly important was the production of tables for navigation. The errors in current tables led to repeated miscalculation of ships' positions, and shipwreck. Not many ships would have to be saved to pay for any number of machines. The project secured unprecedented government support and proceeded steadily for a number of years. Neither technology nor organization were adequate for such a project, but Babbage's work led to crucial advances in machine tools affecting the whole development of British manufacture. Joseph Whitworth, the great pioneer of machine tools and of precision manufacture with interchangeable parts, learned his trade working on Babbage's Engine.

In 1827 Babbage suffered a devastating blow: Georgiana died after childbirth and his home was broken. In deep despair Babbage departed on a world tour, planning to visit China and the Far East. Frustrated in his travel plans when the Battle of Navarino closed the route to Asia, Babbage spent eighteen months in Italy, Austria, and Germany. Meetings with members of the Bonaparte family and liberal nationalists stimulated the militancy of Babbage's youth, while discussions with men of science urged new methods of scientific organization In September 1828 Babbage attended a meeting in Berlin of the Deutsche Naturforscher Versammlung organized by Alexander von Humboldt. The meeting was on a huge scale. The highest ranks of society filled the audience, while ambassadors and royalty crowded the side boxes to hear von Humboldt's opening address. No such scientific meeting had ever been held in England, and Babbage formed the opinion that the social position accorded to men of science was of high importance to the development of science itself. He determined to see that a similar organization was launched in England, and his report on the Berlin meeting published in the April 1829 issue of the *Edinburgh Journal of Science* led to the formation of the British Association for the Advancement of Science.

Babbage returned to England late in 1828 as the 'era of discussion' began. Parliamentary reform was in the air, and all the changes that the pioneers of the Analytical Society had worked for in science since 1812 now appeared as practical possibilities. Babbage leased a house in Dorset Street, Manchester Square, where his glorious

Saturday evening soirées were held. Attended by two or three hundred people from a wide range of society, in the middle third of the nineteenth century the soirées were major events of the London season. Babbage often entertained liberal figures from the Continent, and at a soirée in 1835 the young Cavour first met Alexis de Tocqueville. During the Reform period Babbage engaged in an extraordinary range of activities. He organized several campaigns for Liberal candidates and himself twice stood for election to the newly-reformed Parliament; he launched a devastating attack on the Royal Society, which the active men of science mostly felt was in a mess; and wrote a major book on political economy.

In 1830 Babbage published his most polemical book, *Reflections on the Decline of Science and some of its Causes*. At that time the Royal was not so much a professional body as a gentleman's club, while Babbage and his scientific friends wished to turn it into the organizing centre of British science: in the 1820s the British scientific movement had a radical tinge that it has never since quite recovered. The book has a militancy deriving from the rising Reform movement, and one feels Babbage must have enjoyed writing it. The Society's general malpractice, incompetence, and rank amateurism had led to practices that were quite disgraceful. Babbage had no difficulty showing that minutes of the Council had been forged, the President had entirely improperly been nominating members of the Council without even the formality of an election, the method of appointing scientific advisers to the Admiralty was a scandal, and one of them, Captain Sabine, who had been awarded the illustrious Copley Medal no less, was a charlatan. Panizzi, the celebrated librarian of the British Museum Library, was to have similar problems with the Royal Society a few years later. Such episodes are not always welcome institutional memories, and apologists for orthodoxy have found themselves dancing rather embarrassed pirouettes around the subject.

Arising largely from his work on the Calculating Engine, Babbage wrote the first work on political economy authoritatively to place the factory on centre stage. This book, *On the Economy of Machinery and Manufactures*, had an important influence on John Stuart Mill, who took his discussion of the division of labour from Babbage, and, perhaps curiously for so militant a disciple of Manchester's gospel of free trade as Babbage, on Karl Marx. It will be recalled that Marx had the idea that factories were growing bigger as the result of the development of production technology, while workers were being brought together in the factories, proletarianized, and organized by the processes of production. Marx thought the trend was set to continue as technology advanced, and he figured it might have some interesting historical consequences. It will also be recalled that this set of ideas was taken up by Lenin and others, and developed for the era of finance capital and imperialism, and did indeed lead to some dramatic historical happenings, like the Russian Revolution. Marx took the idea that factories were continuing to grow larger, and the analysis on which it was based, with proper acknowledgement be it said, from Charles Babbage. The analysis proved valid until the 1950s or 1960s – there is little point in trying to define precisely the top of so rough a curve – when development of the new computer-based technologies threw the whole process into reverse as intelligent machines replaced men and factories employed fewer people. Connoisseurs of human folly may be amused to note that whereas anti-Marxists have never accepted the first part of this analysis, Marxists have, at least until very recently, been similarly reluctant to accept the second.

*

Babbage's continental tour of 1827 and 1828 had come at a bad time for work on his Calculating Engine, just when the scale of work was beginning to expand as design progressed to fabrication. On his return to England Babbage took urgent steps to regularize the position. He secured greatly increased government support, particularly from the Duke of Wellington. His biographers have missed this completely, but from the point of view of the history of technology the Duke comes out of it remarkably well. The engineers always looked back to Wellington's premiership as a benign time for engineers. It is ironical that after the Reform Act that he had so championed Babbage lost government support permanently.

During this period Babbage advanced a whole range of proposals with a modern ring: life peerage, the decimal system, decimal coinage, ideas that derive from earlier French practice. He urged industry to adopt rational cost accounting and scientific management, and to follow economic theory firmly rooted in extensive statistics; altogether a rare combination of ideas for the time.

In 1834, as the Reform movement began to wane, support for the first Difference Engine was no longer forthcoming, although Babbage had solved the essential technical problems and a small version of the Engine that was assembled worked perfectly. Deprived of government support for the first Difference Engine, Babbage gradually expanded work on more general and powerful calculating machines until the great series of Analytical Engines began to appear. The Analytical Engines were general purpose programmable calculators. During an extraordinary and prolonged period of creative activity Babbage developed many of the concepts that are now familiar in the digital computer, including: separate store and mill, microprogramming, fast carry-column, fast multiplier/divider, punched card input and output, and a whole range of peripherals.

In 1836 Babbage published his only essay in philosophy, the *Ninth Bridgewater Treatise*, which he called a fragment. Babbage's concept was the apotheosis of Newtonian determinism, as consistent as mechanistic determinism can ever be. In Babbage's thought there is a relation between a commodity moving freely under economic forces in the capitalist system, and a free particle in a Newtonian field of force: both are the best of possible systems, and therefore, from the theological point of view, the actual systems. Free will was simply put aside in a separate compartment. His God was a Being of Science and Programmer who had defined the entire future of the universe at the Creation as a sort of infinite set of programs: miracles were merely subroutines called down from the heavenly store. Few others at the time had the remotest concept of programming, and by the time modern programming was developed in the second half of the twentieth century the self-confident Newtonian world had long since given way to the uncertainties of quantum mechanics. To that extent Babbage's world view was unique.

Meanwhile the government-sponsored project to construct a Difference Engine remained in suspense, without finance, yet without a formal termination. Babbage's successive applications to governments for a decision went unanswered. Only the Prime Minister could settle the matter and the indolent Melbourne was not at all disposed to do so. Support for the project was far from Melbourne's thoughts, while formally discontinuing the project after £17,000 of government money had been spent would have been embarrassing, and would have meant antagonizing Babbage, whom Melbourne knew socially, and his friends among the Whigs.

Successive governments' treatment of Babbage led his friend Charles Dickens to create the most celebrated government department in literature, the Circumlocution Office of *Little Dorrit*. Here Dickens seems to be making himself a spokesman for the engineers, as he had done for so many groups in society, warning 'that Britannia herself might come to look for lodgings in Bleeding Heart Yard, some ugly day or other, if she overdid the Circumlocution Office'. By the 1820s Babbage and his friends had seen the dangers for British industry if scientific methods were not applied generally. They fought for the systematic application of science on a national scale, and lost. The consequences of that defeat remain the subject of active debate. British science did indeed develop and expand later in the nineteenth century with legendary success, but in remarkably complete isolation from industry.

The present-day weaknesses in British industry derive in large measure from trends that developed in the 1830s after the Great Reform Act. This was the period when the country turned its back on any idea of universal education, and became profoundly suspicious of science, particularly of applied science. On the Continent attitudes to science crystallized out under the direct influence of the Enlightenment, two or three decades earlier than in Britain, but the differences were even greater than the time gap might suggest: it was an altogether different era. Nor is it simply a question of the difference between English empiricism and Continental Cartesianism. Although a detailed analysis is still lacking, the basic reasons must be found in the spread of industry, whose unsavoury consequences were being widely felt, and in growing fear of the rising working-class movement. For example in 1834 Dr Arnold wrote to a correspondent of the Trades' Unions as 'a fearful engine of mischief, ready to riot or to assassinate', adding, 'and I see no counteracting power'.

A central problem was the want of formal scientific and technical education in Britain. The few institutions providing technical education, such as the school at Dowlais started by Lady Charlotte Guest, provided middle managers for British industry, but the public schools were inimical to science. For example chemistry became derisively known as 'stinks'. Dr Arnold of Rugby had understood the importance of what he called 'physics', but considered it unsuited to the education of that great empire-builder, the Christian gentleman. When John Josiah Guest wanted advice on steel mills he could go to Bessemer, and throw into gear developments on the largest scale, but as the sons of the founders of British industry went to public schools and became landed gentry, industry languished technically, and was generally technologically obsolescent even at the time of its greatest economic success. It mattered little whether, like the Guests, the owners handed management over to semi-educated professional managers with neither the knowledge nor the status and social position to make the big decisions; or, like the Crawshay-Williams, sought to maintain direct control. The problems that developed during this period were those with which governments are still wrestling: inadequate technical education at all levels, a poor skills base, weak and unscientific management.

Attempts to introduce adequate scientific and technical education in Britain have been continually frustrated, with the churches playing a particularly sorry role in the saga. Scientifically trained people have been rare figures in the administrative civil service, where a culture of classicists and historians prevailed during the nineteenth and twentieth centuries. The scientifically educated few were expected to leave their training in the foyer. The senior positions in British Government, both in the civil service and amongst the political classes, have been occupied by the scientifically illiterate, with consequences, from defence procurement to BSE, which have again and again proved disastrous since the Second World War. Of course government departments have their scientific advisers, but that rarely suffices if the top people are quite incapable of grasping the technical essence of the underlying issues.

During the 1830s the annual gatherings of the British Association were the scene of many scientific social activities. Babbage was instrumental in launching the statistical section of the Association, and, arising from its meetings, what was to become the Royal Statistical Society. In 1838, and on a much larger scale in 1839, at Babbage's instance the meetings of the Association were accompanied by exhibitions of the products and manufactures of the district where the meeting was being held. These exhibitions derived from earlier French exhibitions and were in turn precursors to the Great Exhibition of 1851. There was always something comical about the endless backslapping and mutual congratulations at the Association's meetings, and Dickens parodied them delightfully as The Mudfog Association for the Advancement of Everything.

In 1840, at the invitation of the Italian mathematician Plana, Babbage gave presentations of his plans for Analytical Engines to a meeting of Italian natural philosophers in Turin. As Plana put it: 'Hitherto the *legislative* branch of our analysis has been all powerful – the executive all feeble . . . Your engine seems to give us the same control over the executive which we have hitherto only possessed over the legislative department.' It is an eternal disgrace that no similar opportunity was ever offered to Babbage in his own country. The young General Menabrea, later to be Prime Minister of the newly-united Italy, prepared a report on Babbage's presentation for the *Bibliothèque Universelle de Genève*.

During this period Babbage went widely into society, and one of his friends was Ada Lovelace, Byron's daughter. Ada was a remarkably competent student of mathematics, which was very difficult for a woman at the time, and she became fascinated by the Calculating Engines. Ada prepared a translation of General Menabrea's article, and added a far longer series of notes on the Analytical Engines. These notes incorporate Babbage's views on the general powers of the Engines, and on many aspects are the best statement we have. Ada has been called the world's first programmer. This is nonsense: Babbage was. Ada's programs, if that is the right word for them, were student exercises. She was able to find the odd slip in Babbage's work; no more. Her technical contribution was nil. Ada was Babbage's 'beloved interpretress'. As such her achievement was invaluable. Babbage's work on the main series of Analytical Engines continued until 1847 or 1848. He then produced detailed plans for a second Difference Engine using simplified and improved methods developed for the Analytical Engines.

Throughout this period Babbage continued to engage in a quite extraordinary range of activities. He had given the young Isambard Kingdom Brunel introductions to help him get his start in railway engineering. Now Brunel repaid the compliment and placed extensive facilities at Babbage's disposal, including a stripped down carriage for measuring equipment and a multichannel pen recorder. He conducted an operations research study of Brunel's wide gauge railway that had few rivals until Blackett and Bernal's work during the Second World War on military matters, such as the effectiveness of anti-aircraft guns, during actual operational conditions. Babbage proposed the system of occulting lights that was adopted for light-houses all over the world. Joseph Henry, the first secretary of Washington's Smithsonian, later described Babbage's technical work thus:

> Hundreds of mechanical appliances in the factories and workshops of Europe and America, scores of ingenious expedients in mining and architecture, the construction of bridges and boring of tunnels, and a world of tools by which labor is benefited and the arts improved – all the overflowings of a mind so rich that its very waste became valuable to utilize – came from Charles Babbage. He, more perhaps than any man who ever lived, narrowed the chasm [separating] science and practical mechanics.

Babbage's work has a wide scope, crossing all the artificial but heavily fortified frontiers of academic disciplines, and this has led to endless misunderstandings, but nothing has been more misunder-stood than the Engines themselves. It was repeatedly stated that the Engines were impractical and would not work. However, some thirty years ago, when studying the drawings and notations, the late Maurice Trask and I formed the opinion that the Engines were entirely sound. To ask whether they would indeed have worked is not really meaningful, as too much can go wrong in such a project, while on the other hand many corrections and advances would have been made during actual construction. However, the question can be put slightly differently: would it have been technically feasible for, say, Whitworth and Babbage to have constructed an Analytical Engine during the 1850s? Careful analysis suggested that the prob-lems were financial, organizational, even political, but technically the project in itself was perfectly feasible. We advanced a plan. First make Difference Engine 2; then if wished, one of the other Difference Engines; then proceed by stages to an Analytical Engine, probably following plan 28A. Thanks particularly to the work of Allan Bromley and Doron Swade, Difference Engine 2 was constructed, and now shows its paces in the Science Museum. It works perfectly. One looks forward to the time when it is joined by an Analytical Engine.

In a series of manuscript notes written in the early 1840s Babbage sketched out one of the earliest essays in what was later to become marginal value theory. Babbage was very fond of airing his ideas, and one wonders whether he met and discussed them with William Stanley Jevons, perhaps at a meeting of the Statistical Society.

Among Babbage's more puzzling activities was code-breaking, on which he spent an enormous amount of time, even querying in his autobiography whether he had spent too much of his life on the subject. Nothing that remains quite explains this concern. Certainly Babbage produced highly original and entirely unrivalled work on the theory of code-breaking and planned to write a book on the subject, but his practical efforts seem quite out of proportion. He had a good English dictionary remade as a set of twenty-six dictionaries, the first comprising the one letter words, the second the two letter words, and so on. Plurals of nouns, comparatives, superlatives of adjectives, forms of verbs and so forth were added, and a new edition of the dictionaries prepared; then another set, arranged according to the alphabetical order of the *second letter*; and so on. A number of people have come to suspect that Babbage was conducting a sort of private Bletchley Park in the middle third of the century, either for the Foreign Office or for the Admiralty.

The period of the Great Exhibition was a relaxed time for Babbage. He had put aside the Calculating Engines after more than a decade of intensive work, and went much into society, while crowds thronged his Saturday evening soirées. During the Exhibition an occulting light in one of Babbage's upstairs windows flashed messages to passing friends, a model of lighthouses to come. It was also at this time that Babbage proposed the ophthalmoscope, later developed by Helmholtz. Regularly attending the Exhibition himself, Babbage was much in demand as an expert guide to machinery, and often accompanied the Duke of Wellington.

The Great Exhibition has been to some extent misunderstood. The emphasis was more on luxury than manufacture. Even in the industrial section there was a sorry want of system among the mass of disparate items that had been brought together. In the hands of mediocrity the Industrial Commission had failed to give the clear scientific direction that industry badly needed. During the decades of mid-Victorian prosperity Britain could look back to the Great Exhibition with satisfaction, confident in her commercial superiority and the strength of her industries. Only a few, like Babbage and

Playfair, could see that fundamental weaknesses were developing. The slow introduction of labour-saving machinery when compared with the United States; glaring weakness in scientific and technical education; a lack of systematic application of science to technology: these were the signs that should have caused the greatest concern. But in those balmy years it must have seemed quite unreasonable to worry about a few clouds. Over the drawing rooms of the middle classes, self-confident and self-important, and not greatly worried about the oceans of misery upon which his affluence floated, Podsnap reigned.

*

Babbage's youngest son, Henry Prevost, returned from India with his family and stayed with Babbage for a three-year furlough, bringing much needed family warmth. When Henry returned to India he left a lonely Babbage behind. Ada Lovelace died in appalling circumstances, leaving Babbage much distressed. Undaunted, Babbage launched a second phase of work on the Analytical Engines, seeking to make them simple enough for construction with his private resources. A few years later he noted: 'The *constructor* of the *navy* might as well be required to *pay* for the building of a new ship he has devised as the inventor of the Anal[ytical] Engine to manufacture it.' The work follows his usual procedures: simplify and generalize. This is the period when the Analytical Engines come closest to the modern computer, embodying an extraordinary range of concepts, including multiprocessing and array processing. He even developed an advanced system of pressure die-casting in the attempt to make manufacture cheaper.

Even in old age Babbage could be formidable. At the time street musicians had become a public nuisance and were continually interrupting Babbage's work, but where others merely complained Babbage took action. On 25 July 1864 'Babbage's Bill' became law. We find Augustus de Morgan writing to John Herschel: 'Babbage's Act has passed and he *is* a public benefactor. A grinder went away from before my house at the first word.'

Charles Babbage died on 18 October 1871, his ringing hearty laugh, lively conversation, and unlimited fund of anecdotes sadly missed by his close friends. His life had spanned a great era of British industrial development. Born as the Industrial Revolution was gathering momentum, Babbage grew up while Britain was establishing herself as the unchallenged industrial leader of the world, and himself played a worthy role in developing Britain's industrial technology. But his great plan for the systematic application of science and modern management to industry had been ignored by successive governments. By the time of his death the country's endemic weakness in the newer science-based industries – to have such serious consequences in the twentieth century – was beginning to be more widely recognized. To Babbage it seemed so unnecessary, the fruit of short-sighted policies.

It is misleading to think of Babbage as an early scientist. Rather he was all his life a natural philosopher. Babbage's intellectual roots reached deep into the Enlightenment, and the tension between this eighteenth-century background and the advanced nature of his technical developments gives his work its peculiar flavour.

Babbage died in the consolation of his heterodox beliefs. He was leaving for a better world where he would find his beloved Georgiana, and perhaps, as a reward for his efforts on this earth, he might be permitted to investigate the Celestial Programs.

* * *

REFERENCES

Detailed references to the subject can be found in other studies by the author:

Charles Babbage, Pioneer of the Computer (Oxford University Press/Princeton, 1982).

Science and Reform, Selected Works of Charles Babbage (Cambridge University Press, 1989).

'Whiggism in the History of Science and the Study of the Life and Work of Charles Babbage', *Annals of the History of Computing* (1990), vol. 12, no. 1, pp. 62–7.

Laurent Bonnaud

AIMÉ THOMÉ DE GAMOND (1807–76): A PIONEER OF THE UNACHIEVED

How can visionaries involve their contemporaries and future generations in complex technological adventures? This might seem an odd question but the story of Aimé Thomé de Gamond justifies it. Born in the peaceful provincial town of Poitiers in 1807, Thomé de Gamond is a man of many exceptions. He ranks among the great engineers of his century without having built a single project. He enjoyed a fertile imagination, a technical and scientific culture at the crossroads of rapidly expanding disciplines, and an astonishing talent for international public relations. His actions reflected the coexistence of a deeply rooted humanism and of efficient ways of thinking related to logical positivism. He worked alone most of his life but generously shared his knowledge. What has Thomé de Gamond actually left? Nothing more than a political essay and some blueprints for various railway lines and great engineering works. His major achievement was to popularize the idea of building a permanent link across the English Channel. Embracing the role of Thomé de Gamond in this topic is to capture the essence of his life.

Thomé de Gamond was educated in the exiled Bonapartist society in Germany and Holland before returning to France. As a member of the Saint-Simonian society, he took part in the political debates of the 1830s, an experience that finds a reminiscence in his late essay on a federative French Republic. The rest of his life was exclusively dedicated to finding the best way to cross the Channel. From 1856 onwards, Thomé de Gamond disclosed the results of his research in government spheres and engineering circles in Britain and France. When he died in the most extreme poverty aged sixty-nine, the idea of boring a tunnel to link both countries was supported by prominent railway managers and the cream of the Franco-British financial world. The trend was admittedly towards the development of communication. But Thomé de Gamond was not the only promoter and certainly not the most famous. How did such a fruitful but isolated mind achieve such a successful promotion of his peculiar new idea?

A Variegated Education (1816–32)

His family belonged to the gentry of Poitou and was openly Bonapartist. This was sufficient reason to be banned under the proscription law of 1816, made by the Restoration regime to get rid of some of its opponents. The Thomés lived in Bavaria and Belgium. In 1824 Aimé went to the college in Augsburg with Louis Napoléon Bonaparte. He showed a growing curiosity and a remarkable intellectual precocity. He desired to know not only sciences, but also politics and economics. He read with great appetite and readily met new personalities to exchange ideas. William I of the Netherlands granted him free education without examination obligation and with the request that professors would help the pupil with private tuition. Within five years the student obtained doctorates in medicine and law and a degree in hydrographic and mining engineering at the School of Water Staat in Brussels, jewel of the Flemish hydrographic know-how. Even if the worth of degrees without examination may be questioned, no doubt he acquired there a feverish interest for engineering sciences.

As Thomé de Gamond turned back to France in 1829, he filled in blanks in mineralogy with Dufrénoy at the Museum and the School of Mines, and in geography with Elie de Beaumont at the College of France. He completed his solid background attentively reading the works of the father of hydrography, Charles François Beautemps-Beaupré. Asking for more in midst of plenty, he met Louis Cordier, president of the General Mine Council and professor at the Museum of Natural History. Louis Cordier had belonged to the scientific mission sent with Napoleon in Egypt. As a member of the institute, he remembered plans for a Channel tunnel exposed there around 1802. Their author was a mining engineer called Albert Mathieu-Favier. He had presented his scheme to Napoleon. Nothing remained of Mathieu-Favier and his tunnel but an engraving showing the Imperial Army marching through a wood-propped gallery, as navies fought on sea and French squadrons of hydrogen balloons were being maintained at a respectful distance by British gunners hanging from kites. Considering that tunnels at that time were still dug with picks – with the occasional help of gunpowder, fire and water to break solid rocks – the construction would have lasted decades. In addition to this, Mathieu-Favier apparently did not consider at all the geological structure of the Straits, which had never been surveyed.

Thomé de Gamond related this genuine idea with an essay published in 1753 by Nicholas Desmarets. The *Dissertation sur l'ancienne jonction de l'Angleterre à la France* relied on texts of antiquity and contemporary observations to demonstrate that England was physically linked to the Continent up to the late Ice Age. The ensuing separation had been caused by erosion and thawing ice, not by any geological disaster. Consequently, the Secondary-era chalk and marl layers that formed the Straits of Dover should run unbroken between the shores. Desmarets neither proved it scientifically nor came to the idea of building anything across the Channel, but Thomé de Gamond reflected that this was an assumption of unlimited value to a tunnel promoter. If it was true, it should be possible to bore through the most impermeable layers. The development of mining and railway technologies was propitious to such an enterprise. Since 1824 Marc Isambard Brunel and his team had been digging under the Thames. The first passenger railway service had just been inaugurated in France and the first railway tunnel was built soon afterwards. The British had transformed the old French word '*tonnelle*' (arbour) into 'tunnel', and this Franco-British word was now in current use on both sides of the Channel. In 1830 the news that a train had been driven at a speed of 44 miles per hour amazed the world. George Stephenson's *Rocket* was more than a success: it was a revolution.

A Tunnel is in the Air (1833–56)

Aside from colleges and libraries, Thomé de Gamond frequented the Saint-Simonians in Paris, named after Claude Henri de Rouvroy, Earl of Saint-Simon. Young engineers – most of them from the elitist Polytechnique School – scientists and artists, all dreamed of getting rid of war and poverty by suppressing the frontiers and distributing work according to each capacity. The development of communications played a crucial role in this philosophy – an understandable task for people educated to build bridges, harbours and canals. After the death of their mentor, Prosper Enfantin turned the Saint-Simonians into a mystical community with dedicated uniforms and a 'cloister' in Paris. The whole episode ended before the court on account of outrage upon decency. Some members like Enfantin and the economist Michel Chevalier were even sentenced to jail. All the same, the Saint-Simonian networks irrigated the French political and business life during the century. Thomé de Gamond was sympathetic to their ideas but kept a reasonable distance. He found an alternative group identity as a reserve officer of the French Army engineering corps and started to apply his knowledge in the management of family factories and estates. He occasionally stuck to studying with subjects like agriculture of the Lower territories around Royan or hydrographic changes at the mouth of the Seine and the Escaut.

During his stay on the northern coasts of France, he reinforced his conviction that the building of a permanent link across the Channel was the greatest challenge of his time. The link was not just a question of lessening the discomfort of passengers for their short journey across the Channel but a universal symbol for peace and intercourse between nations. The second conviction was that there was no point in planning any kind of durable link without investigating the geology of the Straits of Dover. There was only one method: methodically survey the possible routes and prepare a geological map of the site. Thomé de Gamond was resolved to risk his own skin and spend all he was worth on the enterprise.

From 1833 onwards, with the exception of a break in 1842, Thomé de Gamond dedicated himself entirely to the Channel crossing. He undertook three sounding campaigns and soon became a familiar, although original figure to the fishermen of Boulogne. He dived from a rowing boat with the help of his daughter, the pilot and sailors. He first experimented a primitive version of Sièbe's diving suit, but suffocated and fainted during the test. Giving up this 'waterproof winding sheet', he skin dived from the boat's deck, but drew no more than 6 metres' rope. With a bag full of pebbles in each hand, he could reach 15 metres but with his head down and he had to drop the bags to swim back to the surface. Thomé de Gamond calculated precisely how many seconds he needed to collect samples. As a result, he tried again with four stone-loaded bags for ballast, two of them fastened around his ankles, two held in his hands. A belt of air-filled pig bladders helped him to rise back to the surface. Lint over the ears and olive oil in the mouth protected him against water pressure and he tightened calicoes around his head against shocks. He dived down to 100 feet in this equipment. Once attacked by a conger eel, the engineer could fortunately be quickly dragged out of the water. When the sun shone through the sea, Thomé de Gamond could observe white shells scattered over the seabed and banks of soles gliding around. When not diving, he sounded the ground with a long gaff, clipped sample rocks and constantly improved his methods and equipment. Like fisherman Gilliat in Victor Hugo's *Les Travailleurs de la mer*, Thomé de Gamond used all his mental and physical resources in his single combat with nature. He proceeded scientifically, accurately writing down every evening the observations of the day. Thomé de Gamond was prompted by the fear of dying prematurely without any witness able to record his work 'outside the illiterate people whose material assistance was necessary to me and a . . . young girl aged seventeen who zealously faced unavoidable privations to follow and support her father'. When he had gathered enough evidence to assert the continuity of strata in the Straits of Dover, he sent a memorandum to the chief engineers of the General Councils of Mines on one side, of Bridges & Roads on the other side, two official bodies supervising mining and tunnelling and transport infrastructure projects.

At the same time, he deployed a technical creativity – though often far from realistic – to seek without prejudice the most feasible way to cross the Channel. The first idea he had in mind in 1834 was the most obvious apart from the bored tunnel: an immersed cast-iron telescopic tube laid in a prepared cutting across the Channel. It would have been difficult to transport the 200-feet-long elements up to the middle of the Straits. The iron would have quickly rusted and seepage could be expected between the telescopic components. Thomé de Gamond abandoned the concept and worked on a concrete vault that would be maintained on the Channel floor by the water pressure. His first sketch of a bridge is from 1836, an imposing construction of wrought iron and granite piles between Dover and Calais. Comfort and security was left unconsidered: a bridge would not have withstood the violent Channel storms and created a shipping hazard. Was a fixed link really the best solution? A year later, Thomé de Gamond gave thought to an integrated transport system: a giant paddle-wheel ferry, large enough to carry four trains or a hundred horse carriages. The boat, interestingly enough built of concrete, would commute between two moles, 8.6 miles long altogether. On the plans of 1840, the piers extended continuously between Dover and Blanc-Nez Cape to become a causeway. A passage for the ships would be provided by swing bridges. No need to say the idea raised fury among fishermen and pilots of the region, though it inspired a similar project from Gustave Robert in 1860. Another fantastic scheme, probably designed in co-operation with English engineers, was a 100-feet gauge railway laid on the seabed and supporting an iron gantry whose top would rise 50 feet above high-water level. Four trains would have taken their places on the structure and been cable-hauled by steam engines located on the shores. In 1855, having exploited all combinations and convinced of the geological continuity, Thomé de Gamond decided that a bored tunnel was the best solution, thus arriving back at his first idea.

In 1856 he prepared a detailed scheme for an 18.3-mile-long single railway tunnel that would connect the two railway systems at Eastwear Point and Cap Gris-Nez. The boring would last six years through the soft and homogenous Upper Jurassic chalk and emerge in the Lower Cretaceous strata near the Kentish coast. The gallery would be vaulted with stones, lit by gas lamps and ventilated by tubes emerging through artificial islands. Thomé de Gamond announced an astonishing travel time of six hours between Paris and London, a clear competitive advantage against the six days needed with the post-coach or even the twelve hours' train journey. But passengers travelling on open third-class coaches would certainly be able to report accurately on the degree of advancement of ventilation technology. An essential component of the profile was the Varne Bank, a shelf of rocks located 10 miles off Folkestone and 12 feet below the surface at high water. Thanks to the Varne Bank, the tunnel could be dug from four points instead of two. Making use of the most advanced bridge-building techniques, Thomé de Gamond proposed to sink a shaft with a 350-foot diameter in a cofferdam at the northern tip of Varne, 50 feet below the seabed. He developed an idea of Mathieu-Favier's that suggested building '*l'Etoile de Varnes*', a subaqueous railway station to take a rest, have a refreshment or simply enjoy the view of the Channel. In Thomé de Gamond's mind, the Etoile was a kind of modern Babel, an international harbour with docks for transatlantic ships, an exchange station between ocean liners and trains – what would be called an intermodal platform. The expected cost of the project was £6.8 million including railway approaches to Boulogne on the French side.

Thomé de Gamond had carried on the first rational and maybe practicable study of the question and, after more than twenty years' solitary work, several reasons induced him to publicize his results. He showed himself idealistic and pragmatic at the same time. The context was highly favourable with the boom of railways and the exhibitions of London in 1851 and Paris in 1855. Ever more foreigners visited Britain. The idea of intercommunication between nations as a mean to facilitate trade and preserve peace was highly considered. British and French engineers reflected upon ways to suppress great natural obstacles: the Suez Canal was being dug, the first drill for the Mont-Cenis tunnel was given, plans for a Panama canal circulated. Mining technology was radically changing with the first hydraulic drills. Bartleet had constructed a steam boring machine for the Mont-Cenis tunnel, which Thomé de Gamond judged of some interest.

The engineer from Poitiers was not the only pebble on the beach and he wanted to keep the lead. For more than twenty years, projects had been submitted to the General Inspection of Bridges and Roads without obtaining any kind of official recognition. Only in 1855, a physician named Prosper Payerne suggested building an archway under the sea. James Wylson wrote to the *Illustrated London News* to propose a submerged tunnel. The abbot Angelini proposed to sink a prefabricated iron tube between Cap Gris-Nez and a point between Folkestone and Dover. There was even a plan to run a submarine railway without the costly pleasure of a tunnel around it – and another fantastic scheme with neo-gothic towers in the middle of the Channel. One day would come when a more realistic proposal would be encouraged from the State and – who knows? – receive a concession. In addition to that, the strict Thomé de Gamond wished to keep the enterprise 'in the purely technical region, and to preserve it as much as possible from contacts with speculators and parasites, who try to turn every question to mercantile advantage'. He clearly warned the private industry – namely the railway and building companies – against carrying out the project before more complete investigations had been realized. On the contrary, the co-operation of governments could give the project 'the authority of a large experimental sanction'. He wanted the governments to finance experimental works and control the rest of the undertaking. As these would prove a success, private money would then not be lacking for boring the main tunnel. Was not finance a secondary matter in comparison to the common interest of the two nations and peace in Europe? As a jurist, he was more concerned with the administrative agreements to be obtained for experimental works and the necessity of a treaty between the two countries. There was another conclusive reason. Thomé de Gamond was forty-nine, physically and financially diminished from his campaigns. He could not carry on himself the soundings that were still necessary. He realized the project was too ambitious for a single head and identified the fields to be completed with official support. He would from now on concentrate himself on this political challenge.

Imperial Will and Engineer's Disputes (1856–70)

The self-proclaimed Emperor Napoleon III was an Anglophile. He had spent several years exiled in London and was fluent in English. Moreover he nurtured a strong technical and economical curiosity, willingly receiving entrepreneurs with innovative concepts. The Saint-Simonians worshipped him. This was a good omen. The Empress Eugenie was related to the Suez builder Ferdinand de Lesseps. In the college of Augsburg, three sons of proscripts had studied simultaneously: Louis Napoléon Bonaparte, Thomé de

Gamond and his cousin Adolphe Thibaudeau, whose father assumed a senatorship under the Second Empire. The proscripts of 1816 formed a closed and powerful society and Thomé de Gamond knew how to use it.

He and his cousin were appointed on 20 April 1856 at the Tuileries palace. The pioneer brought his profiles and geological samples. The Emperor informally put his hat upon the plans to fix them, examined the samples in their case, listened attentively and asked numerous questions. Thomé de Gamond had meticulously prepared the meeting and answered thoroughly, evoking the extra-territoriality of the run and the possibility to batten down the frontiers under Eastware and Cap Gris-Nez. He also proposed plugholes to flood the tunnel.

'That this process is practicable will perhaps suffice,' said the Emperor, 'to hope it will never be used.'

The expected decision came immediately. Napoleon III suggested Thomé de Gamond meet the Secretary of State for Public Works and set up an international scientific commission. The idea was new: never had an industrial problem in France been supervised by an international commission. For Thomé de Gamond, this was a unique opportunity to obtain official recognition for his project through agreement from the administration of Public Works and declaration of public utility in France, and through parliamentary procedure in Britain. Meanwhile Eugène Rouher, then Secretary of State for Agriculture, Trade and Public Works, sang a different tune. Under the pretext that meeting would be made difficult by different languages and distances, Rouher preferred a national commission. Thomé de Gamond had no alternative than to insist it would be left as open as possible and would concentrate on the geology sooner than the construction. Rouher promised to invite the General Council of Mines, of Bridges & Roads, and the hydrographic services of the Navy.

The 'Official Commission for the Submarine Tunnel' started to work in May 1856. Among its members was the geologist Elie de Beaumont. Thomé de Gamond assisted at the meeting of the General Council of Mines in January 1857. Although the Mines and the Bridges & Roads administrations' views were slightly different, the first being far more favourable, the Commission accepted in principle to solicit £24,000 credits from the French Government, should the British Government agree with experimental borings. The Mont-Cenis works should also be considered before making a decision. The debates were kept secret in order to leave the Commission uninfluenced by press comments. But the journalists were quick to take up the question. The *Moniteur*, the *Débats*, the *Gazette de France* and many others marked wild enthusiasm. 'England become continental! What a beautiful dream!' wrote *Le Siècle* in October 1857.

Thomé de Gamond had always considered that the tunnel was a political question and that nothing could be done without a British initiative. Therefore he embarked on a steamer and crossed the Channel. He was received by Prince Albert and Prime Minister Palmerston. The Prince shared with Napoleon III a strong technical curiosity and was seduced by the idea. But Palmerston bitterly commented: 'You would think differently if you had been born in this island', and turning to Thomé de Gamond: 'What? You pretend to ask us to contribute to a work the object of which is to shorten a distance which we find already too short?' These were of course different views than those expressed by John Bright and Richard Cobden, who saw the tunnel as 'the true arch of alliance' between Britain and France. As Queen Victoria, reputed to be easily seasick, transmitted her blessings 'in her personal name and in the name of all the ladies of England' if Thomé de Gamond succeeded, Palmerston moderated himself and declared: 'This project will be carried out because it is respectable, and because it is favoured by all the ladies of England.' His Government had no major objection against the project. But the most earnest supporter of Thomé de Gamond was the French Ambassador Jean de Persigny, who desired 'fervently that the Government would devote the necessary funds for a great experiment'. By the end of the year, they drafted together an official agreement to conduct experimental works, as recommended by the Official Commission. They also tried again to form a bi-national scientific commission. The *Illustrated London News* announced it would be presided over by the two chairmen of the exhibitions of London and Paris.

Thomé de Gamond widely advertised his plans in railway and engineering circles. He sent a striking 180-pages-thick essay to the French Academy of Science and the French Geographical Society, to the Royal Society of London and the Institution of Civil Engineers.

He developed in it the attractive vision of a continuous road between England and India. Was not the tunnel the missing link of the great route?

Charles Couche, a manager of the Northern Railways that served Boulogne, congratulated the engineer for bringing 'this great problem within the region of serious discussion . . . Your learned investigations alone have given it body'. He referred explicitly to the Saint-Simonist ideals: 'Nations begin to understand that it would be wise to assign for their commonwealth part of the sacrifices they have so generously perpetrated to destroy one another'. The economist Michel Chevalier advocated the tunnel cause as vividly as he encouraged the free trade agreement. Louis Delebecque, deputy for the Pas-de-Calais department and a railway supporter, praised 'the sincerity and the order which reign in your exposition of facts, as well as in the strictness of the reasoning by which you deduce them'.

Thomé de Gamond thought it opportune to obtain the co-operation of the so-called triumvirate, the three most famous British engineers of the time. He knew Isambard Kingdom Brunel since their youth. Thomé de Gamond had visited the Caledonian Canal and the Liverpool & Manchester Railway with his father, Sir Marc Isambard, in 1827, as the last was working on the Thames tunnel. Joseph Locke was working on the London to Southampton route when Thomé de Gamond had introduced him to his cousin, Adolphe Thibaudeau, who was trying to raise funds for the railway line between Paris and Rouen. This meeting eased the penetration of English capital in the project. The contacts with Robert Stephenson were more tenuous. Stephenson had worked with Saint-Simonians and got involved in the Suez Canal project as it has sometimes been claimed that Thomé de Gamond had. We have found no evidence of this fact.

In spite of his excellent contacts, Thomé de Gamond achieved very little at this stage. Orsini's failed assassination attempt against Napoleon III, on 14 March 1858, put an end to this first attempt to obtain official recognition for the tunnel project. Orsini was an Italian *carbonaro*, but he allegedly prepared his coup from England. Thomé de Gamond was politely informed, maybe by Napoleon III himself, that circumstances were 'inopportune' to promote a project for a submarine tunnel between the two countries. 'We ought to

know to keep it for better times,' said the mysterious personage.
The regime stiffened, Anglo-French relations froze. Persigny was
recalled 'and replaced by a soldier' noted Thomé de Gamond
bitterly. For the second time since 1802, the tunnel was severely
plagued by political considerations. Thomé de Gamond was equally
unfortunate with his British colleagues. Isambard Brunel, Joseph
Locke and Robert Stephenson died prematurely in 1859 and 1860.
Although Thomé de Gamond judged Stephenson to be 'the type of
a perfect gentleman' Stephenson had unexpectedly kept his French
colleague and his tunnel at a distance as he had done with Ferdinand
de Lesseps and his Suez Canal. 'He seemed then to follow the view
of Palmerston, and influenced by his attitude on the new question of
great cosmopolitan works, he maintained some reserve.'

In 1859 Britain was divided. Invasion fears surged up again
following diplomatic tensions with Paris. But the new Chancellor of
the Exchequer, William Ewart Gladstone, did not believe that a war
with France was inevitable and worked actively to obtain a commercial treaty with the neighbouring country, which had the approval
of industry. The free trade agreement between Britain and France,
prepared by Richard Cobden, John Bright and Michel Chevalier,
was signed in 1860. The tunnel was on the air. In February 1862
the continental business manager of the South Eastern Railway
declared to *Mechanic's Magazine* that a Channel tunnel would be 'a
paying speculation' with under £12 million construction costs.

Such statements encouraged the President of the Institution of
Civil Engineers, John Hawkshaw, to commission the geologist Hart-
sinck Day to investigate the Straits of Dover. Day worked from
1865 to 1867 between South Foreland and Sangatte and concluded
the continuity of strata. Hawkshaw knew Thomé de Gamond's
report and his scheme was a very similar single tunnel with two rail-
tracks. But in opposition to the French engineer, the builder of the
Severn tunnel was convinced that the tunnel should be bored
through the grey Cenomanian chalk, not through the less homogenous Jurassic layers. Hawkshaw explained to Cobden that he
would seek a guarantee of interest from the Government and
undertake trial borings. Cobden was deeply convinced that transport
systems were providing union between people and he supported the
project enthusiastically. But Palmerston was still governing. 'Wait
until the Old Man dies,' suggested Cobden. Both men died in 1865.

Hawkshaw then met Gladstone, to convince him that the expected traffic would cover the costs of the work. 'Who cares of traffic?' answered the Chancellor of the Exchequer. 'Can the tunnel be built? That is the only question.' But he refused to engage a single penny of the Treasury in the whole affair.

William Low started working on the question in 1865. He was another thoroughly experienced tunnel engineer though as familiar with collieries as with railways and less glamorous than John Hawkshaw. His lecture before the Institution of Engineers created a surprise. Low proposed to bore two single-railway tunnels. The twin tunnel offered two significant advantages: the galleries would be connected by cross-passages and be ventilated through the piston effect of incoming trains: in case of fire or any other prejudice in a gallery, it would be easy to escape in the other. They would be cheaper. Low also favoured the younger Cenomanian grey chalk lying above Thomé de Gamond's strata.

Both British engineers worked isolated up to 1867, while Thomé de Gamond endeavoured to restore his finances. The Exhibition of Paris in 1867 gave everybody an opportunity to come back on the stage. Thomé de Gamond's blueprint was not fundamentally differ-ent from his former plan. He presented a tunnel one mile longer with cuttings into the cliffs instead of bored approach tunnels. The route would still run under the Varne Bank but the shaft would be three times larger and deeper, to allow trains driving on a spiral railway – a design favoured by the consortium Euro route in the 1980s. The estimated construction time varied between eight and ten years and it would cost £7.2 million including approaches and rolling stock.

On 17 April 1867 William Low presented his plan to Napoleon III. It was an audacious coup. Neither Low nor his secretary George Thomas spoke French and the hearing was in English. Low had considerably developed the mode of ventilation and Napoleon III expressed himself smiling: 'I see perfectly you will give us English air through one tunnel, and we will repay it by sending a current of French air by the opposite tunnel.'* The Emperor declared himself ready to do all he could to support the scheme and to transmit Low's written proposal to the Ministry of Public Works, but nothing

* Submarine & Continental Railway Company, *Report*, 1882.

happened. During the summer, Low sent his plans to Thomé de Gamond. The pioneer was not shocked by the twin-tunnel concept. He was so keen on finding a successor that he answered Low at once. He was sceptical on the proposed route, which he knew from his ferry scheme, a few miles north from his, but saw no serious obstacle to it. Thomé de Gamond did not want to be fully active any longer. He would confine himself to acting as an adviser and hoped nevertheless to receive some emoluments later from promoting the company. 'I have always hoped to live long enough to become the co-adjutor of an English engineer,' he said. 'Providence has willed that you should be that man.' He put his work at Low's disposal. Low then associated himself with James Brunlees, an expert in steep climbing railways and stationary engines on inclined planes.

At the end of the year 1867, Thomé de Gamond, William Low and James Brunlees established a Channel Tunnel Committee in Paris and London, whose mission was to define the best project to link the two shores and to incorporate companies to run and operate it. Lord Richard Grosvenor, chairman of the London, Chatham & Dover Railway, agreed to preside over it. Like most tunnel supporters, he was a Liberal. Grosvenor's reputation and experience and the interested support of the LCDR would enlarge the fame of the project outside engineers' circles. The new triumvirate submitted its proposal to the Committee on 7 February 1868. The scheme, presented in two languages and named *Chemin de Fer sous-marin de détroit de Calais* or *Anglo-French Submarine Railway*, was Low's twin tunnel, modified according to Thomé de Gamond's suggestion and co-undersigned. Two driftways would be intended as a future tunnel. They should cost £2 million. If the trial proved successful, the driftways would be converted into twin tunnels. As the undertaking would not be rentable for some time, the promoters were anxious to ascertain if the governments would grant them a subvention, or at least a guarantee of interest to 5 per cent on £5 million for fifty years against a right of control on the works.

John Hawkshaw reacted strongly against the Committee and observed on 18 March 1868 that he had been engaged for two years in research that the French Government approved. He declared that Thomé de Gamond had made many attempts to rally him in 1867, which he had declined, because his investigations were not com-

pleted. Brunlees pleaded not guilty considering that 'a project of this
kind should be opened to the world',* and due to his respectability,
he invited Hawkshaw to join the Committee. The express condition
was that Low's project would be the only one to be considered and
that the three engineers would be equal in competence.

Indifferent to these controversies, dispensed to pay the £250 fee
to the common fund, Thomé de Gamond agitated the French
engineering circles to create a pendant of the London Committee.
He achieved his last mission for the great cause successfully when
he rallied Michel Chevalier and Paulin Talabot of the Paris-Lyon-
Méditerranée Railway. The report sent on 10 May 1868 to the
Secretary of Napoleon III was signed by nearly all those who had
participated in the project in the last three years; 170 personalities
petitioned in its favour, aside from the numerous patronage committees – a testimony of the popularity of the idea in both countries.
The project was presented to the Emperor in an audience on 17
June. A scientific commission was routinely set up under the pre-
cedence of the mining engineer Charles Combes, a former member
of the first Official Commission, and reported to the ministry on 2
March 1869. It was accepted that the grey chalk offered 'reasonable
chances of success' and that driftways were the best exploration
method. But the president was unsuccessful in resolving considerable
divisions on the financial question. Invoking the Mont-Cenis, half
the members considered that a project of this size and importance
should be supported by the governments. The other half insisted on
the disproportion between cost and revenue and the absence of a
traffic forecast and construction time estimates. It was impossible to
say in what manner the tunnel would increase the traffic between
England and France. The chairman restricted himself to reflecting
the drift between the General Council of Mines and its counterpart
of the Bridges & Roads. The report was communicated to London
with a positive appreciation from the French Government. On such
a weak basis, the first Gladstone Government again denied any
financial support for the experimental works. The Chancellor of the
Exchequer even declared that this was 'rather a wild proposition'
and that the Government would not pay attention, 'at that time at

* Submarine & Continental Railway Company, *Report*, 1882. Letter Brunlees to
  Hawkshaw, 21 March 1868.

any rate'.* The Channel Tunnel Committee then decided to raise private funds after obtaining official authorization. It was a major setback for the promoters.

The Franco-Prussian War, which burst out in 1870, put a temporary stop to diplomatic negotiations engaged on both sides. When the Committee started to work again, Thomé de Gamond had faded away. Low had designed a sound scheme that laid the foundation for generations of tunnel promoters and was finally built in its modern shape in the 1980s. But Hawkshaw took the lead in the Tunnel Committee. Their struggle culminated in 1873. For this reason, the after-war period would be characterized by the conflicting involvement of railway companies. The rivalry between London, Chatham & Dover defending Hawkshaw's profile and the South Eastern Railway promoting Low's ruined the first trial borings in the early 1880s.

However, Thomé de Gamond had reached his personal goal. His comments of April 1869 reflect a very personal view of the situation. He wrote:

> Ever since the Exhibition, the question of the Submarine Tunnel has made great progress in a practical point of view by the formation of an Anglo-French Committee of promoters and eminent engineers of the two countries henceforth united in mental fraternity to prepare for the execution of the project. The ends we proposed in this Exhibition are therefore attained. Our labours, heretofore solitary, are now mingled with those of our colleagues in a work wherein the individuality of each of us will be absorbed for the execution of a final plan.

When he died in 1876, he left his daughter with no other resources than an ability to give piano lessons, and the Channel Tunnel Company created in 1872 paid her an annuity in recognition of her father's achievements.

From Thomé de Gamond's investigations and design little remained. Low and Hawkshaw were united in rejecting the southern route via the Varne Bank. His great merit is to have made the tunnel credible in engineering circles through a thorough geological investigation, and to have given it a political visibility. The further

---

* Bright, John, *Suez Canal and Channel Tunnel: Peace or War with France?* (London, C.F. Roworth, 1883), p. 29.

corporate developments have based themselves on this legitimacy. The idea of a permanent link across the Channel had acquired a momentum that it would never lose.

* * *

BIBLIOGRAPHY

All quotations without footnote are from Thomé de Gamond's essays, whose main titles follow:

Etude pour l'avant-projet d'un tunnel sous-marin entre l'Angleterre et la France reliant sans rompre charge les chemins de fer de ces deux pays par la ligne de Grinez à Eastevare, avec la carte du tracé projeté et le profil du tunnel traversant le diagramme géologique du massif submergé (Paris, Victor Dalmont, 1857), 180 pp.

Carte d'étude pour le tracé et le profil du canal de Nicaragua . . . Précédée de documents publiés sur cette question par F. Belly (Paris, 1858).

Etudes de travauz publics. Mémoire sur le projet du chemin de fer de Seine-et-Oise . . . destiné à relier les trois réseaux du nord, de l'ouest et d'Orléans par Versailles, avec la carte du tracé et les profils étudiés (Paris, 1865).

Mémoire sur les plans d'un projet nouveau d'un tunnel sous-marin entre la France et l'Angleterre produits à l'exposition universelle (Paris, Société des Ingénieurs civils de France, 1869).

Account of the plans for a new project of a submarine tunnel between England and France (2nd edn.) Reproducing the autobiographic account of 1867, with an atlas of plates, etc. (Paris, Dunod, London, Savill, Edwards & Co., 1870), 2 vols., 111 pp.

République François. Justice! . . . Mémoire sur l'établissement de la République fédérale en France, etc. (Paris, 1871).

A broader history of the Channel Tunnel can be found in the author's book: *Le Tunnel sous la manche: deux siècles de passions* (Paris, Hachette, 1994).

David Gilmour

RICHARD COBB

First encounters with Richard Cobb were often disconcerting, especially for aspiring undergraduates confronted by the History Fellows of Balliol College. Two of the dons tried to put you at your ease, a third seemed always half asleep, but Cobb was alert and rather unnerving, talking with jerky gestures, sharp eyes glinting behind thick-lensed spectacles. There was something alarming, too, about his appearance, the gaunt, bony features and the slight, emaciated body – a condition he blamed on German U-boats for depriving him of sugar as an infant in the First World War.

My own interview in December 1970 was a disaster. In the 'interests' section of my application form, I had made the mistake of including my membership of the Committee for Freedom in Angola, Mozambique and Guinea – an organization that was bound to provoke Cobb, whose politics were whirring rightwards at the time. He seized on it and brusquely asked which liberation group in Angola I supported and why. On my admission that I knew only about the MPLA, he recited the acronyms of the others before turning to the *révolte nobiliaire* of 1787–8: what, he enquired, were the aims of its leaders? Demoralized by Angola, I couldn't remember who the leaders were, let alone what they wanted, and a difficult silence followed until Maurice Keen, the great medievalist, sallied out beyond his period to ask me about the Battle of Waterloo. What should have been a straightforward discussion ended in surly disagreement over whether Wellington had been unduly cautious about his right flank, and I left the room convinced that I would be seeing no more of Cobb, Keen or Balliol. A week later my school received a letter from the senior History don announcing that I had passed in spite of a poor Latin paper; 'To soften the blow,' he added, apparently without irony, 'perhaps you could tell him how much we enjoyed hearing about Angola.'

Successful interviewees usually saw Cobb for the second time the following October when, in his rooms high above the Front Quad, he taught de Tocqueville for the 'prelims' examinations. A naturally shy man, he seemed overawed by the large number of unkempt strangers who filed into his sitting room; certainly he treated us long-haired youths with elaborate politeness, formally addressing us as Mr Gilbert, Mr Gilmour and so on. Only during the second term, when he taught us singly or in pairs, did he relax and use Christian names. I remember sitting on an enormous, badly upholstered sofa, with the springs touching the floor, and being invited to imagine how many vast female bottoms must have sat there for it to have acquired its shape.

His tutorials were memorable occasions introduced with a discussion (or more usually a monologue) about people and things he strongly disliked at the time: cricket, the Common Market, President Pompidou, Vienna, enthusiasm, 'poor foolish Lefties', and his perennial hate-figure, Robespierre (one of his hobbies was identifying potential Robespierres in the Balliol junior common room, though he claimed to find them in other places as well, 'lurking behind the windows of ticket-offices or as deacons in Baptist tabernacles'). After twenty minutes or half an hour, you read your essay while he fidgeted, opening a window, straightening a carpet or noisily moving from one chair to another. And then he talked about the essay subject, often for no more than twenty minutes, yet with such clarity and perceptiveness that you came away feeling you had learned all the essential points about Bourbon Spain or eighteenth-century Poland.

If you had the tutorial before lunch, the last ten minutes might be spent in the Worcester College buttery (he moved from Balliol on his appointment to the Chair of Modern History in 1973), and quite often this would lead on to lunch. Wary of vegetarians and teetotallers, he liked people who shared his capacity for enjoying food and drink. He assumed that Julian Critchley, the irreverent Tory MP, must be 'a Good Thing' because he liked 'eating'; similarly, he welcomed the appointment of his successor at Worcester, Norman Stone, on the grounds that he had *une bonne descente*, especially of whisky and vodka. A devotee of Abbot's Special ('the nectar of Suffolk beers') and French red wine, Cobb never scorned lesser beverages. In 1962, between marriages, he spent a day in a Sofia hotel – waiting for a telephone call from a beautiful Bulgar in apparent need of rescue – reading *The Leopard* (in French) and getting so drunk on rose brandy that he began to sweat attar of roses. A few weeks later, he went to Vienna to fetch the girl, only to discover that she did not want rescuing after all – a disappointment he countered by going on an extended cafe crawl, buying a great deal of local wine for himself and anyone he met in the course of a long night, which finally ended when a barman confiscated his passport until he returned with enough money to pay the bill (an operation that took five days, not because of a cash-flow problem but because he was unable to identify the right cafe in daylight).

Cobb was a brilliant and very funny talker, especially at meals when the panorama of his interests and prejudices – backed up by an astonishing memory – was given full exposure. His likes and dislikes were often transferable, but there was a small, consistent list of improbable heroes – Walpole and Baldwin were his favourite prime ministers, while he sometimes proclaimed that Louis XVIII was France's 'last decent ruler' – and a longer, rather more interesting catalogue of Detested Persons, which included Napoleon, Hemingway, Graham Greene, P.G. Wodehouse, Le Corbusier, Haussmann ('the Alsatian Attila'), Malraux ('a narcissist and trifler'), poets (especially Baudelaire, though he appreciated Pope for his malice), the Elizabethans in general, and the staff of the Archives Nationales in Paris. Sometimes one might be moved to dispute – one couldn't leave unchallenged the view that Wodehouse was a lousy writer who deserved to be hanged as a traitor in 1945 – but it was more entertaining just to listen to the monologues and occasionally do a little prompting.

The list of Detested Persons, onto which certain colleagues occasionally drifted, might suggest both a talent for hatred and an habitual intolerance. But in fact he was a poor hater, as he himself admitted, because his hatreds were inconsistent, 'swivelling round ... like a mad barometer'. And he was mainly intolerant of other people's intolerance, of those impatient to inflict their own disagreeable or self-righteous views (especially when political or architectural) on others. The only people he consistently disliked were puritans, 'miserabilists', Enemies of Pleasure, Propagandists of Virtue, people who were not at all like that 'Good Thing' Critchley.

In the 1960s and 1970s Cobb became a richly anecdotal figure, the university's most notorious eccentric, famous for his humour, feasting, outspokenness – and scholarship. People remembered the stories – such as how he and Maurice Keen kept the Master of Balliol awake all night by singing Irish songs beneath his windows – but they did not forget that he was a great, an original, and also a very prolific historian. Despite the teaching, the revelry, and the time spent with Margaret (whom he married in 1963) and their young sons, he published in a single decade (1969–78) three volumes of essays and four major works on the social history of the French Revolution, each of them based on archival research he had carried out in France.

*

Cobb was born in May 1917, the son of a member of the Sudan Civil Service. He saw little of his father, who was usually abroad, and spent his early years with his mother and grandparents at Frinton, Colchester and Tunbridge Wells. All his life he remained loyal to flat landscapes close to the North Sea and the English Channel, a geography that stretched from Kent past the East Anglian estuaries to Cambridgeshire and the Fens. (But not beyond: he did not like hills and could not see the point of Scotland, which looked on the map as if it had been 'torn out of a piece of paper'; the best thing about the place, he said, was that its topography made it unsuitable for cricket.) In France he ranged further inland, not just between the bleak sea front of Le Havre and the flat lands of the Pas de Calais, but to Rouen and Amiens and beyond the Île de France to the wooded valleys of the Yonne and the Upper Seine. He loved Lyon, where he did much of his research, but he seldom went further south, except to Marseille and in later life to Perpignan. Like Maigret, one of his favourite characters in fiction, he never cared for the heat or the scent of aromatic herbs. You would never find Cobb among the immaculate stone villages of the Dordogne or the Lubéron. He was a winter man with a taste for harsh geography, for the stark angularity of quaysides and canals, the wide horizons of the Beauce, the blackened brick streets of Roubaix and Lille.

The most important event of Cobb's education took place

neither at his public school (Shrewsbury) nor at his Oxford college (Merton) but in between when, at the age of seventeen, his mother sent him to Paris to learn French. The experience of staying with a family on the Grands Boulevards provided the catalyst for a lifetime's immersion in France and French history. During university vacations he returned to work in the Archives Nationales and in 1938, under the distant supervision of Georges Lefebvre, he began research on an obscure leader of the *hébertistes* who was guillotined in 1794. For a time he was an ardent defender of revolutionary zeal, but fortunately this did not last: he later considered Robespierre and Saint-Just to be the two most repellent figures in French history.

Had it not been for Hitler, he might have remained permanently in Paris. As it was, he could not resume his research until 1946, although he learned a good deal about northern France in the months after D-Day, stationed in agreeable and not very dangerous billets in Normandy and the north-east. On going back to the Archives, he abandoned his unpleasant *hébertiste* and turned to the revolutionary armies sent out from Paris and other cities during the Terror to enforce the new order in the provinces and requisition food supplies for the urban population. For nine years he pursued their obscure members through departmental and communal archives, rescuing them from the dust of innumerable boxes in Normandy, Lille, Lyon and Paris. He loved provincial research and wrote many of his early articles for journals such as *Annales de Normandie* and *La Revue du Nord*. As he once remarked, his history was not French history but French provincial history, even if his favourite province was Paris.

It was an unconventional career, and he was an unambitious historian: for a long time he had neither formulated aims nor an appetite for academic appointments. Financing his research by teaching English, he allowed himself the luxury of deflection, of being directed down unexpected channels, of pausing in his pursuit of the revolutionary armies to linger over the love letters of a *guillotiné* or an eyewitness account of the September massacres. Not until 1955, at the age of thirty-eight, did he accept a lectureship at Aberystwyth, succeeded by a research fellowship at Manchester in 1959 and a brief appointment at Leeds before returning to Oxford as a Fellow and Tutor at Balliol in 1962. Yet he did not relinquish his French identity. He kept a room in Paris for long research visits, and for the first fourteen years in Britain nearly all his work was written and published in French. Only in 1969 did the massive volumes on the revolutionary armies give way to works in English, a book of essays (*A Second Identity*) being closely followed by *The Police and the People, Reactions to the French Revolution* and *Paris and its Provinces*.

Cobb's approaches to French history are encapsulated in the titles of these and lesser-known works. *A Second Identity* and *A Sense of Place* indicate his commitment to France and sensitivity to French topography, while *People and Places* and *The Police and the People* suggest his concern with individuals and their relationships with authority and the places they live in. The 'second identity' went beyond an extraordinary knowledge of the French archives and an ability to write books in French. It defined another persona, one that thought, felt and said different things on the other side of the Channel. Little pleased him more than when Frenchmen mistook his nationality. '*Vous êtes Belge?*' they might ask, or better still, '*Vous êtes du Nord?*', for he loved to be mistaken for an inhabitant of one of the great textile towns of the north-east. In Paris he sometimes claimed he was *bruxellois*; in Lyon he might pretend to come from Roubaix. Even when his nationality was discovered or admitted, he was delighted when the stranger beamed and said, '*Monsieur Cobb, vous êtes bilingüe*' – so long as the compliment was not paid by the Québécois, whom he accused of massacring both languages.

A retired *inspecteur général* from the south-west once told him that he spoke French with the facility of '*un titi parisien*' – an observation that sets him apart from other English historians pre-eminent in the studies of another country, for no one has ever suggested that Sir Raymond Carr spoke Spanish like a Madrid Teddy boy or that Denis Mack Smith employed the vocabulary of *un ragazzo di borgata*. Not many people, perhaps, would regard it as a compliment, but for Cobb, the least pompous and most unpretentious of men, it was the best he ever received. For it demonstrated that he *belonged*, that he had crossed the line and acquired that alternative identity which enabled him to become such a fine writer and historian of France.

This identity, combined with a strong sense of place and a unique prose style (he often found it impossible to complete a sentence in fewer than two hundred words), created memorable depictions of ambience. Although he claimed to be 'totally unpoetic', a phrase of his evokes a Paris street like a sentence in Simenon or a song by Piaf. Some of his best writing can be found in brief sketches of the gradients of Lyon, of middle-class houses in Touraine, of townscapes of mills and brick chimneys and back-to-back terraced houses. In *The End of the Line*, his last book, he described an all-night cafe in Rouen, smelling of coffee, cheroots and stale Kronenbourg, populated by sailors, railway workers, women waiting for fishing boats to come in, lonely old men desperate to see out the night. To many people the scene would seem banal, depressing, perhaps even repellent. But such was the power of his evocation and sympathy that it becomes intensely moving.

For Cobb, history was never just a matter of spending long days in the archives: it had to be walked, observed, smelt, drunk and above all listened to, in cafes, buses, parks and railway stations. In Paris he was a persistent boulevardier, especially of unfashionable boulevards in the middle of the night, a man who walked a good deal from choice or from loneliness or because he had missed the last métro home (or because he did manage to catch it but then fell asleep and woke up at the terminus). But it was seldom random walking. He was very much a creature of routine and fixed itineraries, needing to establish a pattern in every town he stayed in for any length of time: to walk the same streets each day, to take the same bus at the same time, to read the local papers, to recognize the customers who drank aperitifs in the *tabac*. He needed routine and familiar faces because they represented security and reassurance, because they made him feel that he belonged to his temporary home while observing it from the vantage point of a cafe or a quayside or his much-loved *platforme d'autobus*.

An appreciative reviewer in the *TLS* once suggested that his weakness was the inability 'to bring himself to sympathise with those who seek to exercise power, be their motives good or evil'. In the introduction to his next book Cobb replied, characteristically, that he did understand people who sought power for purely evil motives because they at least had 'human proportions'. The phrase, an important and recurring one in his work, helps explain his innate sympathy for nearly everyone he was writing about except for self-righteous pleasure-haters and authoritarians. Like his friends, most of his subjects had 'human proportions'. And, indeed, they were

often the same sort of person. He wrote with such intuition about
the poor of revolutionary France because he knew their descendants
in the 1940s and 1950s: peasant farmers, prostitutes, criminals,
légionnaires, black marketeers – his closest French friend was a
deserter and thief. In the archives or on the street he read, listened
and observed; he did not make judgements. He was naturally on the
side of the unheroic, the ordinary and the uncompetitive. He sympathized with people who tried to avoid taking part in wars and
revolutions, and he understood why the Parisians preferred to
surrender their city rather than allow Hitler to destroy it. He
sympathized with a woman from Picardy whose head was shaved
for *collaboration horizontale* with a German – she certainly had
'human proportions' – and, however much he disliked the Vichy
regime, he made the effort to try to understand why people supported it.

'I have never,' wrote Cobb, 'understood history other than in
terms of human relationships', a view that set him against Marxists,
sociologists, computer historians and anyone else who tried to
'impose a false sense of unity and simplicity on a subject which has
neither'. He loathed historians who spent their time debating theories or imposing structures or trying to find a Grand Design for
events that were spontaneous and chaotic and usually unintended.
He once told a Yugoslav historian, who had asked him for advice
about 'methodology', that 'one just went to the records, read them,
thought about them, read some more, and the records would do the
rest': all the historian had to do 'was to be able to read and, above
all, to write clearly and agreeably'.

Cobb's own approach to history was very much an individual's
on individuals, a continuous attempt to get beyond or under the
rhetoric, to see how events affected individual lives. He insisted on
looking at the French Revolution not through its politics and its
institutions but through human experiences, a process he called
'rediscovering the individual'. Thus from his pages the *sans-culottes*
emerge not as a uniform body of people acting out of class considerations but as individuals who did this or that for reasons of family,
geography, temperament, habit, selfishness or pure chance. And
the Revolution itself seems slightly more human, or at any rate
less effective and oppressive. If it did little for *les petites gens*, it
did not prevent a great many of them from getting on with their

lives without busybodies constantly telling them what was good for them. Cobb's works reveal the irrelevance of the Revolution to most people's needs and interests. What meaning did it have for poor girls from Lyon who had been seduced and abandoned when pregnant? Of what possible value were Robespierre's self-righteousness and insistence on virtue to people who could recognize the 'outriders' of hunger and knew that famine was on the way? This was surely Cobb's principal achievement: to have given the Revolution its human proportions, to have shown us what it meant not for Robespierre and Danton and subsequent generations of revolutionaries but for millions of individuals who had to endure the events while trying to get on with the business of living their lives and looking after their families.

*

Death in Paris, which appeared in 1978 and won the Wolfson Prize, was Cobb's last work based on his research in the French archives. Subsequently he published another volume of essays (*People and Places*), *Promenades* (with the subtitle, *A Historian's Appreciation of Modern French Literature*), and a long essay on the German occupations in France during the world wars. In 1984, the year he retired from his Chair, he was awarded the Légion d'honneur. Although he went on writing, chiefly about his early life, this marked the end of his career as an historian of France. Sadly, his reputation then declined, mainly, perhaps, because he did not belong to any school of history; as he himself put it, he was too much of a *frondeur* to want to do anything like that. At the same time he was too much of an individualist and too lacking in self-importance to wish to found one himself. A couple of days before his death, he wrote that, just as he had never been a participant in anyone's cult, 'there could never be a Cobb cult'. He had many pupils, inspired by his teaching and his example, who have become major historians. But they did not become disciples: they knew his genius was unique and inimitable.

Cobb celebrated his retirement year with an eccentric stint as chairman of the judges of the Booker Prize. Frustrated in his attempt to award the prize to the Scottish novelist Allan Massie, he strove successfully to exclude Martin Amis and Lisa St Aubin de Terán from the shortlist; at the final meeting of the judges, he torpedoed the chances of J.G. Ballard, thereby enabling the award to be made to an unambitious novel by Anita Brookner. In his speech at the prize-giving dinner he then shocked the assembled literati by remarking that he had never read Joyce or Proust. The claim was widely regarded as both provocative and untrue, but he insisted privately that he had never read Proust and did not intend to do so unless he was sent to prison for a very long time; he disliked reading things that were *vachement intellectuels*, complicated books about ideas.

As he seems to have read every other French novelist, even the most obscure and provincial, it was a pity he refused to read a man whose writing had many things in common with his own. Of course he might not have seen the point of Swann – he was always more comfortable with the eccentric and the anarchical than he was with the upper middle class – and certainly he would have preferred to spend half an hour with Gaby la Landaise, a good-natured prostitute who lived close to the Porte Saint-Denis, than with the Duchesse de Guermantes in the 'Faubourg'. But he would surely have admired the quality of Proust's memory and the style of his prose, its charms as addictive and idiosyncratic as his own. (On balance, Proust had the longer paragraphs, Cobb the longer sentences.)

Although he did not start producing books about himself until he was over sixty-five, Cobb did not suffer from Proust's need to regain Time before he could begin writing. For him the past was never wasted, never lost; it remained with him always, suffusing his research with his experiences, determining the way he thought and felt and wrote. No doubt this helped him make such a successful transition from history to autobiography. *Still Life: Sketches from a Tunbridge Wells Childhood* quickly established itself as a classic memoir and, although it was succeeded by two slighter volumes, the sequence ended memorably with the posthumous publication of *The End of the Line*.

For those who enjoyed reading about his second identity, 'le Cobb' encountering the Parisian underworld, it was rather alarming to witness the reassertion of his first incarnation, 'the Cobb' who talked about his 'beloved Manningtree' and announced that he had never felt more English, more Protestant or more middle class. Yet his nose for ambience and his ear for dialogue were as acute in England as in France; he was wonderfully observant of the social prejudices and vigilant snobbishness of the south-east. *Still Life* contains an hilarious description of the ladies of Tunbridge Wells returning by train from a day spent in Harrods and Swan & Edgar, while an earlier essay evokes the inter-war years in London, 'the Bloomsbury boarding-houses kept by declining ladies, the stale smell of genteel loneliness'. *Something to Hold Onto* is largely about his uncles and grandparents, people who seem eccentric to the reader only because their lives were so utterly banal: his Uncle Primus preserved his sanity by private ceremonies such as winding the clock, tapping the barometer, and timed-to-the-minute walks in Colchester – and lost it when this routine was destroyed by his parents' deaths and his enforced retirement to a boarding house at Clacton-on-Sea. If this seems untypical Cobb, the theme at least is familiar: the importance of routines, rituals and itineraries in people's lives. And in his too, for amid the jumble and eccentricity of his existence, he retained a little of the Uncle Primus – he loved steam irons, found ironing soothing, and liked to hang out the washing.

Attempts were made in his last years to lure him back into the French orbit. He was commissioned to write a book on Simenon; he wanted to produce an 'anti-revo' work on the Thermidorians. Neither was done. He admired Simon Schama's *Citizens*, a very critical chronicle of the French Revolution, but disliked other recent work on the subject – especially the contributions of an American feminist historian who, he complained, ranted 'endlessly about something called "Discourse"'. He became so 'utterly fed up' with the bicentennial celebrations of the Revolution that he refused to go to any conference anywhere, even Barcelona, if he was expected to say something positive about the subject. In 1990, however, he agreed to go to Spain with Raymond Carr because he had been assured that the theme of a conference in Zamora was that the Revolution 'was a pretty bad thing for all concerned'.

'Do you think they make wigs in Spain?' he asked before setting off; he was developing a tonsure, he reported, and the back of his head tended to get very cold. The idea of covering it with a wig made from some 'silky señorita's hair' appealed to him enormously. Being the least vain of men, he did not buy a wig (instead he started wearing a cream coloured corduroy cap from South Carolina), but he returned full of enthusiasm for Spain: Zamora was wonderful, the language was superb, the Castilians were the most hospitable people in Europe. As for the women ('It is terrible really, but in my seventies I still observe with great interest female anatomy'), their beauty made him wonder why he had spent half a century studying France instead of Spain.

The last remark wasn't serious, of course, for it is difficult even to imagine *l'étonnant Cobb* (as *Le Monde* once called him) without France. It reflected an old man's disenchantment, his sense of loss at the disappearance of familiar places, *his* France of the 30s and 40s, the last moments of the Third Republic and the early years of the Fourth. Much of physical Paris may have survived, but for him its human proportions had gone: he yearned for the time when the markets were still at Les Halles, when artisans still lived in the Marais, when even Pompidou himself had not thought of the Pompidou Centre. 'People have not changed much,' he wrote, 'but places certainly have, and everywhere for the worse.'

It is difficult to write about his last years without a feeling of anguish. He sold his house in Oxford and, after a short stay in Normandy, went with Margaret and their youngest son William to live in Whitby, where they used to go for holidays. But trying to live in Yorkshire, without friends and with little money, was miserable for all of them. He became ill and depressed; he threw away letters and books, he stopped writing, he seldom talked, he even gave up hanging out the washing. Things improved when they returned to the south in June 1994 and moved into a little house in Abingdon. He came to Balliol for lunch and said he was 'going downhill but not too fast'. At home he and Margaret (who did the typing) struggled to complete *The End of the Line*. On 15 January 1996, two days after he wrote the 'Endpaper', he had a heart attack and died.

In September 1975 he had written to apologize for not coming to my wedding because he had been in hospital having tests on his kidneys. He would have to watch 'the demon drink', he said, before adding that he had had a 'pretty good run as far as that's concerned'. In fact the 'pretty good run' lasted another twenty years, during which the demon continued to fuel and brighten his gift for friendship. Notoriously he made enemies, but he made a larger number of friends – and he kept them. He was an emotional man, a sentimentalist, easily touched. At his farewell lunch at Balliol, he wept on recalling how much he owed Maurice Keen, even though his new college was only 300 yards away from his old one. And he was overcome too, when asked to say something at his seventy-fifth birthday lunch at the *Financial Times*; all he could manage apart from gratitude was the observation that he, born in May 1917, had outlived Leningrad.

The friends remain. Some attend an annual dinner in his memory. More retain a large number of letters that are brilliant, funny, irreverent, libellous and currently unpublishable. In May 1996 an even larger group went to his memorial service in Oxford where the Chaplain of Balliol, inviting the company back to the College for tea, added with a smile, 'In honour of Richard, wine will be served.'

Michael Ignatieff

BERLIN IN AUTUMN

By common consent Isaiah Berlin enjoyed a happy old age. The autumn of his life was a time of serenity. But serenity in old age is a philosophical puzzle. Why did he manage to avoid the shipwreck that is the more common fate of us all?

The obvious answer is that he was exceedingly fortunate. He married happily, late in life, and he enjoyed both good health, good fortune and a growing reputation. His life between 1974, when he retired from the presidency of Wolfson College, Oxford, and his death in 1997, were years both of ease and increasing public recognition. Berlin's editor, Henry Hardy, began editing and re-publishing his previously unpublished essays and lectures and this transformed Berlin's reputation, giving the lie to Maurice Bowra's joke that like our Lord and Socrates, Berlin talked much but published little.[1] He lived long enough to see his reputation, which had been in relative eclipse, blossom into what he referred to as posthumous fame.

Certainly, Berlin's serenity in his final years owed a great deal to good fortune. But there are temperaments that frown even when fortune shines, and even those with sunny temperaments find mortal decline a depressing experience. So Berlin's serenity is worth trying to explain, both for what it tells us about him and for what it tells us about how to face our own ageing. I want to ask whether his serenity was a matter of temperament or a result of conviction, whether it was a capacity he inherited or a goal he achieved, and in particular whether his convictions – liberal, sceptical, agnostic, and moderate – helped to fortify him against the ordeals of later life.

Being philosophical about old age implies being reconciled or being resigned or some combination of the two. I want to ask whether Isaiah was resigned or reconciled and in what sense philosophy helped him to be philosophical in either of these senses.

From Socrates onwards, philosophy – especially the Stoic tradition – has made the question of how to die well among its central preoccupations. Indeed until philosophers became academic specialists devoted to the instruction of the young and the maintenance of that walled garden known as professional philosophy – in other words until the second half of the nineteenth century – one of the central tests of a philosophy was whether it helped its adherents to live and die in an instructively rational and inspirational fashion. The great modern example of the philosophical death is David Hume, whose good-humoured scepticism made him one of Isaiah's favourite philosophers. The story of Hume's death, told in James Boswell's journals and in Adam Smith's memoir, became a cause célèbre in the Enlightenment.[2] In the summer of 1776, Boswell returned repeatedly to Hume's house in the final days, awaiting some wavering that would indicate that the philosopher had recanted and embraced the Christian faith. No such wavering occurred. Hume went to his death with all the good humour of Socrates, joking with Boswell about what he might say to Charon the boatman when they met at the banks of the Styx. The jokes sent a shiver through every fibre of Boswell's errant but Christian soul. After visiting Hume for the last time, he found a whore in the streets of Edinburgh and coupled with her within sight of Hume's bedroom, as if wishing to embrace the carnal in order to drive the tormenting fear of death out of his mind. So a philosophical death was both a noble spectacle and a metaphysical puzzle.

Hume's death placed him securely in the grand philosophical tradition going back to Socrates. But his philosophical positions broke with the assumption that philosophy should teach men how to live and die well. His philosophical writings maintained – and his own experience of life deepened this into a settled conviction – that while philosophy could clarify the terms of mental and moral debate, it could not generate meaningful reasons to live or die.[3] In particular, it was not a substitute source of the consolations provided by religion. Indeed, the search for metaphysical consolations was bound to be insatiable and profoundly unsettling. If men were seeking for serenity in their final hours, they should not seek it in philosophy. Hume himself had little to say about the sources of his

own serenity, but they owed more to temperament than to conviction, more to the sense of a life fully lived and enjoyed than to any
received or formulated set of Stoic opinions.

The same proved true of Isaiah Berlin. He was a Humean sceptic
from the time he came up to Oxford in 1928, an agnostic in religion
and a sceptic in philosophy. As it happened, a modern twentieth-
century form of Humean scepticism was just then coming into the
ascendant in Oxford analytical philosophy. While still in his twenties
in Oxford, Berlin became one of the founding fathers of 'logical
positivism'. While the immediate origins of this view were the
Vienna School – Wittgenstein, Carnap, Schlick and Weisman –
Hume remains grandfather and its most characteristic Anglo-Saxon
exponent.[4] Logical positivism strengthened Berlin's Humean distrust
of metaphysics and what the Germans called *Lebensphilosophie*.
Philosophy, as the logical positivists conceived it, had to emancipate
itself from the Socratic heritage of asking questions about the
meaning of life and the manner of a good death. It would never
achieve results; it would never make progress as a discipline unless
it rigorously excluded unanswerable questions from its research
programme. This view of philosophy was in turn a view of life. It
was central to this view that if you persisted in asking questions
about the meaning of life, you had not understood life in any degree.
Life was life and its plausibility was a matter of sentiment not a
matter of argument. Philosophical propositions were of no use at all
in living or dying, and to ask philosophy to console was to mistake
what it was.

Although Berlin eventually broke with the scientistic and reduc-
tive style of logical positivism, he was deeply marked by its anti-
metaphysical bent. Philosophy's function was to clarify common
terms of argument, to elucidate the nature of moral choices, and to
interpret certain puzzles in the relation between the mind and the
world. It was not a substitute for religion and had nothing to say
about death or how we should face it. Like most of the analytical
philosophers of his generation, Berlin felt that unless philosophy
kept the demarcation line with metaphysics clear, it would lose all
claim to rigour, seriousness and self-respect.

These views, developed in late adolescence, made him deeply
sceptical, when he reached his eighties, about the very possibility
that philosophy could assist one to be philosophical about old age.

He was not scornful of those who sought the comfort of systems of belief, but he did not stand in need of one himself. He thought of ageing and death in consistently materialist terms and believed, accordingly, that death held no terrors since, logically speaking, it was not an event in life. This formulation, adapted from Wittgenstein's *Tractatus*, implied both that death was not to be feared, since it could not be experienced, and also that death was only the end, not the defining property of life.[5]

Yet we cannot leave the matter there. Berlin the anti-metaphysical philosopher may have been sceptical of the very idea that philosophical propositions can shape the encounter with death, but when it came to deciding upon his own funeral, he chose the Jewish Orthodox form of service rather than a Reform or non-denominational service his agnostic beliefs might have logically entailed. This reflected a choice of allegiance and belonging, rather than a commitment of faith. He could subscribe to the rituals of Judaism without subscribing to their content. He did so serenely, refusing to see any contradiction. The faith of his fathers had disposed of these matters of burial and mourning very well for centuries. Why should he quarrel with any of it? His scepticism about matters religious was more respectful than many of his more bone-dry sceptical friends, Alfred Ayer or Stuart Hampshire, for example. Why this is so is not easy to explain. As a refugee and exile, he perhaps needed the reassurance of religious ritual more than his English colleagues; just possibly, he thought that there was a sort of arid presumption in the modernist dismissal of ritual as superstition.

He also differed from them, ultimately, in his view of the relation between philosophical propositions and life. As a logical positivist, he was sceptical about the very attempt to justify life philosophically. But he turned away from philosophy proper in his late twenties in part because he had become fascinated precisely by the ways in which men did use ideas to justify, explain and even modify their lives. As an historian of ideas, he was keenly aware that men do live and die by their ideas. Few philosophers had such a keen sense of the intense interaction between propositions, convictions and temperament. If we are going to look at the impact of Berlin's thought on the manner of his own ageing we shall have to look beyond the impact of logical positivism itself.

All of his thinking associated serenity with belonging: and

belonging with self-knowledge. If he was serene in old age it was because he knew who he was and where he belonged. This personal sense of the necessity of roots informed all of his writing on nationalism. He always located the origins of nationalist feeling in the passion to be understood. People needed to live in communities where they were understood – and not merely for what they said, but for what they meant. To have a national home was to live in a world of such tacitly shared meanings.[6]

He attached more importance to belonging than any other modern liberal philosopher and he had a clear sense of his own origins, as the son of a Baltic timber merchant, born in the Jewish community of Riga in the twilight of the tsarist empire. Despite going into exile he kept up a strong sense of connection to these roots throughout his adult life. This organic connection was possible because his mother remained alive until he was well into his sixties. It so happened that he retired in the year of his mother's death, 1974. When he tried to speak about losing her, he used the German verb: *zerreissen*, meaning 'to tear into pieces'. In the letters he wrote in the week after her death, he went on to say that without such living links to his past he felt accidental, contingent, directionless.[7] Life briefly lost its momentum and point. In time, he recovered it again: his organic capacities for repair and recovery were formidable. It is doubtful that he had more than several months' experience of genuine depression in his whole life, and if his mother's death occasioned one such instance, it was brief.

His equanimity in old age had a great deal to do with the degree to which he made his own life – its needs and cravings – the tacit subject of his work, and through apparently abstract writings about nationalism explored the needs for belonging that were central to his own identity. If this produced equanimity it was because it was done tacitly, with a minimum of self-disclosure, so that his work both revealed his inner preoccupations and helped him to resolve them, without exposing him to ridicule or shame.

Among expatriates like Berlin, identities soldered together in exile often come apart in old age. In retirement, people are brought up short with the realization of how far they have come from their beginnings. Often this past is now in another country and in another time. When this dawns, identity becomes strained. They begin to go to church or synagogue more often, they begin to dream in their languages of origin in an attempt to recover past connections, but more often than not, they begin to have a sense of inner fragmentation. They cannot pull past, present and future together. The span of life is simply too long. There are too many twists and turns in the road.

This did not happen to Berlin. In fact, old age represented a coming together of the Russian, Jewish and English skeins of his identity. During his years as a schoolboy and then as a young Oxford don, he assimilated thoroughly. His accent, for example, impersonated the upper middle class Oxford dons of his acquaintance. But with old age, the Russian and Jewish parts of his identity began to return. His voice became less English with time and more Russian in its vowel sounds. He himself was aware of this. It cannot be accidental that his most extended excursion into autobiography, the Jerusalem prize speech, was given as he turned seventy.[8] In it, he makes a point of saying that his identity consisted of three elements, English, Russian and Jewish, all braided together. The philosophical equanimity of his old age owes a great deal to this recovery of all the elements of his past, this braiding of selfhood. It made him an exceedingly economical persona: no energy was wasted in repression or denial of the origins that made him up.

There was no question of a return to Judaism in old age, because he had never left. While he did not keep a kosher table, he observed the major Jewish festivals and liked to joke that the Orthodox synagogue was the synagogue he did not attend. He had no time for reformed Judaism because he thought it was incoherent to combine religion and rationalism, to reduce an ancient faith to nothing more than an agreeable and modern ethical content. He respected the claims of the ancient Jewish tradition precisely because of their irrational and inhuman content. Igor Stravinsky came to lunch in 1963 and asked Isaiah to suggest a religious subject for a composition he had been commissioned to write for the Jerusalem Festival. Berlin went upstairs, returned with his Bible and read Stravinsky the passage in Hebrew describing Abraham's binding of Isaac. Stravinsky took Berlin's advice and went on to compose a cantata on the theme. The Abraham and Isaac story was a parable for Berlin about the inscrutability both of God's commands and of human life itself. Unlike many of his fellow agnostics, Berlin had a healthy respect for the religious dimension in human consciousness. It also helped to sustain his ultimate metaphysical view that there were a lot of things about the shape of human life that could not be known.[9]

Because he was a famous man, he would be asked, sometimes by complete strangers, to pronounce on the meaning of life. He found this very comic, but his replies were terse and matter of fact. When he was seventy-five, he replied to one such questioner, 'As for the meaning of life, I do not believe it has any. I do not at all ask what it is but I suspect it has none, and this is a source of great comfort to me. We make of it what we can and that is all there is about it. Those who seek for some deep cosmic all-embracing libretto are, believe me, pathetically mistaken.'[10]

These, then, were the metaphysical sources of his serenity: a deep and abiding sense of who he was and where he came from, coupled with a cool and sceptical refusal to entertain questions about the meaning of life, which he thought were beyond the reach of reason.

This is about as far as doctrine and mature conviction will take us in explaining his autumnal serenity and they do not take us very far. We need to look at his temperament, at the attitudes to self and habits of mind, which made it easy for him to greet old age with relative calm.

As his biographer I had expected that when he left Wolfson College, when he was no longer president of the British Academy, no longer Chichele Professor of Social Thought at All Souls, no longer a Fellow at All Souls that he might have felt bereft and denuded, as professional men often are at the end of their careers. Retirement can initiate a period of lonely inner questioning. This did not happen. The reason is that he was never heavily invested in those roles in the first place. He did not lack ambition; he liked to be taken seriously; he could be prickly if he felt his dignity or reputation were attacked; but he also stood outside himself and mocked his own desire for recognition. When T.S. Eliot wrote to congratulate him on his knighthood in 1956, Isaiah replied that he felt as silly as if he were wearing a paper hat at a children's party.[11] He liked recognition – the knighthood mattered deeply – but he held some part of himself back. Irony and a sense of the ridiculous, therefore, were important components of the serenity his friends admired in the autumn of his life.

Of course irony and a sense of humour about the scramble for honour and fame are easier if you've had your share of both. He always said his success had been based on a systematic overestimation of his abilities. 'Long may this continue,' he would say. He had very little to be bitter about, very little to regret. Yet even those who have known a success equivalent to his are often bitter and depressed in old age. He was not.

He always insisted that he was not an essentially introspective man; an observer, certainly, but fundamentally directed outwards rather than inwards. He never kept a diary and his most characteristic forms of self-revelation were addressed outwards in letters and conversation. He thought more about what other people made of him than he thought about himself. He found it easy to distance himself from his own life, to be ironical about himself, because he wasn't imprisoned in his own self to begin with.

He had a particular talent for imagining other lives and that gave him a vantage point from which to see his own. He loved reading in order to lose himself in some other person, often someone radically alien to his own temperament. He had a temperamental fascination with his opposite: figures like Joseph de Maistre, the counter-revolutionary theorist and fanatical hater of bourgeois liberal reformism.[12] In entering into de Maistre's inner world, he could see himself as de Maistre might have seen him, and this capacity for standing outside himself freed him from excessive or burdening investment in his own roles.

Keeping himself apart from his roles followed, I think, from being a) a Jew and b) an exile. His belonging in England was both secure and conditional. Irony and self-deprecation had survival value for any Jewish exile in England. This is one of the reasons that he remained, even in secure old age, a watchful character, acutely aware that he was a sojourner and a stranger even in the Establishment, which took him to its heart.

He also refused to vest his own commitments, ideas and values with existential or historical importance. After the fall of communism, he was constantly asked whether he felt vindicated, and his replies always challenged the premise of the question itself. Why, he asked, should any liberal feel vindicated? History, he always said, had no libretto. To claim that it vindicated him or his liberalism seemed an absurd inflation of both himself and the doctrines with which he was associated. He was also self-knowing enough to realize that he had never risked anything decisive in the struggle against communist tyranny, like Koestler, Orwell, Milosz or Akhmatova. Since that was the case, it was unbecoming to make a show of rejoicing at its fall. He did take quiet pleasure in the fact that communism ended as his own life came to a close. He could look back across the century and feel that the intellectuals with whom he felt the closest spiritual kinship: the anti-Bolshevik writers and artists of Russia's Silver Age, 1896–1917 – chiefly Pasternak and Akhmatova – would have rejoiced to have lived the hours he had been lucky enough to see. In this sense, history did shine on him in his final years.

He was detached from his roles, from his own ideas and from his own posterity. He was fond of saying, 'Après moi le deluge.' Of course, there was an element of pose in this, a very Oxford style of appearing not to care about reputation. In fact, of course, he was a careful custodian of his reputation – worrying whether he should accept such and such an honour, sit at such and such a table with such and such a person, give his name to such and such an appeal. All of this indicates a concern to husband the coinage of his fame. But as to what came after, he always purported to be indifferent.

His attitude to my biography, for example, was complex. Initially he thought it was a ludicrous idea. Why would I want to do such a thing? I can remember him asking. It was only after three years of interviewing – in which I would ask him a question at the beginning of the hour and get to ask him another one at the end – that he broached the issue of what would become of the tapes. The idea of a biography grew upon him as he came to trust me and grow comfortable in my company. As the years passed, he engaged with the project, checking with me about this or that detail, retelling certain stories with a new twist or nuance in order that I would appreciate their significance. But he took a fundamentally passive approach to my project, waiting for the right question before proffering the answer, and I had to wait for years for him to disclose what he took to be the essential elements of his life and thought. He seemed to have little anxiety about posterity. When I asked him how he thought he would be remembered, his replies were always of the form a) how can we possibly know? and b) why should it matter?

This attitude towards posterity was reinforced by the fact that he had no children of his own. He was quite content to be a stepfather to his wife's children, but he never evinced any very strong desire to have any of his own. The patriarchal and paternal instincts – all of which usually go with a desire to shape and mould posterity – were absent in him.

He also never had disciples. There were many former students, friends and associates who liked to say, '*Ich bin ein Berliner*', but he never sought to create a circle who would propagate his ideas and safeguard his reputation. There was no Berlin school, tendency or fraction. He disliked the idea of having to take responsibility for a Berlinian doctrine, with orthodoxy to defend and disciples to promote it.

He watched Henry Hardy, a young graduate student in philosophy, attach himself to his work; supported his editions of his works; greatly enjoyed the revival of his reputation which Hardy's work achieved, but never took any initiative in the relationship beyond benign approval. The same genial detachment characterized his relationship to my biography. Neither Hardy nor I ever thought of ourselves as surrogate sons, disciples or acolytes. He simply did not want this kind of entourage around him and did not want the responsibility.

The final source of his equanimity was in relation to ageing itself. Almost all of us have a quarrel with how old we actually are, and present ourselves as younger or older than our actual age. Biological and phenomenological age are never exactly the same. Isaiah was a complex instance of this. The people who remember him from his early youth always said that he was the oldest person in any room. When he was twenty he was already behaving as if he were a middle-aged man. Stephen Spender, one of his oldest friends, once said to me that he had trouble thinking of Isaiah as having aged at all. He was always 'a baby elephant, always the same baby elephant'.[13] If you see the early pictures of him he is wearing the same kind of three-piece suit that he wore to the end of his life. He valued continuity in the details: the same kind of polished shoes, the same look of cautious bourgeois sobriety as his father. He dressed like his father all his life, and he did so from adolescence onwards. The paradox of his extraordinary youthfulness and vitality, therefore, was that he always thought of himself as a middle-aged man.

He always seemed older than he was and he always remained younger than he seemed.

Age did him many favours. He was not a prepossessing twenty- or thirty- even forty-year-old. It wasn't until he was in his sixties that he looked fully at ease with what he had become. He thinned down, his whole face acquired a certain nobility, as if he were finally growing into the age at which he was most himself.

His vernacular of odd behaviour – going to parties with crisp-bread in a matchbox in his pocket so that he could have his own little snacks – belonged more to the personality of an indulged child than of a sage. In a restaurant he would suddenly begin humming some little Yiddish ditty that he had heard in Hebrew school in 1915. That ability to recover his childhood and be a child again was one of the reasons that he was much loved and that he was never weighed down by life.

The other element of his ageing that he noticed himself was that it rendered him more not less susceptible to pity. In a letter written late in life, he said, 'the proposition that the longer one lives the more indifferent one becomes to the ills that beset one or one's dearests is totally false. I suffer much more from this than I used to and I now realize that there must have been a long period of my life when I was, comparatively speaking, too little sensitive to the misfortunes of others, however close, certainly, of my friends'.

In 1993, one year before his death, Stephen Spender sent Isaiah the following poem, written in China in AD 835, It commemorated their sixty years of friendship:

> We are growing old together, you and I
> Let us ask ourselves 'what is age like?'
> The idle head still uncombed at noon
> Propped on a staff sometimes a walk abroad
> Or all day sitting with closed doors.
> One dares not look in the mirror's polished face.
> One cannot read small letter books.
> Deeper and deeper one's love of old friends,
> Fewer and fewer one's dealing with young men.
> One thing only: the pleasure of idle talk
> Is great as ever, when you and I meet.[14]

That does capture perhaps the final element of what kept both of them young: the pleasure of idle talk, and the idler the better.

Memory, word games and puns, the sheer pleasure of orality, which connected him to the pleasures of infancy all his life. There was nothing that meant more to him than the pleasure of talk. He died tragically of oesophageal constriction, literally unable to get words out of his throat. The condition was terrible to him, and it was the only time I ever saw him depressed, because it made it difficult for him to speak to other human beings and that was what made life worth living. What he seemed to vindicate by his life was life itself. Life could not be philosophically justified; it could only be lived. He trusted life and certainly helped those who loved him to trust it more themselves.

*   *   *

NOTES

1. Maurice Bowra to Noel Annan, undated, 1971; see Noel Annan, 'A Man I Loved' in H. Lloyd-Jones (ed.), *Maurice Bowra: A Celebration* (London, 1974), p. 53.

2. I have discussed Hume's death in my *The Needs of Strangers* (London, 1984) ch. 3. See also James Boswell, *Boswell in Extremes, 1776–1778* (New Haven, 1971), pp. 11–15; Adam Smith, *Correspondence* (Oxford, 1977), pp. 203–21.

3. David Hume, *A Treatise of Human Nature* (Oxford, 1978), p. 264.

4. See Ben Rogers, *A.J. Ayer: A Life* (London, 1999); my own *Isaiah Berlin: A Life* (London, 1998), pp. 80–90.

5. *Berlin: A Life*, p. 83.

6. See 'Nationalism: Past Neglect and Present Power' and 'The Apotheosis of the Romantic Will' in Henry Hardy and Roger Hausheer (eds.), *Isaiah Berlin: The Proper Study of Mankind* (London, 1998), pp. 553–605.

7. *Berlin: A Life*, p. 272.

8. Isaiah Berlin, 'The Three Strands in My Life' in *Personal Impressions* (London, 1998), pp. 255–61.

9. *Berlin: A Life*, pp. 237–8.

10. Ibid., p. 279.

11. Ibid., p. 222.

12. 'Joseph de Maistre and the Origins of Fascism' in Henry Hardy (ed.), *Isaiah Berlin: The Crooked Timber of Humanity* (New York, 1991), pp. 91–175.

13. *Berlin: A Life*, p. 3.

14. Ibid., pp. 287–8.

Fellows' Biographical Notes

Harrison (St Antony's 1995)
To write siege of Breslau by the Red Army in 1945

Harrison has now changed course to offer the Fellowship a new full-length study of Kim Philby, postponing 'Breslau' to a later date. He is currently at Wayne University, USA, teaching, and studying Russian so as to be able to research more effectively into the new Philby material. He reckons the Fellowship provided 'a turning point in my writing career, certainly the most positive stimulus I have had since leaving Oxford in 1979'.

Kee (St Antony's 1971–3)
The Laurel and the Ivy: The Story of Charles Stewart Parnell and Irish Nationalism (1993)

Kee was kind enough to write that: 'The book had to go on the back burner for a while – but for the sense of personal pride in the Fellowship invested, the flame which went on burning slowly for almost another twenty years would, long before, have gone out altogether.'
He is currently working on a biography of François Mitterrand.

Hardyment (St Antony's 1990–2)
No Place Like Home: European Domesticity Since the War

She writes:

I was an Alistair Horne Fellow for two successive years, between 1990 and 1992, working on research into the shape of European domesticity in the twentieth century. Not surprisingly this topic proved too large to encompass in a single book, and so the results of my researches are scattered between books of essays, articles and a short book, *The Future of the Family* (Orion, 1999). The Fellowship was a huge boost to morale, and opened the door to the international community at St Antony's College to me, an inestimable benefit to my research. Now that my own family has grown up, I have changed historical direction, and am currently working on a biography of the fifteenth-century author of *Le Morte Darthur*, Sir Thomas Malory.

Hart-Davis (St Antony's 1976–7)
Monarchs of the Glen: A History of Deer Stalking in the Scottish Highlands (1978)

Hart-Davis writes that his research as a Fellow 'consolidated my interest in land use and nature conservation, and this in turn led to my becoming Country Matters correspondent of the *Independent*, a post I have held ever since the inception of the paper in 1986'.

Author of thirty books, he is currently working on a book about the future of the British countryside.

McLynn (St Antony's 1987–8)
Stanley: The Making of an African Explorer and *Stanley: Sorcerer's Apprentice* (1990)

McLynn considers his two-volume Stanley biography: 'my greatest feat of pure scholarship ... only with the financial subvention provided [by the Fellowship] was I able to produce the definitive Stanley biography. I only wish I had had the financial cushioning of such a fellowship when I was working on my subsequent books.'

Huntford (St Antony's 1986–7)
Nansen (1998)

'For my biography of Nansen, I had rapidly to aquire a working knowledge of Russian history during the early years of the Bolshevik regime. St Antony's was clearly the best place in the country for the purpose, and the timely offer of an Alistair Horne Fellowship gave me the opportunity I needed. The Fellowship also provided a taste of the Oxford republic of letters that I needed just as much.'

O'Hanlon (St Antony's 1972–3)
Joseph Conrad and Charles Darwin: Scientific Thought in Conrad's Fiction (1984)

Meredith (St Antony's 1982–3)
The First Dance of Freedom (1984)

After spending fifteen years as a foreign correspondent in Africa, Martin Meredith found St Antony's College an ideal base from which to gain a wider perspective on the course of contemporary African history. Continuing his link with the college, he followed *The First Dance of Freedom* with an account of South Africa in the post-war era, *In the Name of Apartheid*. His biography of Nelson Mandela was published in 1997. He is currently working on a history of the African elephant.

Clad (St Antony's 1988–9)
Behind the Myth: Business, Money and Power in South East Asia (1989)

In view of Indonesia's turbulent politics and international outcry over East Timor in 1999, James Clad's essay is of particular interest. The book he finished at St Antony's predicted a looming financial crisis in South-East Asia. Professor Clad now teaches at Georgetown University's School of Foreign Service and writes about US policy in Asia.

Adelson (St Antony's 1972–3)
Mark Sykes: Portrait of an Amateur (1975)

Adelson (the only surviving US Fellow) writes: 'The Fellowship and book [*Mark Sykes*] helped me to compete against 349 other candidates for a position teaching Modern British History at Arizona State University, which I have held since 1974. I am now writing a book and developing a television documentary on Winston Churchill and the Middle East.'

Thorpe (St Antony's 1997–8)
Official biography, Anthony Eden

For thirty-three years, Thorpe was a master teaching history at Charterhouse. His life of Selwyn Lloyd was followed by his prestigious official life of Douglas-Home. Subsequent to his attachment to St Antony's while working on his Eden biography, at the personal invitation of Lady Avon, he became a senior member of Brasenose College, Oxford. He writes: 'The opportunities to meet scholars working in related fields led to my becoming a contributor to the *New Dictionary of National Biography* . . . as well as the offer of Senior Membership of Brasenose College, Oxford, where I am now based.'

Grigg (St Antony's 1970–80)
Lloyd George: From Peace to War, 1912–1916 (1985),
which was awarded the Wolfson Prize.

Grigg writes:

> Not only was the Fellowship immensely helpful to me in connection with that work, I also greatly appreciated being a temporary member of such an interesting and varied society as St Antony's. Non-academic historians like myself would never in the ordinary way have the privilege of so mixing with our betters. I feel the utmost gratitude to Alistair for imaginative benefaction, and to the College for entering into the spirit of it and making us Horne Fellows so welcome.

Danchev (St Antony's 1991)
Oliver Franks – Founding Father (1993)

Alex Danchev is Professor of International Relations and Dean of Social Science at Keele University. His essay in this book is drawn from his widely acclaimed biography of Liddell Hart, *Alchemist of War* (Weidenfield & Nicolson, 1998, Phoenix, 1999). He is currently working on an unexpurgated edition of the Alanbrooke diaries, and a genealogy of appeasement. He writes:

> Oliver Franks lived just a few blocks away from the College . . . Meeting him and those who knew him enormously enriched the experience and I think the book too. Professionally it was a momentous year: in the course of it I was elected to the Chair in International Relations at my home university, Keele, at the age of thirty-five. The book appeared in 1993. Some remarkably good reviews helped to convince me that I was on the right track. Life-writing has continued to be the focus of my serial self-education. Plainly, there is a long way to go . . .

Bonham-Carter (St Antony's 1974–6)
Authors by Profession (1994), Vol.1 of *A History of Authorship* based on the archives of the Society of Authors

Bonham-Carter writes:

> I was just too tired to get down to writing [the history of the Society of Authors]. That was where the Horne Foundation saved the situation and my life . . . allowed me to take the time off from office work, do the necessary research and write volume one of the book entitled *Authors by Profession*. This two-volume work remains literally unique, no other work that I know of has tackled the history of the business of writing – but without the generous assistance of the Horne Foundation I would never have got started.

Whittam (St Antony's 1970)
The Politics of the Italian Army 1861–1918 (1976)

Whittam writes:

> It was my wife who spotted the advertisement, and encouraged me to apply and to send off a chapter. Anything connected with St Antony's always caught her eye. We had, after all, been married when I was still a student there, and we had held our reception in the College in 1959.

I shared the Fellowship with Norman Davies who subsequently rose effortlessly like a Polish eagle. I have remained close to the ground, but the Fellowship led to the publication of a book, and to promotion in Bristol University.

I am still there, stoically commuting in from Bath, a city which among its many attractions now boasts a direct train to Oxford.

Horne
His *Seven Ages of Paris* is due to be published by Macmillan in 2001.

Campbell (St Antony's 1980–1)
F.E. Smith – The First Earl of Birkenhead (1984)

Campbell writes: 'Alistair was away the whole of my year . . . but it was a valuable taste of Oxford life for an otherwise isolated freelance; while subsequent reunions have introduced me to several other Horne Fellows. I remain proud and grateful to be one of such a distinguished company.'

Following his prizewinning biography of Edward Heath, he is currently writing a full-length study of Margaret Thatcher. The first volume will be published in May 2000.

Davies (St Antony's 1970)
White Eagle, Red Star: The Polish–Soviet War, 1919–20 (1972)

Graciously Davies wrote at the time: 'Without the boost to my reputation which the Fellowship has obviously given, I would probably be on the dole.' From then on he never looked back. After his bestseller, *Europe*, his history of the British Isles, *The Isles*, has just been published by Macmillan.

Foster (St Antony's 1979–80)
Lord Randolph Churchill: A Political Life (1981)

He writes:

I held an Alistair Horne Fellowship at St Antony's from 1979–80, while on leave from the lectureship I then occupied at Birkbeck

College, University of London. The objective was to finish my biography of Lord Randolph Churchill, which was duly published in 1981 as *Lord Randolph Churchill: A Political Life*. The Fellowship was not residential, and I came and went, much enjoying St Antony's hospitality during the Raymond Carr dispensation. On another level I got to know the University of Oxford and its libraries, and the Churchill book, though originally commissioned by someone else, was published by Oxford University Press: so I was unconsciously being introduced to my future publishers, and my future employer. I was appointed the first Carroll Professor of Irish History at Oxford in 1992, and, after several books dealing with general themes of Irish history, am once again writing a biography: not a 'political life', but the life of a highly political poet, W.B. Yeats.

Davidson (St Antony's 1978–9)
Dumas on Food with Jane Davidson (1978), and *North Atlantic Sea Food* (1979)

Former Ambassador to Laos, Alan Davidson has written many other distinguished books on food. During his fellowship he also worked on the subject entitled 'Science in the Kitchen'. It saw the light twenty years later when the *Oxford Companion to Food* was published in 1999, including some 50,000 words on the scientific aspects of the subject. He writes that his tenure 'helped set in motion a surprisingly large range of activities in the field of food history' but now announces that he has 'had enough of food' for the time being, and intends to concentrate on cinema history. Carole Lombard is the first slice of the cake.

Hilton (St Antony's 1976–7)
John Ruskin: The Early Years (1984)
John Ruskin: The Later Years (2000)

'I found St Antony's worldly in the best possible sense of the word. Furthermore, the College was welcoming to an art historian.' Hilton has been the organizer of numerous exhibitions, including 'Picasso's Picassos', 'Drawings by Miró', and 'Anthony Caro', and has been the art critic of the *Guardian* and the *Independent on Sunday*.

Hamilton (St Antony's 1998–9)
Turner – A Life

Chronologically our most recent Fellow, he writes:

I saw, by chance, an advertisement for the Alistair Horne Fellowship in the back of the *Times Literary Supplement*, and applied. If I had picked up any other magazine to read with my coffee that day, I would probably have missed it. At the time I was working on the beginnings of an idea for a book that would observe the inter-relationships between art and science in the first half of the nineteenth century. I had found, when writing *Turner – A Life* (1997), that Turner had had lasting friendships with scientists, Faraday among them, whose significance and extent had not been fully explored. For the exhibition 'Turner and the Scientists' at the Tate in 1998, I looked at those relationships and their influence on Turner's work more fully.

There remained much more to discover and think about, and, early in the course of my Alistair Horne Fellowship, I planned that the new book would attempt a survey of the cultural landscape of art and science in Britain in the period, the communities and the crossing points. Michael Faraday, and his work as a research scientist and an active and intuitive events organizer at the Royal Institution, fell into place as a natural focus.

The rich opportunity of free access to the university libraries, archives and people in Oxford, and the delight at being welcomed as part of St Antony's College, has been a particular joy and a turning point in my life.

Hyman (St Antony's 1977–8)
Charles Babbage: Pioneer of the Computer (1982)

Constructed of precision-made brass cog wheels, with a reproducibility of 0.002″, and elegantly formed gear teeth, Babbage's 'Difference Engine' was a calculator of dizzying complexity for the early nineteenth century. The code-breakers of Bletchley, like Alan Turing, were deeply indebted to Babbage for his groundwork – and probably Bill Gates, too.

Hyman found the Fellowship provided 'congenial conditions for writing Babbage's biography'. He is currently a freelance computer consultant and science historian.

Bonnaud (St Antony's 1987–8)
Le Tunnel sous la manche: deux siècles de passions (1994)

Bonnaud, the first French Fellow, writes that he was elected to St Antony's to write the history of the Channel Tunnel,

> which did not exist at that time. It surprised nobody at St Antony's
> . . . The consequence of having met Alistair Horne surf on concen-
> tric waves. His influence was immediate in giving precious advice.
> Alistair seems indeed to have a key for all closed doors and I
> wondered how he could be taken off his considerable work and
> generously deliver views on the most esoteric subjects. But he also
> set benchmarks – and this, I am convinced, unconsciously – in
> Humanism. . . . I believe in . . . a permanent dialogue between
> experience and theory. Are these 'Hornian' values?

Gilmour (St Antony's 1996–7)
The Administration of Victorian India

Gilmour comments on the 'loneliness' he experienced during a four-year stretch writing a biography of Lord Curzon, where he felt

> the need to sit down occasionally and talk to people engaged in
> work similar to my own. When I mentioned this to friends, they
> suggested that the Alistair Horne Fellowship at St Antony's might
> be the perfect answer. So I applied for it, was accepted – and spent
> a happy academic year strolling between the College, the Bodleian,
> Rhodes House and various lesser libraries. . . . Oxford and St
> Antony's provided me with enough stimulation to go back to
> documents and avoid a return to journalism and other things
> which I used to regard as 'real life'.

Ignatieff (St Antony's 1992–5)
Isaiah Berlin: A Life (1998)

Michael Ignatieff was born in Toronto in 1947, educated at the University of Toronto and has a doctorate in history from Harvard. He was formerly a fellow of King's College, Cambridge. His books include *Scar Tissue*, *The Needs of Strangers*, *The Russia Album*, *The Warrior's Honour* and *Isaiah Berlin*.

Index

[Note: Page references in **bold type** indicate the main references to subjects; WWI and WWII are used to stand for World War I and World War II.]